Struggling with God

To Professor Pillay

With my thanks

for the faith and hope

you have invested in me.

God bless,

Simon

Struggling with God

Kierkegaard and the Temptation of Spiritual Trial

Simon D. Podmore

James Clarke & Co

In memory of Nöelle Mackie
and in gratitude to Cynthia Lund

James Clarke & Co
P.O. Box 60
Cambridge
CB1 2NT
United Kingdom

www.jamesclarke.co
publishing@jamesclarke.co

ISBN: 978 0 227 17343 5

British Library Cataloguing in Publication Data
A record is available from the British Library

Contents

Acknowledgements

Though Kierkegaard refers to the spiritual trials that haunt his own struggles to write and publish, I am, by contrast, indebted to the support and grace of many others who have sustained me in working on this book. The first-fruits of my convictions concerning the under-examined significance of Kierkegaard's view of spiritual trial were expressed in my *Kierkegaard and the Self Before God: Anatomy of the Abyss* (2011) and a number of articles and papers. The opportunity for more detailed research and reflection on this neglected topic was realised in part by a Kierkegaard House Foundation Fellowship, by the Gordon Milburn Junior Research Fellowship, and by a British Academy Postdoctoral Fellowship, for which I will always be thankful. I am also immensely grateful to the staff and students at the Howard and Edna Hong Kierkegaard Library at St Olaf College, the Søren Kierkegaard Research Centre in Copenhagen, the University of Edinburgh, the University of Oxford, and Liverpool Hope University, as well as members of the Søren Kierkegaard Society of the United Kingdom. I have furthermore been blessed by many individuals, including, but not limited to, the following: Katie Townend, Cathy and Lucinda Townend, Katherine Tetlow, Cynthia Lund, Gordon Marino, Howard and Edna Hong, Daphne Hampson, Murray Rae, Alan Torrance, Leo Stan, Hugh Pyper, John Lippitt, Jon Stewart, Claudia Welz, Pia Søltoft, Helle Møller Jensen, Joel Rasmussen, Johannes Zachhuber, Hartmut von Sass, Paul Fiddes, Pamela Sue Anderson, Peggy Morgan, Clare Carlisle, Chris Hamilton, Anthony Rudd, Bob Perkins, Sylvia Walsh, Andrew Burgess, Merold Westphal, Chris Barnett, Sean Turchin, Craig Hinkson, K. Jason Wardley, Joseph Rivera, Chris Shaw, David Lappano, Victoria Davies, Geoff Dargan, Patrick Sheil, Henry Hollanders, Louise Nelstrop, Andrew Weeks, Duane Williams, Patrice Haynes, Jenny Daggers, Peter McGrail, Andrew Cheatle, Steven Shakespeare, and George Pattison. I am also grateful for the patience and investment of Philip Law and Adrian Brink and all at James Clarke & Co. Ltd who have contributed to the publication of this book. Special thanks go to Bethany Churchard for her excellent work on the text and the cover.

Perhaps above all, I acknowledge the disparity Kierkegaard's lonely lament over the silence concerning spiritual trial and the vast support I have enjoyed in seeking to rehabilitate a Kierkegaardian theology of spiritual trial for a contemporary audience. As I congregate with many others to celebrate the bicentenary of Kierkegaard's birth, I hope that the irony of this does not become lost.

5 May 2013, Copenhagen

Abbreviations

Abbreviations for English Editions of Works by Søren Kierkegaard (1813-1855)

CA   *The Concept of Anxiety* (Vigilius Haufniensis), ed. and trans. Reidar Thomte in collaboration with Albert B. Anderson (Princeton, New Jersey: Princeton University Press, 1980).

CD   *Christian Discourses: The Crisis and A Crisis in the Life of an Actress*, ed. and trans. Howard V. Hong and Edna H. Hong (Bloomington and London: Indiana University Press, 1997).

CI   *The Concept of Irony: With Constant Reference to Socrates*, ed. and trans. Howard V. Hong and Edna H. Hong (Bloomington and London: Indiana University Press, 1989).

CUP I-II   *Concluding Unscientific Postscript* (Johannes Climacus), ed. and trans. Howard V. Hong and Edna H. Hong (Bloomington and London: Indiana University Press, 1992).

E/O I-II   *Either/Or*, 2 vols (Judge William, 'A'; ed. Victor Eremita), ed. and trans. Howard V. Hong and Edna H. Hong (Princeton, New Jersey: Princeton University Press, 1987).

EUD   *Eighteen Upbuilding Discourses*, ed. and trans. Howard V. Hong and Edna H. Hong (Princeton, New Jersey: Princeton University Press, 1990).

FSE   *For Self-Examination* in *For Self-Examination* and *Judge For Yourself!*, ed. and trans. Howard V. Hong and Edna H. Hong (Princeton, New Jersey: Princeton University Press, 1990).

FT   *Fear and Trembling* (Johannes de silentio) in *Fear and Trembling* and *Repetition*, ed. and trans. Howard V. Hong and Edna H. Hong (Princeton, New Jersey: Princeton University Press, 1983).

JFY   *Judge for Yourself!* in *For Self-Examination* and *Judge For Yourself!*, ed. and trans. Howard V. Hong and Edna H. Hong (Princeton, New Jersey: Princeton University Press, 1990).

JP   *Søren Kierkegaard's Journals and Papers*, 7 Vols, ed. and trans. Howard V. Hong and Edna H. Hong (Bloomington and London: Indiana University Press, 1967-78), followed by volume and entry number: e.g. JP 2:1383.

LW   *The Moment and Late Writings*, 7 Vols, ed. and trans. Howard V. Hong and Edna H. Hong (Bloomington and London: Indiana University Press, 1967-78).

PC   *Practice in Christianity* (Anti-Climacus; ed. Søren Kierkegaard), ed. and trans. Howard V. Hong and Edna H. Hong (Princeton, New Jersey: Princeton University Press, 1991).

PF   *Philosophical Fragments* (Johannes Climacus), ed. and trans. Howard V. Hong and Edna H. Hong (Princeton, New Jersey: Princeton University Press, 1985).

PV   *The Point of View For My Work as an Author*, ed. and trans. Howard V. Hong and Edna H. Hong (Princeton, New Jersey: Princeton University Press, 1998).

R   *Repetition* (Constantin Constantius) in *Fear and Trembling* and *Repetition*, ed. and trans. Howard V. Hong and Edna H. Hong (Princeton, New Jersey: Princeton University Press, 1983).

SLW   *Stages on Life's Way* (William Afham, the Judge, Frater Taciturnus, published by Hilarius Bookbinder), ed. and trans. Howard V. Hong and Edna H. Hong (Princeton, New Jersey: Princeton University Press, 1988).

SUD   *The Sickness unto Death* (Anti-Climacus; ed. Søren Kierkegaard), ed. and trans. Howard V. Hong and Edna H. Hong (Princeton, New Jersey: Princeton University Press, 1983).

UDVS   *Upbuilding Discourses in Various Spirits*, ed. and trans. Howard V. Hong and Edna H. Hong (Princeton, New Jersey: Princeton University Press, 1988).

WA   *Without Authority*, ed. trans. Howard V. Hong and Edna H. Hong (Princeton, New Jersey: Princeton University Press, 1995).

WL   *Works of Love*, ed. and trans. Howard V. Hong and Edna H. Hong (Princeton, New Jersey: Princeton University Press, 1995).

Abbreviations for Danish Editions
of Kierkegaard's Works

SKS   *Søren Kierkegaards Skrifter* (København: G.E.C. Gads Forlag, 1997-2007).

Pap.   *Søren Kierkegaards Papirer,* udg. af P.A. Heiberg, V. Kuhr og E. Torsting (Københaven: Gyldendal, 1909-1948) 2. forøgede udg. ved N. Thulstrup, I-XVI, (1968-1978), followed by reference to volume, section, and number: e.g. Pap. X^1 A 59.

Abbreviations for Editions of Works by
Martin Luther (1483-1546)

LW   *Luther's Works,* Jaroslav Pelikan and Helmut Lehmann (eds) (Saint Louis: Concordia Publishing House, 1955-1986), followed by volume, page.

WA   *(Weimarer Ausgabe) D. Martin Luthers Werke: Kritische Gesammtausgabe* (Weimar: H. Böhlaus Nachfolger, 1883-1929), followed volume *(Band),* section *(Abteilung),* page.

Introduction — Struggling with God:
Towards a Kierkegaardian Theology of Spiritual Trial

> For I tell thee truly, that I had rather be so nowhere bodily,
> wrestling with that blind nought, than to be so great a lord that
> I might when I would be everywhere bodily, merrily playing
> with all this ought as a lord with his own.
>
> *(The Cloud of Unknowing)*

There are few passages that can access the depths of the *mysterium
tremendum et fascinans* which the strange story of Jacob's struggle
evokes (Genesis 32:24-31).[1] In his solitude, Jacob is assailed by a
strange figure with whom he struggles throughout the night. As
dawn approaches, the stranger, unable to prevail over Jacob, asks to
be released. Jacob refuses to let go without a blessing. The stranger
asks for his name and responds to Jacob's disclosure with the
declaring that "Your name shall no more be called Jacob, but *Yisra'el*,
for you have striven with God and with men, and have prevailed."
Jacob's name, which had previously revealed his flaw,[2] is replaced
with a new name which is a "name divinely understood" (SUD, 32).
The stranger bestows this gift of a new name — one sanctified by

---

1   As Valentine Cunningham writes: "Here is the *Unheimlich*, the uncanny, at
    its most disturbing: a night-time struggle for supremacy at a river-crossing,
    between a tribal patriarch and an unknown assailant whose identity
    remains crucially shady. Is he angel, good or bad, God Himself? Certainly
    this is a weird opponent, a ghostly antagonist who seems to have started
    out in narratives about ancient demon guardians of river crossings. . . . This
    text haunts precisely because of its imprecision." 'It is no Sin to Limp',
    Journal of Literature and Theology, 6 (4), December 1992, 303-309, 304.
2   'Jacob' is a name which may be etymologically related to 'deception' or
    'supplanter', particularly in reference to the deceptive way in which Jacob
    gain the blessing intended for his brother Esau from their father Isaac (Genesis
    27:36). However, Allen suggests that "The name Jacob has as its probable
    meaning 'May he protect' or in its fullest form. Jacob-el, 'may God protect'".
    Allen P. Ross, 'Jacob at the Jabbok, Israel at Peniel', *Bibliotheca Sacra*, 137 (1980),
    338-354, 353n33. On the significance of names and naming in this passage see
    further Herbert Marks, 'Biblical Naming and Poetic Etymology', *Journal of
    Biblical Literature*, 114 (1) Spring, 1995, 21-42, 35-42.

its unison with the name of God (*El*). In asking Jacob for this name, the stranger ask him to reveal himself; only to confer upon him the blessing of a, *Yisra'el* ('struggling with God'), which identifies him as one who has struggled with men and with God, and prevailed.[1] When Jacob responds in his own desire to know the name of his assailant; to which the stranger replies "Why is it that you ask my name?" (Genesis 32:29). There is no answer from Jacob recorded to this question but he is immediately blessed by the nameless stranger. Despite this enigmatic exchange, Jacob appears to make a mysterious inference from the encounter. Jacob consecrates the sacred ground of his struggle as *Peni'el* (the Face of God), "For I have seen God face to face, and yet my life is preserved."[2] To see God means death ("shall no man see me, and live" Exodus 33:21). Moses' desire to behold the glory (*kavod*) of God is refused, though he is permitted to see "my back parts; but my face shall not be seen" (Exodus 33:23). Despite Jacob's words that he had beheld God face to face and been preserved, it is left in some ambiguity as to whether Jacob struggles with God, with a man, with an angel (Hosea 12:4), or with one of the Angels of the Presence or Face of God (*mal'akim panayim*), a heavenly counterpart who renders his name to Jacob — after all, to see God is to die, even though Moses himself earlier speaks "face to face" with God, as with a friend (Exodus 33:11), and later that his own face shone fearfully radiant from speaking with God on Mount Sinai (Exodus 34:29-30).[3]

---

1 In this sense, while to see God is to die, one should also be paradoxically mindful of "the etymology of the word 'Israel' as 'one who sees God'." Elliot Wolfson, *Through a Speculum That Shines* (Princeton: Princeton University Press, 1997), 50. However, "Israel" might not be read as "he has striven with God", but rather as "El will rule (or strive)", or the proclamation "Let El rule" — a reading supported by the notion that the theophoric element (*El*) generally functions as the subject rather than the object of any personal name to which it is joined. Victor P. Hamilton, *The Book of Genesis: Chapters 18-50* (Grand Rapids: William B Eerdmands Publishing Company, 1995), 334. Another plausible interpretation is 'El struggles [for you]'; though Marks argues that "The story of the wrestling undermines this pious fiction, replacing the divine warrior, guardian of Israel, with the dangerous adversary: "El strives [against you]" (Marks, 'Biblical Naming and Poetic Etymology', 40).

2 Ross contends that the meaning is not that Jacob has seen God "and yet" has been delivered but that seeing the Face of God is itself an answer to a prayer of deliverance (Ross, 'Jacob at the Jabbok, Israel at Peniel', 349).

3 On the ambiguity over the identity of Jacob's assailant in the text of Genesis 32:25ff and its relation to Jacob's meeting with the angels of God (*Mahanayim*) at the beginning of chapter 32 see Tzemah Yoreh, 'Jacob's Struggle', *Zeitschrift für die Alttestamentliche Wissenschaft*, 117. Bd., S., 95-97. Yoreh argues for a subsequent Yahwist redaction which separates these once united texts "in attempt to produce ambiguity with regard to the identity of Jacob's mysterious

Through Luther's exegesis of Jacob's struggle, the question of the Face of God becomes masked by notions of the *Hester Panim* (hiding of the Face; the hidden face of God), and a struggle between the *deus absconditus* (hidden God) and the *deus revelatus* (revealed God): that is to say, Jacob's struggle becomes a cypher for the struggle to recognise the love of God in the face of God's apparent wrath. In his lectures on Genesis, Luther discerns that the struggler is "the Lord of glory, God Himself, or God's Son, who was to become incarnate and who appeared and spoke to the fathers" (LW 6, 130). Insofar as Luther generally affirms the *deus revelatus* in Christ, the identification of the stranger with "God's Son" here seems to also affirm Christ in terms of the *deus absconditus*, or the hidden face of God with which Jacob struggles and which is ultimately also revealed in its hiddenness to him. An identification of the stranger with the *Logos*, as the archetypal idea and mediator, was suggested by Philo (c.30 BCE - c.50 CE) in his consideration of Jacob's change of name in *De mutatione nominum*,[1] and affirmed as the pre-incarnate Christ by Clement of Alexandria (c.150-c.215), as the Logos, the teacher, who anointed Jacob against evil — the Face of God being interpreted as the Word of God by whom God is made manifest and known (*Paedagogus* 1.7.57).[2]

Although the revival of Clement's works post-dated Luther, the latter makes a comparable reading of the Face of God as the knowledge of God revealed through the Word of God in Christ.[3] Yet while Luther, like Clement, discerns a pedagogical element in Jacob's struggle, he also accentuates the dark ambiguity of revelation. Jacob struggles with "God Himself [*Deum ipsum*]" and also with the *deus absconditus*, since — hidden under the opposite (*absconditus sub contrario*) — God appears in the darkness of night as "otherwise" than the God of grace

wrestling partner" (97). Some later targumic and rabbinic accounts render the stranger as the angel *Sariel/Uriel*, who is also referred to in places as *Phanu'el*, the Angel of the Presence or Divine Face, perhaps suggesting a derivation from the place name *Peni'el* (Genesis 32:30). See further Andrei A. Orlov, 'The Face as the Heavenly Counterpart of the Visionary in the Slavonic *Ladder of Jacob*', Craig A. Evans (ed.), *Of Scribes and Sages: Early Jewish Interpretation and Transmission of Scripture: Volume 2: Later Versions and Traditions* (London: T & T Clark, 2004), 59-76, 72-74.

1 Philo, *De mutatione nominum*, (Les Œuvres de Philon d'Alexandrie 18) (Paris: Cerf, 1964), 17, 69-71.

2 On the influence of Philo on Clement see, for example, J.C.M. Van Winden, 'Quotations from Philo in Clement of Alexandria's "Protrepticus"', *Vigiliae Christianae*, 32 (3), September, 1978, 208-213.

3 Luther notes that *Peni'el* means the "face of God", and interprets that "'face of God' is nothing else but knowledge of God. Nobody knows God except through faith in his word" (LW 52, 129-130).

(LW 6, 132). In this sense Luther echoes what Otto affirms as the "non-rational" element of the numinous which is irreducible to the insights of speculative philosophy. Furthermore, Otto discerns a prophetic parallel between the *mysterium tremendum* of Jacob's struggle and Christ's struggle in Gethsemane, insofar as both are engaged "with the God of 'Wrath' and 'Fury', with the *numen*, which yet is itself '*My Father*'".[1] Following a Lutheran hermeneutic, the pre-incarnate son who struggled with Jacob now struggles with the wrath of God — a struggle between the *deus revelatus* and *deus absconditus*, which is only resolved through a submission to the divine will: reflected in this present work as *Anfechtung* (spiritual trial) dissolved through *Gelassenheit* (releasement).

While its central image is agonistic, Genesis 32 depicts a struggle with God that ultimately frees Jacob from the fear and violence of the struggle between brothers. Struggling with God enables him to behold the face of God in the other ("I have seen your face, as though I had seen the face of God, and you were pleased with me" Genesis 33:10).[2] While Jacob refuses to let go of his assailant — only releasing him upon receiving his blessing — the struggle provides a kenotic, even cathartic release from fear. Through the struggle, Jacob is reconciled to the other, to a deeper sense of self, and to a God whose face is presence-in-absence. While the onto-theological veracity of the identity of the stranger remains elusive, *aletheia* is 'unconcealed' through meditation (*meditatio* — one of Luther's three pillars of theology, along with *oratio* and, the prime concern of this study, *tentatio*).[3] What is struggled with is the hermeneutical question: "How does the given biblical text give itself to me to understand it — so that *I* am understood?"[4]

1   *The Idea of the Holy: An Inquiry into the non-rational factor in the idea of the divine and its relation to the rational*, trans. John H. Harvey (London: Oxford University Press, 1950), 85. The 1929 edition of *Das Heilige* contains an extensive citation from F.W. Robertson. 'Ten Sermons, III; Jacobs wrestling, point II; The revelation of Mystery': "There is a sense in which darkness has more of God than light has. He dwells in thick darkness.... When day breaks and distinctness comes, the Divine has evaporated from the soul like morning dew.... Yes, in solitary, silent, vague darkness, the Awful One is near.... That night, in that strange scene He impressed on Jacob's soul a religious awe, which he was hereafter to develop." *Das Heilige: Über das Irrationale in der Idee des Göttlichen und sein Verhältnis zum Rationalen* (München: Verlag C.H. Beck, 2004), 213.

2   I discuss the image of Jacob struggling with God in relation to the struggle for selfhood and recognition in 'The Allegory of Yisra'el', chapter five of *Kierkegaard and the Self Before God: Anatomy of the Abyss* (Bloomington: Indiana University Press, 2011).

3   See John W. Kleinig, '*Oratio, Meditatio, Tentatio*: What Makes A Theologian?', *Concordia Theological Quarterly*, 66 (3), July 2002, 258.

4   Oswald Bayer, 'Hermeneutical Theology', *Scottish Journal of Theology*, 56 (2), May 2003, 131-147, 131.

An unremitting concern with the "mirror of the Word" (JP 4:3902) motivates Kierkegaard's call for "a transition to the subjective" (FSE, 63), such as that which David was grasped by in the prophetic reflection of Nathan "thou art the man" (2 Samuel 12:7).

As mirror, as text, icon, and even idol, Jacob's struggle remains one of our most evocative and ambivalent images, inspiring a pathos which has endured from antiquity and continued to inspire modern and postmodern interpretations.[1] A potent example of the re-imagining of this image in visual art is Jacob Epstein's (1880-1959) sculpture *Jacob and the Angel* (1941). The statue does not depict Jacob struggling as such, but rather a Jacob who has struggled and who now hangs drained and weary in the embrace of the angel. This is not Jacob conquering God; nor is it the angel asking to be released. The angel holds a depleted Jacob up; Jacob does not have the angel in his grasp. Whereas the biblical account shows Jacob as resilient and undefeated, refusing to let go, forcing his opponent to ask for mercy, Epstein shows Jacob as wilting, yet upheld by the angel who is undiminished. Jacob is exhausted by the struggle, he can go no further. Yet he is supported by the very one who appears as his opponent. From one perspective, Epstein's sculpture might constitute a visual and tactile work of midrash — albeit a commentary which contradicts as well as embellishes the original text. From another perspective, however, it might be a presumptuous work of idolatry (Exodus 20:4). At once translucent and condensed, the two figures are formed from the same vivid alabaster rock. They are of one matter, even of one flesh. Catherine Garrett discusses Epstein's sculpture in terms of its potential for revealing meaning in the context of suffering and healing. She describes a vision of intimate ecstatic surrender: "Jacob, slumped with exhaustion, has given in to his opponent. They are so close that a single crack of light separates them. The statue represents the moment before Jacob begs the Angel for a blessing. It is a kind of ecstasy: clasped bodies, skin on skin." It is a work hewn from the raw matter of the artist himself, a dense and tangible manifestation of *Jacob*. "It is the reflection of his whole being on the mystery of pain and the peace that comes when we finally experience and accept a reality we have long resisted."[2]

---

1   For a sketch of some influential ancient, classical, and medieval readings see Ross, 'Jacob at the Jabbok, Israel at Peniel', 339-341. For more postmodern readings see, for example, Roland Barthes, 'La Lutte avec l'ange: analyse textuelle de Genese 32.23-33', *Analyse structural et exegise bibllque* (Neuchitel: Delachaux et Niestle Editeurs, 1971), 27-39; 'Wrestling with the Angel: Textual Analysis of Genesis 32:32-32', ed. Graham Ward, *The Postmodern God: A Theological Reader*, ed. Graham Ward (Oxford: Blackwell, 1997), 84-95; and Maurice Blanchot's 'Être Juif', *L'Entretien infini* (Paris: Gallimard, 1969), 188.

2   Catherine Garrett, 'Making Sense of Healing: Meaning and Spirituality

The emphasis here is on acceptance, resignation, *Gelassenheit* perhaps, rather than *Anfechtung*. The struggle has passed and now Jacob, vanquished, is held by grace in the angel's embrace. Such empowerment might also remind us of Jesus at Gethsemane where, in the dark night of sorrow, he too is strengthened by the appearance of an angel (Luke 22:43). It might be said that the strength of the angel enables Jacob to remain in the struggle. From this image one might infer that it is not that God desires to struggle with us, but that God desires us to struggle with God. The one who struggles has only to not let go — though in truth it is the angel who does not let go. In truth, it is God who conquers 'God' in us. In this there are traces of the spirit of Kierkegaard's 'Upbuilding Discourse', 'One Who Prays Aright Struggles in Prayer and is Victorious — in that God is Victorious' (1844).

A Life and Death Struggle

The Jews believed that to see God was death; the pagans that to see God was punished by madness — it was punished, and yet it was the supreme grace and blessedness. This is what it means to have an immediate relationship to God — it is *eo ipso* to be sacrificed; as I have often said, it means to be hit by a sunstroke of the unconditioned — the greatest possible human suffering and a superhuman blessedness. (JP 4:4479)

---

in Stories of Chronic Illness', Peter L. Twohig and Vera Kalitzkus (eds), *Making Sense of Health, Illness and Disease* (Amsterdam/New York: Rodopi, 2004), 105-124, at 107. Epstein's work of art may thus provide the subject with what Kristeva, with reference to Hans Holbein the Younger's *The Body of the Dead Christ in the Tomb* (1521), calls "an imaginary elaboration" of its own suffering. Julia Kristeva, *Black Sun: Depression and Melancholia*, trans. Leon S. Roudiez (New York: Columbia University Press, 1989), 133. At the same time, as explored below, Christ's suffering and the struggle of Jacob retain an irreducible ineffability, even transcendence or sublimity, which cannot be fully represented. See further my 'Lazarus and the Sickness Unto Death: An Allegory of Despair', *Religion and the Arts*, 15 (2011), 486-519. See also Cobb's discussion of Picasso's *Guernica* (1937) in the context of Lutheran *Anfechtung*: "What makes this a Protestant painting, he [Tillich] claimed, is that 'it shows the human situation without any cover. It shows what is now in the souls of many Americans as disruptiveness, existential doubt, emptiness and meaninglessness.' *Guernica* corroborates Luther's experience of *Anfechtung*, of the desolation of sinful humanity forsaken by God, but now tuned into the frequency of the twentieth century, *Guernica* is, in this sense, in the lineage of the art of the crucifixion." Kelton Cobb, 'Theology and Culture', *The Blackwell Guide to Theology and Popular Culture* (Oxford: Blackwell, 2005), 95.

When Kierkegaard asserts that the relationship between God and humanity can be construed as "suffering, anguish, a death struggle" (JP 4:4725) he does not offer Christianity as its immediate cure. On the contrary, Christianity itself asserts that "there is a life and death battle between God and man; God hates man just as man hates God" (JP 4:4711). This agonistic vision reaches its crescendo in the final year of Kierkegaard's life with the lightning flash of 'The Moment' and its unsettling reminder that "God is indeed a human being's most appalling enemy, your mortal enemy, he wants you to die, die unto the world; he hates specifically that in which you naturally have your life, to which you cling with all your zest for life" (LW, 177). Yet, as this work will explore, the enmity that spiritual trial and temptation bears witness to is the primal enmity between spirit (Ånd) and spiritlessness (Åndløsheden) — a struggle elicited by the dawning realisation that "Spirit is restlessness" and that, as an expression of Spirit, "Christianity is the most profound restlessness of existence — so it is in the New Testament" (JP 4:4361). In contrast to the sensate principles of flesh and blood, which flee from the thought of their own non-being, "spirit is to will to die, to die to the world" (JP 4:4354).[1] As the burning realisation that "Spirit is fire" (JP 4:4355), spiritual trial evokes the liminal point of contact between Spirit and spiritlessness — a burning difference between the nascent self and the Absolute, which, as both its limit and its destiny, seems to threaten its reduction to ashes while also promising its sanctification and transubstantiation into the fire of Spirit. The parlance of spiritual trial strives to speak about this transfiguration of the self as a passing through the flames, as a struggle with God and with the self, in which the restlessness of the self finds rest, grounded transparently in God (SUD, 82).

Yet, as will be explored throughout this work, spiritual trial's process of 'dying to' is not, for Kierkegaard, the annihilation of personal identity within the divine ground or the melting away of all individuality "in the divine ocean" (JP 4:3887). It is the realisation of the deep call of the self to become spirit, to become an *I*, enabled to love God, freely, from out of its own self: "To be *spirit* is to be *I*. God desires to have *I*s, for God desires to be loved" (JP 4:4350). As such, despite the appearance of spiritual trial's more numinous moments of being overshadowed and overwhelmed by the Holy Absolute, the process also reveals a sense that God's omnipotence withdraws, out of love, in order to create the space for something other than God to become itself, thereby expressing divine omnipotence in the ability "to create the most fragile

---

1 See further my 'To Die and Yet Not Die: Kierkegaard's Theophany of Death', Patrick Stokes and Adam J. Buben (eds), *Kierkegaard and Death* (Bloomington: Indiana University Press, 2011), 44-64.

of all things — a being independent of that very omnipotence" (JP 2:1251). Such kenotic creation expresses the divine desire that this self will realise itself as Spirit, as *I*, as freedom, and return to God in love — though with the inexorable possibility that the self may decide to desire itself, "the unfathomable grief of [divine] love" (SUD, 126). While it can be said that all love begins, secretly, in the dark hidden spring of God's love (WL, 9-10), it is also said that the human being is not merely a conduit for the divine flow and return of love. One forms one's own heart in the process (WL, 12), out of which one offers a love that is uniquely one's own and out of which one endeavours to help others to love God.[1] The omnipotence of divine love is manifest as love "even at the last instant by letting him be something for it" (CD, 133). Something intimately related to this may also be said of Spirit. While Spirit may be God-breathed and, as such, a divine spark, an echo of the image of God hidden deep within the human being, Spirit is the love of God which also constitutes the awakening and realisation of the individual self. As a transfigured self, Spirit returns to God, as love, but in personalised form, as a free and desiring self, as Spirit, as passing through the fires of Spirit and spiritual trial, but not devoured by them. In this sense, the self as Spirit resembles the image of God but remains other than God in the freedom of love's reciprocity.

The notion that existence is beset or even driven by struggle does not belong to Kierkegaard alone. His locating of the heart of struggle between God and humanity, Spirit and spiritlessness, is, in part, an attempt to re-awaken a soporific modern Christendom to the shadow-side of the "infinite qualitative difference" between the human and the divine. God may have created human beings free, *ex nihilo*; but what we make of our freedom, its uses and abuses, is laid our *coram deo*. As such, it should not be forgotten that human beings are also comprised of Spirit and the eternal, and that the image of God is constantly at risk of (self-)abasement. We forget that not only is God's absence out there beyond the world, it is also an absence deep within insofar as God, the Holy Other, is also the hidden ground of being, deeper and closer to me than I am to myself.

Yet it is also speculative philosophy's and theology's transgression of the "infinite qualitative difference" that troubled Kierkegaard. Within the Hegelian systematising of his contemporaries both the individual and radical alterity of God were in danger of dissolution.

---

1 In this Hampson aptly discerns a "self-integrity, accountability, and responsibility to ourselves", which affirms the self as more than a "(mere) channel between God and neighbour" and thereby empowered rather than simply made nothing by love. Daphne Hampson, *Kierkegaard: Exposition and Critique* (Oxford: Oxford University Press, 2013), 207, 252.

For Kierkegaard, history, particularly the history of Christendom, has failed to reveal the dialectical unfolding of Spirit (*Geist*) in the world. On the contrary, such a vision serves to obfuscate the agonistic tension between Spirit and spiritlessness that Christianity initially awakened. While a Hegelian view of dialectical sublation or *Aufhebung* affirms a dynamic process of struggle inherent to the world, the meta-narrative of Spirit's progressive unfolding in the world seems deluded and self-aggrandising. On the inter-subjective level, Hegel's Master-Slave dialectic (Lordship and Bondage — *Herrschaft und Knechtschaft*) provides an insightful account of the life and death struggle (*den Kampf auf Leben und Tod*) for recognition in which "each seeks the death of the other."[1] Yet there are potential traces of this struggle in the relation between self and God as explored by Kierkegaard and others.[2]

The recognition that struggle determines the shape of the world is given epoch-defining expression in Charles Darwin's *On the Origin of Species* (1859).[3] Darwin wrote of a "war of nature" formalised via the "general law" of natural selection: "multiply, vary, let the strongest live and the weakest die." It was above all the entropy and suffering generated by a world seemingly at war with itself which provided the deepest wound to theological visions of the goodness and providence of creation.[4] Darwin's exposure of the darker side of nature contributed to Freud's belief that alongside the instinct to grow and preserve life there also existed "another contrary instinct seeking to dissolve those units and bring them back to their primaeval, organic state."[5] Therefore Freud proposed to explain "the phenomena of life"

1   *Phenomenology of Spirit*, B, IV, 187, p.113.
2   See further my *Kierkegaard and the Self Before God*, 101, 160-162; and 'Kierkegaard's Theophany of Death'. Emmanuel Levinas also observes that "In [Kierkegaardian] belief, existence is always trying to secure recognition for itself, just like consciousness in Hegel. It struggles for this recognition by seeking forgiveness and salvation." 'Existence and Ethics' in *Kierkegaard: A Critical Reader*, ed. J. Reé and J. Chamberlain (Oxford: Basil Blackwell, 1998), p.30. See also Jean Hyppolite, *Studies on Marx and Hegel*, ed. and trans. John O'Neill (New York, Evanston, San Francisco, London: Harper and Row, 1973), 133.
3   Hampson suggests that though Kierkegaard did not live to see this work published, related discussions were already part of Kierkegaard's intellectual context in the 1840s (*Kierkegaard*, 131-132).
4   As Philip Kitcher observes in the light of Darwin, "we easily might take life as it has been generated on our planet as the handiwork of a bungling, or a chillingly indifferent, god." *Living With Darwin: Evolution, Design, and the Future of Faith* (Oxford: Oxford University Press, 2007), 126.
5   Sigmund Freud, 'Civilization and its Discontents' (1930 [1929])', The Pelican Freud Library, Volume 12: *Civilization, Society and Religion: Group Psychology, Civilization and its Discontents and Other Works*, translated by James Strachey

according to the "concurrent or mutually opposing action" of the life-instinct, *Eros*, and its counterpart, the instinct of death, or death-drive, *Thanatos*.[1] The destructive energy of *Thanatos*, Freud suggested, needed to be directed outwards so as not to become self-destructive, with *Eros* helping to direct the energy of *Thanatos* towards external objects.[2] From this insight Freud concludes:

> And now, I think, the meaning of the evolution of civilization is no longer obscure to us. It must present the struggle between Eros and Death, between the instinct of life and the instinct of destruction, as it works itself out in the human species. This struggle is what life essentially consists of, and the evolution of civilization may therefore be simply described as the struggle for life of the human species. And it is this battle of the giants that our nurse-maids try to appease with their lullaby about Heaven.[3]

From this perspective of *Eros* and *Thanatos*, temptation might be described as the enticement of *Eros* by objects, which, while life-affirming in one sense, ultimately bring death. This ambivalence evokes the anxiety of temptation: the erotic desire for that which brings death. Throwing myself into the embrace of the flesh may seem like a surrender to the unquenchable life-drive of *Eros*, but in doing so I fall towards death. Yet this fall towards death, to destruction and non-being, is itself tempting. It tempts *Thanatos* in all its desires, drives, and instincts towards dissolution. What is more, in these terms, spiritual trial itself, in all its self-mortifying *passio*, might itself be described as an expression of *Thanatos*, the death-drive internalised and directed against the self — a form of *automachia*, which subsists under the guise of a higher form of *Eros*, a love for God that can only be realised via a death to self. Yet at the same time the mortification of the self, in its *ascesis*, might signify an attempt to apply the death-drive to the excesses of lower forms of *Eros*, which, by surrendering to fleshly and worldly temptations, threatens to destroy the self or cast the soul into eternal death. In this sense, *Thanatos* as self-mortifying *ascesis* seeks to rescue the self from the hedonistic excesses of *Eros*, which itself threatens to overflow itself into *Thanatos*. Such is seen in the pathology of addiction. What began as the pursuit of pleasure or escape becomes bereft and imprisoning. Though it may have origins in some sensual semblance of *Eros*, addiction becomes an expression of the death-drive and a manifestation of demonic despair (Cf. SUD, 108).

---

and edited by Albert Dickson (Harmondsworth: Penguin Books, 1985), 310.
1   *Ibid.*
2   *Ibid.* 311: Freud's notion of the death-drive is itself informed by Arthur Schopenhauer's *The World as Will and Representation* (1818).
3   *Ibid.* 314.

In the struggles of spiritual trial the individual must remain mindful of the possibility that the impulse to become nothing before God may express a pathological desire for insatiable self-mortification. Kierkegaard even warns against such excesses, against the desire to be too much Spirit and against the risk of being burned to ashes in Spirit's fire. Temperance is required, both for the sake of one's sanity and humanity. Only God is purely Spirit. Yet in becoming nothing before God the self in spiritual trial renounces its drive for self-will, it resigns the *apotheosis* of despair. Spiritual trial's death-to-self might therefore be described as a sublimation of the death-drive, directing negative and destructive, perhaps even apophatic and agonistic, energy against that which occludes its relationship with the divine. Spiritual trial thereby comes to affirm life on a higher level, affirming a higher form of *Eros*, which passes through a sublimating process of positive disintegration.[1] In willing to die-to temptation (*Eros*) and despair (*Thanatos*), the struggling self before God aspires to its calling to rest transparently in God. Yet Kierkegaard is also wary of a 'mystical' desire to become as nothing, to be annihilated, swallowed up in the abyss of God, which may also express an attempt to sublimate *Thanatos*.[2] Kierkegaard's vision of spiritual trial, by contrast, also consists in the self becoming itself, as Spirit, as the image of God, but in a realisation of subjectivity that is freed to love God from a heart of its own. It contains a quantum of individuality, a secret of interiority, which is its own and can be claimed by no one else. It is the secret of suffering belonging to the restless self that struggles with God in the longing to rest transparently in God.

Struggling *with* God

While spiritual trial may involve one in struggles against 'the world', 'the flesh', and 'the devil', its ultimate meaning is as a struggle with God — albeit a struggle that takes place in the battleground of the self's relation to the Absolute. 'Struggling with God' is an ambiguous even polyvalent motif. At once it may be presumptuous, agonistic, erotic, hubristic, kenotic, and even blasphemous. One may struggle *against* God, or struggle *with* God *against* the world, the devil, and the flesh — even against oneself. What is more, through a theology of spiritual trial I suggest a form of struggle that can be drawn out from

---

1 Cf. Kazimierz Dąbrowski's theory of positive disintegration by which the self undoes primal superficial integrations in search of a higher, though agonistic, sense of self. *Positive Disintegration* (Boston: Little Brown, 1964).
2 I discuss this further in '*Mysterium Horrendum*: Mystical Theology and the Negative Numinous', Louise Nelstrop and Simon D. Podmore (eds), *Exploring Lost Dimensions in Christian Mysticism: Opening to the Mystical* (Aldershot: Ashgate, 2013).

Luther and Kierkegaard: a struggle that is both *with* God and *against* 'God', a struggle against the appearance of the God of darkness which refuses to let go of the God of love. This is, in Lutheran terms, the struggle against the *deus absconditus*, which struggles to lay hold of the *deus revelatus*. Yet it should be stated that such a struggle is not a struggle with the inner being of God-in-Godself (*deus nudus*) but a struggle with the appearance and the revelation of God. In this sense, the struggle is also a struggle against oneself: a struggle with one's fears and desires, with the idols of the mind. The struggle is therefore agonistic and apophatic: it seeks to free the self from its own delusions and attachments to its own God-images. It struggles with the otherness of God and the limit of the Absolute. And yet this undoing is integral to the self's becoming Spirit, the image of God, grounded transparently and transfigured in God.

Whether from the perspective of agonistic apophaticism or demonic defiance, atheism can itself express forms of struggling with God, or perhaps more aptly with 'God' or the 'God-image'. It is in this sense that Tillich suggests an affinity between the deicidal response of Nietzsche's 'Ugliest Man' (*Hässlichste Mensch*) to the omniscient and omnivorous gaze of God and the *Anfechtung* of Luther.[1] According to the account of Nietzsche's 'Ugliest Man', God sees every dirty recess of his ugliness. His gaze intrudes and devours, knowing no mercy or satiety of his appetite to know and to see. "This most curious, overobtrusive, overpitying one had to die. He always saw me: on such a witness I wanted to have revenge or not live myself."[2] The gaze is shameless in its unremitting exposure of the shame of its object. Thus the gaze of God, even in its pity, also reflects upon the Ugliest Man himself, becoming a mirror in which his ugliness cannot escape consciousness of itself. In retaliation against this consciousness of himself as an object for a seemingly Absolute Subject the Ugliest Man murders God. In his *ressentiment* he cannot bear that such a witness live. Of course, the question of deicide already suggests a potential metaphysical contradiction. If God were truly this Absolute Subject then no object, no matter how resentful and demonically enraged, would be able to overthrow God. Nietzsche's Ugliest Man could therefore be understood as performing an act of *automachia*: he overthrows the super-ego in his murder of God — "the hypostasis of a delirious bad conscience, magnified by the metaphysical dimension into a constant

---

1   Paul Tillich, 'The Escape From God', *The Shaking of the Foundations* (New York: Charles Scribner's Sons, 1952), 44. See also my *Kierkegaard and the Self Before God*, 124-126.

2   Friedrich, Nietzsche, 'Thus Spoke Zarathustra: Fourth Part', *The Portable Nietzsche*, ed. and trans. Walter Kaufmann (London: Penguin, 1982), 378-379.

presence".[1] As shall be explored further in this work, spiritual trial can also confront the self with its own psychogenic projections of 'God'. In doing so, the Absolute limit holds a mirror up to the self — an *auto-phany* rather than a theophany — before which the self cannot bear to stand. Yet the struggle of spiritual trial is also to overcome such dysmorphic images, to resists the temptation to flee or to despair but to press on, in spite of one's self, clinging to the God of love.

It is through his own struggles with the meaning of his *Anfechtung* that Luther reaches a breakthrough. The gates of paradise at which he had hammered for so long were opened by grace. He fled from 'God' to God in the realisation that he himself was the source of his experience of the fear and wrath of God. Yet while Tillich discerns the same desire to flee from God in both Luther and Nietzsche, it is also evident that each understands the place of the individual *coram Deo* quite divergently. As shall be elaborated further in this work, Luther and Kierkegaard envisage a struggle with God that also invokes God in the struggle against the self (along with the idols of 'God', which it has constructed). While Luther and Kierkegaard seek to overcome both 'self' and 'God' through God, Nietzsche, by contrast, desires to overcome God and humanity by aspiring to the evolutionary horizon of the Overman (*Übermensch*). In some revealing comments on Darwin's theory of evolution, Nietzsche asserts "Anti-Darwin" that contrary to Darwinian observations about "the will to life" it is actually the "will to non entity", which Nietzsche sees prevailing all around him. It is precisely Christianity itself that bears responsibility for interfering in the evolutionary will for the survival of the strongest.

By upholding the weak and the disempowered and by fashioning virtue in the form of self-negation, Christianity, in Nietzsche's view, dissolves the struggle and enmity that Nietzsche reifies with the motto: "What does not kill me makes me stronger."[2] Struggle, opposition and enmity serve to ennoble humanity. "We adopt the same attitude towards the 'enemy within'", Nietzsche observes, "there too we have spiritualized enmity, there too we have grasped its *value*. One is *fruitful* only at the cost of being rich in contradictions; one remains *young* only on condition the soul does not relax, does not long for peace." To maintain the self in perpetual struggle against itself may mean a divided self, but it may also mean a self capable of attaining greatness by virtue of the struggle itself. As such, Nietzsche suggests,

---

1 Michel Haar, 'Nietzsche and the Metamorphosis of the Divine', ed. Philip Blond, *Post-Secular Philosophy* (London and New York: Routledge, 1998), 162.
2 *Twilight of the Idols*, (trans. R.J. Hollingdale. London: Penguin Books, 1990), 33.

"One has renounced *grand* life when one renounces war."[1] As J. Keith Hyde aptly observes, Nietzsche's Zarathustra "advocated the Jacobian art of creative combat: 'I wrestled long and was a wrestler, so that I might one day have my hands free for blessing.'" At the same time, Hyde observes, Nietzsche also "warned of the dangers of self-dissolution from constant conflict: 'He who fights with monsters should look to it that he himself does not become a monster.'"[2]

Struggling with God becomes the ideal of Pierre-Joseph Proudhon's *anti-theism* who, appropriating the iconography of Genesis 32, declares that it is human destiny to struggle like Jacob, until death.[3] Resonant with Nietzschean self-assertion, even self-aggrandisement, Proudhon attacks theistic accounts of divine providence in the name of human freedom, dignity, and autonomy. His invocation of Jacob's struggle is almost demonic, even Promethean, in its appropriation. Unlike the normative tradition of Christian readings, Proudhon invokes an eternal death struggle against the theistic view of God, in terms perhaps reminiscent of a Hegelian Master-Slave dialectic. Proudhon thus joins the ranks of *misotheists*[4] who struggle against God, or against ideas of God, from a position of hatred, defiance, despair, humanism, or demonic self-apotheosis. In this company one might find Marquis de Sade's embrace of sin, perversity and temptation as a way of raging against God, Baudelaire's demonic curses against the divine, Albert Camus' moral death sentence on

---

1 *Twilight of the Idols*, 54. The contrasts between Nietzsche's vision of the will-to-power and Kierkegaard's own kenotic view and critique of power are well elucidated in J. Keith Hyde, *Concepts of Power in Kierkegaard and Nietzsche* (Farnham: Ashgate, 2010).

2 Hyde, *Concepts of Power in Kierkegaard and Nietzsche*, 65-66. The first reference is to *Thus Spoke Zarathustra*, trans. R.J. Hollingdale (London: Penguin Books, 1976), 186. The second is to *Beyond Good and Evil*, trans. R.J. Hollingdale. (London: Penguin Books, 1990), 102.

3 See further my 'Struggling with God: Kierkegaard/Proudhon', Roman Králik, *et al* (eds) *Acta Kierkegaardiana. Vol. II: Kierkegaard and Great Philosophers*, (Mexico City and Barcelona: Sociedad Iberoamericana de Estudios Kierkegaardianos, University of Barcelona, Kierkegaard Society in Slovakia, 2007), 90-103.

4 See further the erudite discussion of Proudhon in Bernard Schweizer, *Misotheism: The Untold Story of Hating God* (Oxford: Oxford University Press, 2011), 40-47. Schweizer refers to Proudhon's 1846 *Philosophie de la misère* as the "earliest and possibly the most radical and shocking manifestation" of a "politically inspired misotheism" (40) and Proudhon himself as "a titan of misotheism" (46). Schweizer notes that while Proudon "still held a vestigial belief" in "a personal God" he vehemently opposed "any divine object of worship" (*Misotheism*, 50), equally so if this object, or idol, be a humanist idea of Man himself.

God, and even Elie Wiesel's agonistic protest against divine apathy.[1] As far as temptation is concerned, what better way to struggle against God than to embrace all sins, as each one is a wound to the divine heart, each fall into temptation is a nail in the cross for which the pleasure alone is all mine? From such a stance of struggling against God, might the misotheist wish to invert the Kierkegaardian priority of higher spiritual trial over lower temptation? Perhaps temptation is higher insofar as it entails a life-affirming reclamation of the flesh, an attempt to become coherent with one's own nature? Perhaps spiritual trial constitutes abasement in the form of self-subjection to a jealous and Narcissistic numinous Overlord? Might one be best to flee spiritual trial and press on into temptation? These are temptations that will return to haunt us when considering 'the demonic' as the shadow-side of spiritual trial.

A further vision of struggling with God, which is in part inspired by Darwin and Nietzsche, along with Bergson and Whitehead, is found in the writings of Nikos Kazantzakis. In Kazantzakis' novels, plays, and spiritual writings, themes of rebellion, temptation, the spirit and the flesh are invoked with visceral pathos and all in service to the notion of struggle: namely the struggle to transubstantiate matter into spirit. For Kazantzakis, "*theōsis* takes the form of a struggle, in which substance is transformed into spirit; and indeed, *metousiōsis*, transubstantiation, is our 'highest obligation.'"[2] In his theological manifesto, *The Saviors of God (Salvatores Dei)*, Kazantzakis outlines his vision of the struggle for a form of theosis in which both the human and the divine are united: "Behind all appearances, I divine a struggling essence. I want to merge with it."[3] Yet the divine stranger is a voice deep within Kazantzakis who calls out for help, for salvation, desiring to be liberated from every fragment of matter in a violent struggle for transubstantiation. "The essence of our God is STRUGGLE".[4] God is a whirlwind, a consuming fire, "God laughs, wails, kills, sets us on fire, and then leaves us in the

---

1 On Weisel and the Holocaust viewed in this light see Schweizer, *Misotheism*, 149-172.

2 Pamela J. Francis, 'Reading Kazantzakis through Gregory of Nyssa: Some Common Anthropological Themes', Darren J.N. Middleton (ed.), *Scandalizing Jesus: Kazantzakis's The Last Temptation of Christ Fifty Years On*, (New York/London: Continuum, 2005), 65. However, as Francis also elucidates, Kazantzakis departs from the more Orthodox tradition of Gregory of Nyssa: "In Gregory's anthropology, *theōsis* is the realization of the image of God within us. In Kazantzakis's Bergsonian understanding of the transubstantiation of matter into spirit, we 'save' God" (64).

3 *The Saviors of God: Spiritual Exercises*, trans. Kimon Friar (New York: Simon & Schuster, Inc., 1960), 52.

4 *Ibid.* 92.

middle of the way, charred embers."[1] Yet in struggling with this savage vagabond God humanity is not always overwhelmed: "My God is not Almighty. . . . He is defeated incessantly, but rises again, full of blood and earth, to throw himself into battle once more."[2] God evolves along with the world and humanity. God is savage and cruel, striving through blood and earth; and yet as God stumbles and struggles, God is in need of human compassion. Human and divine salvation is co-dependent: "God is imperiled. . . . He cannot be saved unless we save him with our own struggles; nor can we be saved unless he is saved".[3] We save God by our struggles, sacred and profane, "by creating, and by transmuting matter into spirit".[4]

The eternal struggle between the spirit and the flesh and the tension yet salvific inter-dependence of the human and the divine are dramatised further in Kazantzakis's most infamous novel, *The Last Temptation* (1955). Kazantzakis' Jesus is hunted by God, haunted by a *mysterium horrendum*, which seems intent on both his destruction and his divinization. Christ's temptation expresses the tense duality inherent to all humanity between the 'lower' temptations of the flesh (sexual passion, violence, sedition, intoxication, greed, marriage) and the 'higher' trials of the spirit (sacrifice, martyrdom, divine vocation). This struggle reaches its crescendo in 'the last temptation', which is itself shaped and determined by the very struggle to identify and distinguish between God and the devil, the higher and the lower (*Anfechtung* and temptation). Kazantzakis imagines a struggle with God that faces the darkness of a savage deity who is neither all-holy nor all-powerful, a God who struggles for God's life and for our salvific compassion. While his theology and Christology would have been fundamentally incompatible with Luther and Kierkegaard, he nonetheless provides a passionate illustration of how the struggles, which Lutheran tradition comes to understand in terms of temptation (Gn. *Versuchung* / Dn. *Fristelse*) and spiritual trial (Gn. *Anfechtung* / Dn. *Anfægtelse*), may be seen as two sides of the same coin.[5]

---

1 *Ibid.* 94.
2 *Ibid.* 103.
3 *Ibid.* 105.
4 *Ibid.* 106.
5 See further Simon D. Podmore, 'Crucified by God: Kazantzakis and The Last *Anfechtung* of Christ', *Literature and Theology*, 22 (4), December 2008, 419-435. For further work on Kazantzakis and Kierkegaard see Jerry H. Gill, 'Kazantzakis and Kierkegaard: Some Comparisons and Contrasts', Darren J. Middleton and Peter Bien (ed.), *God's Struggler: Religion in the Writings of Nikos Kazantzakis* (Macon, Georgia: Mercer University Press, 1996). For comparison of Kazantzakis with Luther see Ann M. Pederson, 'Saviors of God: Soteriological Motifs in the Theologies of Kazantzakis and Luther', *God's Struggler*, 93-112.

When he awoke he lifted his face towards the east and saw the sun, a terrible blast-furnace, rising above the sand. That is God's face, he reflected, putting his palm over his eyes so that he would not be dazzled. 'Lord,' he whispered, ' . . . I possess no weapon but love. With that I have come to do battle. Help me!'[1]

The 'Heroism' of Struggle

Within all evocations or imaginings of spiritual struggle there are potential temptations for heroism, hubris, narcissism, even a veiled form of self-apotheosis. After all, what is more sublime and self-aggrandising than struggling with God? Kazantzakis writes in his spiritual autobiography that "Each man acquires the stature of the enemy with whom he wrestles. It pleased me, even if it meant my destruction, to wrestle with God".[2] Such struggle is the substance of poetic memorial, as Johannes de silentio writes:

> Everyone shall be remembered, but everyone was great wholly in proportion to the magnitude of that with which he *struggled*. For he who struggled with the world became great by conquering the world, and he who struggled with himself became great by conquering himself, but he who struggled with God became the greatest of all. Thus did they struggle in the world, man against man, one against thousands, but he who struggled with God was the greatest of all. (FT, 16)

Anti-Climacus himself speaks of the rare "Christian heroism" of venturing "wholly to become oneself, an individual human being, this specific human being, alone before God" (SUD, 5). Yet Kierkegaard is also wary of the humility of spiritual struggle, that there is no roll of honour for such essentially secret struggles, that one should not desire to be more Spirit than God has ordained. In the Lutheran vein, the struggle with God is not a titanic struggle between the heroic solitary individual and God-in-Godself (*deus nudus*) but rather a struggle with the appearance, or even masks, of God. As such, the struggle is made possible by a prior divine kenosis in which God gives of Godself in a form that can be struggled with, which itself reflects the God-image of the self. In this sense, Luther's struggles with a wrathful God are transfigured by the realisation that God is not angry with him, but that he is angry with God. In psychogenic terms, the appearance of the wrath of God is due in part

---

1 Nikos Kazantzakis, *The Last Temptation*, trans. Peter Bien (London: Faber and Faber, 1975), 255-56.
2 Kazantzakis, *Report to Greco* (New York: Simon and Schuster, 1965), 146.

to a projection of the self's own wrath against itself, even against God. The *Anfechtung* is the struggle against this vision of God in which the victory is granted by clinging to the God of love. 'God' is overcome by God. Spiritual trial reminds the struggler of their humility (*humus* — earth): the creature-consciousness of oneself who is but dust and ashes and yet stands before God (Genesis 18:27).[1]

The notion of spiritual struggle attains its apotheosis in the temptations and trials of Christ. This Christological tension between a seductive lower human, or fleshly, and higher divine, or spiritual, will is assumed and interiorised in Paul, such that it becomes central to the narrative of the divided 'I' which is elaborated through Augustine and Luther. While Jesus was tempted, yet without sin (Hebrews 4:15), the tempted follower of Christ is undermined by an indwelling of sin: "For I do not do the good I want, but the evil I do not want is what I do. Now if I do what I do not want, it is no longer I that do it, but sin which dwells within me" (Romans 7:19-20).[2] The desire of Spirit to mortify this enemy within, as well as to withdraw from, or die to, the enemy without — the forces of 'the world' and the devil that elicit the temptation to sin — is expressed through *ascesis*: "the spiritual combat", which, according to Rimbaud, is "harder than men's battles".[3]

Kierkegaard harbours a characteristically Lutheran suspicion towards the self-mortifying practices of individual ascetics and its formalisation in the monastic community. Yet he also suspects that while monastic withdrawal from the world may suggest a self-mortifying desire for self-apotheosis, the consciousness of enmity between Spirit and spiritlessness that the monastery expresses is a vital truth, which modern Christendom is in danger of forgetting. It is in the forgotten pages of old devotional writings that Kierkegaard discovers the category of spiritual trial — a discovery which exposes a lacuna in contemporary Christianity.

The contours of Kierkegaard's rehabilitation of spiritual trial are defined to a significant extent by the demographic of devotional texts he is exposed to. As will be discussed further below, this focus is predominantly oriented around *Die Deutsche Mystik* tradition, and the

---

1 Otto describes this 'creature feeling' [*Kreaturgefühl*] as "the emotion of a creature, abased and overwhelmed by its own nothingness in contrast to that which is supreme above all creatures". *The Idea of the Holy*, 10.

2 "For the desires of the flesh are against the Spirit, and the desires of the Spirit are against the flesh; for these are opposed to each other, to prevent you from doing what you would" (Galatians 5:17). See further *Kierkegaard and the Self Before God*, 16-17. Biblical references are taken from the Revised Standard Version (RSV).

3 Quoted in Olivier Clément, *The Roots of Christian Mysticism* (London: New City, 1997), 130.

Lutheran and Pietistic sources that it helped to form. However, before concentrating this exploration of *Anfechtung/Anfægtelse*, honourable mention should be made of some other notable analogues and antecedents from the wider tradition of Christian spiritual literature. While *Anfechtung* has been assimilated into Lutheran theology, the roots of the term in Roman Catholic theology remains relatively neglected. As I suggest above, the various strains of reflection on spiritual struggle throughout Christian tradition share a common genealogy in the passion of Christ and the trials and tribulations of Paul and the early Christians. Reflections from various traditions centre around such common themes as dying to self and world, resignation, detachment, trust in God, the edification of suffering — all traceable to the sufferings of Jesus and the tribulations of the early church.

One of the most influential and widely translated works of Catholic spirituality (and one to which Kierkegaard does not seem to refer) is Lorenzo Scupoli's (c. 1530-1610) *The Spiritual Combat* (*Il combattimento spirituale*). The first known edition dates from Venice in 1589 and the book is soon translated widely in the seventeenth century, including a German edition (*Der Geistliche Kampf*: the 'combat' (*combattimento*) is not rendered in German as *Anfechtung*). The struggle described by Scupoli is essentially a struggle against the self — that which Nietzsche may have regarded as a spiritualized enmity toward the enemy within. While Alexandre-Louis Leloir's (1843-84) painting *Jacob Wrestling with the Angel* (1865) adorns the recent English translation (2010), in the context of Scupoli's work this image most appositely suggests an allegory for the self's struggle with itself. Scupoli himself makes no reference to the struggle of Genesis 32 and the sense one gets from the work is that any notion of struggling with *God* would be presumptuous, perhaps even blasphemous. And yet it might be said that the soul does struggle *with* God insofar as it struggles on the side of God, on the side of the Divine Will against the lower self-will and against the kingdom of the devil — and in this the spiritual combat shares a kinship with spiritual trial.

Scupoli's work encourages its reader to become as nothing, to resign one's own will completely to the Will of God. Such resignation, even perfection, demands that one does violence to oneself by attacking all evil desires and passions. "Doubtless this is the hardest of all struggles", this struggle against the self, "because by fighting against ourselves, we are, at the same time, attacked by ourselves, and on that account the victory obtained in such a conflict will be of all others the most glorious and most dear to God".[1] By waging war against the enemy within, one aspires not simply to sheer self-negation but to a "virtuous

---

1 *The Spiritual Combat*, (London: Longmans, Green, and Co., 1910), Chapter I, 7.

self-distrust, which is based on genuine humility and experiential self-knowledge".[1] In this sense, the spiritual combat does not aspire to destroy the self but to come to a higher self-knowledge — albeit a knowledge of oneself, which, in all humility, has learnt not to trust the self alone. The aim of this spiritual combat is not therefore a mere death of the self, but, as Kierkegaard himself would concur, it aspires to "purity of heart . . . namely, the putting off the old man, and the putting on the new".[2] Yet this is not called a spiritual *combat* without reason. One possesses a "reasonable will" that stands between the higher "Divine Will which is above it, and the lower will of the flesh which is below it". This reasonable will is constantly "assailed by one of the other; each seeking to attract it, to bring it into subjection, and to rule it".[3] The struggle of the reasonable will is to will according to the higher Divine Will: an inalienable capacity, which God has given the will the freedom and power to attain to, despite the flesh, the world, and the devil conspiring together in assaults against it.[4] Trusting in God and in the freedom of the will against vicious forces, one is therefore called upon to "fight valiantly, and never to throw down your arms, nor flee, however many wounds you may have sustained".[5]

As one acts contrary to one's own lower will and in accordance with the higher Divine Will, one discovers the path on which the habit of virtue may be acquired. In fact, the more one's virtuous acts are "contrary to the natural will, the more quickly will they produce the good habit in the soul".[6] God prepares a cup of trials and temptations from which one must drink, as in accordance with the Divine Will. All crosses, tribulations, sorrows, and afflictions are ultimately from God who wills that the soul should suffer "both for our quicker growth in holiness, and for other wise reasons unknown to us".[7] This love and service of God is not possible apart from "a holy hatred of oneself".[8] Through this holy hatred, the will is conformed more readily to the Divine Will, which desires "that your nothingness may be swallowed up in the depth of My infinity, and transformed into it. Thus will you be fully blest and happy in Me, and I completely contented in you."[9]

As is characteristic of the literature of spiritual struggle, one must devote oneself to Christ in the moment of tribulation, bearing one's

---

1 *Ibid.* Chapter II, 11.
2 *Ibid.* Chapter X, 29.
3 *Ibid.* Chapter XII, 35.
4 *Ibid.* Chapter XIV, 45.
5 *Ibid.* Chapter XV, 50.
6 *Ibid.* Chapter XXXV, 122.
7 *Ibid.* Chapter XXXVIII, 130.
8 *Ibid.* Chapter LII, 168.
9 *Ibid.* Chapter LV, 187.

cross with him and saying, with all one's heart "Thy will be done." True devotion, as Scupoli understands it, means the will to "follow Christ with the cross on your shoulder, by whatever way He invites and calls us to Himself, to desire God for God, and at times to leave God for God".[1] This final notion speaks to a feeling of absence, even forsakenness, from which Christ himself was not spared. In such moments of banishment or abandonment, one must not give in to the temptation to despair. Rather one must discern such aridity as a grace bestowed upon one by God, who allows some "to be assailed by these spirits of temptation, to bring them back to their knowledge of themselves, and in order that, by feeling their need of Him, they may draw near to Him".[2]

Such desolate moments are also accorded a privileged place in Scupoli's 'Of Interior Peace or The Path to Paradise'. In this considerably shorter work, Scupoli again urges his readers to "except often to feel disturbed" since "from the emotions of your heart, a cloud of dust will sometimes arise".[3] This desolation is, Scupoli again asserts, permitted by God for the greater good of one's soul. One must therefore "Remember that this is the war in which the Saints have carried off crowns of great merit".[4] In this struggle, one is to conform one's will to the Divine Will, as Christ said at Gethsemane, "with a will free and detached" and "with deep humility", "Nevertheless, not my will but Thine be done."[5] Temptations such as these are sent by God for the good of the soul to hinder the pride that inhibits true spiritual progress. In this respect, Scupoli reminds us of the Apostle Paul who, having been caught up in the third heaven where he was witness to divine secrets, "was visited with a troublesome temptation" to remind him of his weakness. Through this thorn in the flesh, Paul remains humble before his divine revelation so that he should not fall into the temptation of presumption.[6] Such divine temptations enable us to better know ourselves, even in the bitterest abyss of apparent God-forsakenness. The inexperienced soul may be tempted to attribute such trials to the devil or to one's own imperfection. But in truth (and here Scupoli accords with Luther and Kierkegaard) such temptation comes "from the Hand of God".[7] While one may imagine that one is forsaken by God, the truth is that such tribulations are a divine blessing. Those who do not recognise this take "Tokens of love" as "signs of hatred,

1 *Ibid.* Chapter LIX, 199.
2 *Ibid.* Chapter LIX, 200.
3 Scupoli, 'Of Interior Peace or The Path to Paradise', Chapter X, *Ibid.* 290.
4 *Ibid.* 291.
5 *Ibid.* 291.
6 *Ibid.* 298-99.
7 *Ibid.* 301.

and imagine that these Divine favours and caresses are blows which come from an enraged heart, and believe that all they do is lost and worthless, and that this loss is irremediable".[1] At this moment, the inexperienced soul may imagine that God struggles against them and that they suffer blows of holy rage. Since it appears that God fights against them they may be tempted to fall into the belief that they are forsaken by God. Yet such wounds are truly caresses of Divine love, and are to be accepted evidence of God's care for the purity of the soul.

This recognition that some temptations come from God for a holy purpose and for the good of the soul is, as will be explored in greater detail, an insight shared by the literature on spiritual trial. Yet Scupoli's Roman Catholic emphasis upon the capacity of the will to freely will the good and to cultivate virtue is not entirely affirmed within Lutheran theology of *Anfechtung*. Kierkegaard ultimately regards spiritual trial as belonging to the religious rather than the ethical sphere — and yet, as will be examined further, he does also affirm the freedom of the will and the ethico-religious development of the self as Spirit, capable of loving God and the other from out of its own redeemed heart.[2] However, such considerations are not confined to questions of Catholic-Reformed convergence and divergence. Scupoli's *The Spiritual Combat* (1589) was itself translated into Greek by the Saint Nicodemus of the Holy Mountain (1749-1809) and subsequently reformulated into Russian by the Russian Orthodox saint Theophan Zatvornik (Theophanes the Recluse, 1815-94) as *The Unseen Warfare*, which had an immense impact upon modern Eastern Orthodoxy.[3] Both ascetic saints were important to the revival of contemplative prayer (*Hesychasm*) and the dissemination of its principle text the *Philokalia* ('love of the beautiful' — an anthology of monumental spiritual writings spanning the fourth to the fifteenth centuries).[4]

The notion of *Podvig* or spiritual struggle spoken of in the Russian

---

1   *Ibid*. 301.
2   In this vein, Daphne Hampson makes the pertinent suggestion that Kierkegaard comes closest to reconciling Catholic and Lutheran theologies, *Christian Contradictions: The Structures of Lutheran and Catholic Thought*, (Cambridge: Cambridge University Press, 2001). Further exploration of Kierkegaard's understanding of sanctification would be a helpful development in this direction.
3   English translation: *The Unseen Warfare*, as edited by Nicodemus of the holy mountain and revised by Theophan the Recluse (New York: Crestwood, 2000).
4   For an excellent treatment of the *Philokalia* from the perspective of contemporary psychology and mental well-being see Christopher Cook, *The Philokalia and The Inner Life: On Passions and Prayer* (Cambridge: James Clarke & Co., 2011).

Orthodox *Philokalia* tradition finds a powerful echo in Sergii Bulgakov's (1871-1944) essay 'Heroism and the Spiritual Struggle' (1909).[1] Bulgakov appeals to *podvizhnichestvo*, translated here as *spiritual struggle*. As Rowan Williams describes, the *podvig* means the "exploit" of "the saintly ascetic" who "is engaged in the cultivation of a style of personal existence within the limits of the created order". As such, the *podvig* "entails *humility* — not self-abasement, but the willingness to learn, connected with the recognition that the world's ills have roots in each individual self, with its passions and tumults". In Bulgakov, this does not "a passive or world-renouncing ascesis" but actually "a culture of sober and conscientious activism, in which all agents examine their actions and responsibilities in the light of the ideal of *obedience* to God, transferring to 'secular' life the attitude of the monk to the duties of the monastic life". In this sense, Williams observes, Bulgakov "unites certain themes from classical Eastern Christian spirituality with something of the bourgeois Protestant ethic".[2]

While Bulgakov esteems the Christian hero as a "spiritual athlete [*podvizhnik*]",[3] his account of *podvizhnichestvo* speaks of a Christian heroism which can be understood as a polar contrast to the "heroism of self-apotheosis", which characterises the self-perception of the Russian intelligentsia.[4] Beneath Divine Providence and Will, the Christian hero "must humble himself in the *podvig* of faith",[5] while authentic *humility* — "the interior and visible conflict with self, self-will, and self-deification"[6] — remains alien to the intelligentsia. As such:

> The *podvizhnik* looks at the limited and distorted world of human sin and suffering, especially as it exists in his own self, with the purified eyes of the spirit, and in so doing brings to light new imperfections; the sense of distance from the ideal is intensified.[7]

1 In *Sergii Bulgakov: Towards a Russian Political Theology*, Rowan Williams (ed.) (Edinburgh: T & T Clark, 1999), 69-112.

2 Williams' 'Introduction' to 'Heroism and the Spiritual Struggle', *Sergii Bulkakov*, 65-66. Williams thus notes Bulgakov's praise for the 'Protestant ethic' according to which "Protestantism is seen as the ground of the development of civic responsibility and political liberties, as well as well as economic advance; Bulgakov had read his Weber conscientiously" (63). Intriguingly, Bulgakov discusses Tauler and Boehme in Sergius Bulgakov, *Unfading Light: Contemplations and Speculations*, trans. Thomas Allan Smith (Grand Rapids: Wm. B. Eerdmans, 2012), Tauler: 146-148; Boheme: 148-149, 170-180. However, there is no explicit mention of *Anfechtung* in this text.

3 Bulgakov, 'Heroism and the Spiritual Struggle', *Sergii Bulgakov*, 93.

4 *Ibid.* 82.

5 *Ibid.* 93.

6 *Ibid.* 97.

7 *Ibid.* 95.

This "humility before God and 'walking in the sight of God' (as this is expounded in the consistent testimony of ecclesial and patristic literature)"[1] is ostensibly commensurate with the Lutheran notion of spiritual trial, as is the sense of intensified distance from the ideal — or what Kierkegaard named as the infinite qualitative difference between the human and the divine. It is a radical sense of sin which is known to the *podvizhnik* yet remains tragically alien to the heroic intelligentsia.[2] Not reducible to the confines of the monastery, "The Christian struggle is a matter of unremitting self-control, war with the sinful and lower levels of one's ego, ascesis of spirit",[3] also manifest in external action in the world. The Christian Saint is the one whose will is, through "ascetic effort [*podvig*] . . . wholly permeated by the will of God": the image for which permeation is the God-man who comes "not to do his own will, but the will of his Father".[4]

Contemporary to Bulgakov, the Spanish religious philosopher and writer Miguel de Unamuno (1864-1936) regarded himself in the line of Augustine, Pascal, and Kierkegaard in his sense of faith as a spiritual struggle beset by tragedy. In *The Tragic Sense of Life* (*Del sentimiento trágico de la vida*, 1912), Unamuno suggests that suffering is itself only surpassed in its anguish by the feeling of "being incapable of suffering and of tears".[5] This feeling of absence is, of course, itself a form of suffering — albeit a suffering that is never able to realise itself, unable to become conscious of itself. Its suffering is expressed as the numbness of being wounded without feeling any pain. It is the dread of nothingness, of non-being. The feeling of suffering, by contrast, affirms our existence according to Unamuno:

> Suffering tells us that we exist; suffering tells us that those whom we love exist; suffering tells us that the world in which we live exists; and suffering tells us that God exists and suffers; but it is the suffering of anguish, the suffering of surviving and being eternal. Anguish discovers God to us and makes us love Him.
>
> To believe in God is to love Him, and to love Him is to feel Him suffering, to pity Him.[6]

1 *Ibid*. 95.
2 *Ibid*. 95-96.
3 *Ibid*. 98.
4 *Ibid*. 100.
5 Cf. Luther's assertion that the worst *Anfechtung* is the absence of *Anfechtung* (*Nulla tentatio — omnis tentatio*) (LW 44, 47); "*Keine Anfechtung haben ist die schwerste Anfechtung*" (WA 3, 420).
6 Miguel de Unamuno, *Tragic Sense of Life*, trans. J.E. Crawford Flitch (New York: Dover Publications, 1954), 207.

Suffering is understood by Unamuno, in terms reminiscent of Kierkegaard's assertion of the tension between Spirit and spiritlessness, as the "the barrier which unconsciousness, matter, sets up against consciousness, spirit; it is the resistance to will, the limit which the visible universe imposes upon God; it is the wall that consciousness runs up against when it seeks to extend itself at the expense of unconsciousness; it is the resistance which unconsciousness opposes to its penetration by consciousness."[1] This notion of resistance is further resonant with Kierkegaard's understanding of spiritual trial as a limit that the unknown opposes to the one who would know. However, Unamuno conceives of this struggle in terms of an opposition between the consciousness of spirit and the unconsciousness of matter — whereas, for Kierkegaard, the opposition can be understood as a struggle between the consciousness of Spirit and the unconsciousness of spiritlessness: matter itself is not necessarily opposed to Spirit, especially insofar as the task of Spirit in selfhood is synthesis the psychical and the physical (CA, 43).[2] In terms that perhaps resound more with Kazantzakis (who had interviewed Unamuno in Spain in 1936) than with Kierkegaard, Unamuno affirms that the work of the love of God "is to endeavour to liberate God from brute matter, to endeavour to give consciousness to everything, to spiritualize of universalize everything".[3] In a vision which is furthermore suggestive of Teilhard de Chardin (1881-1955), Unamuno sees this process as symbolized in the eucharist: "The Word has been imprisoned in a piece of material bread . . . in order that, after being buried in our body, it may come to life again in our spirit."[4]

In *The Agony of Christianity* (*La Agonía del cristianismo*, 1931) Unamuno speaks more explicitly of the *Agonía* (ἀγωνία) as the struggle, *la moral de*

---

1 Unamuno, *Tragic Sense of Life*, 212.
2 On Unamuno's relation to Kierkegaard see Jan E. Evans, *Unamuno and Kierkegaard: Paths to Selfhood in Fiction* (Lanham: Lexicon Books, 2005) and Jan E. Evans, 'Miguel de Unamuno: Kierkegaard's Spanish "Brother"', ed. Jon Stewart, *Kierkegaard Research: Sources, Reception and Resources: Volume 9: Kierkegaard and Existentialism* (Aldershot: Ashgate, 2011), 375-392.
3 *Tragic Sense of Life*, 214.
4 *Tragic Sense of Life*, 214. On further comparison between Unamuno and Teilhard de Chardin see Armand F. Baker, 'The God of Unamuno', *Hispania*, 74 (4), December 1991, 824-833, 827-831. Teilhard de Chardin invokes the image of Jacob in 'The Mass of the World': "like the quietist I allow myself with delight to be cradled in the divine fantasy: but that the same time I know that the divine will, will only be revealed to me at each moment if I exert myself to the utmost: I shall only touch God in the world of matter, when, like Jacob, I have been vanquished by him." *Hymn of the Universe* (London: William Collins & Co., 1970), 26.

batalla, the death struggle against absolute death. Unamuno opens with the words of St Teresa of Jesus: "I die because I do not die",[1] to which one might compare Kierkegaard's motto, gleaned from Hamann *"Periissem, nisi periissem* ['I would have perished, had I not perished']" (JP 6:6154).[2] Both affirm a tension between *Eros* and *Thanatos* of sorts, between spiritual life and spiritual death, resolved through the struggle to 'die to' through which one is delivered from true death to the fullness of life.[3] "Agony, then, is a struggle", Unamuno asserts, with the Kierkegaardian reminder that "Christ came to bring us agony: struggle and not peace."[4] This agony is also central to the passion of Christ himself, even providing a dark devotional focus for worship: "the Christ worshipped on the cross is the agonizing Christ, the One who cries out: *Consummatum est!* And it is this Christ, the Christ of 'My god, my God, why hast thou forsaken me?' (Matt. 27:46), that agonic believers worship",[5] though the agonists struggle for faith in and through doubt itself — a doubt which in turn vitalises faith. "A faith that does not doubt is a dead faith."[6]

---

1   Unamuno elaborates on this quote a few pages later: "He who lives in the throes of struggle, struggling against life itself, lives in agony, agonizes. And he struggles against death as well. Its spirit is summed up in the ejaculation of Teresa of Jesus: 'I die because I do not die.'" *The Agony of Christianity and Essays on Faith*, trans. Anthony Kerrigan (London: Routledge & Kegan Paul, 1974), 5.

2   Kierkegaard avows that this "still is and will be my life motto. This is why I have been able to endure what long since would have killed someone else who was not dead." While Kierkegaard's adoption of this motto probably derives from J.G. Hamann's letter to Johann Gotthelf Linder, 2 May 1764, the original Latin aphorism most likely dates from the Middle Ages. See additionally JP 5:5673. Frater Taciturnus also employs this as the motto for 'Guilty?/Not Guilty?', SLW, 194.

3   Unamuno affirms that there is not a "struggle for life" as such, "but this struggle for life is 'life' itself, and is at the same time the 'struggle.'" *The Agony of Christianity*, 7.

4   *Ibid.* 9. As well as appealing to Jesus, Unamuno also applies the image of Genesis 32 to the tragic and agonistic life of the Roman Catholic theologian Père Hyacinthe Loyson (1827-1912): "Like Jacob, he wrestled alone with the angel of the Lord, from sundown until the breaking of the day, and calling out to him, 'Tell me . . . thy name!'" (98).

5   *The Agony of Christianity*, 10.

6   *Ibid.* 10. In this assertion we may attain a glimpse of why it may be suggested that Unamuno is something of a peculiarly Spanish Lutheran. See José Luis L. Arunguren, 'Sobre el talante religioso de Miguel de Unamuno', *Arbor*, XI, 1948, 485-503. However, Culpepper notes that while Unamuno read some Luther he did not resonate with the depths of Luther's sense of sin and in this sense at least "he remained more [Roman] Catholic than Protestant". R. Alan Culpepper, *Eternity as a Sunrise: the Life of Hugo H. Culpepper* (Macon: Mercer University Press, 2002), 228.

Yet it should also be added that faith that is lost within the abyss of despair is no longer able to recognise itself as faith. It has fallen into oblivion. No valorisation of the iconography of the agony of doubt can bring it back to life. In this sense, any idolatry of struggle must remain mindful and wary of the truly nihilistic horror of despair — mindful that struggle itself does not become the normative dialectical *via negativa* for 'authentic' faith. If one truly believes that struggle is the mark of the inward God-relationship then struggle need not be sought out or ventured in any heroic sense. It will arise as the Absolute limit of the Absolute itself. In this one prays with all humility, lead us not into temptation (Matthew 6:13).

Such emphasis upon the agonistic aspects of Christianity are no doubt vulnerable to the charge that Christian faith valorises, even fetishises suffering. As such, insofar as theology emphasises such Kierkegaardian motifs as the infinite qualitative abyss between the human and the divine, the enmity between Spirit and spiritlessness, the consciousness of sin, the fallenness into anxiety and despair of the human condition, it surely fuels suspicions that the Christian message is one of tragedy played out in the melancholy longing for an eschatological redemption by an absent God. Yet, while there are important insights in such a critique, the theology of spiritual struggle seeks to speak about that which many would rather not speak about: the darker aspect of life's anxious and lonely moments when the divine seems impossibly remote from, even antagonistic towards, the vicissitudes of human experience. The various theologies of spiritual struggle are at their best, even their most humanity-affirming, in their desire to broach this silence. And yet such theologies are at their worst, or most dangerous, when they attempt to formulate a normative and prescriptive *via dolorosa* along which faith *must* stumble on, through the mortifying dark night, after which the light of God dawns at its brightest. No theology of spiritual struggle should be asserted that in any sense excludes or denigrates those who do not or cannot achieve this via. Any theology of spiritual struggle must, as any theology must, be wary of idolatry — even an idolatry of the cross, even the temptation to form an idol of the *passio Christi*, the worship of the suffering Christ, which falls towards a morbid *Christolary*.[1] Such theology should speak to those

---

1 I adapt this term from Mary Daly's *Beyond God the Father* (Boston: Beacon, 1985). I later suggest that the doubt, offense, and ineffability of the incarnation and the suffering of Christ may provoke a spiritual trial which deconstructs all attempts to create an idol of the *passio Christi*. In this respect I appeal to Simone Weil's notion that affliction (*malheur*), even that of Christ, often appears as beneath compassion rather than inviting devotion.

whose lives are already acquainted with this darkness — to break
the silence, and remind us all that no one is finally alone. It should be
wary of seeking to cultivate such desolation even when it promises
a dialectic of consolation.

Love's Struggle with the Darkness of God: Silence, Protest, and Prayer

The question of desolation without consolation gives rise to a form
of struggling with God that is not cultivated in the crucible of self-
mortifying *ascesis*. This struggle is a struggle with the absence or
the darkness of God in the face of sickness and atrocity. The one
who struggles with the hidden face of God (*hester panim*) does not
so much worship the agonising Christ as speaks with the crucified
and with the psalmist, or even remain silent with them, in the cry of
God-forsakenness. In this cry of 'My God, my God, why have you
forsaken me?' (Psalm 22:1; Mark 15:34) there is the voice of protest,
perhaps even a 'Promethean' form of prayer,[1] which struggles with
God, or with the absence, or darkness, of God.[2]

As an image invoked in response to the *Shoah*, struggling with God
symbolises protest against evil and suffering even if such protest
be directed against One who is, paradoxically, also the focus of all
longing for the Good. Struggle is therefore an (imperfect) expression
of our freedom before God; the freedom to struggle with God and
yet not be annihilated. As an image, which emerges in the silence of
the night, Jacob's struggle with God is powerfully assumed as the
motif for the modern struggle with the holocaust in Eliezer Schweid's
*Wrestling Until Day-Break: Searching for Meaning in the Thinking on
the Holocaust* and Steven T. Katz, Shlomo Biderman, and Gershon
Greenberg edited volume, *Wrestling with God: Jewish Theological
Responses During and After the Holocaust*.[3] Schweid's invocation of

---

1   Sheldon H. Blank, 'Men against God: The Promethean Element in Biblical
    Prayer', *Journal of Biblical Literature*, 72, (1), March, 1953, 1-13.

2   I explore this further in 'My God, My God, Why Have You Forsaken
    Me? Between Consolation & Desolation', ed. Christopher C.H. Cook,
    Spirituality, Theology & Mental Health: Multidisciplinary Perspectives
    (London: SCM Press, 2013), 193-210.

3   *Wrestling Until Day-Break: Searching for Meaning in the Thinking on the
    Holocaust* (Lanham, New York and London: University Press of America,
    1994) and *Wrestling with God: Jewish Theological Responses During and After
    the Holocaust*, Steven T. Katz, Shlomo Biderman, and Gershon Greenberg
    (eds) (Oxford: Oxford University Press, 2007). In a 1938 commentary on
    Genesis 32:25 ("And there wrestled a man with him"), Elhanan Wasserman
    suggests that while Jacob is the Pillar of the Torah, the man who opposes

struggling until dawn (Genesis 32:26), may also educe an allusion to
Elie Wiesel's account of the concentration camps, *Night* — in which
all things come to an end; though to be followed by the second and
third works of Wiesel's trilogy, *Dawn* and *Day*.[1] In Wiesel's night,
all meanings are reduced to an abyss. "Just as readers committed
suicide in the nineteenth century, writers did in ours", Wiesel reflects,
"They felt impotent. They realized that once you have penetrated
the Kingdom of Night, you have reached the end."[2] The night is
essentially impenetrable, abyssal. Within it writers realise, in their
guilt and inadequacy, that they have essentially said nothing.[3] Hence,
for Wiesel, "what is called the literature of the Holocaust does not
exist, cannot exist. It is a contradiction in terms, as is the philosophy,
the theology, the psychology of the Holocaust. Auschwitz negates
all systems, opposes all doctrines."[4] The Holocaust is something in
which, as the poet Edmond Jabés also expresses, language encounters
its limit and its dismay. Though it may be possible still to speak of
'God' in this desert of writing, 'God' has become yet another word
for a confrontation with absence. As Jabés declares, "What I mean by
God in my work is something we come up against, an abyss, a void,
something against which we are powerless."[5]

Rubenstein, in *After Auschwitz*, halts at the abyss in silence before
the "Holy Nothingness" (*das Heilige Nichts*) declaring that "*The
infinite God is not a thing; the infinite God is no-thing*".[6] God as *das
Heilige Nichts* thus conveys something of what Arthur A. Cohen
subsequently identifies as the *tremendum* present in the experience
of the Holocaust (*The Tremendum: A Theological Interpretation of the*

---

him is Samael or Satan: "This means that in the [era of the] 'footsteps of the
Messiah' impurity will wage war against study of the Torah (ignorance is
alive and well)", 'Tractate: the Onset of the Messiah', *Wrestling with God:
Jewish Theological Responses During and After the Holocaust*, 30.

1 See also Simon P. Sibelman, 'The Dialogue of Peniel: Elie Wiesel's Les
Portes de la forêt and Genesis 32:23-33', *The French Review*, 61. (5), April,
1988, 747-757.

2 Elie Wiesel, 'Art and Culture after the Holocaust', ed. Eva Fleischner,
Auschwitz: Beginning of a New Era? Reflections on the Holocaust (New York:
KTAV Publishing House, 1977), 411.

3 *Ibid.*

4 *Ibid.* 405

5 In Paul Auster, 'Book of the Dead: an Interview with Edmond Jabés',
ed. Eric Gould, *The Sin of the Book: Edmond Jabés* (Lincoln and London:
University and Nebraska Press, 1985), 19.

6 *After Auschwitz: History, Theology, and Contemporary Judaism* (Baltimore
and London: The Johns Hopkins University Press, 1996), 298. Yet "Holy
Nothingness" does not equate to God's annihilation for Rubenstein; rather
"God as the 'Nothing' is not absence of being, but a superfluity of being" (*Ibid.*).

Holocaust). In evoking the Ottonian notion of the *tremendum* in the Holocaust, Cohen concedes, "I have promised only to cross the abyss. I have not promised to explain it. I would not dare."[1] In similar vein, Rubenstein himself admits that he still cannot reconcile himself to loving this holy abyssal God: "I cannot. I am aware of His holiness. I am struck with wonder and terror before His Nothingness, but I cannot love him. I am afrighted before Him. Perhaps, in the end, all I have is silence."[2] Rubenstein does not struggle and prevail over a vanquished God; "Unlike Altizer", he confesses, "I cannot rejoice in the death of God. If I am a death-of-God theologian, it is with a cry of agony."[3]

Yet the night of silence is also broken by cries of protest, even by prayers. For Blumenthal, protest against God, protest in thought and also in prayer, in liturgy, in teaching, is legitimate, even right such that the one who protests feels able to stand face to face God with God on the day of judgement. But such protest is itself a struggle that some cannot follow. To those Blumenthal ascribes a "heretical denial. See no evil. Hear no evil. Speak no evil — especially with God."[4] Yet both Blumenthal and Wiesel demonstrate an openness to the possibility of *dystheism*: the notion that God may not be perfectly good, even the possibility that God may be, at least capable of, evil. This possibility, this fear, may also be latent in the cry of 'My God, my God, why have you forsaken me?'.

Such a possibility also haunts the theology of spiritual trial: Luther struggles with it in his own *Anfechtungen*, which in turn informs his reflections on the struggles of Jacob and Abraham. In his reflections upon *Anfechtung* Luther speaks of a struggle against a God who appears as "otherwise", which is also a struggle with God, on the side of God as love (LW 6, 125-132). The same is evident in the *akedah* in which Abraham is confronted by the appearance of God as "an enemy and a tyrant" (LW 4, 94). Kierkegaard's *Fear and Trembling* (1843) also

---

1 Arthur A. Cohen, *The Tremendum: A Theological Interpretation of the Holocaust* (New York: Crossroad, 1981), 108.

2 *Ibid.* 264 (This is a recount of a conversation with a Polish Roman Catholic Theologian).

3 *After Auschwitz*, 264. Rubenstein earlier declares, "*I believe that radical theology errs in its assertion that God is dead.* Such an assertion exceeds human knowledge. . . . It is more precise to assert that *we live in the time of the death of God* than to declare 'God is dead.' *The death of God is a cultural fact. We shall never know whether it is more than that*" (250). Original emphasis.

4 David Blumenthal, 'Despair and Hope in Post-*Shoah* Jewish Life', *Bridges: An Interdisciplinary Journal of Theology, Philosophy, History, and Science,* (Fall/Winter 1999) 123. See also David R. Blumenthal, *Facing the Abusing God: A Theology of Protest* (Louisville: Westminster/John Knox, 1994).

acknowledges this fear, though it enshrouds and refracts it within a meditation on silence. Ultimately for Luther and Kierkegaard the struggle for the God of love in the face of the darkness of God is the most harrowing form of spiritual trial. In such spiritual trial, as if confronted by the Face of God as *mysterium horrendum*, one must struggle against the darkness by grasping for life itself on to the God of love. The struggle with God-forsakenness — which encompasses both abandonment by the love of God as well as confrontation with the darkness of God — is named by Kierkegaard as "the last spiritual trial [*Anfægtelse*]" (JP 4:4699).[1] Elsewhere Kierkegaard calls the God-forsaken cry "freedom's ultimate spiritual trial [*Anfægtelse*]" (JP 4:4611), the ultimate expression of Christ's voluntary suffering, the free submission to the most unthinkable desolation of God.

The cry of God-forsakenness, as expressed by the psalmist and invoked by Jesus on the cross, shows prayer at its most agnostic and agonistic. Yet the doubt and despair, which this cry evokes, also testifies to a broken-hearted love. Love struggles with the darkness of God because love hopes for the theophany of the God of love.

The temptation of spiritual trial is the temptation to despair (*tentatio desperationis*), the temptation believe that God is none other than the God of despair.[2] Yet the higher 'temptation' — which 'tempts' Spirit to awakening — is the divine call of love itself, of Spirit, the presence of love already announcing itself as the *desire for God*. The love for God is itself evidence of the love of God, insofar as all love begins in the secret hidden spring of divine love (WL, 9-10). As a loving

---

1 Luther speaks of God-forsakenness (*desertio gratiae*) as "the last and most serious temptation to unbelief" (LW 6, 131). Rupp identifies God-forsakenness as the final of six waves of attack in Luther's notion of *Anfechtung*: The first wave is the experience of nakedness and shame before creation. The second wave is condemnation by all creation. The third wave is condemnation by the words of scripture. The fourth wave is the Gospel itself adding to the terror of the Law. The fifth wave constitutes the soul turning from Christ. Finally, the soul is tempted to believe it is God-forsaken, predestined to damnation (*tentatio de praedestinatione*). Gordon Rupp, *The Righteousness of God: Luther Studies* (London: Hodder and Stoughton, 1953), 238-239.

2 In a manner resonant with Luther and Kierkegaard, Boulton reads the lament of God-forsakenness as a "Yes to impossibility", which "works against the tyranny of possibility, which is to say, works against the despair that attends the apparent exhaustion of possible remedies to crisis". Matthew Boulton, 'Forsaking God: a Theological Argument for Christian Lamentation', *Scottish Journal of Theology*, 55 (1), 2002, 58-78, 75-76. Consistent with the theology of spiritual trial, Boulton interprets this liturgical lament in terms of "forsaking God by clinging to God's promise over and against God" (58). I discuss this further in relation to Kierkegaard in 'My God, My God, Why Have You Forsaken Me?' Between Consolation & Desolation'.

struggle with the darkness of God, spiritual trial is the struggle to realise the love of God as the God of love. In this sense, the way of spiritual trial is also the way of prayer — even the prayer that cries in protest against God, or is silent in its unknowing or despair.

Invoking the image of Jacob's struggle with God, Juan de los Angeles (1536-1609), following Jerome, describes prayer in terms of a "loving struggle between God and the soul" wherein one "really and truly prevails over God, and [. . .] conquers God".[1] The spiritual essence of the struggle of prayer is ultimately love, though a wounded love, which even in the abyss of divine darkness still longs for the love of God. "Only to love is it given to struggle with God, and God in his love wants nothing more than to be loved in return."[2] Similarly for Kierkegaard, God desires to be loved out of freedom and the heart of selfhood, transfigured as Spirit (JP 4:4350) — though becoming Spirit elicits the spiritual struggle with spiritlessness. While Kierkegaard's works describe many forms of struggling with God — whether in the defiance and offence of unbelief or presumption (CD, 69-70) in the struggle of "despair of the forgiveness of sins" (SUD, 114) — it is ultimately through the loving struggle of prayer that one truly struggles with God.[3] It is through prayer, as the two hands of love and despair grasped together in faith, that one engages in the struggle with God. In temptation and spiritual trial, this struggle also transpires as a struggle against the self.[4] Spiritual trial thereby

---

1   Juan de los Angeles, *The Loving Struggle Between God and the Soul*, trans. Eladia Gómez-Posthill (London: The Saint Austin Press, 2001), 17. He also asserts the ostensible paradox that "God himself, the omnipotent, the impassible God is wounded in his heart by the gentle, blushing, loving gaze of the soul" (28-29). I discuss Juan de los Angeles' appeal to the motif of Jacob's struggle in *Kierkegaard and the Self Before God*, 100 and 104. Juan de los Angeles' reflections bear the mark of influence from the Flemish mystic John of Ruysbroeck (1294-1381) and the Rhineland mystic Johannes Tauler (c.1300-1361), among others. On his relationship with German mysticism see José Miguel López Cuétara, 'El misticismo alemán en la obra de Fr. Juan de los Ángeles', *Verdad y vida*, 64 (247), 2006, 577-612.

2   *The Loving Struggle Between God and the Soul*, 17.

3   One must not lose sight of how, "for all his warfare imagery and warnings against bypassing the possibility of offense, [Kierkegaard] also describes the struggle of faith in terms of falling in love. Such love must be taught, and even commanded". Jason Mahn, *Fortunate Fallibility: Kierkegaard and the Power of Sin* (Oxford: Oxford University Press, 2011), 168. See further WL, 17-43.

4   "So the struggle goes; the struggler contends with God in prayer, or he struggles with himself and in his prayer calls on God for help against himself" (EUD, 397). As Pattison describes: "In this strife, this holy war [for self-mastery], then, the self must wrestle itself to a standstill and, in doing

speaks of the struggle to transfigure the self as Spirit, as the image of God, which loves God from a heart of freedom, and which comes to recognise the love of God as the inexorable presence of God — a divine spark which, though its light may become overshadowed by the abyss of absence, contains a fire that can never be finally extinguished.

Outline

Consideration of the themes and figures referred to in this introduction suggests that a more comprehensive comparative account of the broader theme of spiritual struggle would be a significant and compelling venture. Immediately I am tempted to attend to affinities between *Anfechtung* and the *desolatio* of John of the Cross and Teresa of Avila,[1] which in turn inspires comparison

---

so, discover its actual inability to be itself. . . . For in this annihilation [of the self] we learn that, since we cannot bring about the unification of the self by our own efforts, the achievement of authentic selfhood depends utterly and solely on divine grace. The annihilation of the individual is his transfiguration in God." George Pattison, *Kierkegaard: The Aesthetic and the Religious* (London: SCM Press, 1999), 169. Kierkegaard also writes that: "This is how God fights. . . . God in heaven fights by shifting the attack to the side of the attacker. When impatience, like a rebel, wants to attack God, the consciousness of guilt attacks the rebel; that is, the attacker ends up fighting with himself. God's omnipotence and holiness do not mean that he can be victorious over everyone, that he is the strongest, for this is still a comparison; but it means, and this bars any comparison, that no one can manage to fight with him" (UDVS, 286).

1 I compare this further in 'My God, My God, Why Have You Forsaken Me?' Between Consolation & Desolation', 193-210. On significant resonances between Luther's *Anfechtung* and John of the Cross' notion of the dark night of the soul, see further Catherine Connors-Nelson, 'Touched by the God of Grace: The *Anfechtung* of Luther and the Dark Night of John of the Cross', *Studies in Spirituality*, 9, (1999), 109-139; and Donald Christopher Nugent, 'Mystical and evangelical theology in Martin Luther and St John of the Cross', *Journal of Ecumenical Studies*, 28 (Fall, 1991), 555-565. I also compare Lutheran *Anfechtung* with John of the Cross' notion of *desolatio* in 'The Dark Night of Suffering & the Darkness of God: God-forsakenness or Forsaking God in "The Gospel of Sufferings"', in ed. Robert Perkins, *International Kierkegaard Commentary: Upbuilding Discourses in Various Spirits* (Macon, Georgia: Mercer University Press, 2005), 229-256 and *Kierkegaard and the Self Before God* (Indianapolis: Indiana University Press, 2011). See also the treatment of the desolatio of Teresa of Lisieux by Waltraud Herbstrith, *Therese von Lisieux: Anfechtung un Solidarität* (Frankfurt: Verlag Gerhard Kaffke, 1974).

with Simone Weil's unsettling notion of 'affliction' (*malheur*).[1] However, the focus of this present work must be mostly confined to Kierkegaard, his sources, and inheritors.

The possibility of solidarity in the midst of the solitude of suffering is key to chapter one's examination of the secrecy and silence which surround the category of spiritual trial. As well as attending to the possibility of consolation in the face of ineffable struggle, I also identify how particular problems with translating the word *Anfægetelse* may have contributed to its under-representation in much of Kierkegaard scholarship. Furthermore, this chapter introduces Kierkegaard's discovery of the category within forgotten old devotional literature, a recovery which is examined in greater depth in chapter two. In particular, the treatments of *Anfechtung* in Johannes Tauler and the *Theologia Deutsch* are elaborated, alongside Kierkegaard's relation to mystical theology and the pietistic tradition.

Chapter three focusses more intensively on Luther's theology of *Anfechtung*, examining how the struggle with the darkness of God relates to the dark nights of melancholy and the temptation of despair. This genealogy of *Anfechtung* culminates in chapter four with a study of two of Kierkegaard's other key sources for his view of spiritual trial: Johann Arndt and Jacob Boehme. In the light of these treatments of *Anfechtung* in German mystical, Lutheran, and Pietistic theology, chapters five and six turn to a reconstruction and exegesis of Kierkegaard's own reflections on temptation and spiritual trial. Here the continuities and innovations of Kierkegaard's thinking are elucidated within the context of his wider authorship. A Kierkegaardian theology of spiritual trial is elicited further in chapter seven's more constructive account of Spirit and desire, restlessness and rest, in relation to the dialectic between struggle (*Anfechtung*) and releasement (*Gelassenheit*). The eighth and final chapter further develops a theological account of temptation and spiritual trial, drawing upon Kierkegaard and his sources while also engaging with subsequent thinkers. Ultimately I suggest that while the *via* between struggle (*Anfechtung*) and releasement (*Gelassenheit*) can be symbolised by Christ's prayer at Gethsemane — "nevertheless, not my will but your will be done" — a theology of spiritual trial might also affirm the task of theology itself as an expression of love's protest and struggle with the darkness of God.

---

1 See, for example, Simone Weil, 'The Love of God and Affliction', *Waiting for God*, trans. Emma Craufurd (London: Harper Perennial, 2009), 67-82. Weil describes Affliction as concentrating the "infinite distance separating God from the creature . . . into one point to pierce the soul in its center" (81). A study of spiritual struggle could also be expanded further to encompass considerations of inner *jihad* in Islam as well as notions of agonistic spiritual interiority and practice in other religious traditions.

1. The Secret Struggle:
Lost in Translation

> I myself was the one who acted, I struggled with God [*jeg Streed med Gud*]: frightful collision! [*frygtelige Collision!*]
>
> (JP 6:6385)

Whether Jacob struggled with God-in-Godself, with a man, or with an Angel of the Presence or Face of God remains a *mysterium*. The realisation that it was Jacob, or as Kierkegaard's harrowing 1849 journal entry confesses, "I myself", is inescapable in its *tremendum*. Whether or not I struggle with God, with 'God', with the devil, or with an angel may remain uncertain — a form of doubt which is itself an expression of spiritual trial. The realisation that *I myself* am the one who struggles cannot be denied. The "frightful collision!", which Kierkegaard invokes, stands as a cypher for an ineffable dimension of spiritual trial. "I myself". There is no other who can exchange places and struggle in my place — even though Christ has already assumed all trials and temptations in his passion. While the God-forsaken Christ endures the forsakenness from which all others are finally spared, it is still "I myself" who must also face temptation and spiritual trial — even though I do not necessarily struggle alone. In this respect, the "frightful collision" speaks to the irreducible *sui generis* nature of subjectivity, of each individualised acting self, each unique personalisation of Spirit. At the same moment, it affirms the irreducible alterity of the God with whom one struggles: the Wholly Other with whom one collides across an "the most chasmic qualitative abyss [*Qualitetens meest svælgende Dyb*]" (SUD, 122). Yet spiritual trial, as a collision with the "absolutely different" (PF, 45), also testifies to a kenotic self-giving on the part of God: the Absolute gives itself, albeit in the appearance of a limit, to be struggled with and even beyond. Through this struggle, the Wholly Other reveals itself as the *Holy Other*, and the self that struggles restlessly in the abyss (*Afgrund*) *before God* discovers its rest, grounded transparently in God ("*gjennemsigtigt grunder i Gud*"; SUD, 82).

The "frightful collision" of spiritual trial therefore expresses a dreadful and silent liminality. It witnesses to the dreadful responsibility of one created, *ex nihilo*, in the anxiety of freedom before God. As such, this category signifies something that cannot be fully expressed. It must remain within the secret interiority of the self before God, a silent sanctum, which, as the struggle of prayer, cannot be fully represented to the other.[1] This ineffability of the struggle is perhaps epitomised in the Kierkegaardian representation of Abraham. Here Johannes de silentio presents the one who had previously made intercession for Sodom and Gomorrah — "Behold now, I have taken upon me to speak unto the Lord, which am but dust and ashes" (Genesis 18:27) — now falling silent before the command to sacrifice his own son. Yet Abraham's secret resides in the tension between the appearance that "He did not challenge heaven with his prayers" (FT, 22) and his esoteric promise to Isaac that "My son, God will provide Himself a lamb for a burnt offering" (Genesis 22:8): that is, between silence and the word. The *"horror religiosus"* (61) of Abraham resides in the tension between his ostensible willingness to conform to the darkness of God and the realisation that, even in his silence, Abraham is struggling with God. "Thus did they struggle on earth: there was one who conquered everything by his power, and there was one who conquered God by his powerlessness" (FT, 16).[2]

This kenotic struggle is, however, enshrouded in the sublime, even numinous silence of Abraham's "ordeal" (*Prøvelse*): an "absolutely transcendent" (R, 210) category that takes the incommunicability of temptation and spiritual trial to ineffable heights. For those in temptation and spiritual trial, however, even the more mundane forms of religious suffering bring the self into a secret relationship with the divine. This relationship is marked by deep a silence, which signifies "divinity's mutual understanding with the single individual" (FT, 88), a silent communion with the God who "sees in secret and recognizes the distress and counts the tears and forgets nothing" (FT, 120). In learning silence one becomes "a divine child" who in silence concentrates upon one's "divine origin" (JP 4:3978). As such, it is difficult to speak authentically, indeed to write with any

---

1 I explore this further in 'Mysticism's Secret: A Silent Prayer of Unknowing', ed. Hartmut von Sass, *Stille Tropen: Zur Rhetorik und Grammatik des Schweigens* (München: Karl Alber, 2013).

2 Abraham's victory can be elucidated with reference to the victory of Luther's own "Knight of Faith": the Canaanite Woman (Matthew 15:22-28), of whom Luther asserts "she is no simpleton in matters of faith; she is rather a Knight of Faith who wins the victory over God himself." WA 20.280.17. Cited in Rupp, *The Righteousness of God*, 112. In his Lectures on Genesis, Luther also compares the Canaanite Woman who struggled with and conquered God with the struggles of the patriarchs Jacob and Abraham (LW 6, 139-141).

clarity, about the religious suffering, which "ought to be a secret and be before God in secret" (CUP, 489). This emphasis upon the secret of sufferings is woven throughout Kierkegaard's writings, such that Martin Andic describes it as "an inside knowledge of the Spirit of God", which is at the same moment "an open secretly freely confided to anyone who truly wants it and is willing to take the divine way of hardship."[1] In this regard, Andic reads Kierkegaard's 'The Gospel of Sufferings' as evoking "a *secret* wisdom"[2] that conveys what it means "to know [*gnomai*] the love of Christ which surpasses knowledge [*tes gnoseos*]" (Ephesians 3:19).[3] The knowledge of God's love is a secret, open to all; and its secret is held in suffering. The *metanoia* of this secret knowledge is the "transfiguration" of the one who struggles with God; and the transfiguration of such a one is "to reflect the image of God" (EUD, 400).

In 'The Gospel of Sufferings' (1847) Kierkegaard offers the melancholy suggestion that those who despair in the thought of God-forsakenness would be better to incite the love of God in them to "blaze just by the thought of the horror that God was not love, because if God is love, then he is also love in everything", in all that is known and unknown, "in the dark riddle that lasts a day or in the dark riddle that lasts seventy years" (UDVS, 268). Andic aptly calls this "a proof from desire: the Divinity exists, because I love and desire it 'even if it does not exist'",[4] or even if it does not exist for me.[5] Such a 'proof' could be developed further with reference to the notion that all love has its origins in the secret spring of divine love (WL, 9-10). As such, love for God is itself love of God, the presence of God latent in the abyss of divine absence. This view is developed further in chapter seven in relation to the desire of Spirit — which itself is in the process of realisation of its hidden divine source as the image of God.

---

1 See further Martin Andic, 'The Secret of Sufferings', Robert Perkins (ed.), *International Kierkegaard Commentary: Upbuilding Discourses in Various Spirits* [*IKC: UDVS*], (Macon: Mercer University Press, 2005) 199-228, 200.
2 Andic, 'The Secret of Sufferings', 221.
3 *Ibid.* 223.
4 *Ibid.* 210.
5 Cf. Simone Weil's notion of loving God in detachment from the consolation of God's existence; in which, nonetheless, God's existence may become manifest. *Gravity and Grace* (London: Routledge, 2002) 15. During the absence of God there is nothing to love, except perhaps love itself. However, as Andic astutely observes, a key difference between Kierkegaard and Weil is that whereas Weil aspires to a particular form of detached union with God, Kierkegaard pursues "imitation" which leads to "likeness, with ever-increasing difference". Andic, 'The Secret of Sufferings', 227.

There is a further consolation offered by Kierkegaard to those lingering in the dark night of spiritual suffering. While such suffering individualises, forming a secret of sufferings that cannot be fully revealed to the other, it also initiates the self into a "covenant of tears" with the divine (EUD, 264). Directing the sufferer to the consolation of the *passio Christi*, this sacred covenant offers release from the silent self-enclosure (*Indesluttethed*) of despair: "you who are tempted, whoever you are, do not become silent in despair, as if the temptation were suprahuman and no one could understand it" (WA, 121). This divine-human solidarity endures its most abyssal yet ineffable moment in Christ's cry of God-forsakenness: words that "are consoling to those who imitate" Christ, even to those in the depths of despair whom "the prototype consoles by showing that this, too, belongs" (JP 4:3903). Echoing the spirit of Gregory of Nazianzus (330-389) that "*The unassumed remains unhealed*" and the Lutheran theology of the *communicatio idiomatum*, Kierkegaard discerns all human temptation and spiritual trial as endured and overcome in Christ.[1] Yet at the same time as it provides the "prototype" (*Forebilledet*) for human "imitation",[2] the *passio Christi* is not reducible to human experiences of tribulation. As saviour, Christ's suffering exceeds and prevails over all temptation, ordeal, and spiritual trial and, in doing so, redeems even the experience of God-forsakenness itself. Abandonment is itself redeemed through the God-forsakenness of Christ, which, in its pure innocence, is infinitely qualitatively different from the experience of those who have in some way already abandoned God. Christ's passion is both human, yet "it is also superhuman", and, as such, "there is an eternal chasmic abyss between his suffering and the human being's" (UDVS, 281).

---

1 By invoking the *communicatio idiomatum*, Lutheran theologians were able to speak of the suffering and even death in relation to the divine person of Christ, though this remained distinguishable from the divine nature, which remains immutable and impassible. See Lee C. Barrett, 'The Joy of the Cross: Kierkegaard's Appropriation of Lutheran Christology in "The Gospel of Suffering"', ed. Robert Perkins, *IKC: UDVS* (Macon, Georgia: Mercer University Press, 2005), 257-285, 260-261. Barrett explains that "in any of Christ's episodes of suffering, the human nature experiences the anguish, while the human nature wills endurance and supports the beleaguered human nature in its tribulation" (261). See further Barrett's essay on the faithfulness of Kierkegaard's adoption of Lutheran Christology and its situation in relation to human *pathos* in this discourse. Also see further David Law, *Kierkegaard's Kenotic Christology* (Oxford: Oxford University Press, 2013).

2 Echoing his critique of the censorship of spiritual trial, Kierkegaard observes that "The fact that we are completely silent about the requirement of 'imitation' has altogether demoralized Christendom" (JP 4:4700).

In light of such eternal difference, Anti-Climacus speaks about God's "unfathomable grief of love" (SUD, 126) in bearing the possibility of offence, the inexorable and kenotic divine gift of freedom which God will not violate. This sorrow is foreshadowed in Johannes Climacus' discussion of the god's unrequited love and the agony of disclosure which seems to promise either the death of the beloved or the death of love itself (PF, 30). Kierkegaard's writings, however, do not aspire to fathoming the secret inner life of the Godhead — particularly insofar as attributing the kenosis of God-forsakenness, even the death of God, to the inner life of the divine nature, above and beyond the divine person of Christ, might lead to the excesses of Speculative and Hegelian thought. Kierkegaard's discourse on 'The Gospel of Sufferings' exemplifies his concerns. This discourse is beset with *aporiae* and images concerning the hiddenness, darkness, otherness, and presence-in-absence of God — and yet it does not seek to sublimate these difficulties through metaphysical theodicy.[1] The discourse is Christocentric yet concerned with personal inwardness — its concern is not with a speculative doctrine of kenosis as such but rather with the question of humble imitation through personal kenosis.[2] The suffering Christ provides a consolatory yet ineffable icon for temptation and spiritual trial. There is a danger of making a Christolatory of the *passio Christi*. Christ's suffering is beyond us; as divine it is above us. As base humiliation and the scandal of offence might we also say, with Weil, that Christ in his affliction is not above as but below us, beneath even pity and compassion such that compassion for the afflicted is an "impossibility" and yet a "miracle"?[3] Kierkegaard therefore warns that *mysterium horrendum* of the suffering of Christ should be spoken about in "fear and trembling . . . because human thought is as little able as human language to depict or clearly make out the depth of this horror. This is why we should speak with the circumspection of humility or humbly be silent about how Christ suffered" (UDVS, 270).

---

1 See further my 'The Dark Night of Sufferings and the Darkness of God: God-forsakenness or Forsaking God in "The Gospel of Sufferings"', *IKC: UDVS*, 229-256. I suggest that these motifs can also be related to the hiddenness of God in *Fear and Trembling* as well as John of the Cross. See also the penetrating essays in the same volume: David Kangas, 'The Very Opposite of Beginning with Nothing: Guilt-Consciousness in Kierkegaard's "The Gospel of Sufferings" IV', *IKC: UDVS*, 187-314; and David Law, 'Wrongness, Guilt, and Innocent Suffering in Kierkegaard's *Either/Or, Part Two*, and *Upbuilding Discourses in Various Spirits'*, *IKC: UDVS*, 315-348.

2 Barrett also makes a similar observation in 'The Joy of the Cross', 272.

3 Weil, 'The Love of God and Affliction', *Waiting for God*, 69.

Lost in Translation: The Silence of Spiritual Trial

I am like a chaplain in a monastery, a spiritual advisor to the
solitary etc. — but I cannot involve myself in the nonsense that
is now called piety, religiosity. Spiritual trial [*Anfægtelse*] is
literally never spoken of any more. (JP 6:6459)

There is, however, another form of silence which, perhaps in an even
more troubling sense, disturbs all discussion of spiritual trial. This is
the silent omission of all reference to spiritual trial, which Kierkegaard
discerned as a sickness in the life of Spirit. Whereas Luther and his
followers could find support in "a social dimension to the healing of
the *anfechtung* (assault) of sickness and death", turning in the face of
"death's agonies", towards "support in the fellowship and faith of the
church",[1] Kierkegaard found himself to be quite alone. Kierkegaard's
above lament from 1849 expresses a deep nostalgia for an apparently
archaic notion of spirituality that has fallen silent in the midst of the
bourgeois complacency of modern Christendom. It is in light of this
absence that Kierkegaard confesses himself to be the lonely and under-
appreciated figure of "a chaplain in a monastery, a spiritual advisor
to the solitary", offering solace to the peripheral and the secluded,
whom, he fears, may neither heed nor require his counsel. Spiritual
trial is never spoken of anymore, and in this silence Kierkegaard
discerns the dreadful triumph of spiritlessness over spirit, perhaps
even the slow death of Christianity: "when spiritual trials disappear,
Christianity disappears — as it has disappeared in Christendom" (JP
4:4950). Despite this modern dissolution of the pathos of *Anfægtelse*,
Kierkegaard is insistent that the rhetoric of *Anfægtelse* — expressed
by such anxious souls as Tauler, Luther, Arndt, and Boehme; and
discovered in the arcane pages of "older and better devotional
literature" (JP 4:4384) — is not merely an outmoded idiom that haunts
Christianity from a bygone dark age. Rather, the tension of the God-
relationship expressed by *Anfægtelse* is the stigmatic mark of authentic
Christianity; and its disappearance in modern Christendom is a lacuna
in which authentic Christianity becomes endangered.

In spiritual trial the existential horizon of Christianity becomes
all-encompassing. "Spiritual trial [*Anfægtelse*] is the expression of a
concentration upon Christianity as the only object. That is why most
men have no spiritual trials" (JP 4:4365). Kierkegaard repeats his
impassioned plea for the recovery and redevelopment of the archaic
notion of *Anfægtelse* within modern Christianity: "Because religion is
not taken seriously nowadays in Christendom, there is never a hint

---

1   Dennis Ngien, 'The Art of Dying: In Luther's Sermon on Preparing to
    Die', *The Heythrop Journal*, XLIX (2008), 1-19, 9.

about spiritual trials [*Anfægtelser*]. Life is just not lived religiously; this can be proved indirectly by the disappearance of spiritual trial" (JP 4:4372). Despite Kierkegaard's often extravagantly dramatic evocations, however, *Anfægtelse* is not the exclusive privileged preserve, or authenticating mark, of the extraordinary Christian, the martyr, or the mystic. Rather, *Anfægtelse* may arise in personalised form for each single individual in even the most mundane vicissitudes of life. "If one puts on the religious for everyday use then spiritual trials [*Anfægtelser*] are bound to come" (JP 4:4364). And yet, while the individual struggle with spiritual trial signifies "authentic Christian religiousness", Kierkegaard is left at a loss as to where it is manifest in modern Christendom: "whether or not such a person like this is to be found, I do not know; I have never seen one" (JP 4:4372).

As Kierkegaard provocatively describes it, it seems that most individuals have prescribed to Vigilius Haufniensis' ironic recommendation that "The most effective means of escaping spiritual trial [*Anfægtelse*] is to become spiritless, and the sooner the better" (CA, 117). In similar vein Kierkegaard advises his readers to "Never involve yourself with God so long that any spiritual trial [*Anfægtelse*] has a chance to begin; if you think about God once a week and bow before him the way the others do, I guarantee that you will never be subjected to spiritual trials" (JP 2:1354). Given Kierkegaard's insistence on the recovery of the category of *Anfægtelse* for modern inwardness, it is notable, perhaps even ironically so, that this spiritual trial has remained so under-examined, over-looked, and unrecognised — particularly amongst the wealth of English language studies of Kierkegaard. Over one hundred and fifty years after his lament over the decline of *Anfægtelse* and his impassioned forays into its literary rehabilitation, it might appear that Kierkegaard's lament has itself passed into anachronism. Kierkegaard himself never made a comprehensive monographic conceptual study of the category, as he did, for example, with anxiety and despair. Furthermore, the manifest difficulties in translating *Anfægtelse* have no doubt contributed to the relative obscurity of a category that fails to feature as prevalently as accounts of anxiety, melancholy, and despair in accounts of Kierkegaard's thought.[1] As such, before entering further

---

1 Spiritual trial is absent from the illuminating treatment of anxiety, melancholy, and despair in Vincent A. McCarthy's *The Phenomenology of Moods in Kierkegaard* (The Hague and Boston: Martinus Nijhoff, 1978). However, Brian Gregor has written a perceptive treatment in 'Kierkegaard and the Phenomenology of Temptation', ed. Jeffrey Hanson, *Kierkegaard as Phenomenologist: An Experiment* (Evanston: Northwestern University Press, 2010), 128-148. However, while Gregor observes how the phenomena of anxiety (*Angest*) and spiritual trial (*Anfægtelse*) "are often interwoven, and at times even seem to coincide" (129), his careful

into an exploration of Kierkegaard's understanding of *Anfægtelse*, I shall outline how the difficulties in translating this category may have contributed to the dissolution of the term in Kierkegaard scholarship, and how such difficulties might further emphasise a need for a more comprehensive exploration of *Anfægtelse* in Kierkegaard's writings.

Anfægtelse: 'Temptation', 'Trial', 'Test', 'Tribulation'

Firstly, a note of caution: reading in a language which is not one's own first language often elicits a temptation to over-determine ideas in a nominal sense. The reality is that Kierkegaard's own use of the terminology is not always consistent, ideas are in development, and, ultimately, semantics are not reducible to etymology. A degree of English-language Luther scholarship has constructed *Anfechtung* as a defining feature of a distinctly Lutheran *theologia crucis* while eclipsing the origins and endurance of the term in Catholic theology. Furthermore, Luther himself does not always enforce a formal distinction between temptation (*Versuchung*) and spiritual trial (*Anfechtung*) along strictly lexical terms. Returning to the Hebrew and Greek sources in his German translation of the Bible, Luther renders what in the Latin Vulgate had been *tentatio* as both *Versuchung* and *Anfechtung*. In the context of Jesus' temptation in the wilderness, Luther refers to *Versuchung* (Luke 4:13: 'And when the devil had ended every temptation [*Versuchung*], he departed from him until an opportune time'); while in the context of Jesus' anguished prayer in Gethsemane he invokes the idiom of *Anfechtung* (Luke 22:42-46).[1] In setting Jesus' counsel on temptation in relation to his own anguish, the suggestion is that just as his disciples have, or should have, kept with him throughout his trials, so they will have to endure their own *Anfechtungen* (Luke 22:28; Luther also has Paul speak of serving Christ 'with tears and with trials' / '*mit Tränen und unter Anfechtungen*', Acts 20:19). It might be inferred through a Kierkegaardian lens that *temptation* refers to the lower seductions symbolised in Jesus'

distinguishing of these terms does not acknowledge the differentiated category of ordeal (*Prøvelse*). Kierkegaard's treatment of spiritual trial will, however, be included in an illuminating forthcoming study from Heiko Schulz, 'Das entfallene Herz. Zur Dialektik der Anfechtung bei Søren Kierkegaard', *Anfechtung nd Reflexion, vol. II: studien zur philosophie und theologie sören kierkegaards* (Berlin/Boston: Walter de Gruyter, 2013).

1 'Father, if thou art willing, remove this cup from me; nevertheless not my will, but thine, be done.' . . . And when he rose from prayer, he came to the disciples and found them sleeping for sorrow, and he said to them, 'Why do you sleep? Rise and pray that you may not enter into temptation [*Anfechtung*]' (Luke 22:42-46).

temptation by the devil in the wilderness, while *spiritual trial* is evoked by Jesus's prayer in Gethsemane, the anguished collision of the human and divine will, of fear and love, resolved through the kenotic death-to-self, which pledges "Nevertheless, not my will but thy will be done".[1] Yet while Kierkegaard formalises distinctions between temptation (*Fristelse*) and spiritual trial (*Anfægtelse*), as well as the "transcendent" category of the ordeal (*Prøvelse*), this is an innovation that is not consistently explicit in Luther, Tauler, the *Theologia Deutsch*, Arndt, or Boehme.[2] Furthermore, as Sylvia Walsh observes, the Greek verb *peirazein* can be read within the temptation narratives (Mark 1:12-13; Matthew 4:1-11; Luke 4:1-13) in the double sense of "to test, and to seduce and entice".[3] As a form of testing, the temptations of Jesus echo the Hebrew Bible. As for Abraham, so for Jesus it is ultimately God "who puts him to the test", albeit, as with Job, "through the agency of the figure of Satan".[4] In other words, both senses of what Kierkegaard would proceed to distinguish as *lower* and *higher* forms of temptation and spiritual trial are already implicit in the New Testament Greek *peirazein* as well as in the Latin *tentatio* — which Luther employs as a cognate for both *Versuchung* and *Anfechtung*. Yet Luther evidently proceeds to invest the latter with the agonistic pathos which resonates through Arndt, Boehme, and Kierkegaard. It actually appears that the formal differentiation of temptation and spiritual trial may be an innovation of Kierkegaard's own distinction between *Fristelse* and *Anfægtelse* (e.g. CUP, 410; JP 4:4382) — though this may reflect the prior distinction between

---

1 It is pertinent that Jesus' temptations follow the descent of the Holy Spirit upon him. Viewed through a Kierkegaardian lens this could be seen to foreshadow the view that struggle and temptation erupt with the awakening of Spirit. The temptation is not only an attempt at seduction but also a testing of the willingness to follow the calling of the Spirit.

2 I have, however, suggested that Kierkegaard's rarefied treatment of the ordeal (*Prøvelse*) is analogous to Luther's notion of the "that sublime temptation [*de sublimi illa tentatione*]" in which the patriarchs Abraham and Jacob struggle "against God Himself [*Deum ipsum*]". Simon D. Podmore, 'The Sacrifice of Silence: *Fear and Trembling* and the Secret of Faith, *International Journal of Systematic Theology*, 14 (1), January 2012, 70-90.

3 Sylvia Walsh, 'Moral Character and Temptation', Paul Moser and Michael McFall (eds), *The Wisdom of the Christian Faith* (Cambridge: Cambridge University Press, 2012), 121. See further Walsh's discussion of Kierkegaard on temptation and spiritual trial (123-128). Walsh also invokes Kierkegaard at the conclusion of the essay, ending with the affirmation that "God does not allow us to be tested beyond our strength and always provides the way out so that we can endure our spiritual trials while striving to become the persons of moral character we are intended to be" (137).

4 Walsh, 'Moral Character and Temptation', 121.

tentatio seductionis and *tentatio probationis* (though spiritual trial —
Anfehctung/Anfægtelse — also can encompass *castigationes paternae*:
the *paideia* to paternally educate believers). This distinction is not
followed, for example, by the great Lutheran theologian Dietrich
Bonhoeffer (1906-1945) in his 1937 reflections on *Temptation*, which
are clearly indebted to Luther's theology of temptation. The original
German title is, however, *Versuchung*, though much of its content
is concerned with what is often understood by many in terms of
Anfechtung (which only appears once in the German text — though
notably in reference to "the highest spiritual trial of Christ", "*die
höchste Anfechtung Christi*", which Bonhoeffer identifies as coming
from the devil).[1]

Nonetheless, Thulstrup suggests that Kierkegaard's various and
ostensibly diffuse descriptions of *Anfægtelse* do all "point in one specific
direction, namely towards the original, etymological, and figurative
sense of the word: attack, offensive struggle [*fægte/fecht* — 'fight'] — and
the difficulties which man enters in the state of trial". As such, Thulstrup
proposes that, "If this basic meaning is maintained, the variegated use
is not difficult to understand, and SK's meaning becomes even clearer
when one examines what he says about the origins of trial, its place in
existence, its modes of operation and forms, and its conquest."[2] This
is a perceptive hermeneutic principle, especially insofar as *Anfægtelse*
expresses a struggle against limitation which may beset any position in
life. Focussing on the etymological centrality of *fægte* — 'fight', however,
it becomes evident that one of the most challenging tasks in translating
Anfægtelse is precisely how to preserve the key linguistic feature of a word
which has no equivalent in many other languages, English included. It
is, in part, due to this difficulty that Kiekegaard's notion of *Anfægtelse*
remains under-examined, partially understood and frequently glossed-
over in English language studies.

The interpretative difficulties are rendered more complex by the
discovery that Kierkegaard's own understanding and development of
this term is a work in progress — even one that does not announce
conclusive end. The terminology of *Anfægtelse* appears early in
Kierkegaard's authorship and endures through to the end, becoming
less of a feature in the later publications, but of greater concern in
Kierkegaard's private writings of the same period.[3] Julia Watkin's

1   *Versuchung* (Munich: Chr. Kaiser Verlag, 1954), 60.
2   Niels Thulstrup, 'Trial, Test, Tribulation, Temptation', ed. Marie Mikulová
    Thulstrup, *Bibliotheca Kierkegaardiana: Some of Kierkegaard's Main Categories*
    (Copenhagen: C.A. Reitzels Forlag, 1988), 116-117.
3   Niels Thulstrup calculates that in the *Papirer* and *Samlede Værker* "the
    word trial (and the verb to try) is often used; from the earliest entries to

impressive *Historical Dictionary of Kierkegaard's Philosophy* does not ascribe an individual entry to *Anfægtelse* but rather contains this term, along with ordeal or test (*Prøvelse*), under the entry on "Temptation": "There is temptation as trial or test (*Prøvelse*) and temptation as spiritual trial (*Anfægtelse*)."[1] However, as shall be explored, Kierkegaard's (re) development of *Anfægtelse* goes beyond the notion that it is merely a "higher" temptation — even perhaps eclipsing the theme of temptation (*Fristelse*) in his works. As Watkin's herself states: "Temptation as spiritual trial (*Anfægtelse*) occurs specifically in the situation where the individual is endeavoring to live a life where his or her relationship with God takes first priority. The trial arises in whether the individual is or is not meant to go the one step further that she or he thinks God is requiring."[2] Here there is suggestion of the more positive and unique aspects of *Anfægtelse*: aspects that constitute its evolution beyond the confines of what is evoked by mere "temptation".

The forthcoming edition of *Kierkegaard's Concepts* from the *Kierkegaard Research: Sources, Reception and Resources* series provide distinct entries for temptation and spiritual trial. Sean Turchin's entry on 'Temptation' (*Fristelse* — noun; *Friste* — verb) astutely notes the occasional elision between temptation (*Friselse*), spiritual trial (*Anfægtelse*), and ordeal (*Prøvelse*) in Kierkegaard's writings as his intentional development of both subtle and emphatic diffferentiations between these intimately related terms. The distinctions and intersections of these terms are also acknowledged in Geoffrey Dargan's 'Trial, Test, Tribulation' (*Anfægtelse* — noun). The entry title of notably omits the Hongs' customary adjective 'spiritual' — which is understandable insofar as not all references to *Anfægtelse* in Kierkegaard's works are situated in the religious; though in its most intensified religious form *Anfægtelse* arises in relation to the awakening of *Spirit*. Above all though both Dargan and Turchin trace the nuanced and distinctive development of Kierkegaard's treatment of these key terms and have made important and, in my view, faithful contributions to a renewed understanding of the importance of temptation and spiritual trial in the Kierkegaardian corpus.[3]

---

the final years, about 175 times in all. Whereas it is frequently found in the earlier works and less frequently in earlier Pap., the reverse is true during the later years of SK." 'Trial, Test, Tribulation, Temptation', 109.

1 Julia Watkin, *Historical Dictionary of Kierkegaard's Philosophy* (Lanham, Maryland, and London: The Scarecrow Press, 2001), 255.

2 Watkin, *Historical Dictionary of Kierkegaard's Philosophy*, 255.

3 Sean Turchin, 'Temptation'; and Geoffrey Dargan, 'Trial, Test, Tribulation', Steven Emmanuel, William McDonald and Jon Stewart (eds), *Kierkegaard Research: Sources, Reception and Resources: Volume 15: Kierkegaard's Concepts: Tome VI* (Aldershot: Ashgate, forthcoming). I am very grateful to Sean

Dargan notes a twentieth-century definition of *Anfægtelse* as "doubt", "concern" or even "suspicion" concerning veracity, as well as the nineteenth-century sense of "attack", "challenge" or temptation from the devil.[1] A 1998 Danish-English dictionary also defines *anfægtelse* firstly as "scruple (religious scruples); temptation" and secondly as "contestation". However, perhaps the prevailing contemporary application lies in the second meaning of *contest* — albeit not a spiritual contest between the human and the divine, but a legal contestation of the validity of, for example, a promise or the legality of a marriage.[2] In this sense, the adjective *anfægtelig* means "contestable".[3] According to a Danish dictionary from 1859, however, the complexion is somewhat different. As Robert Widenman outlines, *at anfægte* was defined during Kierkegaard's time as:

> Actually to assault with arms, but used [in this sense] figuratively only. *At anfegtes* (to be tempted [*fristes*]) by the Devil; *anfegtes* (to be insulted) with respect to one's honor; *anfegtes* (to be plagued) by sufferings, by severe illness. The son's misfortune does not *anfegte*(r) him (it does not touch him, he does not take it seriously, to heart). *Anfegtelse, en.* Temptation [*Fristelse*] uneasiness anxiety of the mind.' (*Anfegtelse* is an older spelling).[4]

However, even these varied meanings — of being tempted (*fristes*) by the Devil, to be plagued by sufferings, or afflicted by anxiety of the mind — cannot do sufficient justice to the pathos that spiritual trial assumes in Kierkegaard's writings. And yet the polyvalence of Kierkegaard's treatment of this category threatens to render any endeavour to translate *Anfægtelse* as tortuously contrived. Nonetheless, Widenman argues that Kierkegaard went to exhaustive lengths in the study of language and communication to ensure that he arrived at "a terminology that would not engender ambiguity" such that "the various terms and expressions permeating his authorship show a remarkable consistency in meaning and application —

Turchin and Geoffrey Dargan for providing me with advance copies of their entries prior to publication.

1 Dargan refers in the first instance to *Ordbog over det Danske Sprog*, published by Det Danske Sprog-og Litteraturselskab, Copenhagen: Gyldendal, 1918-56, vol. 1; and secondly to Molbech's 1833 *Dansk Ordborg*.

2 Similarly *Anfechtung* is part of contemporary German legal lexicon: e.g. *Anfechtungsklausel*: 'avoidance clause'.

3 *Dansk-Engelsk Ordbog* (Copenhagen: Gyldendal, 1998).

4 *Dansk Ordbog*, 2nd edn, ed. Chr. Molbech (Copenhagen: Gyldendal, 1859). Cited in Robert Widenman, 'Kierkegaard's Terminology — and English', ed. Niels Thulstrup, *Kierkegaardiana VII* (København: Munksgaard, 1968), 122.

even when Kierkegaard does not supply us with a definition".[1] In his 1968 essay, 'Kierkegaard's Terminology — and English', Widenman's avowed purpose is to take "a closer look at those words and expression which in the past have been the cause not only of difficulties but also of a departure from Kierkegaard's terminology".[2] Among those considered, Widenman confesses that *Anfægtelse* "is perhaps the worst of them all, there existing in English not even an approximation to it in meaning, while it nevertheless constitutes an important category in Kierkegaard's religious thinking".[3]

Widenman concludes that the various English expressions coined to compensate for the lack of an English equivalent "just do not help at all and are, if anything, distracting".[4] As such, Widenman acknowledges David Swenson's obligation to incorporate the German equivalent *Anfechtung* in the absence of a satisfactory English term for the Danish *Anfægtelse* when making the first English translation of *Concluding Unscientific Postscript to the Philosophical Fragments* (1846).[5] "Much as I should always hesitate to import into English foreign, unknown words", Widenman concedes, "the lack in this instance is so glaring that it becomes a necessity". However, Widenman immediately arbitrates that *Anfechtung*, "when it pops up in the middle of an English sentence, brings with it the savor of an unpleasant, contagious disease, for which reason the Danish *anfægtelse*, which at least is pronounceable in English, is much to be preferred."[6] Widenman's comments may bear the mark of personal (dis)taste, but his point is nonetheless legitimate: if a foreign word is to be imported into English — especially one that is a cognate of the original — why not simply insert the Danish original itself?[7] However, perhaps English-language readers familiar with German theology may have some prior acquaintance with the term *Anfechtung* and therefore the particular significance of *Anfægtelse* may be more available by way of this German cognate. Nonetheless, the German *Anfechtung* may encourage the tendency to overlook the category as a

---

1 Widenman, 'Kierkegaard's Terminology — and English', 113.
2 Ibid. 116.
3 Ibid. 122.
4 Ibid. 123.
5 *Concluding Unscientific Postscript*, trans. David F. Swenson and Walter Lowrie (Princeton, New Jersey: Princeton University Press, 1941).
6 Widenman, 'Kierkegaard's Terminology — and English', 123-4.
7 Swenson's use of *Anfechtung* incurs the rather awkward translation, "Within the sphere of religious suffering there lies the special type of religious conflict the Germans call *Anfechtung* [*Anfægtelse*], which category finds its determination only in this connection." (CUP [Swenson and Lowrie translation], 410).

relic of Lutheran spirituality — rather than appreciate Kierkegaard's innovative attempt to refine and rehabilitate the pathos of *Anfægtelse* for a generation oblivious and desensitised to its significance.

Where Swenson employed the German *Anfechtung* in the 1941 English translation of *Concluding Unscientific Postscript*, Walter Lowrie (who was completing the translation after Swenson's death on 11 February 1940) felt compelled to preserve the word in lieu of a satisfactory English translation despite his own preference for "trial of temptation".[1] In his 'Editor's Preface', Lowrie confides that "Even in the part for which I am responsible, I have been scrupulous not to use the terms I prefer but the locutions he [Swenson] had chosen."[2] As such, Lowrie notes his reservation whereby he "cannot assume that all readers are acquainted with the exact sense of the German word which is used here".[3] Indeed, it could not be assumed that everyone who consulted this translation of *Concluding Unscientific Postscript* — particularly those approaching it from a more strictly philosophical perspective — would be familiar with the Lutheran understanding of *Anfechtung* which Johannes Climacus was consciously evoking. Gordon Rupp's influential historical study of Luther's theology, *The Righteousness of God*, which brought a taste of prevailing German and Scandinavian Luther research to an English-language audience, did not appear until 1953. In this work Rupp elucidates Luther's prevailing motif of living *coram Deo* (in the presence/ before the Face of God) alongside the anxious sense of *Anfechtung* that this elicits. Furthermore, by the point of Swenson and Lowrie's translation of *Concluding Unscientific Postscript* in 1941, the existentialist gloss, which Paul Tillich and others would lend to Luther's *Anfechtung*, would not have been readily available to English readers. For example, Tillich's essay on 'The Transmoral Conscience', which describes Luther's struggles with *Anfechtungen*, or "tempting attacks", as "the state of absolute despair" or "the bad conscience", appeared in 1945, four years after Lowrie and Swenson's *Concluding Unscientific Postscript*.[4]

---

1 *Concluding Unscientific Postscript*, trans. David F. Swenson and Walter Lowrie. (Princeton, New Jersey: Princeton University Press, 1941), 569n.8: Dr. Swenson uses here [p. 410f] the German word *Anfechtung* (to translate the kindred Danish word *Anfægtelse*) because unfortunately we make no distinction in English between temptation and temptation, between the temptation which repels and the temptation which attracts. . . . Commonly I translate this word by 'trial of temptation,' but this does not quite serve to make it clear that what we are dealing with is the repellant temptation, not the enticement of pleasure.

2 'Editor's Preface', *Concluding Unscientific Postscript*, ix.

3 *Concluding Unscientific Postscript*, 569 n.8.

4 The essay first appeared in *The Crozer Quarterly*, XXII (4), 1945, and

Beyond *Anfecthung*

As will be elaborated in subsequent chapters; the meaning of the term *Anfechtung* itself has evolved, and devolved, through medieval mystical thought, through Lutheran and Pietistic literature, and twentieth-century existentialist philosophy and theology. Furthermore, Kierkegaard himself wrote "at a time when the Danish orthography was not yet fixed, and when the Danish language contained many words and expressions which have since either disappeared completely or undergone radical modifications in meaning."[1] As such, while the cognate *Anfechtung* indicates the Germanic etymology of the Danish term and preserves the central notion of 'fight' (*fecht*) residing at the heart of *Anfægtelse* (*fægte*), it may seem to be a case of translating one anachronism via another.[2] Furthermore, English translations of the German *Anfechtung* again are subject to the challenge of satisfactory rendition. Clearly the English word 'temptation' is insufficient and risks obscuring the difference between temptation (*Versuchung/Fristelse*) and *Anfechtung/Anfægtelse*. The Lutheran notion of *Anfechtung* has been expressed as "the trial of faith by various temptations",[3] as "the trial of faith, the temptation from above",[4] as "tempting attacks" imprisoning the consciousness of sin with "a feeling of being enclosed in a narrow

---

subsequently in 1948 in James Luther Adams' collected translation of several of Tillich's essays, *The Protestant Era* (Chicago, Illinois: The University of Chicago Press, 1948; 2nd impression 1951), 145-46. Academic German translations of Kierkegaard's works were available during the 1910s, though some independent translations had appeared as early as the 1870s. Like Barth and Bultmann and, in a rather different direction, Heidegger, Tillich was already under Kierkegaard's influence by the time Swenson and Lowrie's translation of *Concluding Unscientific Postscript* appeared in English. "In Germany, however, it [*Concluding Unscientific Postscript*] has had an incalculable influence upon theology, and a new philosophy, the so-called Existentialist Philosophy, has been prompted by it. Perhaps it will make its way slowly in England and America." 'Editor's Preface', *Concluding Unscientific Postscript*, xi.

1 Widenman, 'Kierkegaard's Terminology — and English', 114.
2 Furthermore, as André Clair observes, "On peut imaginer l'ironie de Kierkegaard voyant un concept capital rendu en américain par un terme allemand!" 'La Catégorie Kierkegaardienne de Tribulation: Discriminer Entre L'Éthique et le Religieux-Chrétien', *Revue des Sciences Philosophiques et Théologiques*, 5 (81), October 1997, 630n.1.
3 Rupp, *The Righteousness of God*, 235.
4 H.V. Martin, *The Wings of Faith: A Consideration of the Nature and Meaning of Christian Faith in the Light of the Work of Søren Kierkegaard* (London: The Lutterworth Press, 1950), 101.

place from which there is no escape".[1] This conceptual similitude between *Anfechtung* and *Angst* (form Latin *angustiae* — 'narrows') is particularly elucidating, particularly in Luther's sense of the captivity and claustrophobia of the anguished conscience (WA, 1.557.39). Kierkegaard himself observes how "Anxiety [*Angst*] is the most terrible kind of spiritual trial [*Anfægtelse*]" (JP 2:1401) — though in Kierkegaard anxiety is evoked by the vertiginous fear and desire of freedom and possibility as well as by the narrowing *Angst* of spiritual trial in which the individual is captured, even imprisoned, by the Absolute. Anxiety belongs to both temptation and spiritual trial.[2]

As Kierkegaard's expansive category of anxiety illustrates, conceptual meaning can be compromised by tight philological focus. Similar difficulties have been addressed in translations of Kierkegaard into other languages that, like English, do not possess a cognate term for *Anfægtelse*. On one single page of his French translation of *The Concept of Anxiety* (1935), Paul Petit variously renders *Anfægtelse* as "*harcèlements de l'esprit*" ['harassments of the spirit']; "*travaille à temps*" and "*scrupules de conscience*".[3] Elsewhere in this translation, Petit uses "*conflits intérieur de l'esprit*"[4] [interior spiritual conflicts] and "*scrupule religieux*"[5] [religious scruples]. Petit's 1949 translation of *Concluding Unscientific Postscript* employs "*épreuve*" ['test', 'trial', 'ordeal'; *malheur*] in order to differentiate *Anfægtelse* from "*tentation*" ['temptation'].[6] However, as Clair rightly observes, "*épreuve*" is perhaps a better translation for Kierkegaard's term *Prøvelse* ['trial' or 'ordeal'].[7] As Clair further elucidates, Paul-Henri Tisseau's translations of Kierkegaard's writings provide a multiplicity of possible terms for *Anfægtelse*: "*doute religieux*" ['religious doubt'], "*inquietude*", "*tribulation*", "*anxiété*", "*adversité*", "*lutte intérieure*" ['interior spiritual struggle'], "*crise*", and "*horror religiosus*" — the latter being a term employed in *Fear and Trembling* to describe the Johannes de silentio's approach to the figure of Abraham.[8] Clair aptly

1 *The Protestant Era* (London: Nisbet and Co., 1951), 162.
2 See below and 'Chapter Six' of my *Kierkegaard and the Self Before God*.
3 *Le Concept De L'Angoisse*. Trad. du danois par P. Petit (Paris, Gallimard, 1935), 169 (CA, 117).
4 *Le Concept De L'Angoisse*, 174 (CA, 120).
5 *Le Concept De L'Angoisse*, 206* (CA, 143*).
6 *Post-scriptum aux miettes philosophiques*, Trad. du danois par P. Petit (Paris, Gallimard, 1949 and 1989), 310.
7 "[M]ais on remarquera que ce terms convient mieux pour render le danois *Prøvelse*." 'La Catégorie Kierkegaardienne de Tribulation', 630n.1.
8 'La Catégorie Kierkegaardienne de Tribulation', 630n.1. In the same note, Clair adds that in his translations of *Fear and Trembling* and *Concluding Unscientific*

warns that just as the many translations of *Anfægtelse* draw attention to the complexities of the term, they also risk misleading the reader.[1] Finally Clair proposes a translation of *Anfægtelse* as "*inquietude spirituelle*", an echo of Augustine's *Confessions* 1.1, "*quia fecisti nos ad te et inquietum est cor nostrum donec requiescat in te*": "because you have made us for yourself [or *towards* yourself — *ad te*: re. the Latin Bible, *ad imaginam* — God made us towards God's image] our heart is restless until it finds rest in thee".[2] This evocation of Augustinian longing also affirms the erotic restlessness of Spirit, aspiring to realise itself *towards* God as the image of God, in search of rest in God, which, as I suggest further in chapter seven, underlies a Kierkegaardian understanding of spiritual trial.

A Spanish equivalent of the French "*inquietude spirituelle*", "*las inquietudes del espíritu*", is employed in Demetrio G. Rivero's translation of *The Concept of Anxiety* (1965).[3] Elsewhere, in the same place that Petit turns to the French "*scrupule religieux*", Rivero changes from "*las inquietudes del espíritu*" to "*escrúpulos*".[4] The consistency between the French and Spanish is rendered clearer when it is observed that the passage in question is a note exploring the difference between *Anfægtelse* and 'the demonic' with particular reference to the anxiety about going to Communion (CA, 143* in the English Thomte and Anderson edition). In this context, the monastic notion of 'scruples' may be entirely appropriate. However, scrupulosity (from the Latin *scrupulus* — 'pebble', meaning an aggravation of conscience out of proportion to the reality of its size) also possesses pejorative connotations. For example, it was a common slur against Luther that he was merely a 'scrupulant', a victim of a monastic sickness of the soul to which his tortuous struggles with *Anfechtung* bear pathological witness. However, while scruples may be one form that *Anfægtelse* can take, it does not suffice as a comprehensive translation of the term in all its permutations.[5]

Postscript Tisseau describes *Anfægtelse* as "*une tribulation spirituelle*" but "*elle n'est pas une épreuve* ['test'], *connue comme telle lorsqu'elle est passée.*"

1 "*Pourtant, si la multiplicité des termes a l'avantage d'attirer l'attention sur la complexité du concept, elle risque d'égarer le lecteur.*" Clair, 'La Catégorie Kierkegaardienne de Tribulation', 630n.1.

2 "*[O]ù l'inquiétude n'est pas quelque vague anxiété, mais signifie un tourment qui met radicalement en question toute la personnalité devant l'absolu et qui est vécu comme une épreuve. On se souviendra du début des Confessions de S. Augustin: 'inquietum est cor nostrum donec requiescat in te'*" (Ibid.).

3 *El Concepto de la Angustia* (Madrid: Ediciones Guadarrama, 1965), 216 (CA, 117) and 221 (CA, 120).

4 *El Concepto de la Angustia*, 257* (CA, 143*).

5 See further my 'The Lightning and the Earthquake', 577n44.

Indeed, it is doubtful that any one word will be sufficient to convey the varieties of *Anfægtelse*. One of the earliest attempts to capture the term in English is found in Alexander Dru's 1938 translation of *Anfægtelse* as "tribulation" in his first edition of Kierkegaard's selected journals.[1] "Tribulation", which possesses a substantial heritage in the theological and biblical lexicon, derives from the Middle English *tribulacion* and refers primarily to a state of oppression or affliction.[2] Furthermore, the Latin etymology (Latin *tribulatio*, from *tribulare* to press, oppress), begins to convey the sense of *Angst* (from the Latin *angustiae* — 'narrows') inherent to *Anfechtung/Anfægtelse*. However, as mentioned above, *Angst* in the Kierkegaardian corpus also has a strongly vertiginous as well as a harrowing nuance: it expresses the awakening of subjectivity and freedom as well passivity in the grip of affliction. As such, I suggest that "tribulation" does not sufficiently convey the intensification of subjectivity evoked by Kierkegaard's *Anfægtelse*, the etymological and figurative centrality of 'fight', or the relation between *Anfægtelse* and temptation (*Fristelse*). In his 1965 selected translation, *Søren Kierkegaard: The Last Years, Journals 1853-1855*, Ronald Gregor Smith employs "temptations of thought"[3] and "tempting thoughts"[4] for *anfægtende Tanker* — a phrase translated by

1   *The Journals of Søren Kierkegaard: A Selection*, ed. and trans. Alexander Dru (London, New York, Toronto: Oxford University Press, 1951 [1938]). G.E. Arbaugh uses "spiritual tribulations" in 'The Devil', *Bibliotheca Kierkegaardiana Vol. 5: Theological Concepts in Kierkegaard*, ed. Niels Thusltrup and Marie Mikulová Thulstrup (Copenhagen: C. A. Reitzels Boghandel, 1980), 268.

2   As a possible alternative, 'Affliction' (from the Latin *afflictare* or *afflict*; from *affligere: fligere* — to strike) transmits some sense of the notion of fight (*fægte*) central to *Anfægtelse*. Affliction also conveys an older (religious) sense of 'self-mortification', of being 'cast down', 'humbled', as well as being in a state of suffering. Nonetheless, as with 'trial' and 'tribulation', 'affliction' conveys passivity, even victimhood, too readily. In this sense, perhaps "conflict" (from the Latin *conflictus* —'collision', from past participle of *confligere*, 'to strike together') may be more apt, insofar as it refers to a prolonged fight, or struggle between opposing forces, or a collision of principles. As such, in the Kierkegaardian context *conflict* may help to evoke the dialectical tension of the "infinite qualitative difference" between self and God, the antagonism between Spirit and spiritlessness, so central to Kierkegaard's expressions of the meaning of *Anfægtelse*. But more than this, 'conflict' implies a mutuality in the struggle between self and God (*con* — 'with') which is lost in other translations and suggests that this is also a relational notion in which the resolution of the fight is derived in dialectic with the other with whom one struggles (as *con-science* implies a 'with-knowing').

3   Ronald Gregor Smith, *Søren Kierkegaard: The Last Years, Journals 1853-1855* (London: Collins, 1965), Pap. XI² A 33, p. 198.

4   *Søren Kierkegaard: The Last Years, Journals 1853-1855*, Pap. XI² A 132, p. 256.

the Hongs as "thoughts that try the spirit" (e.g. JP 4:4383). Here it could be said that an attempt is made to distinguish "temptations of thought" from mere "temptation" by emphasising the mental aspect of *Anfægtelse* over the traditionally carnal connotations of fleshly "temptation". However, once again the centrality of struggle (*fægte*) is diminished; as is the sense of *Anfægtelse* as something more than a diverse or inverted form of temptation.

The Diary of Søren Kierkegaard, edited by Peter P. Rhode and translated by Gerda M. Anderson in 1960, uses "sore doubts" for *Anfægtelse* in an entry from 2 July 1855.[1] According to Rhode, "doubt" is what Johannes Climacus means in his discussion of *Anfægtelse* in *Concluding Unscientific Postscript*. However, while Kierkegaard's wider treatment of *Anfægtelse* may be understood in close relation to doubt — particularly as it pertains to doubts over one's salvation and the temptation to despair over one's apparent God-forsakenness — "doubt" would be too reductive a term. Furthermore, doubt (*Tvivl*) itself resides at the etymological root of "despair" [*Fortvivlelse*], and despair itself, like anxiety, can be a form of *Anfægtelse* — but *Anfægtelse* is not reducible to any single term of doubt, despair, or anxiety. As Kierkegaard's wider authorship attests, *Anfægtelse* may have its origins, not only in doubt, but also in the imagination (*Phantasi*); anxiety; offence; freedom; the tension of Spirit; and, perhaps above all, in the "infinite qualitative difference" between humanity and God. Furthermore, Rhode's assertion that doubt manifests itself as "religious fear, a fear of the Good" also evokes Kierkegaard's category of "the demonic", characterised as "anxiety about the good" (CA, 118), an anxious force which Vigilius Haufniensis explicitly distinguishes from *Anfægtelse* (CA, 143*).[2] The demonic wants to lead one *away* from the good, which *Anfægtelse* struggles to engage with, and towards the evil in the shadows of which it seeks to escape the glaring light of the Holy. In this sense, the demonic may be understood as a form of temptation (*Fristelse*) rather than *Anfægtelse* — though the demonic seeks out temptation from a defiance of the good rather than a mere weakness of the (fleshly) will. As such, the demonic might be construed as the temptation of the self in despair (*tentatio desperationis*) to will to be itself, in demonic defiance of the good (SUD, 70-74).

---

1 *The Diary of Søren Kierkegaard*, ed. Peter P. Rhode and trans. Gerda M. Anderson (New York: Philosophical Library, 1960), 201. See also JP 1:731.
2 Vigilius Haufniensis also comments that even though Joseph von Görres' *Die christliche Mystik* (Regensburg and Landshut, 1836-42; ASKB 528-32) contains "a superfluity" of material on spiritual trial, "Görres does not always know how to distinguish between the demonic and spiritual trial. Therefore the work should be used with care." CA, 143*.

In light of these differentiations, Lowrie's more descriptive translation of *Fristelse* as "alluring temptations" and *Anfægtelse* as "deterrent temptations" also seems unsatisfying.[1] His "trial of temptation" from his 1941 translation of CUP also may not serve to sufficiently represent Kierkegaard's distinction. Furthermore, the terminology of "trial" might be thought too passive, even too close to the transcendent category of "ordeal" (*Prøvelse*). Nonetheless, this word prevails in the Hongs' translations of *Anfægtelse* as "spiritual trial". Although "spiritual trial" may imply passivity and employs two words to represent one distinctive category, the Hongs' translation does help to elicit the vital relationship between *Anfægtelse* and "Spirit" [*Ånd*] in Kierkegaard's theological anthropology. "Spiritual trial" thus alludes to the restlessness and *passio* of Spirit in tension with 'spiritlessness' [*Åndløsheden*] — in terms of which *Anfægtelse* might be understood as a trial by fire, a transmutation of the self via the metamorphosis of Spirit.

In her play *The Gayety of Grace*, Edna Hong imagines a conversation with Kierkegaard and Luther in which *Anfechtung* and *Anfægtelse* are both rendered by "spiritual assault".[2] This term effectively indicates the 'fight' central to both the German and the Danish, while the subsequent description of an "unholy combination" of "Doubt, Depression, Despair" affirms the thematically expansive and inter-related facets of "spiritual assault". However, it may be overly pejorative to affirm this dark trinity as an "unholy combination" insofar as for Luther and Kierkegaard spiritual trial can provide a *via negativa* to an encounter with the Holy.

Using the allegory of struggling with God and the loving struggle of prayer, as well as the notion of *agonia* and *passio*, my reluctant preference would be for *spiritual struggle*. This, however, is not without reticence. The adjective "spiritual" is ultimately expedient for affirming the almost *sui generis* nature of *Anfægtelse*: it is ineffable in its secrecy between self and God; it is bound to the alterity of Spirit. Furthermore, as a form of *passio*, it is not identical with the suffering of illness, disaster, accident — though it may describe a

---

1 *For Self-Examination* and *Judge For Yourselves! and Three Discourses*, trans. Walter Lowrie (London: Oxford University Press, 1941).

2 "LUTHER: If I have profound insights, Madame, it is because I have often experienced profound spiritual assault. *Anfechtung* it is called in German. S.K.: *Anfægtelse* in Danish. But it is one and the same, and I, too, had many an attack.
I: Is it what we call mental depression today?
LUTHER: It is an unholy combination of the three damned D's: Doubt, Depression, Despair." Edna Hong, *The Gayety of Grace* (Northfield, MN: Postscript, Inc., 2008), 62.

state of spiritual reflection, prayer, or even protest in response to such experiences. Emphatically, such suffering should not be sanctified in its name. In this, spiritual trial should be understood according to a different world-view and account of divine providence than the medieval view of Luther, for whom illness is abruptly traceable to divine and demonic sources, even such that the Black Death might be understood under a rubric of *Anfechtung* to be spread by evil spirits, yet ultimately under the decree of divine punishment. One of Kierkegaard's most profound innovations is to exorcise Luther's obsession with demonic and satanic sources for spiritual trial, to emphasise its psychogenic elements, and to ultimately re-inscribe it within a framework of human freedom and anxiety.

"Spiritual", however, does not simply rarefy all notions of *Anfægtelse*. In the "old devotional writings", to which attention will turn in the next chapter, there is counsel for those in the thralls of *Geistliche Anfechtungen*, whereby *Geistliche* refers specifically to the life of the Holy Spirit (*Der Heilige Geist*). Many contemporary eyes, however, will perceive "spiritual" in more expansive or cosmopolitan terms than Kierkegaard intended. Yet Kierkegaard employs Spirit in relation to becoming a self (SUD, 13), and in this respect he affirms a universal and relational theological anthropology more than a dogmatic pneumatology. Having said this, a further problem which confronts us is that *spiritual* trial is not always *spiritual*. As *On the Concept of Irony with Continual Reference to Socrates* (1841) observes, and as will be explored further in this work, it might be said that every position in life has its *Anfægtelser* (CI, 166). Yet insofar as every *Anfægtelse* emerges within the context of the struggle for selfhood it might be traceable to the life of Spirit, whether consciously or not.

As Niels Thulstrup has observed, "The English words temptation, test, trial (ev. spiritual trial), tribulation and allurement do not cover all the meanings of the Danish word '*anfægtelse*' (from German 'Anfechtung') as used by SK in various simultaneous meanings."[1] Nonetheless, each translation can help to educe important aspects of what Kierkegaard explores under the rubric of *Anfægtelse*. However, the problem of translation is that of privileging one meaning to the exclusion of other aspects of *Anfægtelse* and, as such, I do not wish to add to the confusion on this matter by proposing yet another English translation.[2] Ideally, what is required is a translation which points towards the specialization of the original, while also allowing space

1 Thulstrup, 'Trial, Test, Tribulation, Temptation', 105.
2 "The different meanings in which SK uses the word trial [*Anfægtelse*] show the difficulties of formulating a definition in which due concern can be paid to both the contents of the term and its range." Thulstrup, 'Trial, Test, Tribulation, Temptation', 116.

for the varied and impressionistic meanings which Kierkegaard explores under the rubric of *Anfægtelse*. In lieu of such a term, and with the caveats explored in this chapter, I work with the Hongs' prevailing term *spiritual trial*.

"Whatever be the choice", Widenman concluded, "let it be hoped that in future revisions and translations the cumbersome and meaningless expression hitherto employed will be discarded."[1] At the time that Widenman's essay was published (1968), the first volume of *Søren Kierkegaard's Journals and Papers*, edited and translated by Howard V. Hong and Edna H. Hong, assisted by Gregor Malantschuk, had recently become available (1967). This contained a reference to "spiritual trial" duly followed by the Danish in square brackets [*Anfægtelse*] on page 169, entry 416:

> [. . .] before he succeeds in arriving at the Christian conviction, he is confronted by many struggles [*mangen Kamp*] and much spiritual suffering [*mangen sjælelig Lidelse*] when doubt [*tvivl*] arises. When, finally, he achieves conviction, he undergoes spiritual trial [*Anfægtelse*], i.e., reason asserts its claims once more before it finally subsides. (JP 1:416 / Pap. I A 95 19 October 1935)

The Hongs' translation has since endured and generally eclipsed previous attempts to render *Anfægtelse* in English.[2] For instance, while Alistair Hannay's 1996 selection of Kierkegaard's journals occasionally translates *Anfægtelse* as "tempting thoughts",[3] echoing Ronald Gregor Smith, for the most part Hannay echoes the Hongs' "spiritual trial".[4] In recent years, the emerging new English translations of Kierkegaard's works from the Søren Kierkegaard Research Centre Foundation at Copenhagen University, retain the terminology of "spiritual trial", at least in some instances. For example, the above passage from the Hongs' translation (JP 1:416 / Pap. I A 95) is rendered in the new

1 Widenman,'Kierkegaard's Terminology — and English', 124.

2 The Hongs' provide a useful list of previous renderings of *Anfægtelse* in earlier English translations of Kierkegaard's works, including: "tribulations"; "trials"; "temptation(s)"; "base temptation"; "terrors"; "exertion"; "anxieties"; "assaults of the spirit"; "assault of doubt"; "temptation of doubt", "temptations of religious scruples and doubts", "assaults of temptation"; "trying doubts"; "trial and temptation"; "trials of temptation"; "doubts and temptations"; "temptations to doubt"; "evil temptation"; "trials and temptations"; "*Anfechtung*"; "alarms"; "spiritual trials"; "torments of anxiety"; "trepidation". See 'Spiritual Trial' in *Søren Kierkegaard's Journals and Papers*, Volume 4, 694.

3 Alastair Hannay, *Søren Kierkegaard Papers and Journals: A Selection* (London: Penguin Books, 1996), 626. See also JP 4:4384 / Pap. XI² A 132.

4 For example, Hannay, *Søren Kierkegaard Papers and Journals: A Selection*, 645. See also JP 1:731 / Pap. XI² A 422.

translation thus: "When he has finally reached it, a spiritual trial faces him, i.e., reason once more presses its claims before its total downfall."[1] However, in the new edition "spiritual trial" is not followed by the bracketed Danish original [Anfægtelse] as it frequently is in the Hongs' translations. As such, readers of Kierkegaard's works in English may once again pass over a highly significant term in Kierkegaard's writings. The waters are further muddied by what follows in the new translation of this particular journal entry. The Hongs' translation of this entry continues to say the following:

> The reason why these doubts are able to appear a second time (for that which appears now, a second time, under the name of spiritual trial [Anfægtelse], is what we in the first instance called doubt) is that they were not dismissed in the first place through debate but through displacement by another force or growth. The reason these spiritual trials [Anfægtelser] do not continue through a Christian's life is not because they have been struggled with, for we clearly saw that they do not want to get involved with them, but one can benumb himself in a certain respect, once can become spiritually deaf in one ear so that it is impossible to arouse him. (JP 1:416 / Pap. I A 95, 19 October 1835)

In the new translation of the same entry, while the first instance of Anfægtelse is duly translated as "spiritual trial", the subsequent second and third instances of Anfægtelse and Anfægtelser (quoted above in the Hongs' translation) are rendered by the English words "temptation" and "temptations".[2] This change seems somewhat inconsistent given the consistent use of Anfægtelse and Anfægtelser, rather than Fristelse(r) [temptation(s)], in the Danish original.[3]

In the second volume of the Copenhagen Research Centre edition, "spiritual trial" is again used in one instance: "It is and remains the most difficult spiritual trial when a pers. doesn't know whether insanity or sin is the reason for his suffering. Here freedom, otherwise

---

1 Journal AA:14. 19 October 1835, Bruce H. Kirmmse general editor, *Kierkegaard's Journals and Notebooks: Volume 1 Journals AA-DD* (Princeton and Oxford: Princeton University Press, 2007), 27.

2 "(for what now makes its second appearance under the name of temptation is what from the earlier standpoint we called doubt). . . . It is not because they have been beaten down that these temptations do not persist through a Christian's life, since Christian's, as we saw, would have no truck with them. . . . " Journal AA:14, 19 October 1835, *Kierkegaard's Journals and Notebooks, Volume 1 Journals AA-DD*, 27.

3 Journalen AA:14. 1935, *Søren Kierkegaards Skrifter 17 Journalerne AA. BB. CC. DD* [SKS], ed. Niels Jørgen Cappelørn *et al* (København: Fonden for Søren Kierkegaard Forskningscenteret, 2000), 33.

used as the means with which to fight, has become dialectical with its dreadful contrasts."[1] However, elsewhere, "trying difficulties" is introduced to convey "*Anfægtelser*": "If one is to clothe oneself in the religious every day, then trying difficulties arise."[2] Evidently, the effort to render and interpret *Anfægtelse* carries its own trials and temptations — namely trials of meaning, source and discernment, which are themselves integral to *Anfægtelse* itself. In light of its secrecy and ineffability, it is notable that the linguistic confusion surrounding *Anfægtelse*, and its relation to "temptation" (*Fristelse*) in particular, still eludes definitive resolution.

From the perspective of this present study, however, the numerous possibilities for translating *Anfægtelse* are indicative of the many dimensions of spiritual struggle. All can be forms of *Anfægtelse*: tribulation; temptation; spiritual inquietude; contestation; spiritual assault; trial of temptation; tempting attacks; the trial of faith, the temptation from above; *harcèlements de l'esprit*; *travaille à temps*; *scrupules de conscience*; *conflits intérieur de l'esprit*; *scrupule religieux*; *épreuve*; *malheur*; *doute religieux*; *adversité*; *lutte intérieure*; *crise*; *tribulation spirituelle*; *horror religiosus*; *acidia espiritual*; desolation; tribulation; temptations of thought; thoughts that try the spirit; sore doubts; test; ordeal; assaults of the spirit; assault of doubt; assault of temptation; temptations of religious scruples and doubts; evil temptation; alarms; torments of anxiety; trepidation; trying difficulties; affliction; spiritual conflict; spiritual struggle; spiritual trial. To this might be added anxiety, despair, melancholy, offense — all of which can be interpreted under the rubric of *Anfægtelse*. While lexical enquiry may deliver a sense of the polyvalence, anachronism, secrecy, even sheer untranslatability of the word itself, this present study seeks to develop a constructive theological and philosophical account of the meaning and content of this elusive category. In order to trace and develop Kierkegaard's understanding of *Anfægtelse*, the sources of this notion in mystical, Lutheran, and Pietistic thought should first be explored. It is therefore to an exploration of that which Kierkegaard venerates as the "older and better devotional literature" (JP 4:4384) that this study now turns.

---

1 Journal JJ:242, Bruce H. Kirmmse general editor, *Kierkegaard's Journals and Notebooks: Volume 1 Journals AA-DD* (Princeton and Oxford: Princeton University Press, 2007), 200. Cf. JP 4:4586 / Pap. V A 49 n.d., 1844.

2 Journal JJ:291, Bruce H. Kirmmse general editor, *Kierkegaard's Journals and Notebooks: Volume 2 Journals EE-KK* (2008), 213. Cf. JP 4:4364 / Pap. VI A 2 n.d., 1844-45. However, the third volume of Kierkegaard's journals retain "spiritual trial": for example, NB:203 (Pap. VIII I A 93) and NB:208 (Pap. VIII I A 98). I am grateful to the general editor Prof. Bruce Kirmmse for providing me with early versions of these translations and for entertaining a constructive discussion on the topic of spiritual trial.

2. The Old Devotional Books:
Anfechtung in Tauler and the *Theologia Deutsch*

Voices in the Wilderness

Kierkegaard's rehabilitation of the idiom of spiritual trial (*Anfægtelse*) testifies to a prolonged search for edification in what he referred to as "the old devotional books" and the "older and better devotional literature" (JP 4:4384). In discovering the notion of spiritual struggle affirmed and elaborated in these echoes from previous centuries, Kierkegaard glimpsed the possibility of consolation in the midst of lonely desolation. While the subjective content of personal spiritual trial remains incommunicable, the solitude of Kierkegaard's own struggles with spiritual trial could be broken. Yet at the same moment, these works also exposed the damning silence of contemporary Christendom on such matters. According to Marie Mikulová Thulstrup's valuable reconstruction, Kierkegaard's sojourn through these texts lead him through a study of Pietism, mystical theology, and finally to the Church Fathers. In his readings in the spiritual ancestry of Christianity, Kierkegaard discovered an inward authenticity and pathos, which he discerned as conspicuous by its absence in modern Christendom. In this seemingly forgotten treasury, he read of rigorous self-mortification and of the flight of the soul into the abyss of God, of the imitation of the passion of Christ and meditations upon the divine compassion for human suffering. Such 'upbuilding' visions, Kierkegaard reflects, arise from a long forgotten belief that human beings are, above all, *Spirit*:

> It is fortunate, after all, that we have the old devotional books to hold to. How in the world would we acquire these mental states in our age. That which made its appearance by treating man as spirit, all these conditions of soul, inwardness — is cured nowadays by vacation trips to a spa, by leeches, bloodletting, and all that — but we are all Christians. (JP 4:4461)

Although the notion of spiritual trial and the tension between Spirit and spiritlessness intensified in the final attack upon Christendom, by 1850 Kierkegaard's interest in the Pietist and mystical literature appears to have increasingly deferred to the authority of the Church Fathers, "the final stopping place in SK's search for exemplars of the view of [Christianity] which he emphasized and wished to document".[1] In them, Kierkegaard found the heart of Christianity — imitation of Christ, suffering, and bearing witness — affirmed at its early consolidation.[2] Such suffering and sacrifice was nurtured in the cradle of the desert, in the ancient struggle between Church and 'the world', which had seemingly become dissolved in the apostate union of Christendom. One might expect that the view of temptation and spiritual struggle forged in the crucible of the desert to have been decisive to Kierkegaard's own exploration of temptation and spiritual trial, yet Kierkegaard's works do not render this genealogy explicitly. However, in a now famous journal entry from 1839, Kierkegaard affirms an implicit continuity between earlier insights concerning sicknesses of the solitary soul — spleen, *acedia, tristitia* — and a contemporary diagnosis of "what my father called: *a quiet despair*" (JP 1:740; 1:739).

While spiritual struggle (*ascesis*) was an inevitable nemesis upon the attempt to relate oneself to the Absolute, *asceticism*, as the deliberate attempt at cultivating an absolute relation to the Absolute remained a difficult concept for Kierkegaard. In his suspicion towards monastic withdrawal and an implicit desire for self-apotheosis in *ascesis* Kierkegaard demonstrates himself to be, at least partially, an inheritor of the customary Lutheran rejection of asceticism which permeated his theological text-books. At the same time, however, Kierkegaard expressed his own opinions on the faults and merits of ascetic practice and disposition.[3] In light of the Constantianian revolution through which the persecuted church triumphs as Christendom; monasticism and asceticism come to signify a rejection of the false elision between Spirit and the world. This refutation echoes in Kierkegaard's polemics against the spiritlessness of Christendom in which he expresses a nostalgic idealisation of early Christianity. In fact, despite his frequently pejorative references to ascetic ideology and practice in earlier works, Mikulová Thulstrup contends that asceticism is silently present in Kierkegaard's discussions of "dying

1   Mikulová Thulstrup, 'Studies of Pietists, Mystics, and Church Fathers', ed. Marie Mikulová Thulstrup, *Bibliotheca Kierkegaardiana: Vol. 1: Kierkegaard's View of Christianity*, (Copenhagen: C.A. Reitzels Boghandel, 1978), 71.

2   For example, Kierkegaard makes the observation that "The Church Fathers were right in observing that to pray is to breathe" (Pap. IX A 462 n.d., 1848), which parallels a key idea in *The Sickness Unto Death* (SUD, 40).

3   See Marie Mikulová Thulstrup, 'The Role of Asceticism', ed. Marie Mikulová Thulstrup, *Bibliotheca Kierkegaardiana: Vol. 2: The Sources and Depths of Faith in Kierkegaard*, (Copenhagen: C.A. Reitzels Boghandel, 1978), 154-55.

to the world, the single state, renunciation, suffering in the interest of a good cause".[1] Furthermore, according to Stan, Kierkegaard does not singularly oppose asceticism; rather, "In times of spiritual degradation or destruction, when religion is turned into commodity in line with democratic capitalist ideals, the commitment of monks achieves a certain respectable value in his eyes."[2] Nonetheless, the ideal of monasticism is at the same time moderated by Kierkegaard's view of the "imperfection of deterioration of all humans and martyrs, with apostles included".[3] In this respect, Kierkegaard acknowledges that the monastery "is an essentially dialectical element in Christianity", which contemporary Protestantism may need once more, if only as something "out there like a buoy at sea in order to see where we are, even though I myself would not enter it" (JP 3:2750).

Marie Mikulová Thulstrup's genealogy suggests that Kierkegaard's devotional reading passed through the Pietists, to the mystics, and came to rest with the Church Fathers. I suggest, however, that his views on temptation and spiritual trial are principally formed by the reflections of Pietistic and mystical literature.[4] As such, this chapter

1 Mikulová Thulstrup, 'The Role of Asceticism', 155.
2 Leo Stan, 'Chrysostom: Between the Hermitage and the City', ed. Jon Stewart, *Kierkegaard Research: Sources, Reception and Resources Volume 4: Kierkegaard and the Patristic and Medieval Traditions*, 46-65, 56. Kierkegaard refers several times in his journals to the ascetic Church Father Johannes Chrysostom (c.347-407), though nothing of note for this present study. See JP 1:574; 1:575; 1:576; 1:577; 2:1891; 3:2757; 3:2758; 3:3161; 4:4466; 4:4665; 6:6716.
3 Stan, 'Chrysostom: Between the Hermitage and the City', 63.
4 Furthermore, although he owned a significant amount of the original works of the Church Fathers, many of Kierkegaard's references to them derive from Friedrich Böhringer, *Die Kirche Christi und ihre Zeugen* (Zurich: 1842-58). Mikulová Thulstrup, 'Studies of Pietists, Mystics, and Church Fathers', 70-71. For example, in an entry from 1851, Kierkegaard quotes Ambrose (c.340-397) via Böhringer: "The wounds which we get for Christ's sake are not wounds by which life is lost but by which life is propagated. . . . I beseech you to let this battle take place — but you are only spectators!" (JP 4:4669. See further references to Ambrose in JP 3:2609, 4:4210 and FSE, 276). The two most explicit journal references to Irenaeus (130-202) are also reliant upon Böhringer (JP 2:1483; 4:4046). There is one solitary reference to Polycarp (69-155) (JP 1:429) and to Justin Martyr (100-c.165) (JP 4:428) in the journals. References to Origen (184/5-253/4) in both the published and private authorship are of little substance to this study (E.g. PF, 277; CUP 1, 96-7; BA, 344, 346; JP 2:1894; 3:3162; 3:3546; 4:3851). Kierkegaard makes numerous references throughout the published and unpublished works to Tertullian (160-220), again via Böhringer (e.g. CI, 552; PF, 53, 294; CA, 27, 230, 249; Prefaces/Writing Sampler, 194; UDVS, 418; CD, 459; SUD, 157-8; JP 1:542; 1:559; 1:616; 1:817; 2:1196; 3:2379; 3:3790; 4:4095; 4:4764; 4:4765; 4:4766; 4:4767; 4:4768; 4:4769; 4:4770; 4:4771; 4:4772; 5:5831). He possesses a

will sketch Kierkegaard's references to Pietists and mystics, before devoting particular attention to specific sources of the notion of spiritual trial (*Anfechtung*) in the mystical writings of Johannes Tauler (c.1300-1361) and the fourteenth-century *Theologia Deutsch*. The other key sources of Martin Luther (1483-1546), Johann Arndt (1555-1621) and Jacob Boehme (1575-1624), insofar as I take them to resonate more deeply with Kierkegaard's treatment of spiritual trial, receive more detailed treatment in the following chapters.

Pietists and the Upbuilding

Kierkegaard's relationship with Pietism begins with his own upbringing shaped by his father's intimate relation to the tradition. Michael Pedersen Kierkegaard (1756-1838) came from the pietistic region of Sædding in West Jutland and carried his strong links with him to Copenhagen, where he become a member of the governing board of *Brødresocietet* — the Moravian Society of Brothers. Furthermore, Kierkegaard intensified his own personal investment through his reading of *upbuilding* literature (*Erbauungsliteratur*). Despite the critical

---

particular affinity with Tertullian's (often misquoted) aphorism "*credo quia absurdum* [I believe because it is absurd. The original Latin reads *certum est, quia impossibile*; it is certain because impossible, from *De Carne Christi*]". There are a few references to Clement of Alexandria (c.150-c.215) throughout Kierkegaard's works, though none of note for this present study (e.g. See further R, 225; Prefaces/Writing Sampler, 99; BA, 333; CA, 227; JP 2:1154; 2:1724; 2:2080; 3:2878; 4:3861). One can find a few references to Cyprian (c.200-258) in the private writings but none within the published works (e.g. JP 1:543; 2:1924; 3:2663; 3:3467; 3:3596). There are also two journal references to Gregory of Nyssa (335-394) though nothing of pertinence to this work (JP 1:264; 3:2667). Kierkegaard makes numerous references to Augustine (354-430) throughout his works, often via Böhringer, though none pertain directly to the themes of spiritual trial or temptation that are central to this present study (See further CI, 173, 520; EUD, 434, 534; CA, 27, 121, 230, 235, 245; Prefaces/Writing Sampler, 175; SLW, 147, 338, 601, 701, 724, 746; TA, 17; UDVS, 417; WL, 196, 269, 400, 502-3, 522; SUD, 176; LW, 644; BA, 293, 378; JP 1:29; 1:191; 2:1154; 2:1193; 2:1197; 2:1199; 2:1210; 2:1268; 2:1269; 3:2400; 3:2551; 3:2580; 3:2584; 3:2759; 3:3614; 3:3642; 3:3667; 4:3864; 4:4047; 4:4299; 4:4470; 4:4670; 4:4877). As far as later Church authorities, there are two journal references to Pope Gregory VIII (c.1100-1187) (JP 2:1134; 3:3787) and several references to Anselm (1033-1109), again mediated through Böhringer, in both his published and unpublished works (JP 1:20; 1:21; 2:1423; 3:3615; CI, 368; CUP 2, 249) — though in describing Christianity as "the divine combat of divine passion with itself", Kierkegaard evokes Anselm's satisfaction-theory of the atonement as a struggle between divine righteousness against sin and reconciliation through love, a struggle seemingly forgotten in modern Christianity's lenient view of God (JP 1:532).

tone of many of the works concerning Pietism that he read, Kierkegaard found a valued Christian authority in the pietistic works themselves.[1] His esteem for figures venerated within Pietism is evident in the many references that he makes in his writings. Kierkegaard makes numerous references, for example, to the French Roman Catholic bishop and advocate of Quietism François de Salignac de La Mothe-Fénelon (1651-1715), in *Stages on Life's Way* (1845) in particular,[2] and at several points throughout his journals and notebooks.[3] Fénelon gradually developed, as Šadja describes, "from an accidental dialogue partner . . . into a trustworthy spiritual authority, whose advice eventually played a crucial role in Kierkegaard's uneasy decision making in summer of 1849".[4] As attested by a "troubled" entry dated 25 June 1849, Fénelon's words were particularly resonant with Kierkegaard's own anxiety over his personal vocation:

> I have been troubled by something I read somewhere in Fenelon, that it must be frightful for a man 'from whom God had expected more or upon whom God had counted for a decision of greater amplitude.' On the other hand I was struck by what I read today in Fenelon. . . . And especially what I read yesterday in Tersteegen's Christmas sermon. . . . 'The wise men went the other way,' for we should always be ready to follow God's guidance. (JP 6:6426) [5]

During this decisive biographical period, in which Kierkegaard agonises over whether and how to press on with his authorship, he also seeks counsel in the religious writings of the German Reformed

---

1   See Marie Mikulová Thulstrup, 'Studies of Pietists, Mystics, and Church Fathers', 61. See further this article and Marie Mikulová Thulstrup's *Kierkegaard og Pietismen* (Copenhagen: Munksgaard, 1967), along with Christopher A. Barnett's extensive and illuminating study *Kierkegaard, Pietism and Holiness* (Farnham: Ashgate, 2011) for a fuller exploration of this relationship.

2   See SLW, 566, 596-97, 720, 722, 746.

3   See JP 1:818; 3:3435; 4:4638; 4 :4863; 5:5736.

4   Peter Šadja, 'François de Salignac de La Moth-Fénelon: Clearing the Way for *The Sickness Unto Death*', ed. Jon Stewart, *Kierkegaard Research: Source, Reception and Resources Volume 5: Kierkegaard and the Renaissance and Modern Traditions: Tome II: Theology* (Aldershot: Ashgate, 2009), 129-147 at 129. Via Fénelon Kierkegaard comes to especially admire a line from Teresa of Avila (1515-82) which notes how Christians too often abandon prayer before it can become a purifying trial (JP 3:3435; Šadja, 139).

5   See further Peter Šadja, '"The wise men went the other way": Kierkegaard's Dialogue with Fénelon and Tersteegen in the Summer of 1849', *Acta Kierkegaardiana III: Kierkegaard and Christianity*, Roman Králik et al (eds) (Toronto and Šal'a: Kierkegaard Circle, 2008), pp. 89-105.

Gerhard Tersteegen (1697-1769), to whom he makes several substantial references.[1] As Šadja and Barnett both note, Kierkegaard refers only once in his published works to Tersteegen, adopting his words as a motto for *On My Work As An Author* (1851), albeit without including him by name.[2] Nevertheless, in his private writings Kierkegaard describes Tersteegen in 1850 as "incomparable", declaring "In him I find genuine and noble piety and simple wisdom" (JP 4:4757). In Tersteegen's metaphor of the three wise men three stages of spiritual life can be discerned: the beginning; on the way; and at the journey's end, rejoicing in Jesus. Kierkegaard evidently resonated most profoundly with the second stage, that of being on the way but not having yet arrived as blessedness (JP 4:4754).[3]

Among the Pietistic tradition, Kierkegaard also makes reference to Lutheran theologian Johann Gerhard (1582-1637), who had come deeply under Johann Arndt's influence (JP 4:3918; Pap. VIII 1 A 349-50). From Gerhard, Kierkegaard found another source of encouragement for the notion of the imitation of Christ — although Kierkegaard's own tendency was more expressly towards an emphasis upon suffering persecution at the hands of the crowd, as Christ himself had done.[4] Kierkegaard also makes several approving references to the Lutheran devotional writer Christian Scriver (1629-93), whose *Treasure of the Soul* he owned in all five of its volumes.[5]

---

1   Kierkegaard notes Tersteegen's observation concerning the hiddenness and love of God (JP 2:1390) and acknowledges a parallel with Tersteegen concerning the faith in the face of despair evoked by the thief crucified beside Christ (JP 4:4040). See also JP 4:4750; 4:4751; 4:4752; 4:4753; 4:4754; 4:4755; 4:4756; 4:4759; 4:4760; 4:4761; 4:4762; 4:4763; 6:6762. See also references to Tersteegen in the published works: PV, 2, 275, 311; *Letters & Documents*, 486.
2   Šadja, '"The wise men went the other way"', 97. See also Christopher B. Barnett, 'Gerhard Tersteegen: Reception of a Man of "Noble Piety and Simple Wisdom"', ed. Jon Stewart, *Kierkegaard Research: Source, Reception and Resources Volume 5*, 245-257, at 246.
3   Šadja, '"The wise men went the other way"', 99.
4   See Mikulová Thulstrup, 'Studies of Pietists, Mystics, and Church Fathers', 63.
5   See Barnett, *Kierkegaard, Pietism and Holiness*, 82-84 for an excellent overview of Kierkegaard's ownership of seventeenth century pietistic literature. Comments concerning Scriver are apparently exclusive to Kierkegaard's private writings, though they are mostly positive in tone. In particular, see JP 1:726 from 1851: "Scriver says that it is good to have business with death — the advantage is ours ('to die is gain')." See also JP 3:2327 from 1851: "Scriver says that the soul, the human soul, is God's rest, or that God rests in it — that this glorious gift to man is just as extraordinary as it would be for a subject if a powerful prince were to rest his head on his breast." See also JP 3:3456; 3:2325; 3:3200; 4:3951; 4:4468; 6:6644.

In the Pietists, Kierkegaard found a resonant existential emphasis upon inward faith and the imitation of Christ through suffering. At the same time, however, he was also keen to dissociate himself from the dogmatic polemics of the Pietists concerning the doctrine of sanctification as well as what could be called the more moralistic or abstinent tendencies of strict external pietism.[1]

The Mystics: Speculation, Union, and Nothingness

The Pietists' emphasis upon "the *via negativa* leading to *imitation*" and the interior life of self-negation, "the concept of 'dying to' (*Afdøen*) that played a crucial role in Kierkegaard's late understanding of Christian discipleship", in turn led Kierkegaard back to the writings of the medieval mystics from which they commonly derived.[2] Nonetheless, while the genealogy of such concepts is traceable to earlier mystical works, Kierkegaard's relation to the mystics and the mystical tradition remains a befittingly opaque area of inquiry. In nineteenth-century western thought, the notion of 'mysticism' was emerging distinctly as an area for modern analysis of the nature of 'religion' and 'religious feeling'. Kierkegaard was not without his own suspicions towards what was being shaped by some as an esoteric facet of Christian thought.[3] Mystical theology was itself being claimed by some as part of the heritage of Speculative Idealism, with figures such as Hegel and Schelling read as inheritors to the visions of such luminaries as Meister Eckhart (c.1260-1327/8) and Jacob Boehme (1575-1624).[4] This

---

1 See Mikulová Thulstrup, 'Studies of Pietists, Mystics, and Church Fathers', 65.

2 Peter Šadja, 'Tauler: A Teacher in Spiritual Dietethics: Kierkegaard's Reception of Johannes Tauler', ed. Jon Stewart, *Kierkegaard Research: Sources, Reception and Resources Volume 4: Kierkegaard and the Patristic and Medieval Traditions*, 276-77.

3 Of particular concern for Kierkegaard was Johann Joseph von Görres' (1776-1848) *Die Christliche Mystik* (1836–1842): a series of biographies of the saints, and exposition of Roman Catholic mysticism — which also covered magic, demonology, spiritualism. The nineteenth century also witnessed a burgeoning interest in the Jewish mystical tradition of the Kabbalah, traces of which features in Boehme and in some speculative philosophy. For example, Adolphe Franck (1809-1893), *The Kabbalah: or, The Religious Philosophy of the Hebrews* (*La Kabbale ou Philosophie Religieuse des Hébreux*. Paris, 1843), translated into German as *Die Kabbala Oder Die Religions Philosophie Der Hebraer* (1844). Also Christian D. Ginsburg (1831-1914), *The Kabbalah: its Doctrines, Development and Literature* (1865); and the first partial translation of *The Zohar* into English in 1887, and *The Kabbalah Unveiled*, by Samuel Liddel MacGregor Mathers (1854-1918), a founding member of the Golden Dawn.

4 See further, for example, Peter Šadja, 'Does Hegelian Philosophy of

opened the way to claims that such Christian mystical theology,
even theosophy, was in some way a supra-rational forerunner of
the omniscient Speculative system.[1] As a rarified form of religious
experience, the apparent claim of certain mystics to a direct knowledge
of God might seem at odds with Kierkegaard's emphasis upon indirect
communication and the infinite qualitative difference between the
human and the divine. On 11 July 1840, Kierkegaard pronounced the
indictment that "Mysticism does not have the patience to wait for God's
revelation" (JP 3:2795). Rather than awaiting the descent of God to the
human, the entry of eternity into time and the divine's gracious crossing
of the infinite qualitative abyss, mysticism, by this critique, storms the
heavens through its exertions toward attainment of knowledge of
the Mind of God itself. Speculative mysticism, despite claims to the
nothingness of the soul, might be suspected of a self-apotheosis of the
mind itself. Insofar as Eckhart seems to desire to know the Godhead as
wüste (desert), in its nakedness, before the enrobing of all names,[2] such
mysticism apparently violates the Lutheran caveat that God-as-God-
is-in-Himself, the *Deus nudus*, is unknowable to us, and, as such, the
hidden ways of God are not to be enquired into.[3]

Kierkegaard already professes a similar suspicion as early as 6
June 1836. Commenting on Matthew 11:12, "From the days of John
the Baptist until now the kingdom of heaven has suffered violence,
and the violent take it by force", Kierkegaard wonders:

Religion Distort Christian Dogmatics and Ethics? (The Debate on Spec-
ulative Mysticism)', *Acta Kierkegaardiana Volume 4: Kierkegaard and the
Nineteenth-Century Religious Crisis in Europe*, Roman Králik *et al* (eds)
(Toronto and Šal'a: Kierkegaard Circle, 2008), 64-83.

1   The entrance of Kierkegaard's nemesis and former tutor the Hegelian
    theologian Hans Martensen (1808-84) with the 1840 publication of
    his book *Meister Eckhart: A Contribution to the Elucidation of Mysticism
    in the Middle Ages* (*Mester Eckart: Et Bidrag til at oplyse Middelaldrens
    Mystik* (Copenhagen: C.A. Reizel, 1840) is unlikely to have enamoured
    Kierkegaard to this way of reading. Martensen's book may in part account
    for Kierkegaard's complete silence on Eckhart despite, as will be explored
    further in this work, the potential points of similitude in their thought.
2   E.g. Sermon Sixty, *The Complete Mystical Works of Meister Eckhart*, trans.
    Maurice O'C Walshe (New York: Crossroad 2009), 310; Sermon Sixty-
    three, 318-319.
3   Luther renders this prohibition as a central principle of *De Servo Arbitrio*.
    However, the situation concerning both Eckhart and Luther is far more
    nuanced, as explored further in this work. Bengt Hoffman traces Luther's
    numinous sense of the hidden face of God in *The Bondage of the Will* to *Die
    deutsche Theologie*. 'Introduction', *The Theologia Germanica of Martin Luther*,
    trans. Bengt Hoffman (New York/Ramsey/Toronto: Paulist Press, 1980), 16.

May not Matthew 11:12 properly be interpreted as referring to the mystics . . . who think that they have a direct relationship to God and consequently will not acknowledge that all men have only an indirect relationship (the Church — in the political domain, the state). (JP 3:2794)

And yet, alongside his above comment on the impatience of mysticism from 1840, in the same year Kierkegaard also writes with appreciation about the voice of the mystic that passes down through the ages to be embraced, in its quiet authenticity, by kindred spirits:

As with certain bird cries, we hear a mystic only in the stillness of the night; for this reason a mystic generally does not have as much significance for his noisy contemporaries as for the listening kindred spirit in the stillness of history after the passage of time. (JP 3:2796)

Furthermore, by 1850 Kierkegaard writes with esteem of the "divine nothing" of the mystics, comparing it favourably with Socratic ignorance as a "devout fear of God" and suggesting that such nothing is actually incongruous with Speculative philosophy, since "The system *begins* with 'nothing'; the mystic always ends with 'nothing'" (JP 3:2797).

What is understood at any moment by modern constructions of 'mysticism' and 'mystics' will be decisive for determining Kierkegaard's relation to such ideas. Kierkegaard's own evaluations are contaminated by Speculative Idealism, by a vague picture of 'oriental' mysticism not atypical of nineteenth-century western thinkers, and by a Lutheran suspicion towards world-renouncing ascetic withdrawal. However, in terms of conceptual and devotional content, Frits Florin adroitly describes mysticism as "the point or moment of tangency between the finite and the infinite, which presupposes total openness, freedom and emptiness of the soul". So conceived, Florin thus suggests that mysticism "is reminiscent of the category of 'adoration' or 'worship' [*Tilbedelse*] in Kierkegaard, the 'maximum for a human being's relationship with God, and thereby for his likeness to God, since the qualities are absolutely different.'"[1]

The notion of "tangency" is pivotal. Any moment of contact between the finite and the infinite might imply a violation of the "infinite qualitative difference" between the human and the divine. And yet Florin's reference to Kierkegaard's notion of worship is

---

1   Frits Florin, 'Was Kierkegaard Inspired by Medieval Mysticism? Meister Eckhart's *Abgeschiedenheit* and Kierkegaard's *Udsondring*', Dario González *et al* (eds), *Kierkegaardiana 22* (Copenhagen: C.A. Reitzels Forlag, 2002), 173 (the reference that Florin makes is to CUP, 413).

highly apt. To worship, as Anti-Climacus describes in *The Sickness Unto Death* (1849), "is to express that the infinite, chasmic, qualitative abyss between them is confirmed" (SUD, 129). Tangency, or moment of contact, does not necessarily entail union or absorption. And yet Kierkegaard also claims that "worship is what makes the human being resemble God" insofar as "The human being and God do not resemble each other directly but inversely; only when God has infinitely become the eternal and omnipresent object of worship and the human being always a worshipper, only then do they resemble each other" (UDVS, 193). This notion of inverse resemblance is also evoked in Kierkegaard's 1844 upbuilding discourse, 'One Who Prays Aright Struggles in Prayer and is Victorious — in that God is Victorious'. It is only when one "becomes nothing" that "God [can] illuminate [*gjennemlyse*] him so that he resembles God . . . God can imprint himself in him only when he himself has become nothing." It is only when the ocean "becomes still and deep [*dybt*]" that "the image of heaven sinks into its nothingness" (EUD, 399).[1]

These questions of resemblance and union shall be addressed further in this work in relation to the self's struggle (*Anfechtung*) to become nothing before God (*Gelassenheit*). For now, it suffices to at least introduce the possibility of further affinities between Kierkegaardian and mystical theology. As Florin has outlined, there are many familiar themes in mysticism that correlate to metaphors employed by Kierkegaard: "wrestling with God, soberness versus inebriety, prayer as respiration, light and darkness, the well, dizziness, the symbol of the fruit, the moment as a mystical point of tangency".[2] To this list it would also be possible to add: the metaphor of the butterfly emerging from its chrysalis (JP 4:4712), the imagery of fire as Spirit and purification of the soul (JP 4:4355), transparency, the abyss, imitation, spiritual trial, to name but a few. Enticing parallels have inevitably stimulated many other comparative studies of Kierkegaard and mystics. For example, Mikulová Thulstrup has also compared Kierkegaard's view of suffering to that found in mystical

---

1 Cf. Arndt: "Our soul is like wax. Whatever a man impresses upon it, it holds that image. Thus, a man is to see God's image in his soul as in a mirror. That to which a man turns himself will be seen in him. Turn a mirror toward heaven and you will see heaven; turn it toward earth and you will see earth. Thus, your soul will show the image of that to which you turn it." Johann Arndt, *True Christianity*, trans. Peter Erb (New York/Ramsey/Toronto: Paulist Press, 1979), 98. Arndt's imagery is in turn indebted to Eckhart. See further chapter seven.

2 Florin, 'Was Kierkegaard Inspired by Medieval Mysticism?', 177. Florin refers this list to a group of themes compiled by Wim R. Scholtens in *Kijk, hier barst de tall . . . Mystiek bij Kierkegaard* (Kok, Kampen/Altiroa, Averbode, 1991).

texts "with which, to the best of our knowledge, Kierkegaard was not familiar": namely, the works of John of the Cross (1542-91), Thérèsa of Lisieux (1873-97), Teresa of Jesus/Àvila (1515-82), and Francis of Sales (1567-1622).[1] However, it is evident that Kierkegaard makes it difficult to draw out such affinities. Kierkegaard was highly ambivalent about mysticism: at times evoking something ostensibly reminiscent of mystical experience in his journals (e.g. JP 5:5324); whilst also publishing such indictments that could be deemed indicative of an "anti-mysticism",[2] as evinced by Judge William in *Either/Or*.[3] On the question of this ambivalence, Christopher

1   Mikulová Thulstrup, 'Suffering', *Bibliotheca Kierkegaardiana Vol. 7: Kierkegaard and Human Values*, ed. Niels Thusltrup and M. Mikulvá Thulstrup (Copenhagen: C.A. Reitzels Boghandel, 1980), 151. However, while Kierkegaard's direct knowledge of mystical theologians is very limited he would have been able to learn indirectly about such figures as John of the Cross and Teresa of Àvila, for example, through such writers as Fénelon (e.g. note 4 above) and through Tersteegen's *Selected Biographies of Holy Souls* (1733-53) (see Barnett, 'Gerhard Tersteegen: Kierkegaard's Reception of a Man of "Noble Piety and Simple Wisdom"', 250). I have also proposed "an unconscious affinity" between Kierkegaard and John of the Cross in relation to the "sense of the withdrawal of God in human suffering", comparing these two thinkers through "a mutual taste for the analogy of maternal withdrawal as descriptive of the God-relationship." 'The Dark Night of Suffering and the Darkness of God: God-forsakenness or Forsaking God in *Gospel of Sufferings*', Robert Perkins (ed.), *International Kierkegaard Commentary: Upbuilding Discourses in Various Spirits* (Macon, Georgia: Mercer University Press, 2005), 229-256.

2   See David R. Law, 'Kierkegaard's Anti-Mysticism', *Scottish Journal of Religious Studies*, 14 (1993), 102-111. Law concludes that:
    Kierkegaard's emphasis upon God's transcendence could also play an important role in tempering the intimacy of the mystic's relation with God. . . . It is only by an act of grace on God's part and not by the mystic's striving for experience of or union with the Divine that he comes into God's presence. It is in making clear these truths that the value of Kierkegaard's anti-mysticism lies. (109)
    In *Kierkegaard as Negative Theologian* (Oxford: Clarendon Press, 1993), Law elaborates this further suggestion that while Kierkegaard was prepared to employ his knowledge of negative theology in his works (26), the idea of mystical union or absorption within the Godhead remains beyond us (214). In his rejection of the consummation of divine union, Law discerns Kierkegaard as "*more apophatic* than the negative theologians" (34).

3   See Christopher A.P. Nelson, 'Kierkegaard, mysticism, and jest: The story of little Ludvig', *Continental Philosophy Review*, 39 (4), 2006, 435-464. Nelson explores the notion of an indirect engagement with the mystical element in Kierkegaard's writings through the various figures who share the name 'Ludvig' (a name with which Kierkegaard felt a special identification). In *Either/Or*, Judge William recounts the cautionary tale of 'Ludvig Blackfeldt',

Nelson appositely concludes that Kierkegaard has little sympathy with mysticism as "intellectually baffling metaphysical postulates" concerning the nothingness of the self and time and the absorption of plurality into oneness. Yet if 'mysticism' is understood as "not merely 'being drawn up the mountain' (the revelation of truth in mystery), but 'coming back down the mountain' (the ethical-religious side of mystery) — because this is what God does, or rather, this is what God is", then, Nelson declares that the mystical is not only an aspect of Kierkegaard, "but it is arguably the crowning element in his thought".[1]

It may be the case that when Kierkegaard encounters the Christian mystics in a more devotional context — namely via his principle source, the writings of the Pietists[2] — his response is generally affirmative. Through Fénelon, for example, Kierkegaard cites Teresa of Avila with approval:

> They are beautiful, those words by St. Theresa which Fenelon often quotes: 'O, you blind ones, to abandon prayer just when it ought to begin.' . . . When adversity comes and praying becomes a struggle, that is, becomes real prayer, then they abandon it. (JP 3:3435)

However, when Kierkegaard encounters mystical concepts through the adaptations of idealist and speculative thought he is more incredulous.[3] In fact, Mikulová Thulstrup suggests, that such philosophers were responsible for Kierkegaard's unwillingness to embrace "the unio mystica, the soul's union with God, or with descriptions of extasies and visions".[4] Although Kierkegaard was evidently of uncertain mind concerning the validity of mystical

---

a mystic whose ascetic self-torture led to suicide. Nelson views Ludvig Blackfeldt as "the vivid representation of a diabolic mysticism" who discovered "the demonic" form of mysticism, which is "the 'negative' form of infinite freedom, the mysticism that is not properly called 'religious,' the quest of an immediate rapport with the eternal that is characterized by the perpetuity of inclosing reserve and existential despair" (448).

1   Nelson, 'Kierkegaard, mysticism, and jest', 458.
2   Mikulová Thulstrup, 'Studies of Pietists, Mystics, and Church Fathers', 65.
3   See further Marie Mikulová, 'Kierkegaard's Encounter with Mysticism through Speculative Idealism', *Liber Academiæ Kierkegaardiensis Tomus V 1983*, ed. Niels Thulstrup (København: C.A. Reitzels Forlag, 1984), 31-91. Mikulová observes that "In philosophical literature (including textbooks) it was for Kierkegaard impossible to find mysticism depicted as an expression of man's existential (in the Kierkegaardian sense) experience, as a genuine experience. On the contrary, together with faith it was degraded to being the expression of something spontaneous and primitive" (83).
4   Mikulová Thulstrup, 'Studies of Pietists, Mystics, and Church Fathers', 66.

states and visions, he was sufficiently curious to read about them. In particular, Kierkegaard was evidently dubious about *Die christlische Mystik* of Joseph von Görres (1776-1848), which he described in 1844 as "so *unheimlich* [uncanny] that I have never dared read it carefully" (Pap. V B 63). This entry can be identified as a draft pertaining to *The Concept of Anxiety* where Vigilius Haufniensis also notes that one can find an abundance of material on the religious 'spiritual trial' [*Anfægtelse*] in Görres, *Die christliche Mystik*. However, Haufniensis adds the important qualification that "I sincerely admit that I never had the courage to read the work completely and thoroughly, because there is such anxiety in it. But this much I have discovered, that Görres does not always know how to distinguish between the demonic and the spiritual trial. Therefore the work should be used with care" (CA, 143*).[1] Nonetheless, Kierkegaard does elsewhere indicate Görres' work on Francis of Assisi (1182-1226).[2] Ultimately, however, the elision, appropriation and contamination of Christian mysticism by speculative idealism and by modern curiosity with the occult proved sufficient to elicit a significant aversion in Kierkegaard. For the most part, as Mikulová Thulstrup concludes, Kierkegaard was occasionally able to discern a lived expression of Christianity in the mystics,[3] and yet his own notion of "actuality as something immanent, earthly and temporal" did not accord with the idealists' vision of mysticism which ultimately appeared to him as "empty, abstract, unreal."[4]

Nevertheless, there are a number of 'mystics' to whom Kierkegaard refers in his writings. References to that great mystic of love, Bernard of Clairvaux (1090-1153) are confined to Kierkegaard's private

1 It is "No wonder" that Kierkegaard reacted this way, as Mikulová Thulstrup observes, "the book is so affected by the mentality of speculative idealism; it has no Christian intention, but merely describes man's biological basis for mystical life, visions, and allied states such as levitation, and deals with exorcism, witchcraft etc." 'Studies of Pietists, Mystics, and Church Fathers', 69-70. Additionally, Mikulová Thulstrup also identifies such works as Adolph Helfferich, *Die christliche Mystik in ihrer Entwickelung und Denkmalen*, I-II (Gotha 1842. Ktl. No. 571-2) and Moriz Carriere, *Die philosophische Weltanschauung der Reformationszeit* (Stuttgart u. Tübingen 1847, Ktl. No. 458) as evaluating Christian mysticism "according to the speculative principles of idealism" (70).
2 "*Der heilige Franciscus [von Assisi] ein Troubadour*, by J. Görres [Strassburg: 1826]" (JP 5:5492). Elsewhere Kierkegaard refers to Francis of Assisi's stigmata as an image of Christ (JP 1:288).
3 Mikulová Thulstrup, 'Studies of Pietists, Mystics, and Church Fathers', 70.
4 Mikulová Thulstrup, 'Kierkegaard's Encounter with Mysticism through Speculative Idealism', 89.

writings.[1] However, as Mulder observes, there is no clear "single verdict from Kierkegaard as to how we are to regard the 'last of the Fathers'".[2] There are several references to Thomas à Kempis (c.1380-1471), all, with the exception of one reference in *The Point of View of My Work as an Author* (1848/51), within Kierkegaard's unpublished writings.[3] Kierkegaard makes several references to Justinus Andreas Christian Kerner (1786-1862) in both the published and unpublished works — even comparing himself to Kerner in two journal entries (JP 5:5239 and 5:5240).[4] A few references to Alphonsus de Ligouri (1696-1787) can also be found within Kierkegaard's notebooks.[5] Abraham à Saint Clara (1644-1709) is referred to once within *The Concept of Irony* (CI, 28) and within the *Christian Discourses* (CD, 439) and elsewhere within Kierkegaard's notebooks, covering the period 1837 to 1854.[6] Šadja notes that Kierkegaard purchased and read the works of this Baroque Catholic theologian over a sustained period,[7] though most intensively between 1847 and 1848, suggesting that his perception of Abraham à Saint Clara was similar to his regard for "other upbuidling authors" Johannes Tauler and Johann Arndt in his focus upon the imitation of Christ.[8] Kierkegaard also marked passages in Abraham

---

1 See JP 1:201; 2:1517; 2:1930; 3:2722; 3:2899; 4:4295; 4:5015; 6:6703.

2 Jack Mulder, Jr., 'Bernard of Clairvaux: Kierkegaard's Reception of the Last of the Fathers', ed. Jon Stewart, *Kierkegaard Research: Sources, Reception and Resources Volume 4: Kierkegaard and the Patristic and Medieval Traditions*, 23-45, 39.

3 See PV: 222, 327; JP 2:2016; 3:2691; 4:4783; 4:4784; 4:4785; 4:4786; 4:4787; 6:6524. See further Joel D.S. Rasmussen, 'Thomas à Kempis: *Devotio Moderna* and Kierkegaard's Critique of "Bourgeois-Philistinism"', ed. Jon Stewart *Kierkegaard Research: Sources, Reception and Resources Volume 4: Kierkegaard and the Patristic and Medieval Traditions*, 289-98.

4 Also CI, 588; R, 171, 368; CUP.2, 45, 274; JP 2:1826; 4:3993; 5:5205.

5 Notably JP 1:336. Kierkegaard cites Johannes Climacus (525-606), author of *Scala Paradisi*, through Liguori: "There are but few saints; if we wish to become saintly and saved, we must live as do the few." (JP 6:6362). Also JP 6:6297 and 6:6355.

6 See further JP 2:1538; 2:2000; 2:2229; 3:3741; 3:3787; 4:4307; 5:5062; 5:5917; 5:6024; 5:6027; 5:6028; 5:6044.

7 Šadja, 'Abraham a Sancta Clara: An Aphoristic Encyclopedia of Christian Wisdom', ed. Jon Stewart, *Kierkegaard Research: Source, Reception and Resources Volume 5: Kierkegaard and the Renaissance and Modern Traditions: Tome II: Theology* (Aldeshot: Ashgate, 2009), 1-20, at 1. Šadja (14) also notes tacit references to Abraham à Saint Clara in *Works of Love*, particularly with reference to the Christian notion of *like for like* (WL, 382-3).

8 Šadja, 'Abraham a Sancta Clara', 9. See also Peter Šadja, 'On Some Aspects of Kierkegaard's Reading of Abraham a Sancta Clara', *Acta Kierkegaardiana Volume II: Kierkegaard and Great Philosopher*, ed, Roman Králik *et al* (Toronto and Šaľa: Kierkegaard Circle, 2007), 80-89.

à Saint Clara's works concerning martyrdom, prayer, and trusting in God in the light of tribulation and temptation.[1] It is through Abraham à Saint Clara, however, that Kierkegaard learnt much about the Flemish monk and mystic Louis de Blois, known in Latinised form as Lucovicus Blosius (1506-1566).[2] In Kierkegaard's view, Blosius as a spiritual advisor (*Sjelesørger* — soul carer, or physician, of the soul; a phrase he associates with spiritual trial and temptation) puts contemporary clergy in the shade:

> It would be a frightful satire on Christendom if one published a work like Blosius's *Consolatium Pusillanimium*, in order to show what a pastor as spiritual adviser found necessary to say in former days, naturally, because then it was something in which to exist. Nowadays there are no longer pastors as spiritual advisers [*Sjelesørger*] but only as a mere spectators [*Betragtere*], naturally, because it is not lived anymore. (JP 1:381)

As a venerable spiritual advisor and author of the better old devotional literature, it might be wise, as Šadja advises, to consider Kierkegaard's reading of Blosius in continuity with his reading of the medieval mystical tradition of Tauler, the *Theologia Deutsch*, and Thomas à Kempis.[3] Kierkegaard's esteem can be glimpsed in his quotation of Blosius from 1847: "Blosius, p. 613 [*Ludovicii Blosii Opera Omnia*, 1568, ASKB 429]. *Amor Jesu me afficit; Ejus odor me reficit; In hunc mens mea déficit; Solus amanti sufficit* [The love of Jesus affects me; his fragrance mortifies me. My mortal mind fails me; love alone suffices the loving one]" (JP 3:2413). Again the following year Kierkegaard affirms words of Blosius that seem to reflect his own sense of the gravity of Christianity: "Blosius, *Consolatio Pusillanimium*, p. 381. *'Satis rogat, qui morbum* (sin) *agnoscit; vehementer rogat, qui plorat et confidit.'* [He questions sufficiently who recognises death (sin) for what it is; he who weeps over it and firmly believes in it begs the question excessively]" (JP 4:4017).

During this intense period of spiritual self-examination and avowed spiritual trial, Kierkegaard also quotes a rule from "Blosius, p. 407. *Totius perfectionis verissima regula haec est: esto humilis, et ubicunque te ipsum inveneris, te ipsum relinque* [This is the supreme

1 Šadja, 'Abraham a Sancta Clara', 9. Re. Temptations and tribulations See Pap. VIII-2 C 2, 18; Pap. VIII-2 C 2, 26; Pap. VIII-2 C 2, 34; Pap. VIII-2 C 2, 45; Pap. VIII-2 C 2, 49-51.
2 Šadja, 'Lucovicus Blosius: A Frightful Satire on Christendom', ed. Jon Stewart, *Kierkegaard Research: Source, Reception and Resources Volume 5: Kierkegaard and the Renaissance and Modern Traditions: Tome II: Theology*, 30-41, 34-35.
3 Šadja, 'Lucovicus Blosius', 39.

rule for the highest perfection. Wherever you shall have found yourself, leave yourself behind]" (JP 5:6084), which Blosius attributes obliquely to Meister Eckhart. "The core of the rule", as Šadja discerns, "is the famous maxim from Meister Eckhart's *Die rede der underscheidunge* which sums up the essence of self-detachment."[1] Eckhart's *Discourses of Instruction* (Latin *discretio*) centre on notions of passive *Gelassenheit* (releasement) which together with a more active sense of *Abgeschiedenheit* (detachment) "characterizes the one who has emptied himself of his own will. One who has necessarily left himself behind in this way will necessarily be given his form by the will of God, and will become one with God".[2]

The emptying, or kenosis, of the will becomes an insistent theme for Kierkegaard, though he is notably more reticent about the extent of the soul's union with God. It is perhaps revealing that Eckhart talks more of *Gelassenheit* than *Anfechtung*[3] — which, while affirmed by others within the medieval mystical tradition (particularly Tauler) does not emerge as an explicit concern and has not yet become the pillar of agonistic theology that Luther would later form of it. As if synthesising elements of Eckhart and Luther, in Boehme *Anfechtung* becomes the path to *Gelassenheit*. For Kierkegaard, as shall be explored

---

1 Šadja, 'Lucovicus Blosius: A Frightful Satire on Christendom', 37. Eckhart's Middle High German reads: "*Nim dîn selbes war, und swâ dû dich vindest, dâ lâz dich; das ist daz aller beste*" (37n42).

2 Dagmar Gottschall, 'Eckhart's German Works', ed. Jeremiah H. Hackett, *A Companion to Meister Eckhart*, (Leiden: Brill, 2013), 137-184, 147.

3 According to McLaughlin, Eckhart identifies sin as merely one, and by no means the most common source of *Anfechtung*. R. Emmett McLaughlin, 'Truth, Tradition, and History: The Historiography of High/Late Medieval and Early Modern Penance', ed. Abigail Firey, *A New History of Penance* (Leiden: Brill, 2008), 19-71, at 50n167). See also Helmut Appel, *Anfechtung und Trost im Spätmittelalter und dei Luther* (Leipzig, 1938), 13. Eckhart prefigures Luther's vision that a human being flees but cannot escape God, "for every nook and cranny reveals Him. He thinks he is fleeing from, and runs into His arms". Sermon Fifty-Three, *The Complete Mystical Works*, 282. What is ultimately inescapable for Eckhart, however, is the birth of the Son in the soul. Moreover, the idiom of *Anfechtung* is not a central feature of Eckhart. This may also be related to his focus upon the birth of Christ over and above the passion and death of Christ. Christ's detachment in the face of suffering, rather than the *Anfechtung* itself, is featured in Eckhart's treatise 'On Detachment [*Von Abgeschiedenheit*]', *The Complete Mystical Works*, 566-575. In Christ's sorrow unto death it is "the outer man" who suffers while "the inner man" is in detachment (571). Moreover, it is in detachment in suffering rather than through suffering itself that one is brought, via grace, into "the greatest likeness to God", who, even in creation and the incarnation, stands in "unmoved detachment from all eternity" (569).

further, it is the *via* rather than the goal of union itself that is his main literary concern (since, perhaps, the latter may be ineffable). Insofar as he remains attached to the infinite qualitative difference between the human and the divine (a consequence of a Lutheran emphasis upon *creatio ex nihilo*), Kierkegaard is concerned with an unassailable alterity *before God* which mystical union may appear to threaten. And yet, as examined later in this work, Kierkegaard does paint a rather mystical horizon of the self resting transparently *in God* in which boundaries seem to begin to become blurred. The key to this ambiguity, I suggest, is the notion of the self becoming itself as *Spirit*, which, as love and as the image of God, proceeds in some sense *ex deo*.

In light of such motifs, Kierkegaard's relation to the negative or apophatic tradition of mystical theology continues to warrant further exploration. The scarcity of explicit textual invocations, however, ensures unequivocal conclusions remain elusive. There is only one clear reference, for example, to Pseudo-Dionysus the Areopagite, the great exponent of mystical theology of the late fifth to early sixth century, in *The Concept of Irony* (CI, 394). I have found no clear references to Angelus Silesius (1624-77), nor even to Meister Eckhart[1] — though Kierkegaard may have read but declined to make reference to Eckhart in protest against H.L. Martensens' comparison between Eckhart and Hegelian philosophy in his 1840 book *Mester Eckart* (which Kierkegaard owned).[2] Nonetheless, Frits Florin pursues an

---

1 See further, Peter Šajda, 'Meister Eckhart: The Patriarch of German Speculation who was a *Lebemeister*: Meister Eckhart's Silent Way into Kierkegaard's Corpus', ed. Jon Stewart, *Kierkegaard Research: Sources, Reception and Resources Volume 4: Kierkegaard and the Patristic and Medieval Traditions*, 237-253. Šajda does, however, note JP 1:508, where Kierkegaard refers to Martensen's lectures on speculative dogmatics [*Die christelige Dogmatik* (Copenhagen: 1849)], as the point "from which stems the only explicit mention of Eckhart in Kierkegaard's papers. The transcript of the lecture links the idea of pantheism to Eckhart's concept of *unio mystica*" (243). See Pap. II C 28, in Pap. XIII, p. 67.

2 Mikulová Thulstrup, 'Studies of Pietists, Mystics, and Church Fathers', 66. "Martensen paid a lot of attention to mysticism, but he too knew [like many speculative philosophers] of no others besides Eckhart and [Jacob] Böhme, and he read them with the prejudice of a speculative thinker . . . None of the idealists showed themselves to be capable of understanding the Christian mystics as they themselves wished to be understood — as witnesses to God and Christ." Marie Mikulová, 'Kierkegaard's Encounter with Mysticism through Speculative Idealism', 53. Šajda observes that "Martensen's treatise on Eckhart was the most extensive account of the German mystic that Kierkegaard ever came in touch with", though the alliance of speculative philosophy with Eckhart would have deterred him from exploring his though further. Šajda, 'Meister Eckhart', 243. Furthermore, as Šajda explains,

intriguing parallel between Kierkegaard and Eckhart, with particular reference to the two concepts of *Abgeschiedenheit* ('emptying of the inner self') and *Udsondring* ('separation').[1] Furthermore, David Kangas pursues the question of potential influence, distinguishing between Eckhart himself and "the Eckhartian *tradition*", insofar as Eckhart's own texts may not have been accessible. Kangas points to Kierkegaard's reading of "texts whose metaphysical horizon is entirely derived from the thought of Meister Eckhart: the *Theologia Germanica, Die Nachfolgung des armen Leben Jesu Christi* (pseudo-Tauler), Johann Arndt's *Von warhemm Christentum,* Jacob Boehme's *Der Weg zur Christo,* as well as other pietists such as Gerhard Teersteegen". Furthermore, Kangas notes Eckhart's presence, along with Jacob Boehme's, in Franz von Baader's *Vorlesungen über die Speculative Dogmatik* and *Fermenta Cognitionis,* and Martensen's work on Eckhart, which contained extensive quotes from his sermons.[2]

"Although Eckhart's works were never completely forgotten, they did not survive in compact collections, as in the case of Tauler. Most of the later medieval sources quoted Eckhart only implicitly, which together with the fragmentary textual basis contributed to the fact that Eckhart necessarily appeared to the thinkers of the early nineteenth century as a mysterious or even mythic figure." 'Meister Eckhart', 239.

1 Florin surmises that "For both Kierkegaard and Eckhart, negative theology means *kenosis*; it is the impossibility of a direct communication of or about God, an annihilation of an attachment to finitude, the directly sensuous, and busyness. It is a distance from what Kierkegaard calls 'the world' or 'the worldly and Eckhart 'the creaturely'" (181).

2 David J. Kangas, *Kierkegaard's Instant: On Beginnings* (Bloomington & Indianapolis: Indiana University Press, 2007), 9. Kangas also notes the thematic parallels between Eckhart's related notions of *Abgeschiedenheit* and *Gelassenheit* and Kierkegaard's ideal of "becoming nothing" (10). Kangas and Curtis L. Thompson have translated Martensen's work in *Between Hegel and Kierkegaard: Hans L. Martensen'sPhilosophy of Religion* (New York: Oxford University Press, 1997), 149-244. Šajda also observes that Eckhart's ideas were often subsumed within the pietists's readings of Johannes Tauler and the *Theologia Deutsch.* "This approach was continued by Peitist authors like Johann Arndt, who paid more attention to the common ideological legacy of the mystical *doctrina practica* than to the authorship of individual texts" ('Meister Eckhart', 245; also 247-251). For example, "In Book III of *True Christianity,* Arndt repeatedly thematizes Eckhart's teaching that the aim of the soul's purgation is to 'suffer God' [*Gott leiden*]" (248). Šajda asserts that, "in developing an ever-deeper understanding of this concept [of suffering], Kierkegaard came in touch with the Eckhartian ideological heritage through his readings of Arndt and Pseudo-Tauleriana [e.g. *The Imitation of the Poor Life of Christ* which Kierkegaard read in 1848]. Meister Eckhart's concept of a human not as an architect of his own soul's reconstruction, but as a receptive 'sufferer of God's work,' played a vital role in Arndt's radical and recurrent requirement of complete self-emptying

Martensen also wrote on Boehme, to whom Kierkegaard does refer. Potential affinities between Kierkegaard and Boehme are explored in chapter four and Eckhart will also be reconsidered further in chapter seven. Luther and Arndt are considered in chapters three and four respectively. Before turning to their innovative accounts of *Anfechtung*, however, this present chapter turns to the treatments of spiritual struggle to be found in Tauler and the *Theologia Deutsch*.

The Winter of the Soul: Johannes Tauler

In Tauler can be found the seeds of what subsequent thinkers cultivate in their treatments of spiritual trial. Although deeply influenced by Eckhart, Tauler's works are generally regarded as less speculative, more vernacular, perhaps even darker in tone than his Dominican master.[1] This concern is evident in his writings on *Anfechtung*, which in turn nurtured Luther and therefore also Arndt, Boehme, and Kierkegaard himself — though the differentiation between Tauler's works and the Pseudo-Tauleriana was not acknowledged by Kierkegaard or by the sources which he consulted.[2] According to Šadja, Tauler helped to form Kierkegaard's conception of 'mysticism' (*Mystik*), 'the Middle Ages' (*Middelalderen*) and 'monastery' (*Kloster*), as well as exerting an influence on "*imitatio Christi*, which was a key concept for Kierkegaard in the last years of his life".[3] In an entry from 1848, Kierkegaard observes how "In [Johannes] Tauler's *Nachfolgung des armen Lebens Jesu Christi* [*The Imitation of the Poor Life of Jesus Christ*, ed. N. Casseder, 1821], which I am presently reading for my edification, I find (pt. 2, para. 33, p. 137) a striking similarity to

---

of the soul by means of *dying to* the created things *inside* oneself. . . . Therefore, it can be argued that Arndt's presentation of the *metanoia* of the powers of the soul, and thus also of human will, mediated to Kierkegaard insights from the arena of the medieval discussions on the topic, and also as their integral part, the concepts of Meister Eckhart" (250). Barnett also notes Kierkegaard's citation of lines from a hymn of Tersteegen, which aspires to divine union as "Secluded [*abgeschieden*] inside with thee", in which *abgeschieden* alludes to notions of detachment (*abscheiden* — "divided from") and *Gelassenheit* in German mysticism ('Gerhard Tersteegen: Reception of a Man of "Noble Piety and Simple Wisdom"', 156 and n103).

1 See further Bernard McGinn, *The Harvest of Mysticism in Medieval Germany* (New York: Herder & Herder, 2005). Also Peter Šadja, 'Tauler: A Teacher in Spiritual Dietethics: Kierkegaard's Reception of Johannes Tauler', ed. Jon Stewart, *Kierkegaard Research: Sources, Reception and Resources Volume 4: Kierkegaard and the Patristic and Medieval Traditions*, 265-287.

2 Šadja, 'Tauler', 266.

3 Šadja, 'Tauler', 276. Also Florin notes thematic affinities in *Practice in Christianity*. 'Was Kierkegaard Inspired by Medieval Mysticism?', 182.

what I have developed in *Christian Discourses* (third section, second discourse)" (JP 2:1844). Kierkegaard also makes a few passing references to Johannes Tauler in *The Concept of Irony* and *Christian Discourses*, and one further citation in an 1847 journal entry.[1] Šadja summarises the affinity between Kierkegaard and Tauler in terms of their shared emphasis upon the need to:

> die to *all* created realities. Inwardly this requires the constant process of dying to one's own will. The death of one's own will is in both a synonym for the union of human and Divine will by means of the transformation of human will . . . the key to the highest possible similarity to Christ and the peak of earnest discipleship.[2]

In a Sermon For Easter Sunday on 'Union With God', Tauler writes of the need "To die to self" as the need "to totally give up all self-seeking, all multiplicity." In a sentiment to be shared by Kierkegaard in 'Purity of Heart Is To Will One Thing', Tauler declares that "The less thou art multiplied, the more shalt thou be single-minded and single-hearted."[3] Christ, who in the anxiety of death discovers equanimity of wills with God in the prayer "Not my will but thy will be done", is the pattern for this death-to-self: "Christ died a physical death that He might show us the way to die a spiritual death."[4] In this spiritual death, the soul discovers an intimate union with God such that "Whosoever fails to die will fail to live. And whosoever totally dies to self, such a one is wholly made alive in God and without any separation."[5] In dying to self, all is, as Luther would later say, hidden under its opposite (*absconditus sub contrario*): "Life has its hiding place in death", Tauler writes, "consolation has its hiding place in

1 See CI, 274, 546; CD, 401, 462; JP 4:4598.
2 Šadja, 'Tauler', 282-83.
3 Tauler, *The Sermons and Conferences of John Tauler*, trans. Walter Elliott (Washington, D.C.: Apostolic Mission House, 1910), 243.
4 Tauler, *The Sermons and Conferences*, 243. Thus Tauler writes elsewhere of Christ's "sorrow, that he cried: 'My God, my God, why hast Thou forsaken me?' (Matt. xxvii, 46). Joy, that with this cry of desolation He should comfort all sorrowful men." 'Sermon For the Feast of St. Stephen on A Dying Life', 619. Again Tauler writes, "'My God, my God, why hast Thou forsaken me?' (Matt. xxvii, 46). Mayst thou also utter those words with Christ crucified. Our Saviour's head as He hung dying was without support, and in His desolate abandonment, His love gave forth those words." 'Sermon For the Feast of St. Agnes, Virgin and Martyr on Christian Purity', 703.
5 "A man, for example, may die a thousand deaths in a single day, and each is instantly followed by a joyous life in God — death is no longer death" Tauler, *The Sermons and Conferences*, 244. Cf. Kierkegaard's motto *Periissem, nisi periissem*" ('I would have perished, had I not perished') (JP 6:6154).

desolation".[1] Here, in a move that will become characteristic of the path from *Anfechtung* (spiritual trial) to *Abgeschiedenheit* (detachment) and *Gelassenheit* (relseasement), the mortified will follows the agony of Christ in Gethsemane who says "not as I will, but as Thou wilt": "As if to say: I have no will; but Thou, Father, shalt have My will, for I am stripped on My will and dead to it, and now in Thy will I am absorbed and restored to life."[2]

Tauler continues to delve ever deeper into the abyss of the soul's desolation in a 'Sermon for the Second Sunday After Easter'. The aridity that the earlier Christian ascetics expressed through the imagery of the desert, is described by Tauler as "The Winter of the Soul". This winter falls "when the heart has grown cold; when it has neither grace, nor God, nor any Godlike things". Snow and frost "quench the fire of the Holy Spirit there; they freeze up the fountains of grace with a dreadful spiritual coldness".[3] And yet there is a deeper, darker and more desolate winter than the one visited by such aridity. Such a bleak winter, according to Tauler:

> is suffered by a really God-fearing man . . . God seems to have forsaken him. As far as his feelings go, he is dry, dark and cold, devoid of all heavenly consolation and spiritual sweetness.[4]

Such utter desolation is, once again, endured and delivered by Christ, "Our Lord Himself" who "suffered this spiritual winter, being deserted by His heavenly Father and deprived of His help".[5] In his God-forsakenness, Christ provides the lesson for all who suffer their own spiritual winter. All who suffer thus "must with all joy and entire good-will endure this state of abandonment in union with Christ".[6] In patient imitation of Christ, the blighted and frozen soul will discover a hidden joy and divine presence in the midst of apparent absence:

> If they are but overjoyed to follow Him into His winter time of desolation, abandonment by God and all creatures, then will God in actual reality be present with them, and in a manner far more to their advantage than if they experiences the brightest possible summer-time of His sensible favor. No one can fully understand all the good that lies hidden in this stern trial of desolation of spirit, this dark and frozen spiritual winter.[7]

1 Tauler, *The Sermons and Conferences*, 246.
2 *Ibid.* 247.
3 *Ibid.* 272.
4 *Ibid.* 272.
5 *Ibid.* 272.
6 *Ibid.* 272.
7 *Ibid.* 272-273.

In order to hear the presence of the voice of God, one must shut out the howling wind, the roaring world and those many voices of the inner life — only then can one hear "that fatherly whispered, secret word, uttered in the inmost depths of thy soul".[1]

The theme of *Anfechtung* is explicitly addressed in Tauler's 'Sermon for the Twentieth Sunday After Trinity', translated into English as 'On Temptations'. "It is in temptation [*Anfechtung*] that we have our conflict for God", Tauler writes, "and the victory is that a man learns who and what he is".[2] Specifically, one discovers one's "own miserable weakness".[3] God may communicate Godself through the virtues and sacraments, but also through *Anfechtung*:

> Little spots are cleansed away by them; and imperfections are dug out by the roots; by them holy humility is generated and the deep fear of God. By these trials God admonishes us to constantly fly to Him for help, and to entrust the battle to His direction.
>
> O beloved children, put on this noble armor of God, and without doubt you will conquer in your battle with temptations.[4]

Anfechtung is thus for Tauler a purifying process, designed to mortify the self and generate genuine humility and fear of God. Those who relinquish their darkness turn away from the self and walk in the true divine light — a light in which the soul discovers a mystical union with the "divine abyss", which, "inaccessible to our reason", we sink down within "by a boundless lowliness of spirit":[5]

> They are immersed in their origin — God; they are melted into Him amid the deep stillness of all their mental faculties. It is by the holy darkness of the divine solitude that they have sought and found, transcending all intelligence. They are cast away so far from self, that in their union with God they have lost self and all things else, and are conscious now of nothing at all but only God, in whom they are wholly absorbed.[6]

Into this state of "paradise", Tauler warns, demons may enter and assault the soul with *Anfechtungen*, unleashing their "fiery darts" against those "godlike men". But what power might demons have in this divine paradise? The power, Tauler suggests, to tempt the soul to believe in its self-*apotheosis*, to believe that in the process of

---

1   *Ibid.* 274.
2   *Ibid.* 571.
3   *Ibid.* 571.
4   *Ibid.* 571.
5   *Ibid.* 608.
6   *Ibid.* 573.

immersion and melting into the holy darkness, that an absorption *within God* means to *become God*. "Among other evil thoughts", Tauler warns, "they suggest to them that they are actually God Himself: for to yield to this illusion were the deadliest calamity of all".[1] In this sense, *Anfechtung* is sent by God, out of love, to humble the proud: "Such is the case with men who are the great ones of the earth", Tauler observes in a 'Sermon For the Feast of St. Stephen on "A Dying Life"'. "Many a battle must they fight with God and always lose, many a death must they die to self, ere they come to this degree of dying life."[2]

Tauler further develops the different forms of *Anfechtung* in a 'Sermon For the Feast of Our Lady's Visitation, or For the Octave of Her Nativity on Mystical Prayer'. In a manner intriguingly anticipatory of Kierkegaard's decisive distinction between the "lower" temptations of *Fristelse* and the "higher" temptations of *Anfægtelse*, Tauler observes how "worldlings" endure their own temptations, "but in a different way [than the godly], for they arise from their own unmortified nature, from the humors of their flesh and blood all tainted with sin".[3] Such lower temptations are escaped "By striking down his corrupt nature, and steadfastly resisting the evil one, and casting him forth".[4] And yet there exists a higher temptation, a temptation beyond the flesh: "a perfect man has done all this long ago", Tauler observes, "He is already a mortified soul". But the mortified soul is not immune from *Anfechtung*. On the contrary, a mortified soul elicits the demonic forces who struggle against it: "His temptation does not come from within [as do the lower temptations of the flesh], but from without, except the demon may find some remnants of sinful inclination within him, as for example a tendency to anger."[5] Here the higher temptation involves a struggle against forces external to the self: that is, agencies which are not reducible to internal inclinations, although a demon may elicit a sinful tendency that lies latent within the soul.

This apparent hierarchy of *Anfechtung* is again elucidated in Tauler's 'Sermon For the Feast of a Holy Martyr on How to Meet Temptations'. "One kind of temptation", Tauler observes, "is that of

---

1 *Ibid.* 573. In his invocation of *Anfechtung* as a reminder against the illusion of taking oneself to be God Tauler may be mindful of the misreadings and controversies which were involved in Eckhart's charge of heresy. Insofar as divine union entails the nothingness of the 'self' for Eckhart, any claim that '*I* am God' would be (self-)contradictory.

2 *Ibid.* 616.

3 *Ibid.* 626.

4 *Ibid.* 626.

5 *Ibid.* 626.

the external senses".[1] In such instances one is tempted to situate joy in other people, to worry about personal finery, adornments, dwellings — in short, material comfort and prestige. To resist such temptations "We should turn quickly away from them".[2] As for "the other kind of temptation", it "is interior" and more dangerous insofar as it:

> would set up an alien rule in the kingdom of the mind. The activity of the soul and that of the body are mingled together. Our inward turning to God in this life is closely joined to our outward tendencies, and this gives rise to temptations. Scripture says that Satan can transform himself into an angel of light; and that takes place in his temptations while our soul is absorbed in contemplating God.[3]

There is therefore, Tauler warns, extreme danger in the moments during which the soul is absorbed in "the holy darkness of the divine solitude". At such moments the demonic can take upon itself the guise of the divine. Such interior *Anfechtung* is even more dreadful since it is even more deeply hidden in the contemplation of the divine abyss. At such moments the contemplative can even succumb to a "Spiritual gluttony", that is "a temptation to ever crave more favor from God than is necessary in our earthly pilgrimage".[4] In a similar vein, Kierkegaard will also describe the *Anfægtelse* of those who wish to be "far too much Spirit" (JP 4:4373), who will to relate to God more absolutely than God permits for our earthly life. Tauler for his part reminds his listener that since Christ kenotically emptied himself of spiritual comfort so should mere mortals expect, and even embrace the darker moments of absence as they may form part of the *via negativa* towards the presence of union:

> [Christ] gave up all heavenly riches and took a life of the greatest earthly destitution, and was finally abandoned by all creatures, and even cast helplessly back on Himself by His divine Father — as He complained from His cross: 'My God, My God, why hast Thou forsaken me?' (Matt. Xxvii, 46). Now all this was for our instruction; He would teach us to cherish spiritual destitution of all things.[5]

In the dreadful cry of dereliction the God-forsaken Christ becomes the teacher in *Anfechtung* — a pedagogical hermeneutic of suffering

---

1   *Ibid.* 744.
2   *Ibid.* 745.
3   *Ibid.* 745.
4   *Ibid.* 746.
5   *Ibid.* 746.

which subsequent writers will also venerate. In order to be instructed in the way of *Anfechtung*, and to avoid spiritual pride and the deceptions of demonic interaction, Tauler prescribes three specific rules of divine authentication. The first rule is to remember that when *Anfechtung* instructs the believer in likeness to Christ, one must rest assured that "such trials are not due to depraved nature, nor are they suggestions of the evil spirit. All such trials undoubtedly come from God"[1] and are therefore, as Luther *et al* will confirm, for one's ultimate good. On the other hand, whatever distorts one's "likeness to God in Christ is due to an evil cause, either our perverted nature or the wicked demons".[2] Tauler's second rule states that genuine humility before God comes from God alone:

> when he cleaves to God in utter self-abandonment, avowing his total powerlessness to help himself:-when a man is conscious of this interior state, let him be quite sure that it is entirely the work of God. None but God can drive a soul inward to learn and acknowledge its own utter destruction.[3]

The third of Tauler's rules of discernment states similarly that: "Whatever makes a man little in his own eyes; whatever humiliates him under the mighty hand of God and under all creatures in sincere lowliness of spirit; whatever makes him long to be downtrodden and made nothing of: all that without doubt is from God."[4] Thus Tauler concludes his sermon by admonishing his listeners to incessantly humiliate themselves in their own sight and to never forget the dangers of spiritual pride.[5] While Tauler does not render the formal differentiation between spiritual trial and temptation, which Kierkegaard would come to insist upon, his counsel nonetheless prefigures many of the key elements, even dangers, which subsequent writings on the topic would elaborate.

The Hidden Path of Sorrow: the *Theologia Deutsch*

One of the most influential works which would reaffirm Tauler's melancholic insights was a devotional book known as the *Theologia Deutsch* (also known as the *Theologia Germanica*, or *Die Deutsche Theologie*), which, along with Tauler's sermons, came to comprise "a compact spiritual unit" of literature for the sources available to

1 *Ibid.* 748.
2 *Ibid.* 748.
3 *Ibid.* 748.
4 *Ibid.* 748.
5 *Ibid.* 750.

Kierkegaard.[1] The *Theologia Deutsch* was written anonymously in
the vernacular German around 1350, although it came to greater
prominence after Luther discovered a shorter version in 1516
which he had printed, incorporating his own preamble to the text.
Luther wrongly attributed the work to Tauler, though it constitutes
an adaptation of his theology ('Chapter Thirteen' of *Die Deutsche
Theologie* begins by invoking the esteemed name of Tauler). This
was to be Luther's first publication. Two years later in 1518 Luther
came across a more comprehensive version in a monastic library,
which he also published, including a more extensive version of his
preface. In this Preface, Luther affirms how "Next to the Bible and
Saint Augustine no other book has come to my attention from which I
have learned — and desired to learn — more concerning God, Christ,
man, and what all things are."[2] In this work Luther found that which
he had also resonated with in Tauler: the idea that "If the soul is to
gaze or look into eternity, it must become chastened and empty of
images and detached from all created things, and, above all, from
the claims of the self."[3] Despite its medieval inception, Kierkegaard
himself, in an early entry from 1843-44, invokes *Die deutsche Theologie*
as a diagnostic tool for the despair of the present age:

> Those lines in *Die deutsche Theologie* can really be regarded
> as a motto for the times (perhaps according to the author the
> German words do not have this precise meaning — he has
> not intimation of the ultimate of despair): 'If we are no longer
> spiritually rich, we forget God and take pride in being lost'. It
> is this commendation, so to speak, the age wants to have before
> God. This is the way the despair of the age shows that it cannot
> dispense with God, for the clue to its despair is precisely this:
> that there is a God. It is like the girl who, when she cannot get
> her way with her beloved, spites him by falling in love with
> another. She only proves thereby her dependence on him, and
> the clue to her first love is precisely her relationship to the first
> one. In the same way the age wishes to become self-important in
> the eyes of God. (JP:1:744)

Echoing this reference in his discourse on 'Strengthening in the
Inner Being', Kierkegaard invoked the *Theologia Deutsch* in specific
relation to spiritual trial.

---

1 Šadja, 'Tauler', 268.
2 'Preface', *The Theologia Germanica of Martin Luther*, 54. German edition
   consulted: *Theologia Deutsch* / herausgegeben von Herm. Mandel (Leipzig:
   A. Deichert, 1908).
3 'Preface', *Ibid.* 68

. . . Then his innermost being rebelled within him, then he did what is related in an old devotional book: 'he boasted that he was lost,' [*Die deutsche Theologie mit einer Vorrede von Dr. M. Luther und Johann Arnd*, ed. Friedrich C Krüger, 1822; ASKB 634, 41; Cf. SUD, 72-74] and that it was God himself who had plunged him down into damnation. Then the inner being within him froze. (EUD, 97-98)

As with Tauler and subsequent literature on spiritual trial, the example of the suffering of Christ is identified in the *Theologia Deutsch* as the archetype for how one should respond to the appearance of *Anfechtung*. Just as "Christ's soul had to visit hell before it came to heaven", so "This is also the path for man's soul".[1] However, while Christ's soul was wholly *innocent* in its anguish, it is through the *consciousness of sin* that the soul of the believer is first brought into the dark night of *Anfechtung*. The soul is brought down to the abyss of the consciousness of sin, even perhaps to the despair of God-forsakenness, by which it deems itself unworthy to ever come into the presence of God. In the abyssal depths of the consciousness of sin the soul believes that its own damnation to be righteous and just. Yet, in this abyss of contrition over sin, there emerges a living flame of consolation in the thought that God does not, in the end, abandon the soul in hell. "No, He takes him to Himself and the result is that man does not ask for anything but the eternal Good alone and knows that the eternal Good is exceedingly precious. Yes, it becomes his ecstasy, his peace, his joy, his rest, his fullness."[2] Through this one enters the kingdom of heaven, in the luminous presence of which the shadowy kingdom of hell vanishes. Yet, as is characteristic of the dialectical nature of *Anfechtung*, both states — heaven and hell — guide the soul's journey to salvation. There is consolation in desolation, therefore, in the thought that "When a person is in one of these two conditions he is on the right road." What is more, "He can be as safe in hell as in heaven. As long as man is on earth, in a temporal state, he might pass frequently from one to the other, indeed perhaps even during a single day or a single night — and without his own doing."[3]

The notion that spiritual states of heaven and hell are both affirmed as paths in the heart to God is confirmed in the life of Christ. With reference to John 14:27, "My peace I give to you; not as the world gives do I give to you", the *Theologia Deutsch* explains:

---

1 'Chapter 11', *Ibid.* 72.

2 '*Ibid.* 73.

3 *Ibid.* 74.

He means the inner peace that comes in the midst of hardship, distress, much anguish and misfortune [*alle anfechtung and widerwertickeit*], strain, misery, disgrace, and whatever setbacks there are. Through this peace we become cheerful and patient amid tribulations, just as Christ's dear disciples were — and not they alone but all chosen friends of God and true Christ-followers.[1]

In describing the life of following Christ, death-to-self is affirmed as the process of inward self-mortification by which "man should die to himself, that is to say, man's self and his I [*selbheyt und icheyt*] must die".[2] Through obedience, submission and serenity, resigned (*gelassen*) to God, the soul enters a silent, secret place *with* God. And here in the silence of intimacy with God the soul discovers a secret divine empathy: "And all this the soul does in silence, resting in its ground and in a secret, hidden, suffering empathy, enabling it to carry all, to suffer with all."[3] From here the work proceeds to describe a mystical union with God: a secret hiding of the soul in God through which the self is reduced to nothing. In this process of reduction, that which is contrary to God will be experienced as suffering:

> When God and man become one — meaning that God does His work in man — everything contrary to God and man is keenly felt and experienced.
>
> As man is reduced to nothing in that unity and God becomes all, things that have been a suffering to his natural being are diminished to nothing. On the other hand, what goes against the grain of the Divine and is God's suffering inside the created order will remain as part of God's presence as long as bodily and mental life last.[4]

While that which goes against and opposes the Divine Will becomes agonistically conspicuous, even to the point of becoming God's suffering in creation, the moment at which "God takes over in man" can nonetheless be found in "deep humility and poverty of spirit and a chastised and reflective mind". Again, however, this chastened condition is not free from all suffering: "In this mood there is bound to be a secret, hidden sorrow and suffering lasting into

---

1 'Chapter 12', *Ibid.* 75.
2 'Chapter 14', *Ibid.* 77.
3 'Chapter 21', *Ibid.* 88 .
4 *Ibid.* 89-90. Cf. Eckhart, Sermon 13(b), *The Complete Mystical Works of Meister Eckhart*, 109. I return to this in chapter seven.

bodily death."[1] An inexorable facet of such suffering and sorrow is the enduring consciousness of sin, which nonetheless remains with the soul until its final redemption in death: "grief and sorrow over sin [that] should and must remain in a divinized person until he leaves his body in death, even if he were to live until the latter day, or forever." Such grief is itself the source of "Christ's hidden anguish of which no one reports or knows but Christ Himself. Therefore we call it what it is: hidden."[2]

In other words, while the *Anfechtung* of sorrow over sin is grievous to the soul, there is, nonetheless, something divine about such grief. Such sorrow is a dark gift from God, insofar as only God can truly know the depths of sin and only God can reveal it to a person:

> This hidden sorrow over man's sinful condition is an attribute of God's that He has chosen and that He is pleased to see in man. But it is God's attribute above all. Sorrow over sin does not finally belong to man; man is not himself capable of it.[3]

In this sense, the consciousness of sin is ultimately sanctified, insofar as sorrow over sin belongs to God and is brought about in us by God, because no human being is autonomously capable of arriving at such an insight and no person is capable of bearing the full depths of the abyss of true grief over sin — an epistemological insight shared by Luther's observation that God reveals only as much as one can bear of the consciousness of sin, that full knowledge of this abyss would be instant death for a human being (LW 42, 125). This melancholy consolation is echoed in Johannes Climacus' and Anti-Climacus' view that one must learn by revelation from God the depths of sin (PF, 45-47; SUD, 95-96). Even when one wills to despair of one's sin one has merely glimpsed the abyss known unto God. Yet this abyss is already overcome by grace; and this despair already belongs. The melancholy struggle to realise the overcoming of wrath by grace is expressed preeminently in Luther's theology of *Anfechtung*, to which the next chapter now turns.

---

1 'Chapter 24', *The Theologia Germanica*, 95.
2 'Chapter 35', *Ibid.* 110.
3 *Ibid.* 110.

3. *Melancholia Coram Deo:*
Luther's Theology of *Anfechtung*

... nothing but the descent to hell [*Höllenfahrt*] of self-knowledge builds the path to becoming divine [*Vergötterung*].
(J.G. Hamann, *Sämtliche Werke* II, 164.17)

[I]t is equally dangerous for man to know God without knowing his own wretchedness as to know his wretchedness without knowing God. (Pascal, *Pensées*, 446: 586)

Between Melancholy and *Anfechtung*

If, as the axiom of Cicero (106-43 B.C.E.) states, "To philosophize is to learn how to die" then for Martin Luther (1483-1546 C.E.) to *theologise* is to learn how to die in order to receive new life: that is, to die to self in the desire to live before the Face of God (*coram Deo*).[1] For Luther, to theologise is to endure *tentatio* (which Luther rendered in German as both *Versuchung* — temptation — and *Anfechtung*[2]): to live as if dead,

---

1 An acclaimed figure within Renaissance Humanism, Cicero was also among Luther's most frequently cited and approved sources. Luther compares Cicero favourably with Aristotle, 'the philosopher' lauded by scholasticism, even reflecting that if he were a youth he would devote himself to the study of Cicero in conjunction with the Bible (WA Tr, III, 612, no. 5012). See further Lewis W. Spitz, 'Headwaters of the Reformation: Studia Humanitatis, Luther Senior et Initia Reformationis', in ed. Heiko Oberman, *Luther and the Dawn of the Modern Era* (Leiden: Brill, 1974), 103-104.

2 *Anfechtung* is often translated within English language Luther scholarship as (spiritual) trial, test, temptation, tribulation, attack, anxiety, temptation, trial, affliction, tribulation. Scaer highlights the latter four as each reflecting key aspects of *Anfechtung*, while also suggesting that the term itself should perhaps be left untranslated: "*Anfechtung* is perhaps better understood not as one vocable in Luther's vocabulary, but as a one-word theological concept" (David P. Scaer, 'The Concept of *Anfechtung* in Luther's Thought', *Concordia Theological Quarterly*, 47 (1), January 1983, 15-30, 15). Alister McGrath observes that:

   'assault' is probably more illuminating than 'temptation', although the latter is more accurate. For Luther, death, the devil, the world and Hell combine in a terrifying assault upon man, reducing him to be damned, to undergo the purgative kenosis of self-mortification, in order then to experience resurrection through salvation in which the gates of heaven may be opened to the soul on earth. *Anfechtung* (the vernacular expression for *tentatio*, which emphasises the sense of demonic or divine attack — *impugnatio*) expresses this melancholy sentiment and the longing for salvation, which hopes for life in the valley of the shadow of death.

Theology, in Luther's agonistic vision, is not merely a cognitive or speculative discipline but a form of un/knowing appropriated existentially through *tentationem (Anfechtungen)*. In contrast to his inherited "manipulative" method of medieval spirituality — reading, prayer, meditation, and contemplation — Luther asserted a *vita passiva* by which *tentatio* becomes one of the three pillars of the most authentic theology and is in itself the touchstone that teaches one to experience as well as to know and understand the truth: "*oratio, meditatio, tentatio faciunt Theologum* [Prayer, study, and temptation make the theologian]".[1] This essentially receptive life of faith was to be understood in contrast to the classical tradition, which moved, by

---

to a state of doubt and despair . . . a state of hopelessness and helplessness, having strong conceptual affinities with the concept of *Angst*. The terms which Luther himself uses when discussing *Anfechtung* illuminate the various aspects of the concept: it is a form of temptation (*tentatio*), which takes place through an assault upon man (*impugnatio*) [WA 5.381.18-19; 619.27], which is intended to put him to the test (*probatio*) [WA 5.470.10,33; 5.203.35].

Other words such as *persecutio, tribulatio, percussio, mortificatio, perditio* are also used Alister McGrath, *Luther's Theology of the Cross* (Oxford/New York: Basil Blackwell, 1985), 170).

Tentatio may exist before the world (*coram mundo*), before others (*coram hominibus*) and before the devil (*coram diabolo*). The worst form of *Anfechtung*, however, is *tentatio coram Deo*: a fight (*fecht*) with God Godself. A widely disseminated fifteenth-century Latin-German glossary, edited by Johannes Melber and based upon the preaching of Jodocus Eichmann, translates *tentatio* as *versuchniß, anfechtung / pinlich ubel* (*Vocabularius praedicantium sive Variloquus: Johannes Melber de Gerolczhofen*. Hrsg.: Jodocus Eichmann, Straßburg: Drucker des Jordanus de Quedlinburg, c. 1497). The brothers Grimm's *Wörterbuch* offers the following: *Versuchung — tentatio; Anfechtung — tentatio; impugnatio (impug[na]re-anfechte)* ('attack' — in contemporary German *Anfechtung* exists as a legal term referring to the act of 'impugning' or contestation). *Deutsches Wörterbuch von Jacob und Wilhelm Grimm* (16 Bde. in 32 Teilbänden. Leipzig 1854-1961. Quellenverzeichnis Leipzig 1971).

1   See John W. Kleinig, '*Oratio, Meditatio, Tentatio*: What Makes A Theologian?', *Concordia Theological Quarterly*, 66 (3), July 2002, 258. See also Oswald Bayer, *Theology the Lutheran Way*, ed. and trans. Jeffrey G. Silcock and Mark C. Mattes (Grand Rapids: William B. Eerdmans, 2007), 59-64.

intellectual ascent, towards ecstatic contemplation or union with the divine (the *vita contemplativa*). *Contemplation* (or speculative *theoria*) has been replaced by *temptation*, the *vita activa* of works with *the vita passiva* of *sola gratia*, and *union* with the mortal tension of *Anfechtung*. By this transfer, Luther performs an existential[1] Copernican revolution in theology — epitomized by his famous assertion that a theologian is not made from "understanding, reading or speculating", but rather from "living, no rather by dying and being damned [*vivendo immo moriendo et damnando fir theologus, non intelligendo, legendo aut speculando*]."[2] In this one even requires "the right critic, the devil, who is the best teacher of theology. If we don't have that kind of devil, then we become nothing but *speculativi Theologi* [speculative theologians]."[3]

In this orientation towards death and the devil, Luther's religious melancholy appears to fall neatly within the diagnostic rubric of William James' (1842-1910) pathology of the divided self, "the sick soul" who is in need of being "twice born", although in his view of "repentance [Luther] had some very healthy-minded ideas".[4] It is in Leo Tolstoy's (1828-1910) *Confessions* (as well as in John Bunyan's (1628-1688) autobiographical writings, which are more akin than Tolstoy's to Luther's *Anfechtungen*) that James observes a virtually canonical account of religious melancholy. Tolstoy recounts a despairing disillusionment (in modern terms a state of *anhedonia*:

---

1 On the *existential* nature of *Anfechtung* see L. Pinomaa, *Der existentialle Charakter der Theologie Luthers* (Helsinki: Akateeminen Kirjakauppa, 1940); and Randall Stephens, 'An Examination of Luther's Theology According to an Existentialist Interpretation', *Quodlibet Journal*, 2 (2), Spring 2000.

2 WA, 5, 163, 28-29. Exploring parallels between Luther's *Anfechtung* & Hamlet's melancholy (50-53) Tibor Fabiny points out that while Hamlet was finally closer to damnation than salvation, "To that extent he was [according to Luther's own definition] on his way to becoming a theologian". Tibor Fabiny, 'The "Strange Acts of God:" The Hermeneutics of Concealment and Revelation in Luther and Shakespeare', *Dialog: A Journal of Theology*, 45 (1), Spring 2006, 44-54, 53.

3 WA 1:147.3-14, no. 352 / LW 54, 50. *Speculativi*: 1590-1600. From Latin *speculātus*, past participle of *speculor* ("look out"), from *specula* ("watchtower"), from *specio* ("look at"). Hence *speculativi Theologi* gaze out from above, aspiring to see all *Sub specie aeternitatis* (under the aspect of eternity), but without becoming subjectively involved in actuality. Luther's scepticism is clearly paralleled by Kierkegaard's own critique of speculative thought.

4 'The Sick Soul', *The Varieties of Religious Experience* (London & New York: Routledge, 2008), 94. James even suggests that in its emphasis upon "letting go" (Luther might say *Gelassenheit*) the modern "mind cure" movement is "psychologically indistinguishable from the Lutheran justification by faith." ('The Religion of Healthy Mindedness', *Ibid.* 82).

'without pleasure'; in classical terminology *acedia*: 'without care'[1]) from which he is finally saved by a latent metaphysical longing for transcendent meaning — a longing through which the vanity of the world is finally transfigured.[2] While James notes that there is "almost no theology in his [Tolstoy's] conversion"[3] from sick to healthy mindedness, Luther's search for deliverance from melancholy is, by contrast, worked out through a distinctly *theological* hermeneutic: a dark night of despair broken by the new dawn of divine grace. While it is keenly felt in the tending of souls (*die Seelen weiden*), *Anfechtung* also emerges throughout Luther's writings as a way of approaching theology itself: a *via melancholia* which opposes the *via moderna* of scholastic theology. In this sense, à la James, Luther could indeed be described as a sick soul who nonetheless arrives, through the dark night of personal struggle, at some of the theological conclusions of the healthy minded — twice born through the death-to-self of *Anfechtung*. In this chapter, Luther's dialectical theology of *Anfechtung* will be explored; interpreted as the search for a consolatory *metanoia* which, through the palliative care of souls, seeks to prevent melancholy from succumbing to the abyss of despair.

Luther as a Patient of Christendom

On a journey back to Erfurt on 2 July 1505, the young Luther was caught in a dreadful thunderstorm near Stotternheim. Beneath the darkly sublime thunderclouds Luther cried out in fear, pledging his life in anguish into the service of God with the words, 'Help me, St. Anne; I will become a monk'.[4] Despite his father's anger over the waste of a promising legal career, Luther soon entered the Augustinian monastery at Erfurt, taking his monastic vows the following year — vows that he would later come to decisively and in/famously

---

1 Johannes Melber's 1497 *Vocabularius praedicantium sive Variloquus* refers to *accidia* as "*verzweifelung des guden or b[s]ynfallen von guttem*". Bonhoeffer also refers to "The temptation to *desperatio*" in terms of "*acedia*", which as a temptation of the spirit "corresponds to the temptation of *securitas*" (*Temptation*, 140), referring the condition explicitly to Luther in his 1925 essay 'Luther's Feelings About His Work as Expressed in the Final Years of His Life Based on His Correspondence of 1540-1546'. *Dietrich Bonhoeffer Works in English, Volume 9, The Young Bonhoeffer: 1918-1927*, Paul Matheny, Clifford J. Green, and Marshall Johnson (eds), trans. Mary Nebelsick and Douglas W. Scott (Minneapolis: Fortress Press, 2001), 280-281; see also 265-267; 296-297).
2 *Ibid.* 108-113.
3 *Ibid.* 176n1.
4 See Heiko A. Oberman, *Luther: Man Between God and the Devil*, trans. Eileen Walliser-Schwarzbart (New York: Doubleday, 1992), 93.

renounce. According to legend, during the storm a lightning bolt had narrowly missed Luther but killed his friend Alexius. Taking this apocryphal legend as read, Kierkegaard would later discern this event as haunting Luther throughout the remainder of his life: "Luther, as you know, was very shaken by a stroke of lightning which killed the friend at his side, but his words always sound as if the lightning were continually striking behind him" (JP 3:2460).[1]

The formative period of Luther's time in the monastery was marked by deep despair, a spiritual crisis in which the earnest search for divine reassurance could never quite quench the flames of divine wrath that burned within the young man's anguished conscience: "Though I lived as a monk without reproach, I felt that I was a sinner before God with an extremely disturbed conscience. I could not believe that He was placated by my satisfaction" (LW 34, 336).[2] Luther devoted himself intensely to the monastic life but, by his own later admission, in his unfulfilling efforts to fulfil supererogatory "counsels of perfection" he lost touch with the image of Christ as the source of salvation and comfort. In the absence of such life-giving consolation, Luther turned inward and found only the worm of conscience and the abyss of desolation. Under the supervision of Johann von Staupitz (c. 1460-1524), Vicar-General of the Augustinian Order in Germany, Luther was commended to an academic career in the hope of extricating him from the interior solitude of the cloisters. But Luther was to bring his struggles with him into the academy and into his struggles with the Church.

In his 'Explanations of the Ninety-Five Theses', Luther describes the depths of his *Anfechungen* as "so great and so much like hell

---

1 I discuss Kierkegaard's ambivalent view of Luther in relation to spiritual trial further in my 'The Lightning and the Earthquake: Kierkegaard on the *Anfechtung* of Luther', *The Heythrop Journal*, XLVII (2006), 562-578. Kierkegaard's relation to Luther is also a key feature of my *Kierkegaard and the Self Before God*. M. Jamie Ferreira notes how "the more general question of Kierkegaard's relation both to Luther's thought and to the Lutheranism of his day is an important one and awaits comprehensive treatment." *Love's Grateful Striving: A Commentary on Kierkegaard's Works of Love* (Oxford: Oxford University Press, 2001), 11. A brilliant overview of this question is provided in David Yoon-Jun Kim and Joel D.S. Rasmussen, 'Martin Luther: Reform, Secularization and the Question of His "True Successor"', ed. Jon Stewart, *Kierkegaard Research: Source, Reception and Resources Volume 5: Kierkegaard and the Renaissance and Modern Traditions: Tome II: Theology* (Aldershot: Ashgate, 2009), 173-217

2 See further Gérard Vallée, 'Luther on Monastic Theology: Notes on *Anfechtung* and *Compunctio*,' *Archiv für Reformationsgeschichte*, 75 (1984), 290-296.

that no tongue could adequately express them, no pen could describe them, and one who had not himself experienced them could not believe them". Furthermore, had they lasted for "even for one tenth of an hour", he believes that he "would have perished completely and all of his bones would have been reduced to ashes". At such moments both God and creation appear so wrathful that one is caused to feel that "there is no flight, no comfort, within or without, but all things accuse". In this abyss, the soul loses faith in its redemption. In its apparent God-forsakenness "the person is stretched out with Christ so that all his bones may be counted, and every corner of the soul is filled with the greatest bitterness, dread, trembling, and sorrow in such a manner that all these last forever." The soul, "at the point where it is touched by a passing eternal flood, feels and imbibes nothing except eternal punishment". But, mercifully such desolation does not last more than a moment — "the punishment does not remain, for it passes over again" (LW 31, 129). It was ultimately as a theologian — albeit a theologian of trials and tribulations — that Luther was able to discover the salve that could deliver his anguished soul from the depths of *desperatio*. In his dawning epiphany of the doctrine of justification by faith alone, Luther experienced a moment in which he tasted freedom from the anxiety of his failure to fulfill the Law and a renewed sense of deliverance by the gift of grace.

Reflecting on this period, Luther recounts how "Sometimes my confessor said to me when I repeatedly discussed silly sins with him, 'You are fool. Man, God is not angry with you, but you are angry with God'" (LW 54, 15). In acknowledging this potentially psychogenic aspect of his *Anfechtung*, Luther implicitly affirms that his view of an angry God was a, perhaps unconscious, projection of his hatred towards God. If depression is understood as internalised rage, then it could be said that Luther's wrathful God of *Anfechtung* is an externalised projection of an internalised wrath.[1] Trapped in the

---

1 This 'God-image' is not the only product of Luther's projection, according to Erik Erikson's *Young Man Luther: A Study in Psychoanalysis and History* (New York: W.W. Norton & Company Inc., 1962). Luther was able to further externalise his rage by shifting it to the devil. "Luther coped with the destructive drives within himself by projecting them onto the figure of Satan, conveniently provided by the religious cultures of his age. But here also the obstinacy and the intensity of Luther's struggle with Satan, in his later years, did not fall within the range of typical medieval behavior" (Roger A. Johnson, 'Introduction', ed. Roger A. Johnson, *Psychohistory and Religion: The Case of Young Man Luther* (Philadelphia: Fortress Press, 1977), 16. However, as discussed below, the ascription of *Anfechtung* to Satan is ultimately traceable back to God.

circularity of this disguised self-condemnation, the melancholy soul is captured within a narcissistic abyss of melancholy self-reflection.[1] As a consequence of this projection, Luther reflected that "I hated the righteous God who punishes sinners . . . I was angry with God". Despite this hatred, however, Luther fled to the Scriptures for theological deliverance. "Nevertheless, I beat importunately upon Paul at that place, most ardently desiring to know what St. Paul wanted. And I extolled my sweetest word with a love as great as the hated with which I had formerly hated that word, 'the righteousness of God'" (LW 34, 336-337). Wrestling with Romans 1:16-17 on the righteousness of God, Luther was finally, and suddenly, born again through the gates of paradise:

> At last, by the mercy of God, meditating day and night, I gave heed to the context of the words, namely, "In it the righteousness of God is revealed, as it is written, 'He who through faith is righteous shall live.'" There I began to understand that the righteousness of God is that by which the righteous lives by a gift of God, namely by faith. And this is the meaning: the righteousness of God is revealed by the gospel, namely the passive righteousness with which merciful God justifies us by faith, as it is written, "He who through faith is righteous shall live." Here I felt that I was altogether born again and had entered paradise itself through open gates. There a totally other face of the entire Scripture showed itself to me. Thereupon I ran through the Scriptures from memory. I also found in other terms an analogy, as, the work of God, that is, what God does in us, the power of God, with which he makes us strong, the wisdom of God, with which he makes us wise, the strength of God, the salvation of God, the glory of God. (LW 34, 337)

Sola fide (faith alone) and the notion that one is *simul iustus et peccator* (both justified and a sinner) became Luther's Archimedean point and, in his theology of *Anfechtung*, he gave expression to the existential struggle to grasp or, rather, to be grasped by it. Not without some justification did Kierkegaard regard Luther as obsessively concerned with universalising this liberation of the conscience from the wrath of God: "Luther suffered exceedingly from an anguished conscience and needed a cure. Well and good, but", Kierkegaard wonders, "must Christianity therefore be converted *in toto* to this, to soothing and

---

1 While not employing the layered terminology of modern psychology, Luther could be seen to latently anticipate Kierkegaard's later explicit view that spiritual trial can be a fantasy of the *imagination* (JP 4:4383). See further 'The Lightning and the Earthquake', 573.

reassuring anguished consciences" (JP 3:2550).[1] Kierkegaard owned a significant collection of Luther's writings,[2] including Luther's *Postil* — the "principal devotional book" of the time.[3] Nonetheless, his view of

1 As Kim and Rasmussen also conclude, "Luther's mistake, Kierkegaard thinks, was to publicize his own *personal* and *consequent* appropriation of grace, and to prescribe it *universally* as the preliminary movement of faith". 'Martin Luther', 201. Any normative dialectical universalisation is especially problematic given the personalised nature of *Anfechtung* and its essential ineffability. Its opacity, as Bonhoeffer also warns, should caution us against establishing psychological phenomena as the dialectical basis for faith. While Bonhoeffer drew much from Luther's *tentatio* he also voiced his suspicion of basing theology on such psychological basis as Luther's autobiographical reflections on his own *Anfechtungen*. Michael P. De Jonge, *Bonhoeffer's Theological Formation: Berlin, Barth, and Protestant Theology*, Oxford: Oxford University Press, 2012, 120). DeJonge illustrates this observation with a quote from Bonhoeffer's *Act and Being*: "Even temptation [*Anfechtung*], which leads to death, is the work of Christ . . . In principle it is impossible to draw the distinction between real temptation by Christ and temptation as the final grasp of oneself." *Act and Being: Transcendental Philosophy and Ontology in Systematic Theology*, (Minneapolis: Fortress Press, 2009), 142. Bonhoeffer also contends that, "Whether Christ will give himself to the tempted man in grace and faith is always in the balance, therefore temptation [*Anfechtung*] should never be regarded as a dialectical point of transition on the road to faith", and deliverance from such a state is purely a question of grace in Christ. *Act and Being*, trans. Bernard Noble (London: Collins, 1962), 168-169.
2 According to Niels Thulstrup's catalogue of Kierkegaard's private library (1957), he owned:
    Luther's Works in 10 Volumes, ed. Otto von Gerlach, a selection in German of Lutheran apopthegms in 4 volumes, *Table Talks* (a Danish edition of the two 'postils': *Kirchenpostille* and *Hauspostille*), readings of Luther's Sermons in Danish. Also, as Niels Thulstrup writes, Kierkegaard would have been able to orient himself in "Luther's view on trial [*Anfechtung*] especially in the representative collection of quotations based on G. Walch's edition of Luther's collected works (1740-53), edited by F.W. Lomler, G.F. Lucius, J. Rust, L. Sackreuter, and E. Zimmermann, *Geist aus Luthers Schriften* I (Darmstadt 1828), p.118 ff. (Ktl. No. 317-20). SK could read Luther's comprehensive, significant interpretation of the essence of trial in his exposition of the sixth petition in the Lord's Prayer in *Cathechismus Maior* (1529), in *Libri Symbolici ecclesiae evangelicae sive Concordia* (rec. C.G. Hase, 2nd edn, Lipsiae 1837)." Thulstrup, 'Trial, Test, Tribulation, Temptation', 108.
3 'This *Postil* was an important work in Kierkegaard's own collection of devotional literature. By and large, Kierkegaard did not know much of Luther apart from this volume, which he refers to most frequently in his papers.' Jørgen Bukdahl, *Søren Kierkegaard and the Common Man*, ed. and trans. Bruce H. Kirmmse (Grand Rapids/Cambridge: Williams B.

Luther himself is fraught with ambiguity.[1] Reflecting his ambivalence, Kierkegaard also observes that "What Luther says is excellent, the one thing needful and the sole explanation — that this whole doctrine (of the Atonement and in the main all Christianity) must be traced back to the struggle of the anguished conscience.... The anguished conscience understands Christianity" (JP 3:2461). However, Kierkegaard also expresses recriminations towards Luther's own role in making modern Christendom's capitulation possible.[2] Nonetheless, although he revises Luther's emphasis upon the role of the devil in spiritual trial, it is this element of his thought, which resonates most authentically with Kierkegaard's own sense of the individual's situation before God.

Eerdmans, 2001), 20. Significantly, this book is also implicated in an acidic rebuke from Kierkegaard: 'Luther has actually done incalculable harm by not becoming a martyr . . . his later life was not devoid of pointlessness. The *Table Talks* are an example: a man of God sitting in placid comfort, ringed by admiring adorers who believe that if he simply breaks wind it is a revelation or the result of inspiration' (JP 3:2546).

1   Kim and Rasmussen acknowledge that in considering Kierkegaard's discussion of Luther in his journals "we are unable to demonstrate Kierkegaard's direct familiarity with Luther sources other than the Postil, but also recognize that even on its own this collection affords Kierkegaard a carefully wrought elucidation of Luther's key theological positions". 'Martin Luther', 192. In light of Kierkegaard's reliance upon this text, Kim and Rasmussen conclude that Kierkegaard's reading of Luther is, inevitably, fraught with historical restrictions and reductions and incomplete with regard to some of the subtleties of Luther's later protracted struggles. However, they also acknowledge that a richer knowledge of sixteenth-century Reformation history "fails to controvert Kierkegaard's central charge that the history of the Reformation is one of political compromise and increasing secularization" (205).

2   As Kim and Rasmussen observe, "the genealogical roots of Christendom, as Kierkegaard found it in Denmark, had to be traced back to the *accommodations* of the Lutheran Reformation", for which Luther himself is attributed some responsibility. 'Martin Luther', 174. As Hinkson describes further, "Gradually, however, his criticism escalates until it becomes quite biting in the last couple of years, by which time he is convinced that the bargain struck with the world by later Lutheranism cannot simply be attributed to its falling away from Luther — the seeds for the accommodation were somehow present *in nuce* in Luther himself." Craig Hinkson, 'Will the *Real* Martin Luther Please Stand Up! Kierkegaard's View of Luther versus the Evolving Perceptions of the Tradition', ed. Robert L. Perkins, *International Kierkegaard Commentary, Volume 21: For Self-Examination and Judge for Yourself!* (Macon: Mercer University Press, 2002), 41-76, 42. See also Hinkson, 'Luther and Kierkegaard: Theologians of the Cross', *International Journal of Systematic Theology*, 3 (1), March 2001, 27-45.

In his famous Freudian psycho-biography, *Young Man Luther* (1958), Erik Erikson (1958-1993) adopts "as a kind of motto" Kierkegaard's observation that Luther "is a patient of exceeding import for Christendom".[3] Kierkegaard was finally, according to Erikson, "the one man who could judge Luther with the compassionate objectivity of a kindred *homo religiosus*".[4] To some extent, both Kierkegaard and Erikson each echo a perennial suspicion that Luther was essentially another monastic 'scrupulant', (Latin *scrupulus* — 'pebble', signifying an excessively disproportionate aggravation of conscience). Erikson describes the young monk as typifying "the traditional *tristitia*, the melancholy world-view of the *homo religiosus*"[5] by which, in contrast to the light of the kingdom of heaven, 'the world' is cast in the shadows of infamy and vanity (paralleling James' account of the metaphysics of religious melancholy). In keeping with this disillusionment Luther suffered from the customary *Tentationes tristitiae* — described by Eriskon as "that sadness which is a traditional temptation of the *homo religiosus*".[6]

It could, nonetheless, be argued that Erikson's diagnosis of Luther as a young man in the grip of an identity crisis merely revives suspicions raised over Luther's temperament at the time of the Reformation — including rumours that Luther had actually committed suicide, thus dying in the sin of despair. More recently, others have also suggested "obsessive compulsive disorder" and revived, via the lens of Lacanian psychoanalysis, unoriginal claims of "excremental" fixation.[7]

---

3   Erikson, *Young Man Luther*, 13.

4   *Ibid.* 13.

5   *Ibid.* 40. Luther referred both to his own "*melancholia* and its spiritual equivalent of *tristitia*. Sadness, for him, was simultaneously a salutary means of comprehending one's own weakness and a pathology of the soul. It was both to be fought as a devilish temptation, and to be welcomed as provoking a turn to God for help". Angus Gowland, 'The Problem of Early Modern Melancholy', *Past & Present*, 191, May 2006, 77-120, 104). A related dialectic is at work in Luther's theology of *Anfechtung*, as explored below.

6   Erikson, *Young Man Luther*, 34.

7   E.g. LW 54, 29. Following Erikson's modern psychoanalytic approach and the work of Donald Capps (*Men, Religion, and Melancholia*, New Haven: Yale University Press, 1997) grounding *melancholia* in childhood beatings and the Freudian internalisation of the lost object (the mother being symbolised by 'God'), Luther has also been diagnosed as suffering from obsessive-compulsive disorder (externalised as satanic temptations) (Allan Hugh Cole, Jr., 'A Spirit in Need of Rest: Luther's Melancholia, Obsessive-Compulsive Disorder, and Religiosity', *Pastoral Psychology*, 48 (3), 2000, 169-190). This article argues that far from serving as a relief from his struggles, Luther's conception of religion actually exacerbates his condition and causes him fall at the end of his life into a "quiet — and raging — despair" (188). However,

Luther himself referred to both to his "*melancholia* and its spiritual equivalent of *tristitia*",[1] combined with a hatred of the wrathful God. Although "he has some acid comments on 'scrupulants' in his letters, he never diagnoses his own troubles in those terms."[2] Yet even one of Luther's most sympathetic modern interpreters, the Lutheran theologian Rudolf Otto, observes that while his own discernment of "the numinous" is indebted to Luther, the reformer's "battles with '*desperatio*' and with Satan, in his constantly recurring catastrophes and fits of grace . . . bring him to the verge of mental disorder".[3] If only to acknowledge the limitations of trans-historical diagnosis and modern tendencies to reduce philosophical and theological attitudes to clinical rubrics, it is important to moderate over-pathologisation of Luther's spiritual struggles.[4] While he frequently lays bare his melancholy and even fetishises his "delicious despair", Luther's insight was also capable of transcending his condition, of attaining to the consolatory perspective of a pastoral counsellor, to which his theology of *Anfechtung* bears poignant witness.

Even though Luther renounced the world-denying *tristitia* of the monastery, he never freed himself from the impression that the authentic Christian life would inevitably elicit the opposition of perennial tribulations and temptations. Inevitably, entering into 'the world' would elicit the devious and seductive attacks of 'the flesh'

---

the article relies excessively on Luther's *Table Talks*, without acknowledging the potentially revisionist element in them — a significant problem if one is depending upon them for diagnosis. It is also unclear whether late medieval accounts of melancholy and *tristitia* (which also encompass deliberately adopted philosophical and theological attitudes) can be reducibly equated with Freudian twentieth century treatments of *melancholia* as clinical depression. Erikson's own unsubstantiated speculations that Luther's father, Hans, was violent, an alcoholic, and had murdered a shepherd in his youth are not historically accurate. See Lewis W. Spitz, 'Psychohistory and History: The Case of *Young Man Luther*', 70-77; and Roger A. Johnson, 'Psychohistory as Religious Narrative: The Demonic Role of Hans Luther in Erikson's Saga of Human Evolution', 127-161, both are in ed. Roger A. Johnson, *Psychohistory and Religion: The Case of Young Man Luther* (Philadelphia: Fortress Press, 1977). Through the lens of Lacanian psychoanalysis, Slavoj Žižek has also recently drawn attention to Luther's apparently "excremental" fixation, though such accusations of anal obsession are nothing new. *The Parallax View*, (Cambridge & London: MIT Press, 2006), 187.

1 Gowland, 'The Problem of Early Modern Melancholy', 104.
2 Rupp, *The Righteousness of God*, 116.
3 *The Idea of the Holy*, 102.
4 See also Horst Beintker, *Die Überwindung der Anfechtung bei Luther* (Berlin: Evangelische Verlagsanstalt, 1954), 70-77, which critiques psychological explanation of Luther's *Anfechtung*.

and 'the devil' (who is the Prince of the world — *Princeps mundi*). But Luther attempted to fortify himself psychologically against such onslaughts by interpreting them in the theological light of God's alien work (*opus alienum Dei*: action which is alien to God's nature; through which is discovered *opus proprium Dei* — action which belongs to God's very nature). Through his theology of *Anfechtung*, Luther subjected even the most melancholy of thoughts (the despair of God-forsakenness, the hopeless thought of eternal damnation, the *tentatio de praedestinatione*) to a consolatory hermeneutic of the crucible of *Anfechtung* — in the fires of which even the abyss of desolation may be transfigured into an experience of the infinite grace of God.[1]

Sources of Melancholy

Above all, Luther's writings seek to reassure those who suffer that they are not alone. By disclosing his own anatomy of melancholy, Luther sought to expose the hidden, occult roots of sadness, to unveil melancholy before the mutual light, bringing consolation ('with-solace') among those who suffer, so that none are brought down to that darkest despair that takes root in solitude. In order to become an effective physician of the soul (*seelsorger*), Luther embodied the belief that one must first have searched and attended to one's own soul ("Physician, heal thyself!" Luke 4:23).[2] Confronted and being confronted by the abysses of his own heart, Luther cultivated the pathos requisite for the care of souls (*für die Sevlen sorgen*), enabling

---

1 Luther examines the essential relationship between election and the hiddenness of God in his 1525 treatise *de Servo Arbitrio* On the relationship between the anxiety of predestination and *Anfechtung* see Wolfhart Pannenberg, 'Der Einfluß der Anfechtungserfahrung uaf den Prädestinationsbegriff Luthers', *Kerygma und Dogma*, (1954) 3, 109-39. Luther warns against excessive meditation upon one's own election as leading towards despair. "In Germany from 1560s onwards, this warning was developed into a charge specifically against Calvinism, which was increasingly attacked by Lutherans as fostering melancholy through its terrifying overemphasis on the predestination decree" (Gowland, 'The Problem of Early Modern Melancholy', 106). This Lutheran charge against Calvinism was subsequently revived in Robert Burton's *Anatomy of Melancholy* (Ibid. 107).

2 "In treating Luther's primary concept of the office of pastor, it is necessary to go back to his own soul conditioning. He held, as a cardinal principle, the necessity for the physician to heal himself before he could heal others: 'Physician, heal thyself' (Luke 4:23). He felt that no one could give counsel and advice to others without first searching his own soul, advising and caring for it, before seeking to give such care to others." C. Charles Bachmann, 'Luther as Pastoral Counselor', *Pastoral Psychology*, (1952) 3, 35-42, 35.

him to offer the palliative comfort of consolation (*consolatio fratrum*).[1] Yet Luther and his fellow strugglers did not operate in a lexicon in which the hidden sources of melancholy were reducible to interiority. Luther inhabited a fearful medieval world-view, which regarded most phenomena as susceptible to the manipulation of demons, ghosts, spirits, *succubus et incubus*, as well as the arcane forces of astrology. While the renunciation of his monastic vows freed Luther from the fear that storms were signifiers of divine retribution, he continued to perceive such events as supernatural, or demonic, rather than purely 'natural' events.[2] Luther referred to his nocturnal anxiety attacks as "the devil's bath [*balneum diaboli*]" and made the inference that "All heaviness of mind and melancholy come of the devil".[3] By ascribing melancholy to the external source of the devil, however, Luther actually sought to alleviate some of the internal guilt, which may so easily drive the conscience to the sinful depths of despair. The conscience itself, after all, cannot be trusted since it can become the robber's castle of the devil himself — the *Magister conscientiaa* (Master of the conscience). Therefore, "'Tis a fearful thing when Satan torments the sorrowful conscience with melancholy".[4]

With reference to his own melancholy, Luther writes that "I, Martin Luther, was born under the most unfavorable of stars, probably under Saturn".[5] Such astrological forces and superstitions — which Luther differentiated from the ostensibly demonstrable proofs of astronomy — were, like storms and tempests, to be identified as the orchestrations of the devil rather than the divine: "Astrology is framed by the devil ... ", Luther proclaims, "to believe in the stars, or to trust thereon, or to

1 See further, Henrik Ivarsson, 'The Principles of Pastoral Care According to Luther', *Pastoral Psychology*, (1962) 13 (1), 19-25, 19. Also John T. McNeill, 'The Cure of Souls in Lutheranism', *Pastoral Psychology*, 2 (5), 1951, 11-19; M. Vernon Begalke, 'Luther's *Anfechtungen*: An Important Clue to His Pastoral Theology,' *Consensus*, 8 (July 1982), 3-17; and Won Yong Ji, 'The significance of *Tentatio* in Luther's Spirituality', *Concordia Journal*, 15 (April 1989), 181-188.
2 Richard Marius, *Martin Luther: The Christian Between God and Death* (Cambridge, Massachusetts: The Belknap Press of Harvard University Press, 1999), 28.
3 'Of Temptation and Tribulation', *The Table Talk of Martin Luther*, ed. and trans. William Hazlitt (London: H.G. Bohn, 1857), DCXXXIV, 270.
4 'Of the Devil and His Works', *The Table Talk of Martin Luther*, DCXII, 262.
5 Quoted in Julia Kristeva, *Black Sun: Depression and Melancholia*, trans. Leon S. Roudiez (New York: Columbia University Press, 1989), 119. From Luther, *Tischreden in der Matheisischen Sammlung*, I, 122, 51, as quoted by Jean Wirth, *Luther, étude d'histoire religieuse* (Geneva: Droz, 1981), 130. In her own translation of the passage, Kristeva also refers to the German text of *Tischreden*, ed. Walther Rehm (Munich, 1934), 130.

be affrighted thereat, is idolatry, and against the first commandment."[1]
The presence of melancholy in the soul therefore constituted evidence
of supernatural interference within the innermost being — within the
intimate depths of the conscience itself.

In one of the Table Talks recorded by Dietrich under the title
'Treatment of Melancholy, Despair etc.' (1531), Luther differentiates
between a legitimate melancholy disillusionment toward the infamy
of 'the world' and the more grievous melancholy of the soul before
God (*coram Deo*): "To be gloomy before God is not pleasing to him,
although he would permit us to be depressed before the world" (LW
54, 16). Luther here proceeds to describe how he resists the devil, even
chasing him away by breaking wind. "He often troubles me with
trivialities [trivial sins]", Luther observes. "I don't notice this when
I'm depressed, but when I feel better I recognize it easily" (LW 54, 16).
In other words, when a melancholy mood is present, it is more difficult
to notice how trivial the misdemeanours are that the devil raises up
before the conscience. When melancholy has lifted, scrupulous excess
elapses as the correctly proportionate perspective prevails. Luther
thus describes how counsel from another can be an invaluable source
of comfort for the sufferer. In Table Talk No. 1288 ('Luther Offers
Spiritual Counsel to an Auditor', recorded by Schlaginhauffen) Luther
laments how in the past "I, too, suffered from such trials, and at the
time I had nobody to console me. When I complained about such
spiritual assaults to my good Staupitz, he replied, 'I don't understand
this; I know nothing about it" (LW 54, 133).

---

1 'Of Astronomy and Astrology', *The Table Talk of Martin Luther*, DCCCXLIII,
343-344. Despite such Christian indictments of superstition as Luther's,
the language of astrology endured beyond the Reformation rhetoric of
melancholy. "Renaissance theories of melancholy reinforced the astrological
aspect of traditional medicine. . . . Some even played down or excluded
the planetary influences, but even those who did so often used the same
terminology." M.A. Screech, *Montaigne and Melancholy: The Wisdom of the
Essays* (London: Gerald Duckworth and Co. Ltd., 1983), 25. For example,
Shakespeare: "We make guilty of our disasters the sun, the moon, and the
stars; as if we were villains by necessity, fools by heavenly compulsion."
King Lear, Act I, Scene 2. In Robert Burton's (1577-1640) virtually canonical
seventeenth century anthology *The Anatomy of Melancholy* (published under
the pseudonym *Democritus Junior* in 1621) cosmological, or astrological,
movements are identified as a cause of all life's motions: "I hope, I may
justly conclude with Cajetan . . . that heaven is God's instrument, by
mediation of which He governs and disposeth these elementary bodies;
or a great book, whose letters are the stars (as one calls it), wherein are
written many strange things for such as can read." Burton, *The Anatomy
of Melancholy* (New York: The New York Review of Books, 2001), Part I,
Section 2, Member I, Subsection IV, p. 206.

Here the melancholy perspective undergoes its Copernican revolution: the true source of *Anfechtung* is not the wrath of God, but the individual's own anger *with* God. In order to avoid such scrupulous brooding, Luther prescribes that the melancholic should avoid the interiority of solitude, should cling to the *external* hope of salvation — fleeing from the *deus absconditus* to the *deus revelatus*, to the image of Christ who even accepted the thief on the cross (LW 54, 17). This image is also suggestive of the consolation that Christ suffers *alongside* the soul. But with this *theological* consolation, Luther also advances a pragmatically temperate approach to tangible relief from melancholy:

> When you are assailed by gloom, despair, or a troubled conscience you should eat, drink, and talk with others. If you can help yourself by thinking of a girl, do so. . . .
> Copious drinking benefits me when I am in this condition. But I would not advise a young person to drink more because this might stimulate his sexual desire. . . . Augustine says wisely in his rule, 'Not equally for all because you are not all equally strong.' So he speaks about the body and so we can speak about the illnesses of the spirit. (LW 54, 17-18)[1]

Crossing the Abyss: Treating Melancholy through *Anfechtung*

While acknowledging that, for many, sadness derives from more worldly issues such as "money, honor, study, etc.", Luther frequently reveals that his own "temptation is this, that I think I don't have a gracious God. This is [because I am still caught up in] the law. It is the greatest grief, and, as Paul says, it produces death [II Corinthians 7:10]. God hates it and he comforts us by saying, 'I am your God'" (LW 54, 75). As elsewhere, Luther here aligns his melancholy with his spiritual assaults, his *geistliche Anfechtungen*, the worst among which is the temptation to think that one is the irredeemable object of the wrath of God, that one is God-forsaken. However, Luther suggests that "Anyone who is deeply rooted and well grounded will often imagine that he has neither God nor Christ". In such moments of abandonment, "He will feel nothing but death, the devil, and sin

---

1 Luther is here speaking to an individual who has not been able to find comfort in the Gospel. His advice, cited here in Dietrich's edition of the Table Talks, seems to shock Aurifaber to the extent that in his account of this Table Talk he omits Luther's suggestion to think of a girl while also inserting that "Anybody who is assailed by grief, despair, or a troubled heart and has a worm in his conscience should first of all cling to the comfort of the divine Word" (LW 54, Preface, xviii).

passing over him like a violent storm and dark cloud. But at such times he will not be forsaken, as it seems" (LW 24, 151). Yet despite the imagined appearance of God-forsakenness, Christ will return to the soul and send such light that he will be seen even more clearly than before. The more one suffers in love for Christ the more Christ will manifest himself to the soul, showing the vastness of God's love for one (LW 24, 151). As such, and despite the profundity of such suffering, Luther reminds believers that ideally "A Christian should and must be a cheerful person. If he isn't the devil is tempting him." Such melancholy *Anfechtung* can be combatted by heteronomous appeal to the gracious Word, "Let not your hearts be troubled [John 14:27]. Trust in me,' etc. This is a command of God: Rejoice!" And yet before such a divine command Luther concedes that "I now preach this, and I also write it, but I haven't as yet learned it. But it happens that we learn as we are tempted" (LW 54, 96). Here Luther asserts one of his favoured refrains: that while it may arise in the devil's assaults of anxiety and melancholy, *Anfechtung* should be interpreted as an integral facet of Christian education. While rejoicing may be a divinely commanded goal, the path to joy may pass through the dark night of the *via melancholia*.

In 'A Meditation on Christ's Passion', Luther describes how a true theologian of the cross should dwell upon the passion of Christ in a state of *Anfechtung*, "with a terror-stricken heart and a despairing conscience" (LW 54, 8). Before the *mysterium horrendum* of the cross one should be awe-struck by the numinous immensity of sin and wrath, "for the main benefit of Christ's passion is that man sees into his own true self and that he be terrified and crushed by this" (LW 54, 10).[1] Here Luther proposes an epiphany of self-knowledge discovered in the self-recognition of evil (the revelation of the consciousness of sin). One must, of course, be vigilant lest this melancholy insight into the abyss of one's true self — the self as sinner — causes one to capitulate into the abyss of despair. Viewed through the eyes of faith, the movement of Luther's theology of *Anfechtung* is essentially *dialectical* insofar as it aspires to pass, by a melancholy *metanoia*, from wrath to grace, from sin to forgiveness, from crucifixion (mortification) to resurrection.[2] Therefore, he warns

---

1 Note also that "The real and true work of Christ's passion is to make man conformable to Christ, so that man's conscience is tormented by his sins in like measure as Christ was pitiably tormented in body and soul by our sins" (LW 42, 10). Furthermore, "This meditation changes man's being and, almost like baptism, gives him a new birth" (LW 42, 11).

2 However, this dialectic does not necessarily pertain for those who are in a state of despair rather than faith. Luther, as Grislis explains, "does not say that all *Anfechtungen* necessarily lead through wrath to love. Luther

that "After man has become thus aware of his sin and is terrified in his heart, he must watch that sin does not remain in his conscience, for this would lead to sheer despair" (LW 54, 12). To ensure that this melancholy consciousness of sin does not succumb to the abyss of despair, the acceptance of our shadow-side must undergo a process of sublimation: in order to be saved from the abyss of our own shadow "we must pour this sin back on him [Christ] and free our conscience from it" (LW 54, 12). Therefore, once the conscience is emancipated from the sin that would drag it into despair's depths, one must "no longer contemplate the suffering of Christ (for this has already done its work and terrified you), but pass beyond that and see his friendly heart and how this heart beats with such love for you that it impels him to bear with pain your conscience and your sin" (LW 54, 12). Through this dialectical contemplation, the gaze of the believer now continues to "rise beyond Christ's heart to God's heart" (LW 54, 12) in order to discover the origin of divine love that is revealed in the heart of the Father. In doing so the soul entertains the adversarial shades of melancholy and *Anfechtung* in order to be instructed by them, to learn truth by gazing into the abyss in order to be redeemed from its oblivion — to be saved from falling into the nihilistic abyss of despair by the omnipotent love of God. This is the true and ultimate knowledge of God for us (*pro nobis*), to which the dialectic of *Anfechtung* should finally lead us. One must not remain with the wrathful God of the abyss (the *mysterium horrendum*), but pass through this dark night of God to the dawning of true knowledge of divine grace. Thus finally, as Luther asserts, "We know God aright when we grasp him not in his might or wisdom (for then he proves terrifying), but in his kindness and love" (LW 54, 13).

Insofar as *Anfechtung* describes a purgative dark night, which is finally to be understood as a dialectical stage on the narrow path to a divine hope, Luther ultimately comes to the melancholy conclusion that all our trials are ordained by God, and "where all is as it should be, trials will not pass us by, and we do not seek to avoid them, but to overcome them like a true knight. Of such, Job says, 'Man's life is a struggle or a trial' [Job 7:1]" (LW 54, 72-73). Though one is extolled to become a knight of faith, crossing the abyss cannot be accomplished by a purely human act of volition, since the will is itself in need of

---

insists that there are unbelievers who remain in the *Anfechtungen* and are not freed from the eternal encounter with wrath. For such unbelievers the wrath of God is not an educational measure; the Law does not lead the unbeliever to the Gospel — but only deeper and deeper into eternal wrath." Egil Grislis, 'Luther's Understanding of the Wrath of God', *The Journal of Religion*, 41 (4), October 1961, 277-292, 287.

the gift of divine grace. Deliverance from great *Anfechtungen* can therefore only be found by entreating God for assistance through the humble and diligent act of prayer (LW 54, 73). It is possible to overcome temptation, Luther claims, "if we but cultivate the habit of calling upon God and praying this petition, 'Father, do not lead us into this trial'" (LW 54, 74). And yet, in spite of our pleas for deliverance, God allows us to be "assailed by sin" (as far as each is able to bear it) as a means of attaining to a more profound form of knowledge — albeit an *initially* melancholy knowledge of self and an *ultimately* salvific knowledge of God. Such self-knowledge (as revealed by the consciousness of sin) is a melancholy insight, which only true knowledge of God can save one from, since, according to Luther, for one to know thyself "is to learn that all he is capable of is sinning and doing evil; to know God is to learn that God's grace is stronger than all creatures" (LW 54, 74). Melancholy knowledge is thus saved from the descent into despair by an even more powerful knowledge of the grace of God. Our hearts may condemn us, but God is greater than our hearts (1 John 3:20).

Despite how the anxious conscience may *feel*, even the most melancholy souls are finally spared from the absolute hell of self-knowledge, which would ensue from consciousness of the full extent of one's sin. "If a man were to feel his evil, he would feel hell, for he has hell within himself" (LW 54, 125). The soul is spared this moment of death, though it may undergo a mortification (a death-to-self), which delivers the self from final annihilation. "God has allotted us much tribulation in this world", Luther affirms, "and, at the same time, offered us no other consolation than his holy Word. Thus Christ has promised us, 'In the world you will have tribulation, but in me you will have peace [John 16:33]'" (LW 54, 50). Appealing to seven key aspects, Luther seeks to guide the sufferer towards the consolation of the Word in his 1521 treatise 'Comfort [*Tröstung*] When Facing Grave Temptations [*Anfechtungen*]'. Here Luther's opening statement asserts that, first of all, the sufferer must neither rely upon their own self nor be guided by their own feelings. "Rather, he must lay hold of the words offered him in God's name, cling to them, place his trust in them, and direct all thoughts and feelings of his heart to them" (LW 54, 183). Secondly, Luther warns the sufferer not to imagine that they are alone in being assaulted by *Anfechtung* (since solitude itself aggravates melancholy). As sacred scripture (especially the Psalms) attests, such "trials are not rare among the godly" (LW 54, 183). Thirdly, one should not seek deliverance from *Anfechtung* "without yielding to the divine will", without following the example of Christ, "not my will, but thy will be done" (Luke 22:42; LW 54, 183). Fourthly, one should actually praise God in the midst of *Anfechtung*, just as David does in the Psalms, "For the evil spirit of gloom cannot be driven away by sadness and lamentation and anxiety, but by praising God, which makes the heart glad" (LW 54, 183). Fifthly, one is to thank God for deeming one worthy or being subjected to *Anfechtung* (LW 54, 183); after all, the most dangerous *Anfechtung* is the absence of *Anfechtung* (*Nulla tentatio — omnis tentatio*; LW 44, 47). And yet the blessings that "lie hidden under such trials" must remain unknown to us. "Some have wanted to fathom this", Luther warns, "and have thereby done themselves much harm" (LW 42, 184). Sixthly, one must never doubt the promise of God that God will hear our prayers. God even *commands* us to pray because of this promise that our payers will be heard. Finally, one must cling to Christ, knowing that it is through him alone that the grace of God is given to us (LW 42, 186).

Ad Deum contra Deum:
Struggling with the Devil — Struggling with God

An ostensibly dualistic interpretation of the devil as the source and God as the consolation in the struggle of *Anfechtung* is rendered murky by Luther's disturbing conviction that all suffering comes under divine Providence — that even the Black Death itself, while spread by poisonous spirits of the air, is ultimately the decree and punishment of God. Accompanying this rigorous, unnerving, not to mention melancholic, account of divine Providence, Luther refused to gloss over passages in the Old Testament that speak of God as the source of *Anfechtung*. In the book of Job, for example, Luther perceives quite clearly that 'Satan Was Permitted by God to Test Job'.[1] "The power he uses is not commanded", Luther explains. "Good gracious, no! But our Lord God doesn't stop him" (LW 54, 129). Even the devil is subordinate to divine Providence and therefore "Without God's will and our own consent, the devil cannot hurt us."[2] But while God may *permit* the devil to assail us, Luther is adamant that this permission is not an explicit *directive*. "The power the devil exercises is not by God commanded", Luther reiterates, "but God resists him not, suffering him to make tumults, yet no longer or further than he wills, for God has set him a mark, beyond which he neither can nor dare step."[3]

---

1 Table Talk recorded by Schlaginhaufen, December, 1531, No. 1252.
2 'Of the Devil and His Works', DCXX, *The Table Talk of Martin Luther*, 265.
3 *Ibid*. 263-4. Thus H. Beintker, *Die Überwindung der Anfechtung bei Luther: Eine Studie zu seiner Theologie nach den Operationes In Psalmos 1519-21* (Berlin: Evangelische Verlagsanstalt, 1954) argues that Luther regards God

3. Melancholia Coram Deo

Nonetheless, while the devil may be the one who unleashes his fiery arrows against believers (Ephesians 6:16), Luther's insistence on ultimate divine Providence betrays the implicit, even melancholy, revelation that God is the tacit source of *Anfechtung*. The ascription of *Anfechtung* to the devil is ultimately "tantamount to an ascription to God, the devil being *God's* devil, or 'mask'."[1] This deeply rooted conviction that *God* is the hidden source of *Anfechtung* is rendered more explicit in Luther's 'Lectures on Genesis', particularly in his expositions of Abraham's near-sacrifice of Isaac (Genesis 22) and Jacob's struggle at Peni'el (Genesis 32). Luther's opening caveat in this lecture on Genesis 22 is that Abraham is "the foremost and greatest among the old patriarchs" and, therefore, "he endures truly patriarchal trials [*Patriarchales tentationes*] which his descendants would not be able to bear" (LW 4, 91). His is an exceptional *Anfechtung* at the hands of God that no ordinary believer is called to endure; what is more, "it is impossible for us to comprehend the greatness of the trial" (LW 4, 92). Luther regards the *akedah* as a direct violation of the assertion of James 1:13 (which Luther disdained as an epistle of straw) that nobody is tempted by God. Here, Luther affirms, Abraham *is* tempted by God, tempted by an apparent contradiction in Holy Scripture: specifically, the contradiction between God's promise that "Through Isaac shall your descendants be named" (Genesis 21:12) and his command to "Take your son and sacrifice him" (LW 4, 92).[2] Faced with this dreadful antinomy, Luther reiterates that "The trial [*tentatio*] cannot be overcome and is far too great to be understood by us" (LW 4, 93). Although all is *absconditus sub contrario* ("hidden under the opposite"),[3] God also *reveals* Godself under the opposite (*revelatus sub contrariis*). As such, God's ostensible contradiction of Godself forms a theological antinomy, which cannot be understood by "the flesh", since "the flesh" will either come to the inevitable rational conclusion that God is lying (thus committing the sin of blasphemy against the nature of God) or that God hates me (thereby succumbing to the sin of despair) (LW 4, 93).

In order to render this collision more comprehensible to us, Luther parallels Abraham's trial with the *Anfechtung* in which the tempting

---

as the ultimate source of *Anfechtung*. See also P.T. Bühler, *Die Anfechtung bei Martin Luther* (Zürich: Zwingli Verlag, 1944), which explicates how the devil is God's instrument.

1 Craig Hinkson, 'Luther and Kierkegaard: Theologians of the Cross', 35.

2 Kierkegaard also describes Abraham's ineffable "ordeal" (*Prøvelse*) as resulting from a "terrifying" contradiction between two divine commands. See further my 'The Sacrifice of Silence: Fear & Trembling and the Secret of Faith'.

3 Steven A. Hein, 'Tentatio', *Lutheran Theological Review*, X (1997-98) 38-39.

thought that God has damned us as unworthy enters into collision with the promise of the grace of God. In this *Anfechtung* one is tempted to despair of God; but one must cling to the promise of salvation given through baptism. Of his own wisdom, Luther confesses that "I am unable to resolve this contradiction. Our only consolation [*consolatio*] is that in affliction [*afflictione*] we take refuge in the promise" (LW 4, 93). Luther therefore counsels that:

> we must hold fast to the promise [of grace] and maintain that, just as the text states about Abraham, we are tempted by God, not because He really wants this, but because He wants to find out whether we love Him above all things and are able to bear Him when He is angry as we gladly bear Him when He is beneficent and makes promises. (LW 4, 93)

Unlike us, however, Abraham cannot believe that he is merely being tested by God in this way for his own edification, as a parent treats a child. When God commands the death of Isaac, "He leaves no hope but simply confronts Abraham with a contradiction. And God, who formerly seemed to be his best friend, now appears to have become an enemy and a tyrant" (LW 4, 94). While the events of the *akedah* are disturbing and mysterious, Luther regards that they have been recorded in Scripture for the comfort of believers, encouraging them to have faith in the promise of God, even in the depths of despair. "Wherever we experience the opposite of a promise [wrath rather than the promised grace]", Luther proposes, "we should maintain with assurance that when God shows Himself differently from the way the promise speaks, this is merely a temptation" (LW 4, 94).

In a lecture on Genesis 32, Luther turns his attention to a passage "regarded by all as among the most obscure passages of the Old Testament", one which "deals with that sublime temptation [*de sublimi illa tentatione*] in which the patriarch Jacob had to fight not with flesh and blood or with the devil but against God Himself [*Deum ipsum*]" (LW 6, 125). In a bold theological assertion, Luther dismisses readings that claim that Jacob's mysterious night-time assailant was an angel, insisting instead that "the wrestler is the Lord of glory, God Himself, or God's Son, who was to become incarnate and who appeared and spoke to the fathers" (LW 6, 130). According to Luther's hermeneutic of *Anfechtung*, God disciplines Jacob in order to strengthen his faith. He receives a blessing from God and declares that "I have seen the Lord face to face" and, as such, "new joy and life arises from the sad temptation and death itself" (LW 6, 130). As with his treatment of Abraham and Isaac, Luther reads Jacob struggling with God (or God's Son) as a source of consolation for those in despair. It may *appear* that the will of God is other than God has promised. "To the flesh it cannot seem otherwise than an evil, troublesome, and gloomy will", Luther concedes. However, God takes delight in our melancholy, for "when we are weeping, God is smiling in a most kindly manner, and He takes pleasure in those who fear Him and hope in His mercy" (LW 6, 130-131).

Yet this benign gaze of God may remain hidden from the sufferer. In the temptation to despair (*tentatio desperationis*), which is elicited by such an experience of the evil and gloomy will of God, the heart may believe that it has been "forsaken and cut off from God" (LW 6, 131). This despair of God-forsakenness is "the last and most serious temptation to unbelief" (cf. Kierkegaard, JP 4:4699), which is nonetheless, Luther notes, God's means of disciplining "the greatest of the saints". In the abyss of desolation there is enlightenment — just as fear of the LORD is the beginning of all knowledge and wisdom (Proverbs 1:7; 9:10). Whoever withstands this terrible *Anfechtung* "comes to the perfect knowledge of the will of God" according to which one may say with Jacob, "I have seen God face to face and my life is preserved" (LW 6, 131). However, to attain to the dawning of such knowledge one must struggle through the dark night of fear. To endure such an ephemeral night of desolation one must cling to the eternal consolation of the Word of God — just as Jacob cleaves to his mysterious nocturnal assailant, refusing to let go until he receives a blessing (the new name in which there is new wisdom: *Yisra'el* — struggling with God). Ultimately, *contrary* to the phenomena of the *mysterium horrendum*, the grace and goodness of God vanquishes all wrath. The promise of God for the salvation of believers is thus so eternal and immutable that Luther even asserts that:

> if God Himself appeared to me in His majesty and said: 'You are not worthy of My grace; I will change My plan and not keep My promise to you,' I would not have to yield to Him, but it would be necessary to fight vehemently against God Himself. It is as Job says: 'Though He slay me, yet will I hope in Him' [Job 13:15]. (LW 6, 131)

Here Luther urges the believer to fight against despair, even to fight against God Godself, should God appear as contrary to God's promise of salvation, *to flee to God against God* (*ad Deum contra Deum*). While one cannot help the intrusion of melancholy thoughts, which tempt the believer to doubt the grace and love of God, one should not dwell on such thoughts lest one be tempted to affirm them: "they should remain only thoughts; they should not become axioms that are fixed and speak the final word or are established by our judgment and conscience" (LW 6, 133).

Against such thoughts one should dialectically juxtapose and cleave to the promised Word — which is more unshakeable than the self-indictment of the conscience — to which God only reveals a glimpse of the abyss of sin. By looking to the exalted mystery of Jacob struggling with God, the believer has access to a sublime source of consolation in the face of *Anfechtung*.[1] While most believers endure the assaults of flesh and blood, the world, and the devil, here "is the example of perfect saints and of temptations in high degree [*tentationum in sublimi gradu*]", not even against a good angel, "but against God appearing in hostile form".[2] As with Abraham, so Jacob clings to faith in the promise of God, even when — *absconditus sub contrario* — God appears so dreadfully "otherwise" (LW 6, 132). As Jacob did, so "[i]n this manner, Abraham also fought against GOD, which is one of the most serious and difficult of all struggles." Luther adds that "Although this struggle is not understood and cannot be endured except by the saints" (LW 6, 132), it is nonetheless a source of consolation in our lesser struggles against the devil, who assaults the believer with "a temptation to unbelief, which is a most bitter grief and torment of conscience [*acerrismus dolor et cruciatus conscientiae*]."[3]

There is also a sense in which we all conquer God as Jacob does, insofar as God has already surrendered Godself to us in the kenotic and salvific acts of the incarnation and atonement. In this Luther traces struggling with God (*Anfechtung*) to prayer, to the love for God which overcomes our vision of God's wrathful opposition to us, which allows us to see God as Love. In this sense Luther explains:

> He is not conquered in such a way that He is subjected to us, but His judgement, or his wrath and fury and whatever opposes us, is conquered by us by praying, seeking, and knocking, so that from an angry judge, as He seemed to be previously, He becomes a most loving Father.... It is the fullness of consolation that God exercises us in such a way and exhorts us to fight and shows us that it is to Him a most pleasing sacrifice to be conquered by us.[4]

---

1 "These matters in the saints are too sublime [*sublimiora*] for us to be able to understand them, although they should be read and heard" (LW 6, 135).

2 "For although Jacob does not know who this man is, he nevertheless feels that he has been forsaken by God or that God is opposed to him and angry with him" (LW 6, 134).

3 "For hearts are consumed by trepidation and doubt, and experience alone shows what this grief is; it cannot be declared in words" (LW 6, 132).

4 LW 6, 141. Luther refers to the example of the faith of the Canaanite Woman whom he also calls a knight of faith (Matthew 15), (LW 6, 139-141).

In this theological exposition of *Anfechtung*, Luther locates trials and tribulations at what is for him Christianity's victorious heart of darkness. Before the death of God on the cross, darkness covers the face of the earth for three hours (Luke 23:44), prefiguring the three nights of Christ in the tomb. Finally, from the darkness of the tomb is born the light of the resurrection: life and hope emerging from love's struggle with the wrath of God, bringing dawn to the night of mourning and *melancholia*.

The Consolation of Christ

The elder Luther is recounted as reflecting on a desire to write a book about *Anfechtung*, if he were permitted to live long enough.[1] Luther never lived to fulfil this ambition though, as shall be explored below, the legacy of his focus on *Anfechtung* can be felt in Arndt's *True Christianity* as well as in Boehme's and Kierkegaard's writings. Spiritual trial is for these, as it was for Luther, a virtually perennial and essential facet of the struggle of faith (LW 4, 94-95). Even one as venerable as Jacob may struggle "with weakness of faith",[2] at which point "there appears to him the gloomy face of God [*facies Dei tristissima*], struggling with him and desiring to kill him" (LW 6, 142). Such a melancholy vision of God assails all who are tried:

> when they do not rejoice in the goodness of God which has been clearly perceived but shudder at God's wrath and are terrified. Here all things seem to threaten instant death, all things are black, cloudy, gloomy [*tristia*], unfavorable, and mournful in heaven and on earth. Neither the sun nor the moon shines forth because the heart, overwhelmed in the flesh, is dying, and when that is dead, all things fall into ruin. (LW 6, 143)[3]

---

1 "If I live longer, I would like to write a book about *Anfechtungen*, for without them no man can understand Scripture, faith, the fear or the love of God. He does not know the meaning of hope who was never subject to temptations." See Roland Bainton, 'Luther's Struggle For Faith', *Church History*, 17 (1948), 198. See also M. Vernon Begalke, 'Luther's *Anfechtungen*: An Important Clue to His Pastoral Theology,' 6.

2 Cf. *Fear and Trembling*: "there was one who conquered God by his powerlessness" (FT, 16).

3 Luther later describes Jacob as entering into a fatal state of melancholy after three years of successive trials and loss (Genesis 37:18-20):

> The saintly man will now die; this was his last temptation which without a doubt consumed him, for he spent the rest of his life in the greatest sorrow, in darkness, and the shadow of death [*in summo moerore, in tenebris et umbra mortis*]. . . . Jacob endures his last trial, which kills him, for his most beloved son is lost, his firstborn from his chief wife. (LW 6, 362)

God is, therefore, the overseer of all *Anfechtungen*, by which God ultimately seeks an "enlargement" of the believer through "education", "strength", and "love, faith, hope" (LW 10, 49). While Luther's *Anfechtungen* may appear as an excessively melancholy, even morbidly pathological, hermeneutic, Luther himself regards *consolation* and (self-) reconciliation as its ultimate dialectical *telos*. While to the sensibilities of Enlightened Christendom, Luther's dialectical understanding of God through "fear and trembling and much spiritual trial" (JFY, 213) may seem intolerably melancholy, Luther himself regarded the world without such divine consolation as irredeemably sorrowful:

> Of ourselves we have no consolations but only sorrows, but from God we have consolations. . . . The world, however, is sorrowful, but is not consoled. For that reason many have come out of the sorrow of this age into madness and insanity, since there is bare sorrow, as with lost honor, riches, or love. (LW 11, 249)

Before the horizon of a fallen world yearning in fear for its *eschaton*, Luther offers the suffering soul a palliative, though not curative, consolation. Luther's theology of *Anfechtung* is in part a *memento mori* forged in a world on the brink of apocalypse, in the liminal shadows of which lurk demons and spirits, witchcraft, disease, madness, sudden death and despair.[1] Yet this is only one part of the dialectic of *Anfechtung*: the other side of the abyss of mortification being resurrection. In the closing words of his aptly titled *Luther: Man Between God And The Devil* Oberman suggests that while the medieval *memento mori* reminds us that death surrounds us in life, "Luther's faith allowed him to vigorously turn this on its head: 'In the midst of death we are surrounded by life.'"[2] In his *tristitia* Luther likened himself to Lazarus.[3] This sickness is not unto death. Jesus weeps over Lazarus and, moved by a moment of divine-human compassion, raises his beloved from the darkness of the tomb. In the final hour of death, Luther thus commends believers to a contemplation of *Christus victor*.[4] Through the

---

1 To these should also be noted the opposition of the political world, of papists and princes, which Luther credits as an external source of *Anfechtung*. See further Bayer, *Theology the Lutheran Way*, 60-61.

2 Heiko, Oberman, *Luther: Man Between God And The Devil*, 330.

3 "The true diseases are those of the heart, such as sadness, grief and temptation. I am true Lazarus who is quite tempted by diseases". Quoted in Eric W. Gritsch, *Martin — God's Court Jester. Luther in Retrospect* (Ramsey, NJ: Sigler Press, 1991), 147.

4 "The trilogy of evil — death, sin and hell — will flee before the picture

victory of Christ's death and resurrection, our own death becomes transfigured as a new birth "through the narrow and dark passage of death into new life".[1]

The new birth of death and resurrection is thus — via a soteriological and maieutic metaphysics of melancholy — a deliverance from the sorrows of this world. In the world is melancholy and madness; in the body of Christ is consolation by which one is relieved ('raised up') of the burden of death through resurrection. [2] As a gift of the infinite grace and mercy of God, the sacramental presence delivers believers from "all misery and tribulation [*anfechtung*]", which may be laid upon the community of saints, and, above all, on Christ himself (LW 35, 54). There are, Luther asserts, none more in need of the grace of the holy mass than those with anguished consciences, tormented by sin and afraid of divine wrath, death, the devil and hell. Where such a soul believes in the mass, a divine peace and joy is received, which is greater than any demonic despair (LW 36, 109). "What greater affliction [*anfechtung*] is there", Luther asks, "than sin and the evil conscience which is always afraid of God's anger and never has rest?" (LW 35, 110). Yet there is peace (*Gelassenheit*) in Christ who calls unto him all who are heavy-burdened and in need of rest (Matthew 11:28). Following the example of Christ at Gethsemane, "not my will, but thy will be done", the soul in *Anfechtung* is commended to surrender the will to God, "to wait in confident trust [*Gelassen stehen*]" (LW 35, 264) in God alone. Resting in *Gelassenheit* — a form of 'releasement', "letting be' or 'abandonment', which is a more passive complement to *Abgeschiedenheit* or 'detachment', the soul discovers a union or equanimity of the will with the divine will which dissolves the suffering of alterity. Erikson describes *Gelassenheit* as "a total state of *letting* things be, letting them come and go", including "also the all-Christian condition of accepting total guiltiness, but without

---

of the victorious Christ. Only by appreciating Christ 'for us' (*pro nobis*) can we find solace at this last hour and face the terror of death without fear." Dennis Ngien, 'The Art of Dying: In Luther's Sermon on Preparing to Die', *The Heythrop Journal*, XLIX, 2008, 1-19, 2.

1 Ngien, 'The Art of Dying', 3.
2 It is only after the eschatological resurrection that one will be finally freed from *Anfechtungen*. Egil Grislis, 'The Experience of the *Anfechtungen* and the Formulation of Pure Doctrine in Martin Luther's Commentary on Genesis,' *Consensus*, 8 (April 1982), 24. It is only in heaven that one is finally able to behold God as the God of Love, as Adam beheld God before the Fall. "Yet, until that day arrives for each believer, he must lead a life which is always a life under God's wrath and love." Grislis, 'Luther's Understanding of the Wrath of God', 288.

excessive remorse or melancholy".[1] As will be developed further below, I suggest that its meaning becomes clearer as a counterpoint to the cathartic struggle of *Anfechtung*: as a kenotic release of the self's struggle with God through the death-in-union of the human and divine will. Yet Erikson suggests that while Luther "adored it [*Gelassenheit*] from afar" in Tauler and the *Theologia Deutsch*, he himself remained "intellectually and temperamentally unfit for it, and somehow afraid of it".[2] There may be some truth in this observation, for Kierkegaard as well as Luther; but an empathic reading might conclude that in his dialectical anatomy of *Anfechtung* Luther the theologian attempts to come to the aid of Luther the melancholic. At least in its ideal expression, Luther's theology of *Anfechtung*[3] expresses the desire for a light shining in the darkness, for forgiveness overcoming sin, for grace overcoming wrath, and for the abyss of Christ's suffering overcoming the inner abyss of despair.

---

1   Erikson, *Young Man Luther*, 189. Bainton also describes *Gelassenheit* as a way of escaping the struggle between faith and doubt: "In all this advice to flee the fray Luther was in a way prescribing faith as a cure for lack of faith. To give up the argument is of itself an act of faith akin to the *Gelassenheit* of the mystics, an expression of confidence in the restorative power of God, who operates in the subconscious while man occupies himself with extraneous things." Roland H. Bainton, *Here I Stand: A Life of Martin Luther* (Peabody: Hendrickson, 1977), 177. Luther admired German mysticism's sense of *Anfechtung* and "unconditional resignation to the will of God (resignatio ad infernum)", though his view of mysticsm remains ambigiuous. David C. Steinmetz, 'Ecstasy in Staupitz and the Young Luther', *The Sixteenth Century Journal*, 11 (1), Spring, 1980, 23-38, 24.

2   Erikson, *Young Man Luther*, 189.

3   I have not been able to represent this in all its breadth. Hein recommends, for example, Luther's discussion of *Anfechtung* "found in the *Operationes in Psalmos* (WA 5) and *Luther's Commentary on the First Twenty two Psalms*, trans. John Nicholas Lenker (Sunbury, Penn.: Lutherans in All Lands Co., 1903)" ('Tentatio', 33n5). See also Andrew Pfeiffer, 'The Place of *Tentatio* in the Formation of Church Servants', *Lutheran Theological Journal*, 30 (1996), 111-119; and Heino O. Kadai, 'Luther's Theology of the Cross', *Concordia Theological Quarterly*, 63 (3), July 1999, 169-204.

4. God's Fire in the Soul: *Anfechtung* in Arndt and Boehme

In developing his theology of *Anfechtung*, Luther is, in part, an heir to discussions of scrupulosity in Heinrich Seuse (c.1300-66) and Jean Gerson (1363-1429).[1] Though the term *Anfechtung* also appears within prayer books of the period,[2] Luther's development draws more evidently upon the use of the idiom in the mystical texts of Johannes Tauler (c.1300-61) and the fourteenth-century *Theologia Deutsch*. From his annotations of Tauler's sermons, it is possible to glean a sense of the impact of Taulerian notions of *Gelassenheit* and *Anfechtung* for the young Luther.[3] Yet in his innovative elaboration of the theology of spiritual trial and temptation, Luther draws *Anfechtung* out from the rarefied cloisters of monastic scrupulosity and attempts to drive it into the heart of the common believer, thereby fashioning *Anfechtung* into one of the pillars of the task of theology itself and, as such, establishes a framework for subsequent accounts of *Anfechtung* in Johann Arndt (1555-1621) and Jacob Boehme (1575-1624) — all of whom nourish Kierkegaard's own understanding of *Anfægtelse*. However, Luther's own suspicion towards speculative mystical theology is partially contravened by the more Eckhartian elements of both Boehme and Arndt.

In his *Anfechtung*, Luther is engaged in a struggle with the

---

1 See R. Emmett McLaughlin, 'Truth, Tradition, and History: The Historiography of High/Late Medieval and Early Modern Penance', ed. Abigail Firey, *A New History of Penance* (Leiden: Brill, 2008), 19-71, 49. See also Helmut Appel, *Anfechtung und Trost im Spätmittelalter und dei Luther* (Leipzig, 1938); and Steven E. Ozment, *Homo Spiritualis: A Comparative Study of the Anthropology of Johannes Tauler, Jean Gerson and Martin Luther (1509-16) in the Contest of Their Theological Thought* (Leiden: E.J. Brill, 1969).

2 See, for example, Peter Matheson, 'Angels, Depression, and "The Stone": A Late Medieval Prayer Book', *Journal of Theological Studies*, 48 (2), October 1997, 517-530. However, *"anfechtung"* is here used in a prayer for overcoming the attacks of one's enemies (529).

3 See further Steven E. Ozment, 'An Aid to Luther's Marginal Comments on Johannes Tauler's Sermons', *The Harvard Theological Review*, 63 (2), April 1970, 305-311.

deus absconditus and the *deus revelatus*, rather than the peudo-Dionysian *deus incognoscibilis* or *deus incognitos*. Yet in doing so Luther is referring to the *appearance* of God rather than God-in-Godself, *deus in se*, which, as apophatic mystical theology affirms, is beyond all things and unknowable.[1] Luther's suspicion towards speculative mysticism conveys a mistrust towards attempts to unite with the unknowable *deus nudus* beyond the created order. In this respect, *Anfechtung* ensures that the individual cannot escape the "creature-feeling" of *creatio ex nihilo*, the fearful difference and trembling embodiment of existing *coram Deo*. Yet the endurance of profound mystical elements within Luther might be elucidated by invoking a potential difference between what Bernard McGinn calls "the negativity of apophasis" and "the negativity of dereliction". McGinn illustrates this difference with specific reference to Eckhart whose view of the hiddenness of God has "nothing of the torturous character of Luther's *Deus absconditus*" insofar as Eckhart's vision of the divine nothing (*niht*), unlike "the predestining God of Luther, does not induce fear and anxiety in the mystic". As such, Eckhart's sense of sinking into the nothingness of God "does not result in anything like Luther's *Anfechtung*, or mystical dereliction".[2] In contrast to the dereliction yet intensification of subjectivity, which arises from the subjection and abandonment of *Anfechtung*, Eckhart's union with divine nothingness is beyond knowing and willing and "is rather the cessation of all experience [whereas experience is central to Luther's vision of an anti-speculative theology], i.e. the forms of particularised consciousness that are the hallmarks of created being".[3] McGinn does also acknowledge that both senses of "the negativity of apophasis" and "the negativity of dereliction" are present in some mystics[4] — as I believe they are discernible in the writings of Johann Arndt and Jacob Boehme.

---

1 See further Piotr J. Malysz, 'Luther and Dionysius: Beyond Mere Negations', *Modern Theology*, 24 (4), October 2008, 679-692, 682.

2 Bernard McGinn, '*Vere tu es Deus absconditus*: The Hidden God in Luther and Some Mystics', Oliver Davies and Denys Turner (eds), *Silence and the Word: Negative Theology and Incarnation* (Cambridge: Cambridge University Press, 2004), 103.

3 McGinn, 'The Hidden God in Luther and Some Mystics', 104.

4 McGinn proceeds to consider mystical experiences of estrangement and the wrath of God in several thirteenth and fourteenth-century women. In particular, McGinn points to the example of Angela of Foligno, which he suggests bears comparison with Luther's anguished notion of *sub contrario* (104-106).

"Purified as gold in the refiner's fire":
Johann Arndt (1551-1621)

Through the sixteenth and seventeenth centuries, Arndt's works went through so many new editions that his influence within the devotional life of Lutherans began to overshadow that of Luther himself.[1] Whereas Luther had brought the 'good news' of justification by faith, Arndt addressed the emerging emphasis from justification to sanctification — that is, to the rise of a "piety of interiority and introspection".[2] While Arndt's call to return to an authentically inward Christianity resonated with Kierkegaard, perhaps Arndt's most significant influence upon Kierkegaard can be found in the extent to which reading Arndt encouraged him to reconsider his previous aversions towards contemplating the sufferings of Christ.[3] In his discourse on 'The Thorn in the Flesh' (1844), Kierkegaard refers with great esteem to "an old, time-honored, and trustworthy devotional book", Johann Arndt's *True Christianity* (*Vier Bücher vom wahren Christentum*, 1605-09; "Four Books on True Christianity"), which, Kierkegaard approvingly observes, rightly induces terror in the reader in order to initiate people into the upbuilding — just as "God deals with a human being as the hunter deals with game: he chases it weary, then gives it a little time to catch its breath and gather new strength, and then the chase begins again" (EUD, 344). This sense of dialectical rigour is also affirmed in a journal entry in 1851 where Kierkegaard approves of how "Arndt (as well as the old devotional books)" urges the believer to contemplate Christ's suffering and death in order to truly "get a conception of what sin means to God" (JP 4:4026).

Kierkegaard also discerns comfort as well as terror in Arndt's writings. Under the heading of 'An Upbuilding Observation' in an entry from 1850, Kierkegaard relates with admiration how "In an old devotional book (Arndt) it says that God sleeps as lightly with those who suffer as the mother with a sick child, that she awakens the instant it moves. A masterpiece of pathos, skirting the boundary of distraction" (JP 4:4926). Given such esteem, it is perhaps no surprise

1   Carter Lindberg, 'Introduction', *The Pietist Theologians* (Oxford: Blackwell, 2005), 6.
2   *Ibid.* Furthermore, as Joseph Ballan observes, insofar as Arndt "negotiated a theological convergence of late medieval mysticism, Reformation-era spiritualism and Lutheran Orthodoxy, he is a transitional figure between confessional Lutheranism and Pietism." 'Johann Arndt: The Pietist Impulse in Kierkegaard and Seventeenth-Century Lutheran Devotional Literature', ed. Jon Stewart, *Kierkegaard and the Renaissance and Modern Traditions*, 21-30, 23.
3   Mikulová Thulstrup, 'Studies of Pietists, Mystics, and Church Fathers', 62.

that, where the influence of other thinkers waxed and waned, Arndt's writings remained with Kierkegaard right through to the end of his life.[1] Again, in a late journal entry from 1854, the year before his early death, Kierkegaard invokes the exhortation in Arndt's "devotional book" to think of God in all things (JP 3:3463).

Along with Luther, it is Arndt's *True Christianity* that represents one of the key sources for Kierkegaard's category of *Anfægtelse*.[2] In Arndt's reflections on spiritual struggle it is possible to recognise many of the key traits that become central to Kierkegaard's own treatment. In 'Chapter 12: A True Christian Must Die to Himself and the World and Live in Christ' of *True Christianity*, Arndt appeals to the iconic image of Jacob who "in a battle with the angel . . . saw the face of God". In order to come into God's presence (*Peni'el*), to become an Israel ("God's prince"), one must, Arndt counsels, first be a Jacob: that is, "a victor through the Holy Spirit over your evil lusts".[3] Jacob thus symbolises the struggle against the desires of the flesh, the death-to-self and to the world — a symbolism that situates Jacob closer to Kierkegaard's notion of lower temptation (*Fristelse*) than higher spiritual trial (*Anfægtelse*). In contrast to Luther's view of the sublime temptation (*de sublimi illa tentatione*) of Genesis 32, Arndt does not identify Jacob as struggling with *God* but with an *angel* — through whom he nonetheless comes to behold the Face of God.

Arndt's most sustained comments on *Anfechtung* are located in Book II, 'Liber Vitae Christus', of *True Christianity*. In his Preface to the second of the four books Arndt vows to say something "of the nature and conquest of those deep *spiritual temptations* [*geistlichen Anfechtungen*], with which Satan harasses those that adhere to the Lord, and who endeavor to be faithful to the end".[4] Again ostensibly

---

1 For example, JP 2:1949; 3:3431; 3:3771; 2:1404; 3:2864; 3:3446; 6:6264; SLW, 710; CUP.2, 261; UDVS, 102; BA, 313, 379. Ballan concludes that "Kierkegaard is, perhaps, closer to Arndt than to any other German Lutheran theologian he encountered." 'Johann Arndt', 29.

2 Louise Carroll Keeley, 'Spiritual Trial in the Thought of Kierkegaard', ed. Robert Perkins, *International Kierkegaard Commentary: Concluding Unscientific Postscript* (Macon: Mercer University Press, 1997), 313. Arndt's *True Christianity* was undoubtedly an important book for Kierkegaard's devotional reading. See also George Pattison, *Kierkegaard's Upbuilding Discourses: Philosophy, Theology, Literature* (London/New York: Routledge, 2002), 58.

3 Johann Arndt, *True Christianity*, trans. Peter Erb (New York/Ramsey/ Toronto: Paulist Press, 1979), 72.

4 Johann Arndt, *True Christianity*, trans. A.W. Boehm, [1712]; new American ed. / revised, corrected, and furnished with additional matter from the original German, together with a general introduction by Charles F. Schaeffer (Philadelphia: General Council Publication House, 1917), 158. German edition consulted, *weiland Generalsuperintendenten des*

departing from Luther's identification of God as the ultimate source of spiritual trial, Arndt recognises the devil as a cause of *Anfechtung*, his wrath being elicited (and here Luther would agree), by the proximity of the believer to God. In the face of such demonic assaults (*Anfechtungen*) one is to imitate Christ in prayer:

> In the midst of the agony which he suffered [*angefochten*] on the mount of Olives, 'he prayed the more earnestly.' Luke 22:44. . . . By prayer we learn to practice true humility; for by prayer the highest is united to the lowest; the most High God to the most humble heart.[1]

Prayer therefore represents the moment of intimate tangency between the human and the divine in the face of spiritual trial. There is no greater example of prayer in the face of tribulation than the sacred prayer of Christ at Gethsemane. Yet whereas in his earlier temptations in the wilderness, the devil is the explicit source, tempting him with the flesh and the world, the anguish on the Mount of Olives suggests an *Anfechtung* between the soul and God when confronted by the cup of divine wrath and the sorrow unto death ("Father, all things are possible for you; take away this cup from me: nevertheless not what I will, but what you will", Mark 14:36).

Insofar as Jesus exemplifies struggles with God's wrath as well as the wrath of Satan, there are evidently *Anfechtungen* that are more divine than demonic in origin. As such, Arndt concedes that "The most considerable temptation and obstruction [*Anfechtung und Hinderung*] in prayer seems to be *when God withdraws* [my emphasis] the grace of a fervent and lively devotion." Again, following Christ at Gethsemane, at such times of aridity and the withdrawal of divine grace the soul must pray most stridently, since even more pleasing to God than the prayer of "power and fervency" is the prayer which ensues from *Anfechtung*: "that which climbs up to the throne of grace in affliction, temptation [*Anfechtung*], spiritual dryness, and brokenness of soul, is still more pleasing in his sight." In this sense, the anguished prayer of Christ on the Mount of Olives expresses the longing for grace in a state of devastation — a restless desire which is finally consoled by the vision of an angel of comfort. This is the trembling prayer of a "sick and languishing child" to its father, climbing up to the throne of grace, which softens the father's heart into "paternal tenderness" towards one who, in "weakness of faith" and "poverty of spirit", is without "divine consolation".[2]

Fürstenthums Lüneburg, Vier Bücher vom Wahren Christenthum nebst dessen Paradiesgärtlein (Berlin: Trowitzsch und Sohn, 1831).

1 *True Christianity* (1917), 238.

2 *Ibid.* 238.

Whereas Kierkegaard will later render a decisive distinction between *higher* and *lower* temptations, between *Anfægtelse* and *Fristelse*, Arndt employs *Trübsal* (affliction, tribulation) more or less interchangeably with *Anfechtung*, suggesting that, at least for Arndt, the specific word *Anfechtung* does not necessarily designate a distinct and rarefied concept, as it would later become for Kierkegaard. Nonetheless, there are clearly gradations in severity in temptations and tribulations: from the nemesis of demonic forces avenging themselves against the believer's intimacy with God, to the desolation of the absence, withdrawal, or hiddenness of God in prayer. While the sources of such suffering may be demonic presence or divine absence, Arndt nonetheless also discerns the consolation of divine blessing to be found in *Anfechtung*: "Blessed is the man that endureth temptation [*Anfechtung*]: for when he is tried, he shall receive the crown of life, which the Lord has promised to them that love him — James 1:12."[1]

Furthermore, Arndt avows himself to be "Showing how hope is tested in seasons of adversity [*geistlichen Anfechtungen*]; it maketh not ashamed."[2] Not only is *Anfechtung* a blessing, therefore, it can also be a necessity, since "it is necessary that God should sometimes visit us with crosses and afflictions [*Kreuz und Trübsal*], and deprive us of his good things that we have abused; that so may we learn to praise, and glorify, and depend on him alone."[3] Christian hope must itself be tried by the loss of temporal things; but more than this, it must be tried by higher afflictions, characterised "by the withholding of the communications of divine grace and favor (as commonly happens in great temptations [*Anfechtungen*])". In this state one must "'we must hope even against hope' Rom. 4:18), as we read that Abraham did [cf. Luther]", as through forsakenness "by God himself" one is "properly to be conformed to the image of the Son of God".[4]

Therefore, "in these spiritual trials of the conscience [*Anfechtungen des Gewissens*]", hope itself is "eminently proved and tried [*die Hoffnung geprüfet und angefochten*], whether it is sincere or not".[5] Here the soul is tempted by the anguish of its conscience to believe that it is forsaken by God, cast out from divine grace and into the abyss of despair. And yet, while the soul is tempted to inevitable "impatience, murmuring, blasphemy, or the like", there still remains "some gentle breath of hope, arising from the ground of the heart, by the power of the divine

---

1   *Ibid.* 332.
2   *Ibid.* 341.
3   *Ibid.* 342.
4   *Ibid.* 343.
5   *Ibid.*

Spirit, which contradicts and opposes those unholy suggestions".[1] The spark of hope, the power of the Spirit in the ground of the heart, thus struggles against the temptation to murmur against God; it opposes the "unholy suggestions" of the despairing conscience that it is utterly forsaken by God. Since this struggle, this glimpse of apparent God-forsakenness, is ultimately for the *proving* of the soul, one must rest assured that: "When this combat is over, all his transgressions are forgiven, and all his sins are covered and he himself is like 'a brand plucked out of the fire' (Zech. 3:2); 'or like a piece of an ear taken out of the mouth of the lion.' Amos 3:12." As this sorrow came against one's will it must not be conflated with the sin of "despair [*Verzweiflung*]" but rather as "the sharpest conflict, the severest trial of the Christian's hope [*Probe und Anfechtung der Hoffnung*]".[2]

Through the *apparent* withdrawal of the presence of grace, God therefore refines the souls of God's children who are "purified as gold in the refiner's fire".[3] By such suffering one is taught to trust nothing but God because even "when affliction [*Trübsal*] has taken everything else from us, God alone cannot be taken from us".[4] This hope is certain, despite the *appearance* to the conscience of being forsaken by God: an appearance of God-forsakenness, which by taking away all else, gives rise to the indelible presence of longing and hope in the heart, the presence of the divine Spirit.

Due to the hidden, interior, even secretive way in which *Anfechtung* refines believers, Arndt warns against judging one who is struggling to be weak in faith, or, even worse, imagining them to be cut off and forsaken by God. On the contrary, Arndt enigmatically asserts, "We know that fire is often hidden under ashes, though neither light nor heat appear."[5] A struggling faith might therefore be evidence, not of forsakenness, but of the authenticity of faith and the presence of Spirit: "a *striving faith* is a true faith; for there is a continual struggle . . . between faith and unbelief . . . continually assaulted by temptations to unbelief [*Schwerdtern der Anfechtung*] . . . life is one continued combat".[6]

In 'Chapter LII', Arndt offers further 'Comforting Instructions for those that are Laboring under great Temptations [*geistliche Anfechtung*] in Spirit'. Here consolation is to be derived from the secret realisation that, as Luther discerns, *God* is the ultimate source of *Anfechtung* and

---

1 *Ibid.*
2 *Ibid.*
3 *Ibid.*
4 *Ibid.* 344.
5 *Ibid.* 347.
6 *Ibid.*

that Christ is the soul's exemplar. "It is an undoubted truth that all spiritual sorrow proceeds from God", Arndt asserts. "For 'the Lord killeth, and maketh alive: he bringeth down to the grave, and bringeth up.' 1 Sam. 2:6,7." Arndt continues with a rather melancholy exposition:

> By the 'grave' in this place, is meant such a state of spiritual affliction as, like the grave, is void of all light and comfort. The soul that is thrust down into this prison, looks upon itself as dying and pining away as hated, despised, and persecuted by every creature of God. In this disconsolate state, the poor man cries out with holy David, 'My soul refused to be comforted.' Ps. 77:22. . . . Here it finds no comfort but in silence and resignation, in those unutterable sighs and groans which proceed from the ground of the heart . . . Faith grows weak, hope languishes, and the whole man is feeble, withered like grass (Ps. 38:8,9; 102:3), and ready to perish, were he not inwardly supported by the secret Word and power of God.[1]

The secret source of support in the depths of the grave is revealed in the suffering of Christ, present in all human suffering:

> In this grave or shadow of death, we find our Lord Jesus Christ, when 'his soul was exceeding sorrowful even unto death; and in his agony his sweat was, as it were, great drops of blood.' Matt. 26:38; Luke 22:44. . . . Thus we find Job repeatedly wishing for death. And our blessed Lord himself, under the agonies [*Angst*] of death, cried out, 'My God, my God, why hast thou forsaken me!' Matt. 27:46.

In the desolate cry of God-forsakenness Arndt discerns a secret intimate moment of tangency between Christ and the soul: here is consolation insofar as God remains present in Christ even in the dark hour of forsakenness; furthermore, if Christ himself endured such suffering, the sinful cannot expect exemption. Though Christ cries against God-forsakenness, God is, nonetheless, "continually present" and preserving him "under all his trouble [*Höllenangst* — 'hellish-anxiety']." Yet while in "intimate union with God", God had "so withdrawn his consolations from him, that his human nature [*not his divine nature*] was left desolate and comfortless". If Christ himself, "who was united to the eternal Godhead and anointed with the heavenly oil of gladness", suffered such desolation "surely sinful man has no reason to wonder, when he is brought under the same fiery trial".[2]

---

1 *Ibid.* 349-350.
2 *Ibid.* 350.

By passing through "this furnace of affliction" the soul joins those who "learned faith in the school, and under the discipline of the cross".[1] All is under divine Providence and, as such, one must believe that though tempting thoughts "are suggested to us by Satan. . . . Satan can do nothing but by God's permission. . . . The fiery darts (Eph. 6:16) which the Evil One cast at our blessed Saviour, came indeed from him, and not from God" — although ultimately God permitted Satan "to assault as he did".[2] Permission is granted in order to refine the soul like gold in the fire; and also to act as a nemesis against spiritual pride, vanity and arrogance, which cause God "to withdraw his consolations from us, and to hide himself in thick darkness; so that though we call and cry, and search ever so diligently, we shall not be able to find Him". In this desolate state one is left "hanging, as it were, between heaven and hell", unsure whether or not one has faith, "whether God be angry with us or not, whether we are in a state of life or of death".[3]

At this point of desolation, the soul discovers deep within it a still, small voice of hidden and sorrowful longing for God. To discover this secret longing, the soul has become bereft of all comfort and, stripped of its pride, initiated into the truest knowledge of God. In its "deep and secret sorrow, venting itself in holy sighs, and devout aspirations towards God, and a longing for his favor", the soul learns that peace is found in God alone — an insight that "cannot be learned anywhere but in this school of temptation; in which alone the truest knowledge is to be acquired. And whosoever is unacquainted with this, knows not God and Christ as they ought to be known."[4]

Faith is thereby tried as gold in the furnace, so that the faithful soul "comes forth glorious as gold out of the fire, cleansed from all its dross; so that neither fire, nor water, nor the cross, nor death, nor Satan, can hurt it".[5] Through the fires of temptation the soul if fitted for eternity, having its own will "swallowed up in the will and good pleasure of God".[6] Though to such a one it may seem that "The whole world is to him but one bitter cross; yea, even God himself appears dreadful to him",[7] nonetheless, one must cling to the promise of God: "'if our heart condemn us, God is greater than our heart' (1 John 3:20), yea, than all the world, or the devil himself".[8]

1 *Ibid.* 351.
2 *Ibid.* 351.
3 *Ibid.* 352.
4 *Ibid.*
5 *Ibid.* 353.
6 *Ibid.*
7 *Ibid.* 354.
8 *Ibid.*

Such an individual struggles with the hell of darkness and despair, "so that with his blessed Saviour at the mount of Olives, he is in agony, is very heavy and sorrowful, even unto death. Luke 22:44".[1] Yet in discovering Christ in the abyss one realises that one is not in solitude. Here in the abyss one finds Christ — not only the anguished Christ of Gethsemane but the God-forsaken Christ of Golgotha. With Christ one discovers the consolation in the depths of desolation that ultimately:

> These trials [*Anfechtungen*] are not to be looked upon as tokens of God's anger, but rather of his infinite *mercy*, since he is hereby fitting us to be partakers with them who have through many temptations entered into glory. . . . Nor, lastly, did the Son of God himself, escape severe trials, when his holy body trembled, and his soul was exceeding sorrowful (Matt. 26:38), and he cried out, 'My god, my god, why hast thou forsaken me?' Matt. 27:46.[2]

"God's wrath in the conscience": 'Temptation' in Jacob Boehme (1575-1624)

Consonant with Luther, Arndt appeals to Tauler, explicitly invoking his authority with the observation that "Tauler reckons these spiritual afflictions and trials [*Anfechtungen*] among the singular gifts and favors of God".[3] Kierkegaard's discourse 'Strengthening in the Inner Being' refers to the *Theologia Deutsch* (which Arndt had also prepared his own edition of) in relation to spiritual trial (EUD, 97-98; Cf. SUD, 72-74). Yet where spiritual trial (*Anfægtelse*) is explicitly discussed in Kierkegaard's journals, the only names which Kierkegaard directly invokes are Luther, Tersteegen (in 1850)[4] and Arndt's contemporary and mutual influence Jacob Boehme (in 1841):

---

1   *Ibid.* 356. "With this the soul is oftentimes so afflicted, that it is, as it were, continually dying, yet cannot die" (*Ibid.* 369). In a similar evocation, Anti Climacus describes despair as "the sickness unto death, this tormenting contradiction, this sickness of the self, perpetually to be dying, to die and yet not die, to die death" (SUD, 18).

2   *True Christianity*, 357.

3   *Ibid.* 360. Arndt drew upon Tauler to such an extent that Lukas Osiander II suggested that Arndt's book acknowledge itself as "True Taulerism". Ballan, 'Johann Arndt', 22.

4   "Tersteegen made an excellent point. . . . The scribes knew enough to say where the Messiah was to be born–but they remained passively in Jerusalem and did not go along to look for him. . . .

   Alas, what a difference–the three kings had only a rumor to go on– but it moved them to travel that great distance. . . . Tersteegen did not use the circumstance [*] in this way; he uses it — and splendidly — as

How beautiful, how true, and how profound is what J. Boehme says somewhere [*Christosophia Der oder Weg zu Christo* (1731), 387 ff]: In the moment of spiritual trial [*Anfægtelse*] the important thing is not to have many thoughts but to hold fast to *one*. God give me the strength for this. (JP 1:884).

As shall be considered further in the following chapters, the aspiration of clinging to one single thought becomes a central focus of Kierkegaard's counsel on spiritual trial. Yet while the shared concern with spiritual trial between Arndt and Kierkegaard has received some recognition, the potential contribution of Boehme's thought to Kierkegaard's treatment of spiritual trial remains under-explored.[1]

In addition to the above citation of spiritual trial from 1841, Kierkegaard makes several further references to Boehme.[2] As Kangas also observes, Kierkegaard's reading of Schelling's *Philosophical Investigations into the Essence of Human Freedom and Related Matters* (1809) is vital to establishing his connection with Boehme, since "Though Schelling himself never mentions Boehme, Kierkegaard

the spiritual trial [*Anfægtelse*] it must have been for the kings [to journey outwards] when the scribes, who gave them the information, remained passively in Jerusalem. . . . It is just as suspicious when someone knows about Christianity — and his own life expresses the opposite" (JP 4:4757)

* *In margin*: "Incidentally, in reading an earlier passage in the same sermon I see now that Tersteegen was also aware of what I was about to point out" (JP 4:4758).

1   For example, Ballan, 'Johann Arndt', 24. While Keeley notes the importance of Arndt's *True Christianity* for Kierkegaard's view of spiritual trial ('Spiritual Trial in the Thought of Kierkegaard', 13) I would also add Boehme's *Way to Christ*. Joseph Ballan also noted Boehme's relevance in his paper, 'The Absolute's Own Resistance: *Anfechtung* and Prayer in *Four Upbuilding Discourses* (1844)' Presented at the Kierkegaard, Religion, and Culture Group AAR November 19, 2006 Washington, DC, USA.

2   Of note, Kierkegaard refers to Boehme approvingly in 1847 (JP 4:5010): An excellent statement by Jacob Boehme: [See Moriz Carriere, *Die philosophische Weltanschauung der Reformationszeit* (Stuttgart, Tübingen: 1847), p. 621]

Wem Zeit ist wie Ewigkeit,	[*The one to whom time is eternity*
Und Ewigkeit wie Zeit,	*And eternity is time,*
Der ist befreit	*He is freed*
Von allem Streit.	*From all strife.*]

See also the published works: CI, 285, 369, 387; FT, 345 (possible reference); CA, 187, 236; *Letters & Documents* (LD), 184. In this final reference, from an 1845 letter to Israel Levin, Kierkegaard lampoons Boehme's famous vision in the glittering reflection of the sun in a pewter plate, remarking that the plate would have been embarrassed had it known of it.

wrote in his notes — apparently on the basis of his own reading — that Schelling was essentially paraphrasing Boehme.[1] Furthermore, as Barrett also suggests, Boehme's apophatic notion of the "unground" (*Ungrund*) — the abyssal nothingness preceding the divine self-manifestation which is at once the source of all possibilities and the great mystery (*mysterium magnum*)[2] — may be discernible as an inspiration for Kierkegaard's treatment of freedom, sin, and anxiety in *The Concept of Anxiety* — even if only as mediated by Friedrich Wilhelm Schelling or Franz von Baader.[3] To this I would add that Boehme's thinking may be taken to prefigure Kierkegaardian notions of desire, imagination, the demonic, and inclosing reserve — particularly as articulated in *The Sickness Unto Death*. Barrett himself notes the "self-inclosing desire" by which, according to Boehme, both Lucifer and Adam fall into sin.[4] Furthermore, Boehme's "tripartite anthropology of body, soul, and spirit, with spirit being the locus of freedom"[5] bears comparison to a Kierkegaardian anthropology of Spirit as freedom, as the synthesis of the physical and the psychical.

Kierkegaard owned at least four of Boehme's works (*Beschreibung der drey Principien Göttliches Wesens; Hohe und tiefe Gründe von dem dreyfachen Leben des Menschen, Mysterium Magnum*, and, perhaps most notably, *Christosophia oder Weg zu Christo*), along with several works which referred to Boehme.[6] Explicit references to Boehme are, however, scarce, often passing, and even suspicious of his speculative and sensory aspects.[7] Barrett classifies Kierkegaard's treatment of Boehme according to four categories: firstly, as a "forerunner to speculative philosophy" who is thereby vulnerable

---

1 Kangas, *Kierkegaard's Instant*, 9-10.

2 See Arlene A. Miller, 'The Theologies of Luther and Boehme in the Light of their Genesis Commentaries', *Harvard Theological Review*, 63 (1970), 261-303, which explores Boehme's "alchemical understanding of salvation" (278) in his *Mysterium Magnum*.

3 Lee C. Barrett, 'Jacob Böhme: The Ambiguous Legacy of Speculative Passion', ed. Jon Stewart, *Kierkegaard and the Renaissance and Modern Traditions*, 43-61, 43 and 56.

4 Barrett, 'Jacob Böhme', 49.

5 'Jacob Böhme', 48. Barrett furthermore suggests that Boehme's vision of the tripartite structure of the indwelling of the divine spirit in all things is probably developed "from the Lutheran Eucharistic doctrine of the ubiquity of Christ's body, which maintained that the communication of the attributes of the divine and human natures of Christ to one another resulted in the omnipresence of Christ in the created order. Elaborating this theme, Böhme regarded the entire cosmos as the product of the divine impulse toward self-manifestation" (47).

6 Barrett, 'Jacob Böhme', 51-53.

7 See further, Barrett, 'Jacob Böhme', 53-55.

to the same critique;[1] secondly, Boehme is "ridiculed by Kierkegaard for regarding sensory, imagistic phenomena as an aspect of religious consciousness"; thirdly, Kierkegaard esteems Boehme "for his authentic religious pathos and his antipathy to worldliness"; and finally, Boehme may be read as the direct or indirect root for Kierkegaard's notion of "the groundlessness of freedom and the indeterminacy of anxiety" — though here Kierkegaard renders Boehme's metaphysics in a more strictly psychological framework.[2] It is the third of these aspects that concerns this section on Boehme's treatment of *Anfechtung*.

Whereas Luther expressed elements of apophatic theology's interior darkness (*tenebrae interiores*) through a "negativity of dereliction", he also externalised *Anfechtung*, by extending it to the experience of creation, and even, to Kierkegaard's dismay, somewhat politicised his struggles with *Anfechtung*. In Boehme, the *theologia mystica* is revived as both "the negativity of apophasis" and "dereliction" alongside an interior Lutheran piety. Boehme's desire to integrate the speculative with the agonistic derived from an anguished concern with the existence of evil and suffering — which he came to interpret as the manifestation of divine, demonic, and human wrath. Confronted by the violence of religious, political, natural, and interior conflict, Boehme discerned a perennial struggle between wrath and love manifest in the world all around him, echoing in the world within, yet (un)grounded in the abyss beyond. His responses to these struggles stemmed from visionary mystical illuminations — which revealed the hidden immanence of the divine life in the cosmos — experiences, which he elaborated upon in voluminous writings which integrated elements from alchemy, kabbalah, theosophy, Neoplatonism, neo-gnosticism, Pietistic and Lutheran theology. As such, underlying Boehme's speculative "ontotheological narrative"[3] on the origins of evil there resides a concomitant Lutheran concern with the subjective recognition of evil and its overcoming through a struggle (*Anfechtung*) between the self and God, between wrath and love, in which the self is restored via self-negation and mortification to the primal state of equanimity (*Gelassenheit*): the union of the self-

---

1 Martensen's interest in Boehme, which he had developed through Franz von Baader, would hardly have encouraged Kierkegaard. Martensen also refers to Boehme in his 1840 work on Eckhart (*Meister Eckhart: Et Bidrag til at oplyse Middelalderens Mystik* (Copenhagen: Reitzels Forlag, 1840). In 1882 Martensen published *Jacob Boehme: His Life and Teaching or A Study in Theosophy*, trans. T. Rhys Evans (London: Hodder and Stoughton, 1885).
2 Barrett, 'Jacob Böhme', 56.
3 Cyril O'Regan, *Gnostic Apocalypse: Jacob's Boehme's Haunted Narrative* (Albany: State University of New York Press, 2002), 52-56.

will in the divine Will. This personal interior struggle echoes the cosmological divine struggle between love and wrath incarnate in the struggles of Christ (*angefochtene Christus*).

However, I suggest that Boehme's account of *Anfechtung* also contains elements that distinguish it from the prior tradition and actually anticipate important aspects of Kierkegaard's own attempted rehabilitation of the category, some three hundred years later. Boehme and Kierkegaard both, for example, moderate Luther's primary ascription of *Anfechtung* to the Devil. Furthermore, Kierkegaard's attribution of certain "thoughts that try the spirit" (*anfægtende Tanker*) to "imagination" (*Fantasi*) (JP 4:4383) is a diagnosis also expressed uniquely in Boehme. As such, while the Idealists may have inherited Boehme's speculative aspirations — while Martensen was attentive to the system[1] — his devotional spirit has, in one form or another, endured in the scourge of speculative philosophy. Kierkegaard's appreciation for neglected aspects of Boehme's thought demonstrates

---

1 To illustrate, in his 1882 'Author's Preface', Martensen recounts how "during my younger days I was absorbed in the study of medieval mysticism", Meister Eckhart and Tauler in particular, and that this "led forward, almost inevitably, from mysticism to theosophy, and, consequently, to Jacob Boehme." While his initial interest in Boehme "gradually faded away . . . modern philosophy and theology still kept me in contact with his ideas, during my whole life." He was not drawn the devotional aspects but the speculative 'theosophical' aspects of Boehme, calling his volume Theosophical Studies to indicate that he is not simply studying "Boehme as a historical phenomenon, but the actual problems to the solution of which he has offered so remarkable and renowned a contribution, and which he has so powerfully stirred into activity." *Jacob Boehme*, vi-vii. It is notable that even in Chapter II on the revolt of Satan and the origin of evil, where Martensen observes that "Boehme certainly indicates the possibility of temptation more profoundly than other thinkers have done by his doctrine of the two *centra* — the Nature-centrum and the Light-centrum, Egoism and Love" (204), there is no substantial discussion of Boehme's pastoral or devotional treatment of *Anfechtung*. Martensen explains how "It is necessary that even the angels should be tempted and proved, in order that their holiness may not be simply nature, but may be conditioned by their own free-will" (205), but the metaphysical voluntarism that he proceeds to elucidate is virtually bereft of the pastoral concern with the inward attitude of releasement (*Gelassenheit*), which negotiates the path through *tentatio*. Martensen does consider Boehme's 'Treatise on the Four Complexions' in chapter on 'The Church and the Life of Faith' where he observes how "[i]n his teaching with regard to despondency, Boehme displays a profound knowledge of the human heart" (292). However, again discussion of Boehme's contribution to *Anfechtung*, as understood in relation to the tradition of Lutheran spirituality, is again absent. It appears that Kierkegaard's recent plea for the rehabilitation of this theme was not taken up by his surviving opponent.

that, taken in all its dimensions, Boehme's ontotheology is not existentially disinterested, and, as such, need not fall prey to the foibles of abstraction that he would discern in the very Hegelian thought that would claim Boehme as an ancestor.

Yet in the end, Boehme remains, like Luther, another deeply ambivalent figure within Kierkegaard's writings. Boehme represents the metaphysical excesses of speculative Christian thinking while also serving, as Barrett astutely observes, "as an exemplary model of single-minded, God-oriented religious passion". In other words, Boehme stands before Kierkegaard as "the apparent anomaly of a grand speculator of cosmic proportions who nevertheless manifested genuine pathos",[1] thereby fulfilling both/and, which contemporary speculative theology was manifestly incapable of. While Luther's emphasis upon the hermeneutical role of *Anfechtung* for the task of a *theologia crucis* riled against a 'satanic' speculative theology, Boehme attempts to synthesise the speculative and the devotional in a manner which echoes Tauler and the *Theologia Deutsch*. Like Arndt, Boehme is thus heir to both Luther and Eckhart — to both *Anfechtung* and to the *Gelassenheit* — which had seemed to elude Luther, to the macrocosm of cosmogony and the microcosmic concerns of the individual soul *coram Deo*.[2] It is as if the devotional pathos of Eckhart and Boehme had

---

1 Barrett, 'Jacob Böhme', 43.
2 O'Regan explains, for example, that while Boehme's *Ungrund* evokes the *Urgrund* of the Godhead (*Gottheit*) in Eckhart, Boehme also "completely reverses and transvalues the ontotheological values operative in Eckhart's commentaries and sermons" by emphasising the manifest God over the hidden God, contextualised — though not reducible to — Luther's emphasis upon the *deus revelatus* who is also hidden in revelation (*Gnostic Apocalypse*, 72). However, as O'Regan also observes, Boehme's relation to Luther, "which after all was the issue of Boehme's own day . . . can be read at best as tensional, even if Lutheranism is understood to be open to mysticism and speculative bands of thought. To achieve an adequate understanding of Boehme it is crucial to grasp the ways his discourse fundamentally contests Lutheran thought on such topics as Trinity, Christ, creation, and grace" (21). See also Heinrich Bornkamm, *Luther und Böhme* (Bonn: Marcus und Weber, 1925). Bornhamm makes a few references to *Anfechtung* (e.g. 152, 240, and 259n2 where he refers to an experience that is testimony to the psychology of *Anfechtung*: "*Welches Zeugnis für Erfahrung is die Psychologie dieser Anfechtung!*"). See also Heinrich Bornkamm, 'Renaissancemystik, Luther und Böhme', *Jahrbuch der Luther-Gesellschaft*, 9 (1927), 156-197; Ferdinand August Gerhardt, *Untersuchung über das Wesen des mystischen Grunderlebnisses. Ein Beitrag zur Mystik Meister Eckharts, Luthers und Böhmes* (Greifswald: Doctoral Thesis, 1923), Steven A. Haggemark, *Luther and Boehme: Investigations of a Unified Metaphysic for Lutheran Theological Discourse* (Luther Northwestern Theological Seminary: ThD Dissertation, 1992).

been drained by the Hegelian lens through which nineteenth-century speculative logic viewed its system. *Sub specie aeternitatis*, it seems that the *Anfechtung* of Tauler and Boehme becomes dispensable, such that while speculative theology integrated Eckhartian cosmogony it found no place for the darker nights of the soul that Eckhart himself acknowledged. While much ink is spilt over 'the System', barely a word is whispered about spiritual trial. *Anfechtung* thus becomes the shadow of speculative thinking: secret, unacknowledged; yet, as unsublimated, silently threatening to undermine its omniscient pretentions.

It is revealing that the *Anfechtung*, which his more speculative contemporaries had seemingly passed over as a mere relic of arcane devotion in their efforts to go 'beyond Christianity', became for Kierkegaard the secret philosopher's stone of Christianity's truth. The notion that Boehme confronted Kierkegaard "with the paradox of a passionate, pious practitioner of speculation",[1] is resonant with Rudolf Otto's own discernment that for all Boehme's "pseudo-science of theosophy" and confounded "monstrous science of God [*Monstrum von Gotteswissenschaft*]", it is nonetheless irresistible that "behind the theosophy the consciousness of the numinous was astir and alive as an element of genuine value".[2] This numinous consciousness is expressed through Boehme's notion of *Anfechtung* as a dialectical struggle between self-will and Divine Will — which further illuminates Boehme's account of evil in relation to his central categories of the will, freedom, anxiety, self-negation, and the internal divine dialectic between wrath and love, good and evil. Boehme's metaphysical account of evil must be read alongside a deeply interior desire to reconcile evil within the self.[3] *Anfechtung* evokes Boehme's sense of cosmological struggle (the internal divine dialectic between wrath and love, good and evil) while also providing a personal spiritual call to the self-negation of evil (reflecting Boehme's vision of the human being as a microcosm of the universe within whose soul heaven and hell can be found). The struggle of spiritual trial thus reflects the cosmogonic struggle between love and wrath and, as such, the movement from *Anfechtung* and *Gelassenheit* might be read as a cypher for the genesis, agony, and restoration of all things in God.[4]

---

1 Barrett, 'Jacob Böhme', 43.

2 *The Idea of the Holy*, 107-108.

3 According to Berdyaev (1930), Luther's moral sense of evil is transformed by Boehme into a metaphysical sense. 'Iz Etiudov O Ya. Beme. Etiud I. Uchenie Ob Ungrund'e I Svobode', *Journal Put'*, (20 February 1930), 47-79. However, I suggest that it is evident in Boehme's devotional treatment of *Anfechtung* that Luther's moral sense of the self-recognition of evil is not simply abstracted or dissolved by Boehme's metaphysical system.

4 O'Regan asserts that the "developmental dynamism" of Boehme's "onto-

The Way to Christ

After Boehme's death, his more devotional writings were collated and published by his followers and supporters as *Der Weg zu Christo* (*The Way to Christ*). This collection of writings, written in part at the request of his followers, applies Boehme's metaphysics "to the development of the individual's spiritual life, mapping out a novel *ordo salutis*", which binds personal transformation to a "broader cosmic transformation."[1] Boehme's final writings — in intriguing parallel to Luther's late confession of a desire to write a book about *Anfechtungen* — contain treatises on melancholy, *Anfechtung*, and *Gelassenheit* that assimilate the interiority of Lutheran piety within his speculative system. While a much shorter version was published in 1623 (containing only 'On Penitence' and 'On Resignation' from the subsequent edition), this final anthology, Weeks suggests, provides "a measure of the range of Boehme's devotional writings, as well as the impression of his teachings that his supporters later wished to propagate."[2] This once forbidden text became part of Kierkegaard's collection of venerable old devotional books.

Boehme's treatises 'On True Repentance', 'On Resignation [*Gelassenheit*]', and most explicitly his 'Consolation Treatise On the Four Humours', reveal his debt to Tauler and the *Theologia Deutsch*.[3] Boehme's complex motif of *contrario* (contradiction) can itself be traced in its origins to the Lutheran theology of *Anfechtung* — in its sense of *psychomachic* struggle and dialectical tension between the hidden and the revealed — as well as to alchemical principles of opposition.[4] Consonant with Lutheran and mystical notions of *Anfechtung*, Boehme describes an attack made upon the sinner by the 'Wrath of God': the dark and fiery principle, which sparks in the tender conscience threatening, under the machinations of the Devil (the Master of the conscience —

---

theological narrative" as driven by *eros, kenosis, agon* (themes that I also emphasise in relation to *Anfechtung* and *Gelassenheit* in the closing chapters of this work), expressed through discourses, which tend towards *metalepsis* (85).

1 Barrett, 'Jacob Böhme', 50.

2 Andrew Weeks, *Boehme: An Intellectual Biography of the Seventeenth-century Philosopher and Mystic* (Albany: SUNY, 1991), 206.

3 O'Regan, *Gnostic Apocalypse*, 249n56.

4 O'Regan emphasises that "Though Boehme's view of contradiction finds a starting-point in Luther's reflections on the *sub contrario* and possibly also in his view of *Anfechtung* and the suddenness of divine grace, Luther is at best a point of departure for a form of speculation that he likely would have felt pried too much into the 'deep things of God' (1 Corinthians 2.10), speculation which certainly the Lutheran orthodoxy of Boehme's day thought smacked of ungodly curiosity." *Gnostic Apocalypse*, 75.

Magister conscientiaa), to burn the soul to ashes (cf. JP 4:4355). However, the danger of *Anfechtung* lies in the dark abyss between the two sides of a volatile dialectic between wrath and grace. God may begin the *opus alienum* by allowing the dark fire of Wrath to awaken in the soul; but if this darkness is not transmuted into its opposite, into light, then the soul finds only forsakenness in the abyss of melancholy and despair. In light of these tribulations Boehme's treatises offer consolation to the struggling soul, illuminating the sacred hidden path from *Anfechtung* to *Gelassenheit*. In particular, the ninth treatise, the 'Consolation Treatise on The Four Humours', written on request in March 1624, provides "detailed psychological advice for troubled souls".[1] In its composition, Weeks continues, Boehme "created something like a manual for spiritual counselling" in which "Presumably the diagnoses rely on the experiences of the author."[2]

Boehme's counsel on holding fast to one thought in the face of spiritual trial, a sentiment affirmed by Kierkegaard (JP 1:884) and replicated in his upbuilding discourse 'Purity of Heart is to Will One Thing', is expressed and emphasised at various points throughout *The Way to Christ*, particularly with reference to the *passio Christi*. In 'A Very Earnest Prayer in *Anfechtung* against God's wrath in the conscience' from 'The First Treatise On True Repentance' (1622), Boehme exhorts the struggling believer to relinquish oneself by confessing: "I have refuge in nothing other than in Your holy wounds and death. I sink into you in the anguish [*Angst*] of my conscience. Treat me as You will. In You will I now live or die as You will."[3] In the face of *Anfechtung*, when God's wrath burns in the conscience, one is to surrender all thoughts — even the thoughts of irremediable guilt that the devil shoots like fiery arrows[4] — and fixate on one: the *Anfechtung* of Christ that delivers from the Wrath of God.

Through devotion to the anguished Christ, one dies to self-will, a mortifying *kenosis-in-ekstasis* with the Will of God, as Christ prayed at Gethsemane: "nevertheless, not my will but your will be done". In this spirit Boehme desires union with Christ through mutual death,

---

1 Weeks, *Boehme*, 206. Alongside this, *Der Weg zu Christo* "offers advice to the believer ranging from spiritual exercises for the practice of faith (the booklets on penitence and prayer)" and "For the more advanced readers, there are works of introspective contemplation which show the influence of older German mysticism" (206).

2 *Ibid.* 207.

3 *The Way to Christ*, trans. Peter Erb (New York/Ramsey/Toronto: Paulist Press, 1978), 47.

4 "[P]rotect us from the fiery arrows of the evil one's desires, which he shoots daily at us by the curse of God's wrath that has been awakened in our earthly flesh." *The Way to Christ*, 51-52.

praying to Christ to "Strike down my 'I' in Your death",[1] imploring the Saviour to "Lead my soul's hunger into Your wounds from which You poured Your holy blood and extinguished the wrath in my soul."[2] In Christ, the soul is saved from the fire of divine wrath, dying in the death of Christ, surrendering the will to the Holy Will. In this spirit, Boehme's prayer concludes: "Break the devil's will. . . . Be my will. . . . I give myself fully and completely to You. Amen."[3]

In 'A Prayer in and against Temptation [*Anfechtung*] under the Cross of Christ', Boehme implores Christ to comfort him "with the comfort which the angel in the garden comforted You when You prayed to the Father and sweated Your bloody sweat."[4] This desire for comfort is echoed in 'The Second Treatise On True Repentance' (1623). While, in the stance of confession before the divine gaze, Boehme beseeches God to "crush my soul so that it is in fear before You, continually falling on the ground before You",[5] he also seeks divine deliverance from the very wrath that he invites. When one stands before God's face, exposed in the mortifying nakedness of the consciousness of sin, one should seek salvation from the temptation of despair in the "consolation of forgiveness".[6] In one passage, which reflects the singularity of thought which elicits Kierkegaard's admiration (and harmonising also with *The Sickness Unto Death*), Boehme counsels the one in spiritual trial not to "despair of God's grace" but only own one's own self, one's "own abilities and possibilities":

> Let him bend his soul with all his powers before God, even if his heart clearly says: 'No,' or 'Wait. This is not a good day,' or, 'Your sins are too great; it is not possible for you to come to God's mercy.' Then he will also become anxious, so that he cannot pray to God nor receive comfort of power in his heart, so that it seems to him as if his soul is completely blind and dead to God. But he ought to stand firm and hold God's promise as a certain, unfailing truth, and sigh with dejected heart for God's grace and, in his great unworthiness, give himself to Him.[7]

The focus on *Anfechtung* in Boehme's two treatises 'On True Repentance' (1622 and 1623) is complemented by his treatise 'On Resignation' (*Gelassenheit*) from 1622. *Von wahrer Gelassenheit (De*

---

1 *The Way to Christ*, 49; also 35.
2 *Ibid.* 50.
3 *Ibid.*
4 *Ibid.* 54.
5 *Ibid.* 36.
6 *Ibid.* 69.
7 *The Way to Christ*, 68. Cf. Kierkegaard's discussion of the struggle between despair and possibility in SUD, 114 and CD, 107.

Aequanimitate) pertains to what Weeks names as "the untranslatable classical concept of German speculative mysticism", with *Gelassen* having "roots in the verb for leaving and relinquishing", conveying "abandonment, calm, and selfless serenity". The meaning of this elusive concept can be clarified in dialectical relation to the notion of *Anfechtung* outlined in Boehme's treatises on true repentance. As can be seen from these words, "The attainment of *Gelassenheit* requires abandonment of one's own will",[1] which can be realised through the mortification of the soul in *Anfechtung*.

As such, temptation and spiritual both shadow the state of *Gelassenheit*. Following his baptism, Christ is led into the desert where, confronted by the devil, "He is tempted [*versuchet*] [to see] whether he will remain in resignation to God's will."[2] Again, in Gethsemane, Christ encounters the *Anfechtung* of death — haunted also, one imagines, by the temptation to flee from death — overcome by the prayer of *Gelassenheit* "nevertheless, your will not my will be done". Through this prayer, Christ expresses the restoration of the true primal relationship of "resigned humility toward God". Both Lucifer and Adam "broke themselves off from the resignation out of God", following instead "the desire of the creaturely self" rather than the Divine Will.[3] By taking reason for itself, the self turns in upon itself in an autonomous act of self-possession. Such a grasp at oneself is, concomitantly, a turn away from God. The primal sin of Lucifer and Adam is thereby identified as a form of *hubris*: an apotheosis of the self-will, which renounces resignation itself, valorising one's own reason and creating a false imagination. In a manner, which pre-empts Kierkegaardian notions of "anxiety" and "in despair to will oneself" as "the demonic" and as "inclosing reserve" (*Indesluttehed*), Boehme envisions the fall of Lucifer, and of Adam, and of all human beings, as a turning of the desire of the will inwards, away from the Divine Will. In doing so, the self believes that it is willing its own freedom, that it is becoming its own master; but the truth is that it is a divided and self-alienated self, which inevitably becomes a slave to despair (SUD, 68-70).[4] Furthermore, in its failure to master itself, the fatally flawed self-will leaves itself open to another master, namely the devil, who enters secretly into the soul and there builds his robber's castle, a fortress that he is not eager to leave.[5]

---

1 Weeks, *Boehme*, 208.

2 *The Way to Christ*, 135.

3 *Ibid.* 114f.

4 I discuss this further and in relation to Hegel's Master-Slave dialectic in *Kierkegaard and the Self Before God*, 160-165.

5 *The Way to Christ*, 121.

In order to be freed from this bondage to the satanic self-will, "the soul's will must ceaselessly even in this fiery drive sink itself into the nothing, as into the deepest humility before God."[1] Through *Anfechtung* the self-will dies in union with the death of Christ, trusting in God and becoming restored to the state of *Gelassenheit* from which it had "broken off from God".[2] Through spiritual trial, the "self-will dies to self" and becomes "free from sin".[3] United to the *via dolorosa* through the death of *Anfechtung* to the resurrection of *Gelassenheit*, the soul "completely sinks into God's mercy, desires to die to its self, and desires God's will as leader and understanding, so that it might know and believe itself as a nothing that wills nothing except what God wills."[4] In the thrall of its fallenness, the soul cannot of its own self-will will itself to become nothing. Yet it can *desire* and *believe* in its own nothingness in union with the death of Christ, who has overcome wrath by his own *Gelassenheit* to the divine will. Trusting in Christ, "the soul's will must stand silent in the death of Christ, shelter itself" therein, from where it is enabled by grace to "will nothing other than the mercy of God".[5] If it does not shelter itself in this silence, the soul, remaining in *Anfechtung*, "will walk into the opposition and enmity of the will of God and bring itself into torment".[6] In this respect, the devil himself is captured in the abyss of *Anfechtung*, which burns without the light of *Gelassenheit*. In this state, he endures "an everlasting despair concerning God's grace and continual enmity in that He cannot endure Him in himself and has cast him out".[7]

The Dark Fire of Melancholy

It is in his "Consolation treatise *On The Four Humours [Complexionem]*", where Boehme offers perhaps his most innovative and focused account of *Anfechtung*. Congruent with Luther, Boehme here aligns *Anfechtung* explicitly with melancholy (*Traurigkeit*): a melancholy that places heart and soul under attack (*Angefochtenen*). Melancholy can give rise to *Anfechtung* — as melancholy brooding over sin gives birth to an anxious *tentatio de praedestinatione* — yet, as Boehme proclaims at the opening of his treatise, "All melancholy and fear under which man is terrorized and frightened is from the soul."[8]

---

1 *Ibid.*
2 *Ibid.* 122.
3 *Ibid.* 123.
4 *Ibid.* 126.
5 *Ibid.* 132.
6 *Ibid.* 126.
7 *Ibid.* 128.
8 *Ibid.* 245.

Boehme's consolation treatise is articulated via the prisms of alchemical, astrological, and Galenic idioms. As laid out by classical humour theory, the melancholic nature (*Die Melancholische Natur*) is characterised by the element of "earth, cold, numb, dark, melancholy and hungry for light, ever in fear before God's wrath".[1] Its nature is "dark, dry, gives little being [*Wessenheit*], eats itself in itself, and always remains in a house of sadness".[2] Its opposite is found in the choleric humour according to fire: the choleric soul is "fiery, then wrath, pride, the desire for position in might and splendour enter the man to subject all to itself."[3] In short, it is prone to the *hubris* and *superbia* that characterise the devil's fall from *Gelassenheit*. Therefore, "the angry devil has a powerful entrance to it [the soul] for the fire characteristic serves him."[4] The soul is far from *Gelassenheit* and also from melancholy: it mistakes its own fire-light for God's light, and in its "great pride and pompousness, it wishes also to be considered holy."[5] By its demonic and wrathful self-will it is resistant not only to the death-to-self of *Gelassenheit* but also to the self-abasement of melancholy.

Yet this is not to identify *Gelassenheit* with melancholy any more than mystical self-negation is reducible to pathological self-mortification. Whereas *Gelassenheit* represents an escape from *Anfechtung*, melancholy can easily give rise to it. A soul wrapped in the sable mantle of melancholy burns a dark fire, "depressed and frightened as the earth" and vulnerable to the devil who "sifts it with force always wishing eagerly to bring it into the darkness, to trip it into his kingdom".[6] The devil enters the soul's darkness, frightening it, mixing his imagination with it and tempting it to "despair of God's grace".[7] The devil strives to become the *Magister conscientiaa*, the master of the conscience, establishing his "robber's castle" in the soul. "In no humour is the devil's will more evident (if the soul in God's light [love] is illuminated) than in the melancholy", Boehme warns. "This the tempted [*die Angefochtenen*] know well, if they break his robber's castle for him."[8] The devil tempts the melancholy soul, "He frightens it in prayer (especially at night when it is dark), casts its *imagination* into it so that it thinks God's wrath is on it, and wishes to trip it."[9] He seeks to excite fear in the soul by his demonic

---

1 *Ibid.* 246.
2 *Ibid.*
3 *Ibid.* 250.
4 *Ibid.* 251.
5 *Ibid.*
6 *Ibid.* 253.
7 *Ibid.*
8 *Ibid.* 254.
9 *Ibid.* 254.

imagination — causing the melancholic to imagine the wrath of God burning in the darkness of night. He is a hangman who would bring the soul to embrace death by tempting the imagination with the irremediable impossibility of its salvation. "The devil always eagerly casts the melancholy man's sin before him. He suggests that he might not reach God's grace, is only to despair, kill, drown, hang himself or murder someone else."[1]

Against such melancholy *Anfechtung*, Boehme, following a characteristically pragmatic strain in Lutheran spirituality, prescribes particular remedies against "the Black Devil". Echoing Luther's own counsel, Boehme exhorts one not to become frightened. One is even to ignore the devil, to give him no answer. If he "beats on the soul with his *imagination*",[2] seeking to frighten and incite the belief that one is beyond the reach of God's salvation, then one must "uphold a defiant mind against him saying: 'Look, what's this, Black Jack [*Schwarz Hans*]? I thought you were in heaven among the angels. . . . Has a hangman's servant been made from such a beautiful angel? . . . You are God's servant. Fie on you. Pack yourself away, you hangman's servant."[3] If the devil succeeds in instilling the belief that God has abandoned one because of one's sin, then the devil is ready to strike his death blow. In such terror one must "take up in yourself courage against him in Christ" and remind him (and oneself) of the salvific assurance of Scripture, which promises an ever-open door of grace to you, to all, except the devil himself.[4] In other words, one is to remind the devil of the plenitude of grace towards humanity that concomitantly reflects his own damnation. "Christ is in me and I am in Him, and my sins are in you and you are in hell."[5] Reminding the devil of the potency of Christ to retain his flock, one is to resume the mockery, reminding him that while you are saved by the cross, he is a fallen angel, once beautiful, now resorting to dragging around his sack of sin, a vulgar jailer's servant.[6]

Such defiance, even outright mockery of the devil is quite derivative of Luther's own recounts of his own battles with Satan, particularly in the monastery at Wittenberg. Boehme likewise refers

---

1 *Ibid.* 255.
2 *Ibid.* 256.
3 *Ibid.* While Kierkegaard ultimately critiques Luther's attribution of spiritual trial to the devil, preferring to identify its source in the human *imagination*, he does approvingly cite one of Luther's ripostes: "He says to him: My good Satan, you must really let me have peace now, for you know it is God's will that man shall work by day and sleep by night" (JP 3:2526).
4 *Ibid.* 257.
5 *Ibid.*
6 *Ibid.*

to "the stink of sin", which accompanies or even draws the devil.[1] Following Luther, Boehme also advises the individual not to get drawn in to lengthy disputation with the devil. One should use only a few words, preferably proof texts from Scripture, and avoid any demonic exegesis on its meaning.[2] One is to cling to one singular thought: the grace, the love, the light of God that conquers the dark fire of wrath in the conscience.

However, anticipating Kierkegaard's decisive break from medieval demonology towards modern psychology, Boehme's anatomy of *Anfechtung* does not regard the devil as always at its root cause. In a section 'On the Temptation [*Anfechtung*] [Rising] out of the Complexion and the Constellation' Boehme reiterates and develops his opening sentiment: "Temptation [*Anfechtung*] does not all come from the devil (especially in melancholy men). Most melancholy comes from the thought of the soul [*Einbildung der Seelen*]." And yet melancholy is also a stranger to the soul: "the melancholy humour is dark, has no light of its own as the others [do], but does not belong to the being of the soul [*Wessen der Seelen*]. At this time of external life it is only the dwelling place of the soul."[3] Melancholy therefore is temporary and temporal; it is not our true essence, but a transitory dwelling place between presence and absence, between the external life and the life of heaven. Such melancholy thus expresses a sacred longing for the soul's heavenly origin. Indeed, it is often the case that "the holiest souls become thus covered and melancholy", insofar as "God often allows this to happen so that they might be tested and strive for the noble conqueror's crown."[4]

However, this sense of the sacred interior to melancholy should not eclipse the sense of the vulnerability of the soul in *Anfechtung* to exterior forces. In speculating after its sinfulness, the soul that thinks "that the gates of grace are closed to it" has become prey to a "fantasy [*Phantasey*] from the constellation". Subject to the fantasy of the stars, the devil casts his eyes upon the soul and "shoots his *imagination* into it [and] torments the soul yet more."[5] In light of such external forces, Boehme is emphatic that "no one tempted [*Angefochtener*] by melancholy is to think to himself, when this tests him through the humour [*Complexion*], that it is from God's gracelessness and wrath." On the contrary, "It is a fantasy [*Phantasen*] of the humour and constellation." Ultimately, however, such external assaults

1 *Ibid.* 258.
2 *Ibid.* 258-59.
3 *Ibid.* 260-61.
4 *Ibid.* 261.
5 *Ibid.* 262.

can be consoled by an internal resource of the soul. Anticipating Kierkegaard's proof from desire, Boehme suggests that "As long as there is a spark in man that desires only God's grace and wishes eagerly to be holy, God's door of grace is left open."[1] In other words, as long as one longs for God, feels the pull of God, then the Holy Spirit, "the divine desire itself",[2] is assuredly present. If the Spirit is present, conscious as the desire for God, even the melancholy longing for the absent God, then there is inexorable proof that one is not forsaken. The *Anfechtung* of God-forsakenness is a fantasy, and the pain of desire is, according to Boehme's consolatory logic, proof of God's presence ("It is the pull of the Father in His Son Jesus Christ to Himself").[3]

In light of this consolation, Boehme suggests that one must bear *Anfechtung* "with patience and cast himself into His love and mercy." Furthermore, such sufferings "do no harm to the soul", in fact the soul "is in truth better for them, for since it stands in the house of melancholy, it is neither in the house of sin nor in a [house of] pride and pleasure of the world. God holds it by this in reins away from the world's sinful pleasure."[4] Yet the crucible of *Anfechtung* nonetheless remains a difficult and mysterious trial. "Why is it that the soul must be melancholy for a short while and thereafter have eternal joy?", Boehme ponders, before invoking the consolation of Revelation 7:17: "He will wash away all tears from their eyes. As long as there is only a spark in the soul that longs for God, God's Spirit is in the same spark."[5]

Boehme's emphasis upon the consolatory promise of the Spirit's presence is affirmed in his own invocation of Jacob as an image for the soul's struggle with *Anfechtung*:

He battles correctly with God, as Jacob of old [battled] the whole night, who sees or feels nothing but trusts on the promised word. He conquers God as it was said to Jacob: You have wrestled with God and man and have prevailed (Genesis 32:28). You say, 'Which word is that? Answer: It is this: My Father will give the Holy Spirit to those who ask him for it (Luke 11:13). It is what Christ himself said with His lips: He who will come will lead you into all truth, for he will receive [it] from one and make [it] known to you (John 16:13-14).[6]

---

1 *Ibid.* 262.
2 *Ibid.* 263.
3 *Ibid.*
4 *Ibid.*
5 *Ibid.*
6 *Ibid.* 266-67.

One must cling to the promised word, the presence of the Spirit, like Jacob clings to his assailant; to cling to one thought, as Kierkegaard discerned in Boehme's treatment. Elsewhere Boehme appeals to Jacob's struggle as paradigmatic for the desire and purity of will expressed through prayer.[1] By refusing to let go of the presence of grace one learns to trust the love of God over and above the fantasy of wrath. "So that you will not be in doubt", Boehme asserts to his reader, "know for certain that temptation [*Anfechtung*] and dread only come out of the humour [Complexion]". To illustrate this Boehme draws an analogy with fear of the dark. If one enters at night into a darkened room it is easy to frighten oneself, to imagine that there is something present in the darkness. "[T]he fear comes from fantasy [*Phantasey*]." The same is true of the melancholy giving birth to *Anfechtung*. "Thus it happens to the poor soul in a continually dark room of humour [*Complexion*]. It is afraid that it must live in the dark and is always frightened of the devil and God's wrath."[2] Boehme thus counsels melancholy souls to avoid talk of damnation, to avoid literature that occupies itself with the question of predestination, lest melancholy succumb to fantasy and leave an opening for the devil to ignite the dark fire of *Anfechtung*. Melancholy souls should instead meditate on the light of Christ which overcomes the darkness, as love vanquishes God's wrath in the conscience.

Desire and the Demonic Will: From Boehme to Kierkegaard

Boehme's treatment of *Anfechtung* retains and reinforces a distinctive aspect of German mysticism and Lutheran piety, while making notable innovations, which revise Luther and anticipate Kierkegaard. Unlike Luther, Boehme does not explicitly identify the devil as a dialectical 'teacher' in the school of *Anfechtung*: he remains an invader, establishing his robber's castle in the soul, a fallen angel and hangman's servant, to be mocked and derided (as Luther also does). Ultimately for Boehme, the devil symbolises the fall into evil of the Prince of Angels, of Adam, and of every human being. The devil fell from a position of *Gelassenheit* in relation to the Divine Will, esteeming himself above God, sufficient unto himself and a will unto himself. From his fallenness he seeks to tempt the will-

---

1 "God aids a pure, empty, naked soul in prayer . . . certainly is the will with desire to be directed so to God, that it might say with Jacob when he wrestled the whole night with God: Lord I will not let You go, until You bless me (Genesis 32:26)." *Ibid.* 77.

2 *Ibid.* 267.

to-power in all of us. Desire, therefore, plays an important role in Boehme's metaphysical voluntarism and the account of *Anfechtung*, which expresses the cosmological struggle in personalised form. Yet desire is not simply treated negatively, as the desire for self-will that is elicited in temptation. Boehme's treatment of spiritual trial also discerns a consolation of desire, as expressed most viscerally in the fear that one is God-forsaken, which is itself an expression of one's desire for God. This desire for God — while a melancholy and frustrated longing — is itself evidence of the presence of God in the midst of apparent absence, the spark of God in the soul, which pulls the soul back to God.

By anatomising 'the demonic' in terms of a hubristic self-will and by acknowledging the presence-in-absence of an erotic consolation, Boehme also anticipates significant motifs in Kierkegaard. The demonic, for Kierkegaard, is the pinnacle of the self which in despair wills to be itself, such that there is no salvation — "the second severance" (SUD, 109) epitomised by the despair of the devil himself. Furthermore, Boehme's assertion that "The Holy Spirit is the divine desire itself"[1] foreshadows Kierkegaard's account of Spirit as a profound restlessness, a fiery longing for God, which transmutes and refines the 'self' in the crucible of spiritual trial. Furthermore, Boehme's emphasis upon the roles of imagination (*Phantasey*) and melancholy are re-inscribed in Kierkegaard's own treatment of spiritual trial. While the finer details of their views of imagination may be equivocal, Boehme and Kierkegaard both warn that a melancholy imagination can easily become 'fantastic', fantasising that one is under the wrath of God and that to exist before God is nothing but madness, annihilation, and the temptation to a despair that is secretly demonic.[2] Yet just as he moderates Luther's ascription of spiritual trial to the devil, so too does Kierkegaard's notion of the excesses of the imagination attribute the melancholy delusions, which Boehme might ascribe to the devil's imagination to the human imagination alone (JP 4:4383). Kierkegaard further reduces the devil from the tangible external threat that he is in Luther and Boehme (who relies upon the devil for his account of the genesis of evil), to a symbol of 'the demonic' within a theological anthropology and a psychology of the will in despair. It is to Kierkegaard's own treatment of temptation and spiritual trial that attention now devotes itself.

---

1 *Ibid.* 262.
2 "The fantastic [*Phantastiske*], of course, is most closely related to the imagination [*Phantasie*] . . . therefore a person can have imaginary feeling, knowing, and willing." SUD, 30. See further SUD, 32.

5. Before God in Secret:
Spiritual Trial and Temptation
in Kierkegaard I

This and the following chapter trace the development of the category of spiritual trial (*Anfægtelse*), and the related notions of temptation (*Fristelse*) and ordeal (*Prøvelse*), through Kierkegaard's writings, signed and pseudonymous, published and unpublished. Kierkegaard's numerous reflections on temptation and spiritual trial can be both concentrated and diffuse — not to mention repetitive. Insofar as a comprehensive account of each and every reference is not possible in this space, I will attend to key passages and central themes, noting parallels elsewhere in the authorship. This chapter begins with the earliest sketches in Kierkegaard's private writings and proceeds to Johannes Climacus' more formal development of spiritual trial in 1846's *Concluding Unscientific Postscript*. This text, as is well observed, marks a decisive point for Kierkegaard: the end of the nominal first authorship.

It will become apparent that much of Kierkegaard's most sustained and focussed discussions of spiritual trial can be found in his unpublished journals, notebooks and papers and reveal the distinctive stigma of a deeply intimate engagement with the category. In these pages are found some of the most vivid and complex descriptions of the anguish and pathos of spiritual trial — descriptions of a frequently personal and pastoral tone that convey a sense of how this was a category of intense devotional interest to Kierkegaard. Such passages also frequently reflect the consolatory voice of 'soul-care' found in the old devotional books. While these observations are often paralleled by Kierkegaard's published writings on the subject, they also often demonstrate a greater depth of reflection than one finds in the public corpus. At the same moment, they also affirm how interpersonal communication of its interior details is ultimately unsustainable. In the end, the struggle is silent, a secret of the self *coram Deo*.

Life's Struggles

In a journal entry dated 19 October 1835, Kierkegaard already demonstrates an early acquaintance with the category of spiritual trial and its place in the traditional devotional literature of Christianity. In this extensive reflection Kierkegaard introduces defining themes that will resonate throughout his subsequent deliberations on spiritual trial. In considering Christians "who have not so much sought to bring Christianity into the world as to take themselves out of the world in order to live in Christ" (JP 1:416), Kierkegaard refers to ideas that will become central to many of his later concerns (though his ideas on these themes are not yet as developed as they will subsequently become): the tension between spirit and world; the relation between spiritual trial and doubt (*tvivl*); the erroneous identification of the role of the devil as the source of spiritual trial; and the disappearance of spiritual trial in the life of contemporary Christians. In his deliberation, Kierkegaard is avowedly referring to "those edifying writings which are drawn out of a completely Christian life" and "have served to strengthen a great number of devout Christians in their Christianity". From such writings Kierkegaard infers that before one "succeeds in arriving at the Christian conviction, he is confronted by many struggles and much spiritual suffering when doubt arises". And yet, once one does arrive at the Christian conviction, one is faced with further struggles: "he undergoes spiritual trial [*Anfægtelse*], i.e. reason asserts its claims once more before it finally subsides." At this point, reason may rise up as a nemesis against faith, asserting itself against the believer. In this struggle, it is as if reason becomes the *temptation*: that is, the heteronomous voice of reason, as the sophistry of doubt, tempts one to doubt the substance of one's faith.

While such doubt is crucified by its incommunicability, one should also appreciate that one is not alone in facing such spiritual trial. On the contrary, "the Christian has advance knowledge of these objections and problems, before he has heard them, that they proceed from the devil" — a warning which can be gleaned from the older edifying writings. Following the counsel of such books, the Christian can follow the same tactic that Ulysses employed against the allure of the sirens: "plugging his ears, since one must not allow himself in any way to have dealings with them as coming from the devil, for it was thought that the objections were taken care of in this way". Yet merely becoming deaf to such doubt and spiritual trial, as if they were the whispered temptations of the devil, will not suffice. On the contrary, Kierkegaard asserts that such spiritual trials must be struggled with as one struggles with doubts, which arise from one's own self, rather than from an external satanic source. In this sense, Kierkegaard here declares his recurrent affirmation that "I regard all this talk about the devil as a great Christian evasion" — a criticism that remains throughout the authorship, again featuring in his latest reflections on spiritual trial in the year before his death (JP 4:4384). The truth about the reappearance of "what we in the first instance called doubt" in the secondary form "under the name of spiritual trial" is that they will recur with even greater force by virtue of their initial suppression. Such repression of doubt, stemming from a belief in doubt's satanic origin, serves only to cause the temptation of doubt's siren song to reappear in the more terrible form of spiritual trial. The problem is that such doubts "were not dismissed in the first place through debate but through displacement by another force or growth". Rather than seeking to immunise oneself against such spiritual trials, as if they proceeded as a sirenic enchantment from the lips of the devil, Kierkegaard advocates that the believer should actively struggle with one's doubts, that by acknowledging that doubt belongs to interiority, one should confront rather than evade them — for that which one evades, represses, or displaces, as if "spiritually deaf", will only return and take its revenge upon the soul (JP 1:416).

Kierkegaard returns to consider the source of temptation in a journal entry dated Christmas Eve, 1838, at 11 o'clock. Kierkegaard asks his reader, "Have you really felt the consolation in the reflection: God tempts no one" (JP 4:4001). Kierkegaard here considers a divine rather than satanic origin for temptation. Furthermore, he here suggests what will become a vital and enduring distinction between "tests [*Prøvelser*]" and "temptations [*Fristelser*]": "to be sure, God exposes a person to tests [*Prøvelser*] in order to strengthen and mature him", temptations [*Fristelser*], by contrast, "aim to break, because the tempter believes the one tempted will succumb". In other words, while temptations may be elicited by "the tempter", a test or ordeal (*Prøvelse*) may be something to which God allows one to be exposed in order to forge faith in the dialectical fires of doubt. God desires that one should confront and overcome the test, thereby flourishing in the struggle of faith. Temptations, on the other hand, are sent with the lower purpose of inciting failure. God *tests*; the flesh, the world, and the devil *tempt*.

Several years later, however, Kierkegaard also reaffirms his earlier endorsement of the need to confront and struggle with "temptations [*Fristelserne*]", since if they are avoided they merely "come again all the stronger" (JP 4:4746). Such trials of "great temptations" are ultimately under a secret divine governance:

> You, my listener, you who have been tried in great temptations and perhaps have often fought the good fight and conquered — but, alas, when at times . . . you stood there with a consciousness of having lost the battle and looked out upon the desolation which was your soul, and it seemed to you as if everything were lost and despair beckoned to you, its passion already

intoxicating you, then perhaps these words came to mind: God will make the ending of the temptation such that we can bear it, for the ending of temptation is not always victory . . . and your soul will again become sober and awake (JP 4:4746).

While these reflections resonate with an explicitly devotional tone, at the early point in Kierkegaard's published authorship, spiritual trial is also employed to denote an existential struggle which besets any endeavour to live out an ideal in actuality. In *The Concept of Irony* (1841), Kierkegaard refers to spiritual trial as one example of the existential vicissitudes that may traumatise any attempt to express a speculative ideal. "But we forget that a position is never as ideal in life as it is in the system; we forget that irony, just as any position in life, has its spiritual trials [*Anfægtelser*], its battles, its retreats, its victories" (CI, 166). Life reminds the individual of that which the system cannot assimilate. Kierkegaard is here summarising "what he takes to be one of the central differences between a speculative history and an account of personal life".[1] The situating of spiritual trial in relation to a lived ideal is again evident in *Either/Or* (1843), where Judge William's response to the Young Man speaks of spiritual trial in relation to marriage and ethical struggle. In 'The Esthetic Validity of Marriage', Judge William writes of transforming "the outer trials" of marriage into "inner trials", such that "if one wishes to preserve the esthetic, it is a matter of transforming the outer into an inner trial" (EO II, 123-124).

In 'The Balance Between the Esthetic and the Ethical in the Development of the Personality', Judge William imagines one who when he was a young man dreamed of combat, imagined himself in the arena, with frightened "clusters of girls" watching on in alarm, waving their approval and causing him to forget the difficulty of the struggle. "Now I am older", however, "my struggle has become a different one, but my soul is not less proud". In this struggle, he continues, "I require another judge, and expert. I require eyes that see in secret, that do not weary of watching, that see the struggle and see the danger. I require ears that hear the working of thoughts, that sense how my better nature extricates itself from the tortures of spiritual trials [*Anfægtelser*]" (EO II, 287). It is from such a judge that the ethical struggler will covet an undeserved approval, and from whom he will take the cup of suffering, which he will take gladly and, gazing into the eyes of the judge, drink to "an eternal health" (EO II, 287).

Such struggles are, for Judge William at least, the struggles of the ethical life (EO II, 322). The esthete, on the contrary, "does not give

1 K. Brian Soderquist, *The Isolated Self: Truth and Untruth in Søren Kierkegaard's On the Concept of Irony* (Copenhagen: C.A. Reitzel, 2007), 51.

meaning to actuality": he remains hidden, always holding something of himself back in his disclosure of himself to the world. To disclose himself totally would mean to do so *ethically* (EO II, 322). In this Judge William discerns a dangerous affinity between the esthete's and the mystic's refusal to struggle with the self-disclosing realm of actuality and "spiritual trials [*Anfægtelser*]": a "wanting to play hide-and-seek", which "always takes revenge, and usually in the form of one's becoming an enigma to oneself" (EO II, 322-323). Only the ethical man truly struggles with actuality, since "Anyone who refuses to struggle with actualities acquires phantoms to struggle against" (EO II, 323).

Abraham: Between Spiritual Trial and Ordeal

In the same year as the publication of *Either/Or*, the situating of certain spiritual trials in relation to "the ethical" and "the universal" also emerges as a key orienting theme in Johannes de silentio's *Fear and Trembling* (1843) where it is decisive for the distinctively sublime category of Abraham's "ordeal" (*Prøvelse*). In this enigmatic text the themes of secrecy, self-disclosure, and openness to the world are also explored with reference to a cluster of related terms: the co-ordinates of spiritual trial (*Anfægtelse*), temptation (*Fristelse*), and ordeal (*Prøvelse*), by which Abraham's call to sacrifice Isaac can be interpreted. Silentio opens his 'Exordium' with this reminiscence:

> Once upon a time there was a man who as a child had heard that beautiful story of how God tempted [*fristede*] Abraham and of how Abraham withstood the temptation [*Fristelsen*], kept the faith, and, contrary to expectation, got a son a second time. (FT, 9)

While later in his authorship Kierkegaard will repeatedly identify temptation (*Fristelse*) as deriving distinctively from the "lower" things of the world and flesh, and spiritual trial (*Anfægtelse*) as deriving from the distinctly "higher" God-relationship itself, here silentio's use of "the temptation [*Fristelsen*]" remains faithful to the biblical Danish of Genesis 32, which recounts how "God tempted [*fristede*] Abraham" (FT, 10). And yet silentio also elaborates on the biblical idiom when he proceeds in his 'Eulogy on Abraham' to describe how "Abraham was to be tried [*forsøges*]" and that "it was the Lord who imposed the ordeal [*Prøvelse*]" (FT, 19). As Luther had done, so silentio also renders explicit that Abraham was tempted by *God*, that "it was God who tested [*prøvede*] Abraham" (FT, 20). As Luther speaks of this as one of the "temptations in high degree [*tentationum in sublimi gradu*]", which is reserved only for the highest of patriarchs and most perfect of saints — and which therefore exceeds our understanding (LW 6, 134) — so silentio identifies Abraham's temptation as an "ordeal" [*Prøvelse*] which is too sublime in its profound "*horror religiosus*" to be intelligibly communicated to the other (FT, 21).[1]

As silentio develops the category, it becomes apparent that an ordeal (*Prøvelse*) is essentially a sublime form of temptation, higher even than spiritual trial itself—indeed, so sublime as to rise up into the clouds of unknowing and therein be hidden from our understanding. Before such a patriarchal ordeal (*Prøvelse*) we can only fall silent in fear and trembling. Nor can we expect to experience such an ordeal for ourselves since only a "devout and God-fearing man" who is "worthy of being called God's chosen one" — such as Abraham was — "Only a person of that kind is put to such a test [*Prøve*]" (FT, 31). The ordeal is also an ordeal of love: an ordeal of Abraham's love for Isaac, of his love for God, and an ordeal of his faith in the promise that God is love even when God's face is as if turned to darkness. The inalienable truth of the father's love for his son is essential to his ordeal. For if one "did not love as Abraham loved, then" silentio argues, "any thought of sacrificing Isaac would surely be a spiritual trial [*Anfægtelse*]" (FT, 31).[2]

Silentio proceeds to identify "the ethical" in terms of "the universal": that in which "the single individual" discovers their *telos* and that in which one must express oneself through the negation of one's singularity. If the single individual "asserts himself in his singularity before the universal," silentio infers, "he sins, and only by acknowledging this can he be reconciled again with the universal" (FT, 54). According to the Hegelian schema, the universal is the religious and, as such, any deviation from the universal is a *sin*, a transgression of the universal, which can only mitigated by an act of repentance. As such, when the single individual

---

1   The similarities between Luther's account and *Fear and Trembling* are striking such that Hampson suggests that "it is tempting to think that Kierkegaard must have known it" (*Kierkegaard*, 49). Cf. Luther, WA 43.220 / LW 4: "Abraham turned pale. . . . Who would not hate a God so cruel and contradictory? How Abraham longed to talk it over with someone! . . . If God has slept an instant, the lad would have been dead. I could not have watched. I am not able in my thoughts to follow". Quoted from Roland Bainton's reconstruction, *Here I Stand: A Life of Martin Luther* (Peabody, Massachusetts: Hendrickson Publishers, 2009), 382-4.

2   As Kirkconnell explains further, "the emphasis on Abraham's love for Isaac, a social, moral, and emotional bond, is the element without which Abraham's ordeal is only a 'spiritual trial' — that is, a temptation to evil which ought to be repented and abandoned as quickly as possible." *Kierkegaard on Ethics and Religion: From Either/Or to Philosophical Fragments* (London: Continuum, 2008), 65.

"feels an impulse to assert himself as the single individual, he is in spiritual trial [*Anfægtelse*], from which he can work himself only by repentantly surrendering as the single individual in the universal" (FT, 54). As any position in life has its own spiritual trials (CI, 166) so in this sense does silentio describe the spiritual trial of the universal.[1] Spiritual trial (*Anfægtelse*) here describes the state that accompanies the *impulse* to assert oneself in one's singularity against the universal.[2] Spiritual trial here means being in a state of tension with the universal (which is also, according to Hegelian idiom, the religious). Hence spiritual trial means to be in a state of *sin* against the universal: a state in which reconciliation is only possible via a movement of repentance. Spiritual trial could therefore, in this orientation, be called the nemesis of the universal: the force of the greater universal that opposes the singularity of the single individual. Only by the act of "infinite resignation" to the universal is one's singularity negated and redeemed. This requires an act of repentant surrender (FT, 54).

Faith, however, particularly as made evident in the dreadful and sublime figure of Abraham, threatens to disturb this schema by the introduction of "this paradox that the single individual is higher than the universal" (FT, 55). In other words, Abraham may be in spiritual trial in relation to the universal, but this is not identical with a truly *religious* spiritual trial since the religious is *not*, at least in this moment, synonymous with the universal. Rather the religious is *the absolute*. By *faith* he exists in a state of paradox that raises him above, not below, the universal: "the single individual stands in an absolute relation to the absolute" (FT, 56), which transcends the nemesis of the spiritual trial of the universal. He stands, therefore, in a paradoxical and ineffable state of "ordeal [*Prøvelse*]" before the absolute.

---

1 Illuminating in this respect is Gregor's idea that "On a strictly formal level it is possible to describe temptation as being enticed by the lower, without being committed to a theology or ontology that determines what the lower and higher actually are. Thus, the Nietzschean could recognize the religious as a tempting lowness, while the Christian could see it as the higher." 'The Phenomenology of Temptation', 144n3. In other words, for the Nietzschean, Christianity, particularly as expressed via the death-to-self-will, could be understood as the lower temptation of the will to non-entity, while the will-to-power would be the site of spiritual trial — the higher limit which the Overman (*Übermensch*) should overcome in his self-transcending individualism. Taking this further, one could say that the Overman might also encounter his sublime ordeals that cannot be understood by 'lesser' men.

2 In 'An Observation About Something in Fear and Trembling' from 1850 Kierkegaard also that the "collision here is so high that the ethical is spiritual trial [*Anfægtelsen*]" (JP 3:3130).

"It is certainly true", silentio admits, "that the single individual can easily confuse this paradox with spiritual trial [*Anfægtelse*], but it ought not to be concealed for that reason" (FT, 56). In fact, rather than being concealed, "those who have faith ought to be prepared to set forth some characteristics whereby the paradox can be distinguished from a spiritual trial" (FT, 56). The paradox of Abraham's faith "cannot be mediated", silentio continues, "for as soon as Abraham begins to do so, he has to confess that he was in spiritual trial [*Anfægtelse* re. the universal] . . . then in repentance he must come back to the universal" (FT, 56-57). In other words, as soon as Abraham attempts to "mediate" or communicate the paradox of faith he is returning under the auspices of the universal, revealing himself to be "a tragic hero" and thereby effectively disavowing his ordeal as merely a spiritual trial before the universal. But the paradox of faith's ordeal is that it does not repent before the universal; it transgresses it.

The implication of this transcendent and transgressive position of faith is, however, the realisation that Abraham cannot communicate himself to the universal. "This is why I can understand a tragic hero [who remains in the ethical-universal] but cannot understand Abraham [who has an absolute relation to the absolute]" (FT, 57). And yet silentio does appear to have an idea as to why Abraham would be willing to sacrifice Isaac: he does it "[f]or God's sake and — the two are wholly identical — for his own sake. He does it for God's sake because God demands this proof of his faith; he does it for his own sake so that he can prove it" (FT, 59-60). Silentio thus contends that the unity of these two is "altogether correctly expressed in the word already used to describe this relationship. It is an ordeal [*Prøvelse*], a temptation [*Fristelse*]" (FT, 60). But is silentio thereby seeking to identify "ordeal" and "temptation"? To elucidate, he continues with a decisive clarification of the latter term. "A temptation — but what does this mean? As a rule, what tempts a person is something that will hold him back from doing his duty". Where Abraham is concerned, however, the ethical *is* itself the "temptation": it tempts him away from the will of God and back into the realm of the universal. The ethical becomes a temptation for Abraham because it promises to understand him, to render him intelligible, to mediate and return him as "a tragic hero" to the sanctuary of the others (FT, 60).

This is also the *temptation* of the universal: that it is tempting in its promise to render Abraham intelligible by naming his struggle as a spiritual trial. Both spiritual trial (*Anfægtelse*) and temptation (*Fristelse*) are here elicited by the universal; the ordeal, by contrast, remains in the paradoxical realm of the absolute: it "gives up the universal in order to grasp something even higher that is not the universal" (FT, 60).

Abraham's relation to God is not determined by the spiritual trial of the universal, but by the ordeal of the absolute. Abraham, therefore, does not have recourse to the universal without negating his absolute relation to the absolute. As such, in his sublimity he cannot be rendered intelligible to us. In response to the question "Why?", Abraham can say nothing but only "that it is an ordeal, a temptation . . . a synthesis of its being for the sake of God and for his own sake" (FT, 71). Yet in confessing that this is an ordeal Abraham does not render the ordeal commensurate with reason and language: the confession of an ordeal does not translate the single individual into the universal as a confession of spiritual trial would. "Faith is this paradox, and the single individual simply cannot make himself understandable to anyone" (FT, 71). This ineffability is partly what distinguishes the "knight of faith" from the "tragic hero" (FT, 74). The tragic hero denies the self in expressing the universal; the knight of faith abandons the universal in becoming the single individual (FT, 75). The knight of faith is in a perennial, even sleepless state of being "tested [*prøves*]"; but there remains "the possibility of returning penitently to the universal, and this possibility may be a spiritual trial [*Anfægtelse*] as well as the truth" (FT, 78). This discernment again speaks of a hidden interiority that is inaccessible to the other: "Whether the single individual actually is undergoing a spiritual trial or is a knight of faith, only the single individual himself can decide" (FT, 79).[1] Yet silentio proceeds to argue that "a dozen sectarians . . . are totally ignorant of the solitary spiritual trials [*Anfægtelser*] that are in store for the knight of faith" (FT, 80), thereby appearing to suggest that the knight of faith *does* undergo spiritual trials. However, I contend that these are not the spiritual trials of *the universal*, in response to which the single individual must repent; rather they are the solitary spiritual trials of *the absolute*, from which "he dares not flee" but which he chooses to confront in the fear and trembling of faith.

The questions of silence, secrecy, concealment and hiddenness to which silentio repeatedly returns are now rendered even more explicit. The escape-route from spiritual trial is a return to the universal: a self-disclosure that unveils the single individual and redeems Abraham from the anguish of his secrecy (FT, 82). In contrast to Abraham the knight of faith, silentio considers the figure of the tragic hero, particularly as manifest in Euripides' *Iphigenia in Aulis*. At the moment when Agamemnon is to sacrifice his daughter Iphigenia for sake of

---

1 However, ordeal and spiritual trial are used interchangeably in a draft from 1843: "Yet he could understand that Abraham's ordeal [*Prøvelse*] was the most difficult, because, insofar as doubt arose in his soul, it was only about God's love. . . . But these two spiritual trials [*Anfægtelser*] were of equal degree or of the same intensity" (Pap. IV B 66)

the state, he is silent. But his silence is not the silence of Abraham. His is the silence demanded by esthetics, insofar as, silentio argues, it is unworthy of the tragic hero to derive comfort from another. Yet this silence does not preserve him against the arrows of suffering since "in order to be a hero, the hero also has to be tried in the dreadful spiritual trial [*Anfægtelse*] that the tears of Clytemnestra and Iphigenia will cause" (FT, 87). In other words, the esthetic sphere in which the tragic hero is forged is not without its spiritual trials: it harbours its own anguished pathos, its own tears and silence. But esthetics, according to silentio, "has a way out" of this suffering: "it has the old servant in readiness to disclose everything to Clytemnestra. Now everything is in order" (FT, 87). Now Agamemnon can be understood; now the anguish and spiritual trial of the tragic hero can be made known.

The tragic hero, however, does not possess the dread and loneliness known to the knight of faith. He may weep in consolation with Clytemnestra and Iphigenia. But Abraham has no such relief.[1] He cannot even speak since "he speaks no human language . . . he speaks in a divine language, he speaks in tongues" (FT, 114). And yet, silentio asserts, "At every moment, Abraham can stop; he can repent of the whole thing as a spiritual trial". That is, he can announce that he is in spiritual trial and thus return repentantly to the universal: "then he can speak out, and everybody will be able to understand him — but then he is no longer Abraham" (FT, 115). Unlike the tragic hero, "Abraham cannot speak, because he cannot say that which would explain everything": he cannot make it understandable by saying "that it is an ordeal such that, please note, the ethical is the temptation" (FT, 115). And so Abraham has only silence, even before his only beloved son. And yet, amidst the silence, there is one final word that father does speak to son: a word in which he invests his whole being and which contains the secret essence of the ordeal. "My son, God himself will provide a lamb for the burnt offering" (Genesis 22:8).[2]

Job's Secret Ordeal

The sublime and paradoxical category of the ordeal (*Prøvelse*) also occupies Kierkegaard in the parallel work published in the same year: *Repetition* (1843). In a meditation on the suffering of Job the

---

1 A difference resides in the fact that, as Kierkegaard notes in a draft from 1843, that "Abraham did not sacrifice Isaac for the universal. . . . It was a purely personal ordeal [*Prøvelse*] for Abraham" (Pap. IV B 74) and not for the greater good of his people.
2 This phrase as a hermeneutic key to the secret of Abraham's "ordeal" is examined further in my 'The Sacrifice of Silence'.

book speaks similarly of a "silence [that] hides all horrors within itself as a secret no one dares to name" (R, 206). Job is spoken of, in terms resonant with Abraham's description, as "an exception" whose "secret" is that "despite everything, [he] is in the right" (R, 207). Despite the arguments of his friends to the contrary, Job knows *before God* that he suffers in relative innocence.[1] In clinging to this thought, Job continually resists the temptation to become "demonic": a term used in this instance to designate the state in which an individual "will admit that God is in the right, although he believes that he himself is. He wants, so to speak, to show that he loves God even when God is tempting [*frister*] the lover" (R, 207). Such a "demonic" stance effectively judges God by loving God whilst believing that God is actually in the wrong, and that one is, in truth, the wronged victim of the world. In contrast to such demonic irony, however, Job manifests "the love and trust that are confident that God can surely explain everything if one can only speak with him" (R, 208).

The "explanation" of suffering is affirmed in terms of an "*ordeal* [*Prøvelse*]": a category fraught with difficulties for "science and scholarship", which "exists only for the individual" (R, 209). In order for one to discover the ordeal, the event must "get a religious baptism and a religious name, then one must appear before ethics for examination" (R, 209). Job therefore stands as an anguished exemplar of a liminal category — one who exists, like Abraham, at the paradoxical limits of understanding where "the disputes at the boundaries of faith are fought out" in the "colossal revolt of the wild and aggressive powers" (R, 210). Job therefore becomes a living symbol of the struggle between the human and the divine, assuming its most anguished form in the visceral experience of absurd suffering. But Job is not simply the exemplar of resignation to suffering. His *Gelassenheit* is expressed in the name of human innocence and, as such, "Job is, so to speak, the whole weighty defense plea on man's behalf in the great case between God and man, the lengthy and appalling trial that started with Satan's creation of discord between God and Job and ends with the whole thing having been an ordeal" (R, 210).

This paradoxical category of the ordeal is neither "esthetic" nor "ethical", nor reducible to the "dogmatic", but rather "altogether transcendent". Dogmatics can only know that it *is* an ordeal but it cannot

---

1 Yet Job does not know that he is undergoing an "ordeal" at the time since "if he had this knowledge it would no longer be an ordeal for him". Kirkconnell, *Kierkegaard on Ethics and Religion*, 44. In other words, knowing that one is being tested might render an otherwise inscrutable suffering more intelligible. Silence and ineffability are constitutive of the nature of the ordeal itself.

say *what* the ordeal itself consists of since "This category is absolutely transcendent and places a person in a purely personal relationship of opposition to God", which cannot be explained "at second hand" (R, 210). Like Abraham, Job is not merely "a hero of faith" but one who "he gives birth to the category of 'ordeal' with excruciating anguish precisely" (R, 210).[1] The ordeal cannot be immediately grasped and assimilated but must be struggled with in actuality over the course of a protracted and anxious period of time. In being construed in relation to such a narrative, "ordeal is a temporary category, it *eo ipso* is defined in relation to time and must therefore be annulled in time" (R, 210). It is not simply annulled in relation to eternity — as if from the perspective of an eternal bliss the ordeal becomes as nothing by comparison. On the contrary, the ordeal takes place over a definite period of time and tangible experience of actuality. At the end of this period of the ordeal stands "repetition": the moment at which Abraham and Job, each in their own actuality, receives back something that has been temporally lost. No longer are they in a relationship of opposition to God: "the Lord and Job have come to an understanding, they are reconciled. . . . Job is blessed and has received everything *double*. — This is called a *repetition*" (R, 212). Yet this repetition is initiated by a moment that shatters human understanding. For the Young Man this is signified by the thunderstorm, the numinous theophany from which God speaks in the midst of silence:

> When everything has stalled, when thought is immobilized, when language is silent, when explanation returns home in despair — then there has to be a thunderstorm. Who can understand this? And yet who can conceive of anything else? (R, 212)

Here repetition occurs beyond the limits of human wisdom, in the form of *mysterium tremendum*. For Abraham this is the absurdly impossible possibility of receiving Isaac back again. Likewise for Job, repetition occurred at the moment "When every thinkable human certainty and probability were impossible" (R, 212).

Kierkegaard undertakes a parallel consideration of Job's struggle

---

1 Hans-Martin Barth affirms how for Kierkegaard Abraham is an exemplar of *Anfechtung*, whereas "What Job endured as a righteous sufferer was only superficial compared to what Abraham experienced as the father of faith". Hans-Martin Barth, 'Temptation', ed. Erwin Fahlbusch, *The Encyclopedia of Christianity: Si-Z. Volume 5* (Grand Rapids: Wm Eerdmans, 2008), 335-336, 335. Originally published in German as *Evangelisches Kirchenlexikon* (Göttingen: Vandenhoeck and Ruprecht, 1986). Kierkegaard's works do not bear this out, however, insofar as they venerate both Abraham and Job as examples of the "transcendent" category of the ordeal (*Prøvelse*), which occupies another level to spiritual trial (*Anfægtelse*).

in 'The Lord Gave, and the Lord Took Away; Blessed Be the Name of the Lord', one of 'Four Upbuilding Discourses' from the same year (1843). Job is here regarded as "a teacher and guide of humankind" (EUD, 109) who is treated as a source of comfort for the soul in anguish; he witnesses that "the battle of despair has been fought to the glory of God" (EUD, 110). Job walks alongside a generation as a sign of consolation in the midst of desolation: for those who "innermost being groans in despair and 'in bitterness of soul' cries to heaven", Job walks alongside "and guarantees that there is a victory . . . even if the single individual loses in the struggle, there is still a God who, just as he proportions every temptation humanly, even though a person did not withstand the temptation, will still make its outcome so that we are able to bear it" (EUD, 111).

Temptation (*Fristelse*) is again used here according to the biblical idiom in the sense of trial, test, or ordeal rather than, as Kierkegaard elsewhere employs it, to designate the lower seductions of the flesh. Job was "tried" and yet he was able to say "The Lord Gave, and the Lord Took Away; Blessed Be the Name of the Lord". Through the paradox of faith, Job was able to behold God in all his sufferings, "and therefore he did not see despair" (EUD, 121). Here Kierkegaard asks: "does he alone see God who sees God turn his face toward him, or does not also he see God who sees him turn his back, just as Moses continually sees nothing but the Lord's back?" (EUD, 121).

Although Job's ordeal was an exceptional even sublime test, his expression of faith, can still, Kierkegaard suggests, speak to us in our own personal sufferings (EUD, 123). The category of ordeal is an absolutely *transcendent* category which, nonetheless, relates to the temporal nature of human suffering. But while the sublime ordeals of Abraham and Job do not equate to the life of every believer, in their paradoxical trust and hope in the impossible possibility of repetition, each stands as a sublime exemplar of the nature of faith that echoes in the struggles of every human being.

Temptation and the Changeless God

In 1843 Kierkegaard published the discourse 'Every Good and Perfect Gift is From Above', comprising an extended meditation on the words of the apostle James, "Every good gift and every perfect gift is from above and comes down from the Father of lights, with whom there is no change or shadow of variation" (James 1:17). For Kierkegaard these words are beautiful, deeply moving for the heart and even curative for the soul. Whereas Luther dismisses James as an epistle of straw, Kierkegaard describes these words as "faithful and unfailing, tried and tested, as was the life of the apostle who wrote them" (EUD, 32). Kierkegaard reads these words with reference to the preceding verses, in particular verse 13: "Let no one say when he is tempted, 'I am being tempted by God,' for God cannot be tempted with evil, and he himself tempts no one". The words of James, as Kierkegaard affirms them, serve "to warn against the terribly mistaken belief that God would tempt [friste] a person, to warn against the heart's delusion that wants to tempt God" (EUD, 33). The apostle's emphasis upon the changelessness of God is thus taken as an admonition against believing that God is the source of our temptations and the presumptuous suggestion that one can change God by tempting God — perhaps even "With humble prayers, with burning zeal" (EUD, 35) — into an action that does not derive from the divine self-will.

Yet is it not said that "God tempted [fristede] Abraham" (FT, 10)? Such an anxious thought appears in the discourse as the view of an imagined listener for whom it is commensurate with the melancholy view that "life is a dark saying" (EUD, 37). Kierkegaard addresses such an anxious soul in the following:

> in the secret workshop of your thoughts, you said — no, you did not say it, but there you heard a voice say: God does tempt a person. And the chill of despair froze your spirit, and its death brooded over your heart. If at times life stirred again in your inner being, savage voices raged there, voices that were not your own but nevertheless came from your own being. (EUD, 38)

But this despair gives voice to screams, to prayers of aggression against God, rooted in the agonistic belief that one's suffering and grief are so mighty and one's complaint so great and profound as — perhaps with "demonic" potency (R, 207; SUD, 74) — to "call God out of his hidden depths" (EUD, 38). By this violent despair, one seeks to tempt God out from what is perceived as a divine indifference towards one's demonic innocence and into an open struggle with one's anguished passion. "But heaven shuts itself off to such presumptuous talk", Kierkegaard responds. It is only when the individual comes before God, "crushed in spirit" (EUD, 38), in repentance and humility, that one "humbly confesse[s] before God that God tempts no one, but that everyone is tempted when he is beguiled and drawn by his own cravings [James 1:14]" (EUD, 38).

Spiritual Trial and Inner Strengthening

The above discourse treats "temptation" (*Fristelse*) as originating in individual desire and responsibility, leading to sin and death. Temptation as transcendent test or "ordeal" (*Prøvelse*), may, by contrast, possess a hidden divine origin that ultimately seeks to direct the individual towards the paradox of faith. In 'Three Upbuilding Discourses' from the same year (1843), however, Kierkegaard explicitly treats the category of "spiritual trial" (*Anfægtelse*). Whereas the transcendent ordeal belongs in the rarefied narratives of Abraham and Job, spiritual trial belongs, as Kierkegaard observes near the beginning of his discourse 'Strengthening in the Inner Being', to the inner life of every person who "in all ages does indeed have his struggle and his spiritual trial [*Anfægtelse*], his distress, his solitude in which he is tempted, his anxiety and powerlessness when the witness slips away" (EUD, 84).

Kierkegaard appears to identify spiritual trial as something which is known to all — though elsewhere he will lament that "most men have no spiritual trials" (JP 4:4365). In this discourse spiritual trial refers to the anxiety of temptation as well as the edifying notion of spiritual striving — that is, to both the mundane and the sacred, to the lower temptation and the higher upbuilding. In terms of the latter the experience of spiritual trial can blossom with fruits of hope, which cannot be taken away by the world, "because it is acquired in tribulation and becomes strong through tribulation". One who learns the good from suffering "gained not only the best learning but what is much more — the best instructor — and the person who learns from God is strengthened in the inner being" (EUD, 95).

Subsequently in the discourse, Kierkegaard asks his reader to "Consider him, the person who was *tried*, who was tested in the distress of spiritual trial [*Anfægetlse*]" (EUD, 97). In contrast to prior differentiations from the ordeal (*Prøvelse*), Kierkegaard here suggests a continuity between being tried or tested and spiritual trial. As the knight of faith suffered in a hidden inwardness, which gave birth to no external signifier of his struggle, so too does the one who endures spiritual trial often do so invisibly (EUD, 97). And yet the person in question is not forsaken by others around him — whereas Abraham must become estranged from those around him by virtue of his ordeal. While outwardly all goes well for the person in spiritual trial, inwardly the soul may be "in anxiety, devoid of trust and confidence" (EUD, 97). Under the weight of this incommensurability between internal suffering and external success, "the inner being within him drooped" (EUD, 97). At this moment, it seems to the sufferer "as if it were God himself who laid his powerful hand on him, as if he were a child of wrath", and that such suffering surpasses all explanation (EUD, 97).

The withering inner being now, in a despairing sense, attempts to strengthen itself by way of rebellion: that is, by way of attaining to an almost demonic self-consistency, to boast that he is lost, that he is irremediable, even God-forsaken. Following the old devotional counsel on spiritual trial, Kierkegaard does not confirm an *actual* God-forsakenness, but speaks instead to the inner being who believes this *appearance* of abandonment to be authentic. The inner being had rebelled within Kierkegaard's agonist; but now "the inner being within him froze" (EDU, 98) as he discovers "the explanation: that God was testing him" and in this he "nevertheless did find the comfort, that when God tests the time of testing can certainly become very long, but that God can make up for everything because to him one day is a thousand years" (EUD, 98). Again, Kierkegaard repeats a familiar consolation from old devotional books: that God tests believers and that while the time of testing may seem unendurably prolonged, one should strive to understand the duration of such suffering from the perspective of eternity. With this consolation in mind, "he became more calm in his distress. He did not flee the pain of spiritual trial [*Anfægtelse*]; it became for him a confidant, a friend in disguise, even though he strained his thought in vain to explain his riddle" (EUD, 98). By remaining with his intimate confidante of spiritual trial, the sufferer attains a mindful state of "calmness and humility", perhaps even a state approaching *Gelassenheit*, in which his inner being is strengthened. Dawn breaks upon his soul "in the full assurance of faith, because he who believes God contrary to the understanding . . . learned the most beautiful thing of all, the most blessed — that God loved him, because the one God tests he loves" (EUD, 98). Through this transfiguration, the inner being is able to see beyond the "human distinction" between gift and giver and discern God as "infinitesimally" and "completely present" in this gift (EUD, 99). The realisation that this dark gift is love in which the lover gives themselves is perhaps symbolised in Jacob's realisation that he has been struggling with the Face of God and yet he is blessed. Despite appearances to the contrary, the breaking of dawn transfigures the night struggle as a struggle of love.[1]

---

1   In his discourse on 'The Expectancy of Eternal Salvation' in the following year (1844), Kierkegaard makes one brief reference to spiritual trial, again contrasted with the consolation of eternity. Kierkegaard considers that if one read the words of Paul, "For our affliction, which is brief and light, is preparing for us an eternal weight of glory beyond all measure" (EUD, 261; 2 Corinthians 4:17), without knowing who they were written by, one may deduce that they came from a person who was "not tried in the extreme test, in the mortal danger of earthly distress, of spiritual trial" (EUD, 261) rather than one who "was halted on the road of offense and consequently was indeed tried in the mortal dangers of the soul, that he was caught up in the third heaven and consequently was indeed tempted to have a distaste for earthy life" (EUD, 261). As with the earlier discourse, Kierkegaard employs spiritual trial as a variant of being tried and tested. In 'To Need God is a Human Being's

The Limit of Understanding: The Absolute Paradox

This prolific year of Kierkegaard's authorship, 1844, also sees the publication of two further pseudonymous works: *Philosophical Fragments* and *The Concept of Anxiety*. The latter articulates an important psychological framework, which informs Kierkegaard's wider anatomy of spiritual trial and temptation. The former, however, also develops Kierkegaard's earlier notions of the paradox and prepares the epistemological grounding for a more sustained reflection on spiritual trial which will be elaborated by the subsequent *Concluding Unscientific Postscript*. In the third chapter of *Philosophical Fragments* (1844), the pre-Christian pseudonym Johannes Climacus considers 'The Absolute Paradox (A Metaphysical Caprice)'. Climacus describes that with "which the understanding in its paradoxical passion collides and which even disturbs man and his self-knowledge" as "the unknown", that is *"the god"* (PF, 39). In a critique of the tautological presuppositions inherent within ontological demonstrations of the existence of God, Climacus observes that, in the effort to infer God's existence from the works of the god, "Do we not encounter the most terrible spiritual trials here, and is it ever possible to be finished with all these trials?" (PF, 42).

Climacus does not elaborate here on what he means by spiritual trial but it seems to suggest an epistemological limit encountered by reason in its effort to demonstrate the existence of "the unknown", "the god" who is, after all, "The Absolute Paradox". Here, in empathy with Climacus' earlier statement, the understanding "in its paradoxical passion collides" with an unknown, which "disturbs man and his self-

---

Highest Perfection' from the same year (1844), Kierkegaard makes a passing reference to the understanding that one "is capable of nothing at all" when caught "in the maelstrom of spiritual trial, the outcome of which would seem to have to be more terrible than death" (EUD, 323). In the same collection of 'Four Upbuilding Discourses' Kierkegaard returns to consider the apostle Paul in 'The Thorn in the Flesh'. Again Paul is portrayed as "the most severely tried" who "experienced sufferings that until then no man had experienced" (EUD, 331). In relation to Paul, Kierkegaard seeks to remind his listener that "no one enters the kingdom of heaven without suffering. Just to be reminded of it is instructive, lest the distress of spiritual trial come upon one as unexpectedly as a thief in the night, as birth pangs to one who had no presentiment of giving birth" (EUD, 331). The Apostle has realised this inevitability. His thorn in the flesh then "became a warning, a reminder, that wherever a person goes he walks in danger, that even the one who grasps at the highest is still only aspiring to it, pursued by that angel of Satan, whose assault, just like everything else, must nevertheless serve the believer for good" (EUD, 331). The margin of a draft also contain the words: "like the spiritual trial of sorrow — since once one has become unhappy, one really prospers — but whether it would have been better not to become unhappy at all" (Pap. V B 207:6 n.d., 1844).

knowledge" (PF, 39). In this sense, spiritual trial signifies the existential anguish that afflicts the understanding as it comes up against the limit, even the potential ruin, of its cognition. A demonstration of the existence of the god only emerges from a moment of letting-go, from "a *leap*" (PF, 42-43). The "paradoxical passion of the understanding" collides with the unknown; it encounters the unknown as a "frontier" (PF, 44). The absolutely different marks the point beyond which the understanding cannot think, the mark at which it "cannot absolutely transcend itself" (PF, 45). Therefore, if one "is to come truly to know something about the unknown (the god), he must first know that it is different from him, absolutely different from him" (PF, 46) and this difference can only be made known, paradoxically, from the god itself through the revelation of "the absolute difference of sin" (PF, 47), which, as *Concluding Unscientific Postscript* will elaborate, expresses the offence and suffering of spiritual trial.[1]

The Anxiety of Temptation and Spiritual Trial

Whereas *Philosophical Fragments* considers sin primarily in its epistemological dimensions, in *The Concept of Anxiety*, published only four days after *Philosophical Fragments*, Vigilius Haufniensis develops a psychological account of the fall into sin that underpins Kierkegaard's broader treatments of temptation and spiritual trial. At first glance, Haufniensis' account runs in continuity with the assertion of the Epistle of James "that God tempts no man and is not tempted by anyone, but each person is tempted by himself" (CA, 48).[2] *The Concept of Anxiety* contests the notion of original sin as a sinful nature biologically inherited from Adam, asserting that each individual sins and falls for oneself, just as Adam did. The primal nature of each individual is not sin, therefore, but *anxiety* (*Angest*). The individual is born into the freedom to choose between seemingly innumerable and vertiginous possibilities, before which the self becomes dizzy. In terms of the psychology of temptation, anxiety is described as a desire for what one fears, as a fear of that which one desires. Like the serpent's

---

1 Johannes Climacus also refers to how "self-love" might become "erotic love's spiritual trial. So also with the paradox's relation to the understanding, except that this passion has another name" (PF, 48).

2 Therefore the command, 'Thou shalt not' is not yet a temptation but an arousal of the consciousness of *possibility*. God's prohibition against eating from the tree of knowledge "awakens Adam to the possibility of freedom, and thereby induces anxiety in him" (CA, 44). But in this new awareness of possibility, the "prohibition precedes the temptation" and "what emerges from the prohibition is not temptation, but an awareness of the possibility of freedom." Gregor, 'The Phenomenology of Temptation', 132.

gaze, it fascinates and repels — as a *mysterium tremendum et fascinans* (CA, 103; Cf. WA, 33).[1] Looking back in 1849, Kierkegaard affirms Haufniensis' identification of anxiety (*Angest*) as "the middle term in relation to temptation": in fact, "it is the dialectic of temptation", the fear and fascination by which "the serpent's power is precisely anxiety" (JP 1:102). In this way each individual encounters anxiety, temptation, and fallenness on one's own account and inexorably within one's own sphere of responsibility — guilt itself cannot be transferred between subjective individuals since "whoever yields to temptation is himself guilty of the temptation" (CA, 109).[2]

This serpentine ambivalence speaks to anxiety over an object of temptation's fear and desire. And yet anxiety in relation to temptation may also be an anxiety over nothing (JP 1:102). Furthermore, anxiety can also take the more dreadful form of an anxiety over sin, an anxiety *about* evil which lives and breathes among the pages of the old devotional books. In this state, repentance cannot make one free because repentance itself is fed upon by anxiety: "Every thought trembles. Anxiety sucks the strength out of repentance and shakes its head" (CA, 116). Yet, while in such scrupulosity over sin it may be true that "repentance has gone crazy",[3] it can also represent "the sign of a deeper nature" (CA, 116), which is prepared to contemplate the inner abyss of sin. Such interior contemplation of conscience, Haufniensis laments, is a phenomenon rarely seen in contemporary life:

> And as for spiritual trial, it may be explained as non-existent, or at the most may be regarded as a piquant poetical fiction. In the old days, the road to perfection was narrow and solitary. The journey along it was disturbed by the arrows of the past, which is as dangerous as that of the Scythian hordes. Now one travels to perfection by railroad in good company, and before he knows it, he has arrived (CA, 117[4]).

---

1 See further my *Kierkegaard and the Self Before God*, 174.
2 The reduction of sin to a hereditary sexuality is itself countered by the example of Christ's struggles against the trials and temptations of the human condition: "while it is said that Christ was tried in all human ordeals, there is no mention of temptation in this respect [the sexual sense,] which has its explanation precisely in that he withstood all temptations" (CA, 79-80).
3 In a journal entry from the same year, 1844, Kierkegaard observes that "It is and always will be the most difficult spiritual trial [*Anfægtelse*] not to know whether the cause of one's suffering is mental derangement or sin" (JP 4:4586).
4 "[P]eople in our day learn to know so little about the highest spiritual trials [*Anfægtelser*], and so much more about the pandering conflicts between men and between man and woman, which a sophisticated soirée and society life bring with it" (CA, 120).

Haufniensis' scathing diagnosis of the spiritlessness of the age, as echoed elsewhere by Kierkegaard himself, is not tantamount to advocating immersion in the sort of morbid spirituality in which repentance loses its mind, in which, the worm of anxiety devours the conscience.[1] "The only thing that it truly able to disarm the sophistry of sin is faith", Haufniensis prescribes, "courage to believe that the state itself is a new sin, courage to renounce anxiety without anxiety, which only faith can do" (CA, 117). Faith thereby delivers the soul in spiritual trial from anxiety's "moment of death" (CA, 117), from the shadowy embrace of despair that hauls the self down into the abyssal. Such despair can itself be a demonic temptation, a seduction of the abyss which promises to alleviate the self from any possibility of relating to God.

Spiritual trial is pre-eminently described under the rubric of "ANXIETY ABOUT EVIL": that is, the condition in which the consciousness of sin threatens to overwhelm the soul, causing anxiety to throw "itself despairingly into the arms of repentance" (CA, 115), inducing penitent tears that cannot quench the omnivorous flames of *despair*. As a counterpoint to the 'ANXIETY ABOUT EVIL', Haufniensis proceeds with a related discussion of 'ANXIETY ABOUT THE GOOD (THE DEMONIC)' — a phenomenon about which contemporary theology has had almost nothing to say (CA, 118).[2] In the state of sin there are, Haufniensis describes, two formations. The first is the anxiety about evil described with reference to the spiritual trial of anxiety over sin. "Viewed from a higher standpoint", Haufniensis writes, "this formation is in the good, and for this reason it is in anxiety about the evil" (CA, 119); in other words, it is in its desire for the good that the self becomes anxious about contamination by the evil with which it has come into contact. "The other formation", Haufniensis continues, "is the demonic. The individual is in the evil and is in anxiety about the good. The bondage of sin is an unfree relation to the evil, but the demonic is in an unfree relation to the good" (CA, 119).

It is thus in relation to the good that the demonic feels unfree: in relation to the evil, to sin, it feels some coherence within itself — just like the sinner who plunges into sin for the sake of self-consistency, because only in sin do they feel that they are truly who and what

---

1 In a journal entry from 1837 Kierkegaard already warns about how anxiety can tempt one to believe that one is predestined to damnation. Kierkegaard thus urges that one should be very careful with what one says to children in particular for fear that one remark gives rise to "an anguished conscience in which innocent but fragile souls can easily be tempted to believe themselves guilty, to despair" (JP 1:91).

2 On the demonic see further CA, 118-36, 202-208, 249.

they are (Cf. SUD, 72). "The demonic therefore manifests itself clearly only when it is in contact with the good, which comes to its boundary from outside" (CA, 119). To exemplify this, Haufniensis observes how the demonic in the Gospels appears when Christ draws near (CA, 119; Matthew 8:28-34; Mark 5:1-20; Luke 8:26-39). The demonic thus becomes most conscious of itself once it encounters the "boundary" of the good, the liminal frontier of its redemption and salvation. Insofar as spiritual trial represents a collision between good and evil from the side of the good; the demonic might be understood as a collision from the side of the evil.

Just as talk of spiritual trials has diminished in Christendom, so too has talk of the demonic. And yet, while talk of the demonic is muted by the cacophony of urbane existence, its existence is dangerously more prevalent than we may suspect; in fact, "there are traces of it in every man, as surely as every man is a sinner" (CA, 122). That is to say, every person, as sinner, possesses a trace of anxiety about the good, a fear of the good, a liminal trembling before salvation itself elicited by coming into contact with the presence of the good. In this sense, the demonic could also be avowed as evidence that one has actually come into some form of contact with the presence of the Holy. It is no wonder then that Haufniensis notes that "in the religious sphere the demonic may have a deceptive resemblance to a spiritual trial [*Anfægtelse*]" (CA, 143*). But given this deceptive resemblance how is one to discern whether one is in anxiety about the evil or anxiety about the good, whether one is in spiritual trial or the demonic? "Which it is can never be determined *in abstracto*", Haufniensis cautions. "Thus a pious, believing Christian may fall into anxiety. He may become anxious about going to Communion. This is a spiritual trial, that is, whether or not it is a spiritual trial will show itself in his relation to anxiety" (CA, 143*). In other words, a believer may be anxious about going to Communion due to an anxiety over sin, an anxiety over the abyssal depths of sin which causes the conscience to feel unworthy to partake of the sacrament, the presence. Nonetheless, it also desires the *mysterium tremendum et fascinans* of the Holy, desires the good that can save it from itself. The demonic, by contrast, is anxious about Communion because it experiences an anxiety about the good, an anxiety before the Holy (which it perhaps experiences as the *tremendum*, if not the *horrendum* of a holiness before which it cannot bear to stand). It does not wish to be disclosed by the good and so it flees from the Communion, not because it humbly deems itself unworthy but because the presence of the good makes it anxious: insofar as, like Nietzsche's Ugliest Man, it threatens to reveal the self to itself, threatening the inclosing reserve in which demonic despair hides and maintains itself.

In this sense, Haufniensis states that "Whoever is in a religious spiritual trial wants to go on to that from which the spiritual trial would keep him away [in this instance Communion], while the demonic, according to his stronger will (the will of unfreedom), wants to get away from it, while the weaker will in him wants to go on to it" (CA, 143*). Spiritual trial and the demonic are thus, perhaps resonant with Boehme, distinguished according to *will* and *desire*. One who is in the demonic desires to flee from the good and towards the evil (the self-will); the individual discovers that one is in spiritual trial because one desires to flee to the good (the Divine Will) in order to be delivered from the evil.

Around this period of his authorship, Kierkegaard makes several notable references to spiritual trial in his private corpus. By affirming the inevitability of spiritual trial for Christian existence in a journal entry from 1844-5, Kierkegaard questions the poetic idea that "a sigh without words is the best way to pray to God" (JP 4:4364). While such a stance may posses a beautiful lyricism, it really betrays that "one does not dare or does not want to get involved with the religious"; rather one prefers to sigh without words before the horizon of the religious, to "gaze out upon it as upon the boundaries of existence — the blue mountains". Such a position regards the vista of the religious as beautiful, but it does not engage in a confrontation with the sublimity of the boundaries of the existence. By contrast, "If one puts on the religious for everyday use," rather than merely gazing upon it with a deep sigh of admiration, "then spiritual trials [*Anfægtelser*] are bound to come" (JP 4:4364).

In a further 1845 journal entry, Kierkegaard laments the inadequacy of contemporary preachers when it comes to speaking to those rare individuals whose existence has become acquainted with spiritual trials. Kierkegaard invokes "the law that spiritual trial [*Anfægtelse*] increases proportionately to religious inwardness" and observes that "a completely unthinking person is usually free from spiritual trial". The "person who is being tried . . . will struggle and listen and listen" to the preacher but unless the preacher "scrapes together a few points", perhaps from a pastor's handbook, the struggler rarely hears a word about spiritual trial (JP 3:3467).

Again in the same year Kierkegaard passionately questions why "the religious address in these times treats fortune, misfortune, duty, the seven last Commandments, uses the name of God and of Christ — and almost never draws attention to spiritual trials [*Anfægtelse*]?" (JP 1:634). Immediately following this lament, Kierkegaard proclaims what will become three of his virtual statutes concerning spiritual trial: "Spiritual trial belongs to the inwardness of religiousness, and inwardness belongs to religiousness; spiritual trial belongs to the individual's absolute relation to the absolute τέλος. What temptation [*Fristelse*] is outwardly, spiritual trial is inwardly" (JP 1:634). Despite his critique of the absence of spiritual trials, Kierkegaard's published work, *Stages on Life's Way* (1845), makes little advance on the topic. 'Some Reflections in Marriage in Answer to Objections' by 'A Married Man' contains three passing references to spiritual trial but nothing particularly substantive.[1] In the following year, by contrast, the publication of *Concluding Unscientific Postscript* (1846) brings the category to the fore.

The Suffering of the God-Relationship

In Johannes Climacus' *Concluding Unscientific Postscript to Philosophical Fragments* suggestions of spiritual trial as a limit and a boundary in *Philosophical Fragments* are consolidated further and imbued with an intensified fear and trembling. In his 'Introduction' to this vast work, Johannes Climacus reflects upon the dialectical character of the *Postscript*. He wonders whether "dialectical deliberation" may itself be a spiritual trial for the believer — though *Anfægtelse* is here used in the lower sense of "a temptation that he, keeping himself in the passion of faith, must resist with all his strength, lest it end with his succeeding . . . in changing faith into something else, into another kind of certainty (CUP, 11-12). Through the course of the *Concluding Unscientific Postscript*, it becomes apparent that faith cannot become a *certainty* and that it demands a religious sense of spiritual trial that expresses the limit, the boundary against which the life of faith must come. Prior to this 'higher' consideration of spiritual trial, in 'A Glance at Danish literature' Johannes Climacus recapitulates the roles performed by "temptation" and "ordeal" in *Fear and Trembling* and *Repetition* (CUP, 267) — in relation to which he observes that "An ordeal [*Prøvelse*] is the religious paradigm's highest earnestness, but for the purely ethical an ordeal is a jest, and to exist on trial [*paa Prøve*] is by no means earnestness, but a comic motif" (CUP, 263). Johannes proceeds to describe an ordeal as "a passing through", by which he means that "the person tested comes back again to exist in the ethical, even though he retains an everlasting impression of the terror" (CUP, 266). In an ordeal, which here appears to be synonymous with being tempted, or perhaps more aptly *tested by God* (as Abraham was), "the ethical is a temptation" (CUP, 267).

Yet while Johannes repeats earlier discussions of ordeal and

---

1 "The resolution wants next to triumph over all danger and spiritual trials" (SLW, 163); "every objection, every counter-argument of life is regarded as a spiritual trial" (SLW, 170); he also refers to "the terrible spiritual trial of envy" (SLW, 182).

temptation in the Kierkegaardian authorship, he proceeds to develop a distinctive account of spiritual trial, glimpses of which have already been captured in Kierkegaard's earlier writings. In this work, Johannes Climacus, while himself not a Christian, is seeking to elicit an authentic account of faith as "precisely the infinite interest in Christianity" in relation to which "any other interest easily becomes a temptation" (CUP, 21). In 'The Issue in Fragments', Johannes Climacus suggests that Christendom has been fooled by the pastors into thinking that if only one could remain in church all day then one would become holy. But the pastor tells the congregation that each must leave the sanctuary of the church and go out into 'the world'. "Shame on the pastor for wanting us to think that the fault is with the world and not in us" (CUP, 415). On the contrary, Climacus says that he always thought that a pastor was meant to teach humility, to teach each one to "thank God, who knows a person's weakness, that you are not required to remain here [in church] all day long and do nothing but sing hymns and praise God" (CUP, 415). Were one to remain in the church at all times (that is, to attempt an absolute relation to the absolute) then one would not, contrary to what the Christendom pastor expounds, easily become a holy person. Instead of finding a sanctuary in the solemnity of the church "you perhaps would discover spiritual trials of which God allows you to continue to remain ignorant" (CUP, 415).

Despite this concession, Climacus proceeds to describe spiritual trials as an "essential form" of the God-relationship (CUP, 461), situating it in the stance of the individual before God and thus rendering spiritual trial in more rarefied religious form. Climacus therefore asserts that "Within religious suffering lies the category of spiritual trial [*Anfægtelse*], and only there can it be defined" (CUP, 458). In speaking of spiritual trial, Climacus is here attempting to expose "the religiousness of our day, which pretends to have advanced beyond the religiousness of the Middle Ages" (CUP, 458). Climacus believes that "by trying to assign spiritual trial its place" he will implicitly, even ironically, "call to mind that nowadays one almost never hears spiritual trial mentioned or, if it is mentioned at all, hears it summarily lumped together with temptations [*Fristelse*], indeed, even with adversities" (CUP, 458). In fact, Climacus asserts, "[a]s soon as the relation to an absolute τέλος is omitted and allowed to exhaust itself into relative ends, spiritual trial ceases" (CUP, 458).

If spiritual trial belongs to the religious or the absolute, then 'the ethical' (or 'the universal'), according to Climacus' development, is the realm of temptation (*Fristelse*): as such, they cannot be "summarily lumped together". In this respect, Climacus recapitulates a decisive distinction already formulated by Kierkegaard:

In the sphere of the relationship with God, it [spiritual trial] is what temptation [*Fristelse*] is in the sphere of the ethical relation. . . . In temptation, it is the lower that tempts; in spiritual trial it is the higher. In temptation, it is the lower that wants to lure the individual; in spiritual trial, it is the higher that, seemingly envious of the individual, wants to frighten him back (CUP, 458-59).

While silentio had written of spiritual trial as the temptation of the ethical, Climacus now affirms that "spiritual trial begins only in the sphere of the religious proper, and there only in the final course" (CUP, 459). What is more, one can expect spiritual trial to "quite rightly increase in proportion to the religiousness, because the individual has discovered the boundary, and the spiritual trial expresses the response of the boundary against the finite individual" (CUP, 459). With this in mind, Climacus returns to the example of the Christendom pastor who tells his congregation that they would easily become holy if only they could remain in the holy and solemn sanctuary of the church. On the contrary, Climacus asserts, the reality is actually such that to remain in this sacred space would mean to discover, not one's own inner holiness, but the limit of spiritual trial — in relation to which one would in all likelihood "come off so badly from this activity that he would not exactly want to thank the pastor for it" (CUP, 459).

To wish to exist interminably before the Face of God constitutes an almost hubristic attempt to relate absolutely to the absolute. To relate oneself to the absolute in subjectivity is to discover "the boundary" — articulated elsewhere as the "infinite qualitative abyss" between self and God — such that "spiritual trial then becomes the expression for the boundary" (CUP, 459). In self-conscious indictment of his own lack of intimacy with spiritual trials, Climacus observes that "anyone who is not very religious will not be exposed to spiritual trials either, because spiritual trial is the response to the absolute expression of the absolute relationship" (CUP, 459). Furthermore, this sense of resistance evokes a further distinction between spiritual trial and temptation. While temptation comes from within — from inner fears and desires (anxiety), perhaps elicited in part by external objects — spiritual trial originates in the response to the absolute. As such, "[t]he individual is certainly innocent in spiritual trial (whereas he is not innocent in temptation), but nevertheless the suffering is probably terrible" (CUP, 459). In this respect, while temptation points to a darkness within, spiritual trial orients the self, anxiously, towards an Other. Spiritual trial can thus be understood as encountering the numinous boundary, the limit, between the self and a Holy Other. Climacus therefore asserts that while:

Temptation attacks the individual in his weak moments; spiritual trial is a nemesis upon the intense moments in the absolute relation. Therefore, temptation has a connection with the individual's ethical constitution, whereas spiritual trial is without continuity and is the absolute's own resistance (CUP, 459).

Provocatively in light of the lacuna he discerns in contemporary Christianity, Climacus asserts "That there is spiritual trial cannot be denied"; and yet there is "in our time" (CUP, 460) such silence surrounding its existence that one who suffers from it may easily despair that they are all alone in their suffering. Climacus therefore asks his reader to "Suppose that a person with a deeply religious need continually heard only the kind of pious address in which everything is rounded off by having the absolute τέλος exhaust itself in relative ends" (CUP, 460). Such a person never hears the pastor speak of anything even close to their secret anguish of spiritual trial. Untouched by the blithe piety of the pastor's address, this person "with a deeply religious need" finds that his anxious soul remains without consolation. "He would sink into the deepest despair", Climacus imagines, "since he in himself experienced something else and yet he never heard the pastor talk about this, about suffering in one's inner being, about the suffering of the God-relationship" (CUP, 460). Such a person approaches God and discovers a limit, a nemesis not previously spoken about. The incommensurability between one's own religious suffering and the facile piety espoused by the pastor induces a further despair: a deep sense of solitude, of alienation from the collective experience of contemporary Christendom. Such a person has been failed by the pastor; and yet the tragedy is that such a person imagines that it is they who have failed because no one else seems to have been met with this limit of the absolute, nor do they seem to share these secret inner struggles. Perhaps this suffering is a misunderstanding of the God-relationship; or perhaps others *do* experience this suffering — but it is so easily overcome by them that it is hardly worth mentioning (CUP, 460).

The silence that enshrouds spiritual trial therefore threatens to induce despair in the solitary sufferer. As a person of "deeply religious need" one comes to doubt oneself. Perhaps this experience is not God. Perhaps this is the devil (a crisis of discernment, which itself deepens the spiritual trial). This doubt persists "until, with the same horror as the first time it happened, he discovered the category of spiritual trial" (CUP, 460). In discovering this category the dark secret is opened and the light of consolation breaks through the darkness of solitude. But where might he discover this secret category spoken of? Not among his contemporaries. Rather, "Let him suddenly come upon one of the old devotional books and there quite rightly find spiritual trial described" (CUP, 460). Now one can name the darkness and one is somehow no longer so alone within it. Now one finds the consolation which could not be found among one's contemporaries — "indeed, he would very likely be as happy as Robinson Crusoe was to meet Friday" (CUP, 460). Such a person felt alone among the crowd of the church; now they discover, with a dark joy, fellow-strugglers among the forgotten palliative pages of the old devotional books. What then, Climacus wonders, would such a person now think of the old familiar address they had become accustomed to hearing in church — those words of piety which rang hollow for them and which ultimately failed to connect with the suffering of their inner being? Now the address "should be such that by hearing it one would gain the most accurate insight into the religious delusions of his era and into himself as belonging to that era" (CUP, 460). Such an insight into the religious delusion of the era can even be inferred indirectly, Climacus proposes, simply "by listening to a religious address that does not even hint at spiritual trials" (CUP, 460). The forgetting of spiritual trials thereby becomes a silent wound, which testifies to the delusions of Christendom itself.

The solidarity of the old devotional literature may offer some consolation; but how is one to actually endure a suffering that "remains as long as the individual lives" (CUP, 460)? Climacus ultimately diagnoses that the basis of spiritual trial "is that in his immediacy the individual is absolutely within relative ends"[1] and that the relation must be turned around by "dying to immediacy or existentially expressing that the individual is capable of doing nothing himself but is nothing before God". In this "the relationship with God is distinguishable by the negative, and self-annihilation is the essential form for the relationship with God" (CUP, 460-61). As the old devotional books direct their listener, spiritual trial brings one towards the state of becoming nothing before God, which no amount of reading or writing can sublimate.

The struggle of spiritual trial interrupts the self, exposing its own nothingness before the boundary and abyssal difference of the absolute. Only by becoming nothing is one able to be before God (CUP, 461). Becoming nothing before God is therefore "only another expression for the absoluteness of God" (CUP, 461*).Yet as Climacus has stated at the outset of this discussion of spiritual trial, to exist

---

1 Whereas "[a]s soon as the relation to an absolute τέλος is omitted and allowed to exhaust itself into relative ends, spiritual trial ceases" (CUP, 458).

in an absolute relationship of self-negation, conscious at all times of being in the presence of the absolute, would not mean to simply become holy as God is holy. Rather it would be to experience the inner suffering of spiritual trial, for which each person has their limits — beyond which God will not test one.

Such an absolute God-relationship is ultimately unsustainable within the vicissitudes of life. To say that one is nothing before God is one thing; but to die to immediacy and to express one's nothingness in actuality is another matter (CUP, 463). The dizzying anxiety of the primal self before an immeasurable abyss of possibility is overshadowed by the inescapable dread of the self's nothingness before God. Held "captive in the absolute conception of God", the individual is helpless as a bird imprisoned in a cage, or like a fish cast onto the shore, "lying on the ground outside its element, so, too, the religious individual is captive, because absoluteness is not directly the element of a finite existence" (CUP, 483). Yet even these harrowing metaphors fall short of the all-engulfing anxiety of the absolute. Even, "the bird in the cage, the fish on the beach, the invalid on his sickbed, and the prisoner in the narrowest prison cell are not as captive as the person who is captive in his conception of God, because, just as God is, the captivating conception is everywhere present and at every moment" (CUP, 484). Climacus therefore proceeds further to compare the plight of the religious person as like one who is thought to be dead — yet is alive, hearing and sensing all around him but paralysed, unable to express that he is still alive (CUP, 484). Or, the religious individual "lies in the finite as a helpless infant; he wants to hold on to the conception absolutely, and this is what annihilates him" (CUP, 484). The religious person loses "the relativity of immediacy, its diversion, its whiling away of time"; for such a person, the absolute conception of God threatens to devour, to annihilate, to consume "like the fire of the summer sun when it refuses to set . . . when it refuses to cease" (CUP, 485).

Consumed by the absolute, the religious individual languishes "in the crisis of sickness"; and yet, Climacus adds (anticipating Anti-Climacus' later anatomy of despair), "this sickness is not unto death". On the contrary, one is "strengthened by the very same conception that destroyed him, by the conception of God" (CUP, 488). There is no true solace to be found in the confession of such suffering "before human beings". Rather such suffering "ought to be a secret and be before God in secret" (CUP, 489) — where one also discovers a secret consolation in the presence of the divine and in the thought that God understands the spiritual suffering better even than the one who struggles. A sufferer therefore may be strengthened "with the upbuilding reflection that God", one's creator, knows better than anyone "all the numerous things that to a human being appear to be incapable of being joined together with the thought of God — all the earthly desires, all the confusion in which he can be trapped, and the necessity of diversion, of rest, as well as a night's sleep" (CUP, 489).

The equality of love between God and the individual expresses itself through the absolute difference: that is, in the humility which admits that one is capable of nothing before God. Such kenotic humility is not, Climacus contends, expressed in the monastic flight from the world — an endeavor which expresses an implicit self-apotheosis, "an attempt at wanting to be more than a human being, an enthusiastic, perhaps pious attempt to be like God" (CUP, 492). Rather humility, and humanity, are expressed by way of "humble diversion", by going to the amusement park, or to the deer park, even enjoying oneself there. Through such things one discovers that "the humblest expression for the relationship with God is to acknowledge one's humanness, and [that] it is human to enjoy oneself" (CUP, 493). In other words, rather than being consumed by the absolute fire of the absolute relation to the absolute, one should, in recognition of one's humility, embrace the earth (*humus*) itself. Welcoming "humble diversion", one confesses that no human being can become Spirit absolutely, thereby humbly avowing the presence of the infinite qualitative difference by which one's human nature is "expressed most perfectly" (CUP, 412).

While one must evade the lower temptations of the world, the flesh, and the devil, one should also affirm that God creates the space in which human-divine alterity is affirmed over the pressure to become ecstatic absolute Spirit. Here at the close of the first act of his authorship, Kierkegaard has delivered a passionate yet temperate account of the role of spiritual trial and its limitations. However, this is far from the end of the matter. As the authorship resumes, the spectre of spiritual trial comes to haunt the texts even more intimately. Kierkegaard continues to reiterate and develop the dimensions of spiritual trial, while also drawing out more sophisticated accounts of the role of the devil, of "imagination", faith, will, mortification, freedom, and vocation. In all of this Kierkegaard reveals some of his own anguish of personal reflection and disclosure, a strenuous confrontation with the madness and the mysteries of suffering, and, perhaps above all, contemplation of the suffering of the God-forsaken Christ.

6. The God-forsaken God:
Spiritual Trial and Temptation
in Kierkegaard II

Suffering's Dark Secret

[A]s an old devotional book [Arndt's *True Christianity*] so simply
and so movingly says, 'How can God dry your tears in the next
world if you have not wept?'   (UDVS, 102)

The years following the publication of *Concluding Unscientific
Postscript* (1846) are marked by an intensified struggle with the
question of vocation — a reflective turn mirrored by an increasing
concern with the imitation of Christ and a related consolatory turn
to the suffering of Christ. Focussed by increasingly Christocentric
reflections on spiritual trial, Kierkegaard elaborates his struggles
with questions of faith and despair in the love of God, the meaning
and meaninglessness of suffering, guilt, innocence, and hope
in the impossible possibility of salvation. In the year following
Concluding Unscientific Postscript, Kierkegaard published
Upbuilding Discourses in Various Spirits (1847) under his own name.
In 'Purity of Heart Is to Will One Thing' (developing James 4:8),
Kierkegaard reflects on despair (*Fortvivelse*) as the doubt (*tvivl*), or
the denial "that God is love" (UDVS, 101). This variant of *tentatio
desperationis* is examined in more harrowing depth in 'The Gospel
of Sufferings', which descends into "the dark night of suffering"
(UDVS, 238) and beholds the absolute abyss of Christianity's
despair: namely, the fathomless horror of God-forsakenness. Here
in the dark night one requires the eyes of faith which, despite the
shadows that devour all sight, can nonetheless "see God, since
faith sees best in the dark" (UDVS, 238). The eyes of faith discern
the secret that even the spiritual trial of faith's own desolation is
beneficial for testing and strengthening the faith of the believer
(UDVS, 239). Here Kierkegaard identifies the spiritual trial of
apparent God-forsakenness in a manner consistent with Luther's
struggle with the God who *appears* as *otherwise* than the God of
grace. According to the hidden meaning of the symbolism of a
mother weaning her child, which this discourse shares with *Fear*

and Trembling,[1] the spiritual trial of love's absence, even of the mortifying *in extremis* of God-forsakenness, is only ever on the level of *appearance* — though the experience itself may be no less terrifying for being born of appearance, feeling, or imagination.

In this sense, the believer's spiritual trial of God-forsakenness is to be contrasted with the actual God-forsakenness that Christ bears on our behalf. Christ alone is innocent and, as such, suffers in innocence; we are always guilty before God and as such suffer within the context of our guilt, as being always in the wrong before God. As such, only Christ, as innocent, can truly be said to be forsaken by God; we, by contrast, are already guilty of having in some way forsaken God long before we are able to lament the appearance that God has forsaken us. This is not to assert, however, that we are all utterly deserving, by virtue of our guilt, of all the suffering we endure. Job, for example, "humanly speaking, suffers as innocent", though he is, in an ontological sense, in the wrong in relation to God (UDVS, 283). Speaking about such a figure as Job and his relation to God, Kierkegaard suggests that we may say "that God is testing a person" without accounting him guilty "humanly speaking" (UDVS, 284). Yet where the appearance of our own God-forsakenness is concerned, we are to remind ourselves that we are not truly forsaken by God, that there is only one who knows what it truly means to be forsaken by God, and that because of him no one is truly God-forsaken. This source of God-forsaken consolation is the crucified Christ, the God-forsaken God. In the agonistic antinomy between apparent God-forsakenness and the promise of God's unchanging love, Kierkegaard urges the struggler to flee from despair over desolation to faith in the God-forsakenness of God, thus transfiguring the antinomy of love's desolation within the dialectical upbuilding of spiritual trial.

One is ultimately able to recognise one's own tribulation as one's friend because, unlike the sublime suffering of Christ, "*The hardship is not suprahuman*. . . . 'No temptation has confronted you except the human. God will make both the temptation and the way out such that you can bear it'" (UDVS, 303; 1 Corinthians 10:13). Yet there are times when it may *appear* that temptation is suprahuman; that one may magnify one's temptation in order to minimize one's guilt or to justify oneself. At such moments, one's own temptation appears darkly sublime, to the extent that it transforms one "into a creeping thing in comparison with the size of the temptation" (UDVS, 304). Yet, in the face of such a fantastic vision of temptation, Kierkegaard counters with the consolation that "God be praised, there is no suprahuman temptation" (UDVS, 304), only the human imagination, which makes it appear so.

---

1 I examine this analogy further in my 'The Dark Night of Suffering and the Darkness of God'.

The anxious longing for reassurance of the love of God is also addressed in the same year in *Works of Love* (1847). The struggle is, once more, that of resisting the temptation to despair before the apparent absence of divine love. In these discourses, Kierkegaard discusses the human need to test (*Prøve*) love in the search for evidence of its security (here "test [*Prøve*]" denotes an aspect of inter-personal human activity, not a state which one passively endures at the hand of God). *Divinely commanded love*, by contrast to merely human love, raises us up out of our anxiety for divine reassurance, for "when it is a duty to love, then no test is needed and no insulting foolhardiness of wanting to test, then love is higher than any test; it has already stood the test in the same sense as faith 'more than conquers' [Romans 8:37]" (WL, 33).[1]

The Stigmata of Christianity

During the late 1840s, spiritual trial begins to become a more prominent feature of Kierkegaard's private corpus. In a journal entry from 1847, Kierkegaard describes the appearance of spiritual trial via the metaphor of having recourse to only one spring, only one source from which to draw water: "And so it is when Christianity has become a person's one and only spring that spiritual trials [*Anfægtelser*] also begin". Not only does spiritual trial arise when one puts on the religious for everyday use, it arises when one looks to Christianity in all things, relating all things to God. "Spiritual trial is the expression of a concentration upon Christianity as the only object." And yet such a concentration is a rarity, Kierkegaard laments; "This is why most men have no spiritual trials" (JP 4:4365).

The enduring absence of spiritual trials in contemporary Christendom is again lamented in another journal entry from the same year. Kierkegaard suggests that in place of the usual preaching one hears "about lofty virtues, faith, hope, and love, about loving God, etc." that someone should be honest and proclaim "Never involve yourself with God so long that any spiritual trial [*Anfægtelse*] has a chance to begin; if you think about God once a week and bow before him the way the others do, I guarantee that you will never be subjected to spiritual trials" (JP 2:1354).

In an entry dated on 5 May 1847, Kierkegaard's thirty-fourth birthday, there is a reiteration of what Kierkegaard takes to be the decisive difference between spiritual trial (*Anfægtelse*) and temptation (*Fristelse*). While he warns that "the conditions in both" sin and spiritual

---

1 *Works of Love* also refers to offence towards Christ's "form of a lowly servant" as "the spiritual trial in which faith is tested" (WL, 146).

trial "can be deceptively similar", the difference between the two is that "the temptation [*Fristelse*] to sin is in accord with inclination, spiritual trial [is] contrary to inclination". While temptation is in continuity with internal human desires, spiritual trial is an interruption of the sinful will — it opposes the will with something higher. As such, "The person tempted by inclination to sin does well to shun the danger, but in relation to spiritual trial this is the very danger, for every time he thinks he is saving himself by shunning the danger, the danger becomes greater the next time" (JP 4:4367).

Temptation features again in Kierkegaard's *Christian Discourses* (1848). In his discourse on 'The Care of Poverty', Kierkegaard considers how "those who want to be rich fall into many temptations and snares" (CD, 20). The care of poverty is envisioned as a long and terrible road "everywhere crisscrossed with temptations!" (CD, 20). It is inevitable that the rich man will fall into the temptation that everywhere surrounds him. In this case it is a temptation "into which God has not led him but into which he has plunged himself" (CD, 20). The one who is without the care of poverty, however, avoids such depths by directing their gaze upwards towards God. By contrast, the one who desires wealth gazes down upon the earth and, as such, "[h]e is already in the power of the temptation, because the care [of poverty] is the temptation's most ingenious servant" (CD, 21). This is, as Kierkegaard elucidates, a dreadful temptation: "*the temptation* that in itself is many temptations" (CD, 21), that is the temptation "to lose oneself, to lose one's soul, to cease to be a human being and live as a human being instead of being freer than the bird, and godforsaken to slave more wretchedly than the animal" (CD, 21).

Again, the desire of wealth incurs Kierkegaard's fierce admonishment in the second Christian Discourse, 'The Care of Abundance'. As the rich man wants to become ever richer his desire will never be satisfied by the acquisition of wealth — more is never "enough". Even though he already possesses an abundance he still falls prey to "the temptation that in itself embraces the many temptations" (CD, 35). As with the desire for wealth among those stricken by the care of poverty, so too the wealthy who desire an even greater abundance fall victim to the temptation in which their very humanity is at stake. By falling to such temptation, one willingly enters oneself into a sub-human form of enslavement (CD, 35).

In the same year as these discourses appear, Kierkegaard writes a significant journal entry, which again speaks of the anxiety of sin: in this instance, he identifies the "very special spiritual trial [*Anfægtelse*] when a person in the strictest sense sins against his will" (JP 4:4368). While temptation induces the individual to sin according to inclination (the lower will), Kierkegaard is here writing of a spiritual trial that arises when one is, for example, plagued by "sinful thoughts which he would rather flee, does everything to avoid, but still they come". In one sense such a person is *tempted* by these sinful thoughts, insofar as they appeal to the lower will (the flesh). But in another respect this is also something else, since such thoughts are contrary to the higher will (Spirit). From this perspective their persistence is a source of great distress, which in itself gives rise to "a special kind of spiritual trial": namely "to believe that this [these sinful thoughts] is something he must submit to", not by giving in to temptation, but by enduring such troubling thoughts, acknowledging the tension of being a creature of divided desire. The Spirit must acknowledge the flesh, even though it does not will its desires. This is its spiritual trial. The consolation is that in such a spiritual trial one can believe "that Christ is given to him to console him as he bears this cross, plagued as he is by a thorn in the flesh" (JP 4:4368).

Kierkegaard is, however, resolute that such spiritual trial — the *endurance* of this cross, this thorn in the flesh, with the consolation of Christ — is itself "still a kind of despair". Christ exists not only as the gift of the forgiveness of sins but also, proactively, to save people from sinning. One is not simply to submit to sinful thoughts with a melancholy heart, accepting the ostensibly inexorable presence of the thorn in one's flesh, gazing to Christ for consolation, but doing so through the heavy veil of despair. Rather, Kierkegaard suggests, "By faith in Christ he shall and must become the master of these evil thoughts": that is, faith in Christ is not only the (melancholy) faith in the *forgiveness of sins* — for which the cruciform figure of Christ consoles us in our despair; it is faith in the *overcoming of evil* — the wilful refusal to submit to these sinful thoughts. The true spiritual trial is thus not the surrender to the temptation to melancholy and despair, but the struggle against these thoughts, the desire to master them through faith in Christ.

In this context, the mysterious Pauline reference to the thorn in the flesh (2 Corinthians 12:7) can, Kierkegaard warns, lead to the misunderstanding that one must simply submit to the presence of, rather than strive to master, sinful thoughts. Yet one must hold on to the understanding that such thoughts are, like the sensate seductions of temptation that arise from our lower sinful will, in opposition to our higher will — the will, which wills faith, wills to be as one with the Divine Will. In this vision of the will spiritual trial arises as the higher self of temptation — elicited by the awakened will of Spirit.

Kierkegaard proceeds further to a substantial and involved reflection on the meaning of the struggle he has described: a spiritual trial that he warns is "dialectically complicated almost to the point of madness" (JP 4:4370). The dialectical element which brings the sufferer almost to madness is that the spiritual trial "is to define it teleologically, an educational torture which, whatever else, is intended to break all self-centred wilfulness", or the lower will of the flesh (JP 4:4370). Resonant with the traditional devotional literature, Kierkegaard thus regards spiritual trial as part of God's instruction of the believer aimed, dialectically, at the mortification of the lower selfish will. Through the path of self-submission, the kenosis of the will, one becomes *nothing before God* (JP 4:4370).

While it may be true that "No man knows when help will come, no man knows whether it will come in a short time or in forty years", it is also true that help will come and "the help will consist in this that 'the Savior' comes to mean something different to him." Illustrating this transfiguration of the Saviour, Kierkegaard imagines that the sufferer has probably used all his will-power to ensure that these evil thoughts do not assail him in prayer, or in contemplation of God, "assuming that this must be a monstrous sin" to be avoided at all costs. And yet the Saviour will come to mean something different when he realises that these thoughts can be thought in the presence of God without inducing parasitic guilt. In fact, "his salvation lies right here, in his acquiring the frankness to think these evil thoughts together with God before God — in order to dispose of them", for when these evil thoughts are brought *before God* they can be overcome by the Saviour (JP 4:4370).

When this salvific moment will come to a struggler "no man can say". Grace comes in "a moment [*Øieblikke*]" — the blink of an eye — when all that one has longed and sought for "suddenly is granted and comes to fruition". Impatience can itself be an expression of the "self-centred wilfulness", which longs for an end to or an explanation for the suffering — even if the explanation is that there is no explanation, certainly none that can be expected in this life. In this case the impatient one "wants to resign himself humbly to this and still believe God, love God". Such a person is not like those who out of defiance or despair abandon God; "on the contrary he needs God continually in order to endure this suffering and the meaninglessness of it." Furthermore, by having it settled that his suffering "is and will remain meaningless" he "can now concentrate all his energies upon bearing it patiently, humbly". Yet even in this resignation to the absurdity of one's suffering, God still discerns "a little self-centred wilfulness": a self-willed embrace of the meaningless of suffering that is perhaps closer to despair than it is willing to recognise. Rather than aligning himself with a melancholic resignation to the absurd, God "wants him also to hope continually in the possibility of salvation and that in whatever moment it is offered to him he will receive it with the same joy as in the first moment". This religious hope demands "a new obedience . . . which really lets him feel in what sense God is master" (JP 4:4370). In spiritual trial, therefore, one is able to master sinful thoughts by coming to a sense of the mastery of God.

Despair and the Love of God

Significant portions of the journal entries from 1848 revealingly suggest that spiritual trial both may or may not constitute a form of despair and point towards the substantial and subtle anatomy of despair undertaken in *The Sickness Unto Death* (1849). The existential question of vocation, the anxiety of presumption, which tempts one in the prospect of offering oneself to something higher, appears to prey heavily on Kierkegaard's mind at this juncture. In this year he confesses that he has "been experiencing much spiritual [*Anfægtelse*] thinking about how one dares to withhold direct communication" (JP 6:6230). At the time of writing *The Sickness Unto Death*, speaks of a need of "physical recreation and rest" citing "The proofreading of the last book at such a time, spiritual trial [*Anfægtelse*] with regard to its publication" amid socio-economic difficulties, "seven years of continuous work", reduced to loneliness — "yet constantly producing (Thank God! This is the only thing that helps me. Even in these days I have written something on the new book about the sickness unto death)" (JP 6:6134). Amidst such spiritual trial Kierkegaard is in the grips of a period of intense literary productivity, of deepened self-understanding, and, most significantly, a more profound realisation of the love of God (JP 6:6134).

Spiritual trial, at this intense period in Kierkegaard's life, is identified as something that will enable him to understand himself better — with God's help — and, dialectically, bring him towards a greater joy. In this year, Kierkegaard writes of the spiritual trial that "comes in the weak moments when the soul cannot hold to the absolute" (JP 1:488). Moreover, he speaks of the radical demands of the essentially Christian, the unconditional and "absolute recklessness" epitomised by Christ's exacting command to "Let the dead bury their dead." Spiritual trial at this moment means the absence of explanation in the absolute relation: "to the question 'Why?' one has no why — this is precisely the absolute" (JP 1:488). And yet alongside the radical ineffability of the absolute relation there is also, somehow, ineffable joy. Elsewhere in his journals in this year Kierkegaard professes how "God's love overwhelms me still", wondering at how "a poor human being who from childhood on has fallen into the most miserable melancholy, an object of anxiety to himself" has been helped so much and granted so much by the grace of God (JP 6:6135). Movingly, Kierkegaard rejoices at how God "allows me to weep before him in quiet solitude, to empty and again empty out my pain blessedly consoled by the knowledge that he is concerned for me". Furthermore, through this kenosis of tears Kierkegaard also discerns himself as blessed in that God "gives this life of pain a significance which almost overwhelms me" (JP 6:6135).

Since Easter of the same year, Kierkegaard apparently feels close to a moment of breaking through: he speaks of a hope having been "awakened in my soul that it may still be God's will to lift this elemental misery of my being." Such hope is expressed in a renewed sense of faith by which he declares that "I now believe in the deepest sense". Kierkegaard now feels that he has come closer to himself in the realisation that resignation should give way to the affirmation that "For God all things are possible. . . . For it is despair and blasphemy to confuse one's own little crumb of imagination and the like with the possibilities God has as his disposal" (JP 6:6135). This expresses the inexpressible pathos of spiritual trial: the cathartic *metanoia* about which one must finally affirm silence.

And yet Kierkegaard continues to strive to give expression to his struggles, wondering, "Have I not arrogated too much to myself? Should I not have discussed this matter with others?" (JP 1:610). At this moment one begins to doubt that one has perhaps taken on something which one has no real claim to, that offering one's life is merely a manifestation of presumptuousness — one must, nonetheless, confront rather than flee the doubts which arise within oneself. This is a spiritual trial, which, according to the dialectical rubric of spiritual trial, one must press on with — only now one proceeds with the humility that spiritual trial instils within one's soul (JP 1:610). Writing directly about his own vocation and devotion to ideas, Kierkegaard confesses in the same year that while "I am aware of how much has been granted to me" he is prevented from falling into arrogance and pride by "an enormous responsibility, heavy, heavy memories, many, many trials. Of all these things I cannot speak. . . . Before God I feel less than a sparrow, or just as insignificant" (JP 1:646). And yet, as Kierkegaard also observes in the same year, "What is said of the sparrows is literally true of men: God knows each single one" — no one is insignificant before God and as such it is the task "to maintain longer and longer the thought of God-present-with-me" (JP 2:2007). However, this "God-relationship of singleness in the single individual" can become "diseased" — become melancholy, for example, such that "the middle term of sociality or of 'the other person' is temporarily postulated" for the sake of temperance (JP 2:2007).

There are, however, times when this "disease" can also be "a spiritual trial [*Anfægtelse*], and then it does not at all follow that a person should yield to it and go seeking company [as Luther advises] but should struggle against it and bring love of God to glow as it should." One should struggle against this spiritual trial since its origins derive from the moment when "the deep underlying feeling of infinite unworthiness basic to every true God-relationship becomes overpowering, is not transfigured into a greater joy in God, but oppresses one" (JP 2:2008). In this sense, the potential for spiritual trial is latent within the fundaments of the authentic God-relationship: it arises when infinite unworthiness overpowers all else to the point at which the struggler fears both self and God. The extent of one's sin looms dark and terrible before the eye of the imagination. One is, as *The Sickness Unto Death* elucidates, tempted to despair of/over the forgiveness of sins: "'That a sparrow can live is comprehensible; it does not know that it exists before God. But to know that one exists before God, and then not instantly go mad or sink into nothingness!'" (SUD, 32). The temptation is then to flee from this presence, perhaps to lose oneself within the crowd so that God can no longer see one, or at least no longer see just oneself.

"But a person is not to give in", Kierkegaard affirms, "he is to fight against it, thank God that God has *commanded* that one *ought* to pray to him, for otherwise it is hardly possible to force one's way through the spiritual trial [*Anfægtelse*]." Just as God *commands* love so God has *commanded* prayer. In praying to God, as God has commanded one ought to do, one is to embrace an apophatic veracity: despite *imagining* that one is a sinful object of wrath before God one is "to remember that God is love, the God of patience and consolation, and that God is not one who adopts vain titles but is completely different from anything I am able to comprehend of what he says himself to be" (JP 2:2008).

Given these references to spiritual trial in 1848, it is perhaps surprising that the explicit terminology of spiritual trial does not appear in *The Sickness Unto Death* — especially since much of what is described therein is elsewhere (e.g. JP 4:4370) identified by Kierkegaard as a form of spiritual trial. To a certain extent, it could be argued that the whole book deals with spiritual trial: namely, the spiritual trial of despair. But despair also brings us into contact with another of Kierkegaard's distinctive categories, a category which, as *The Concept of Anxiety* has already disclosed, "may have a deceptive resemblance to a spiritual trial [*Anfægtelse*]" (CA, 143*): namely, *the demonic*. Expressing the self *Incurvatus in se*, the demonic responds to the presence of the good by turning away from it and retreating into its own inclosing reserve. The demonic self becomes anxious before God; but the demonic self refuses to become nothing before God, surrendering its will in harmony with the Divine Will.

The Sickness Unto Death classifies this as "In Despair to Will to Be Oneself: Defiance": a "despairing misuse of the eternal within the self" (SUD, 67). This is the self that does not wish to become itself by first losing itself, by becoming nothing before God. It wishes to master and create itself: "like Prometheus stealing fire from the gods" it steals the thought of itself from God (SUD, 68). Yet in becoming master over itself the self soon discovers that it is "a king without a country, actually ruling over nothing; his position, his sovereignty, is subordinate to the dialectic that rebellion is legitimate at any moment" (SUD, 69). The self desires to fashion itself, to create and rule over itself; but in the end all it has discovered is an inner abyss, an enigma — that is, a self which essentially dissolves at the moment that it grasps in the desire to take hold of itself. While the demonic, in its anxiety about the good, flees from God, the demonic which wills in despair desires, by contrast, to force itself defiantly upon "the power that established it" (SUD, 73). In this sense, demonic despair seeks to struggle with God, "for spite wants to force itself upon it, to obtrude defiantly upon it, wants to adhere to it out of malice" (SUD, 73).

Yet ultimately as the good flees from temptation so the demonic flees from grace. As sin breaks with the good, so "the second severance" seeks to break with the possibility of repentance itself (SUD, 109). Despair over sin can, nonetheless, gives itself "the appearance of something good" (SUD, 111). To illustrate this deceptiveness, Anti-Climacus gives the example of a person who has been addicted to a particular sin, which he has managed to resist for a long time. Then one day he fails to resist, falls into temptation and commits this sin. "[T]he depression that sets in", Anti-Climacus suggests, "is by no means always sorrow over sin" (SUD, 111). On the contrary, it may signify a "bitterness against Governance", a displacement of responsibility for the fact that he has fallen into temptation (SUD, 111). Even though he declares "I will never forgive myself", he is actually betraying a pride over all the times that he had managed to resist the temptation (SUD, 111-12). His melancholy over falling into temptation represents "a movement away from God, a secret selfishness and pride", which is in contrast to the humble response to succumbing to temptation: to thank God that he has been helped in resisting temptation for so long, before God "humbling himself under the recollection of what he has been" (SUD, 112). As is often the tendency in Kierkegaard's authorship, Anti-Climacus finds this position most appositely demonstrated in the older and better devotional literature:

> Here, as everywhere, is what the old devotional books explain
> so profoundly, so experientially, so instructively. They teach

that God sometimes lets the believer stumble and fall in some temptation or other, precisely in order to humble him and thereby to establish him better in the good. (SUD, 112)

Becoming a self *before God*, becoming nothing and resting transparently in God, by contrast to the demonic, therefore requires the willingness to surrender the nothingness of the 'self' (SUD, 110). *Before God* designates the position of willingness to go beyond one's demonic inclosing reserve, to go beyond oneself in becoming nothing (*kenosis-in-ekstasis*), and there perhaps to encounter spiritual trial: the limit of the infinite qualitative difference, which nonetheless opens the self to a Holy Otherness beyond itself. And there, beyond despair, one must be willing to become nothing before God in the transparency of Spirit. The nothingness of the self which in despair wills to be itself gives way to the becoming nothing of the self before God, the self resting transparently *in* God. In despair to will to be oneself gives way, via the trials of restless Spirit, to the rest of *Gelassenheit* — "nevertheless, not my will but your will be done".

The problem of reconciling the divided human will with the Divine Will is also considered in Kierkegaard's discourses from this period. On 14 May 1849 (two months before the publication of *The Sickness Unto Death* on 30 July), Kierkegaard published under his own name a collection of three discourses under the title of *The Lily in the Field and the Bird of the Air* (translated into English as part of the collection of discourses from 1849-51, *Without Authority*). Here Kierkegaard encourages his reader to heed "the Gospel's instruction to learn obedience from the lily and the bird" (WA, 32). If one learns such obedience then one can fulfil the line from the Lord's prayer, "'Your will be done, as in heaven also on earth,' since by unconditional obedience your will is one with God's will and therefore God's will is done by you on earth as it is in heaven" (WA, 32). While this union of the will with the Divine Will does not fathom the mystical depths of *Gelassenheit*, it does here serve as protection against temptation. When one comes to pray "Lead us not into temptation", one should aspire to an unconditional obedience free from all ambivalence, since "if there is no ambivalence in you, then you are sheer simplicity before God" (WA, 32).

Kierkegaard describes this *simplicity before God* as delivering the individual from the gaze of Satan — a glance which searches for the slightest shade of ambivalence, through which temptation attaches itself, though "temptation does not actually come from him" (WA, 33). In order to be safe from the devil one must, therefore, lose all ambivalence and unite the will with the Divine Will. One must hide, perfectly still, in perfect simplicity, *in God* since "the person who by unconditional obedience hides in God is unconditionally secure; from his secure hiding place he can see the devil, but the devil cannot see him" (WA, 33). The devil cannot behold simplicity and so his "glittering gaze that looks as if it could penetrate earth and sea and the most hidden secrets of the heart" becomes blind; and if the devil — the one "who spreads the snare of temptation" — is blind to a person who "by unconditional obedience is hidden in God, then of course there is no temptation for him, because 'God tempts no one' [James 1:13]" (WA, 33).

The theme of temptation returns, this time along with spiritual trial, in one of Kierkegaard's *Three Discourses at the Communion* in Fridays published on 14 November 1849 (also published in *Without Authority*). In the discourse on 'The High Priest', Kierkegaard begins with the words of Hebrews 4:15: "We have not a high priest who is unable to have sympathy with our weaknesses, but one who has been tested in all things in the same way, yet without sin" (WA, 116). As preparation for going to the communion table, Kierkegaard advances the consolation that Jesus *"put himself completely in your place; whoever you are, you who are being tested in temptation and spiritual trial, he is able to put himself completely in your place"* (WA, 120; italics original). No matter what temptation one is enduring there is unity with Christ: whether one is "tempted to fall away from God" one should know that "he too was tempted in this way"; or whether one is "tempted in the great moment of decision, when it is a matter of renouncing everything" then one should recall that "so also was he"; if one endures the temptation of "being abandoned by humanity" then one should rest assured that "so also was he tempted" (WA, 121).

Furthermore, Christ's temptation and trials are of such anguish that they even go beyond that which any human being has endured — they even encompass the dreadful and unknowable moment of God-forsakenness. Here Kierkegaard reiterates the infinite qualitative difference between divine and human suffering, this time invoking the explicit terminology of spiritual trial: "If it is — but no, surely no human being has experienced that spiritual trial, the spiritual trial of being abandoned by God — but he was tempted in that way (WA, 121). Moving freely between the idiom of temptation and spiritual trial, Kierkegaard thus urges his listener to remember that Christ has endured such tribulations, and therefore not to "become silent in despair, as if the temptation were suprahuman and no one could understand it" (WA, 121). As long as one is in temptation, then one will be tempted to despair of the enormity of temptation. Temptation itself is a deceiver. Only by holding out in temptation is the proper perspective attained (WA, 121). To hold out in temptation and spiritual trial is to hold on to Christ, to the one who overcame all trials and temptations and who therefore is the "only one who in truth knows exactly the magnitude of every temptation and can put himself completely in the place of everyone who is tempted: he who himself was tested in all things in the same way — tempted, but who held out in every temptation" (WA, 122).

Yet, as the only one who overcame all temptation Christ retains a decisive difference from us. *"He put himself completely in your place, in every respect was tested in all things in the same way* — **yet without sin**" (WA, 123; italics and bold original). In this final caveat lies the infinite qualitative difference that 'The Gospel of Sufferings' invokes. In this respect "he cannot put himself completely in your place, he, the Holy One — how could it be possible!". The difference between God in heaven and humanity on earth is itself infinite; in which case "the difference between the Holy One and the sinner is infinitely greater" (WA, 123). And yet, because Christ is a High Priest without sin, he is able not only to understand but to stand in our place, to suffer in our place, and make the satisfaction of Atonement in our place.

The Betrayal of Christianity and the Disappearance of Spiritual Trial

These discourses, along with *The Sickness Unto Death*, emerge from a period of profound spiritual awakening and literary productivity. The year 1849 also contains the highest concentration of journal entries on spiritual trial, even though the publications from this period contain few explicit instances of the actual idiom of *Anfægtelse* — despite its importance to prominent themes in these works. It is in this year that Kierkegaard mourns the disappearance of spiritual trials in contemporary Christendom (JP 6:6459; JP 4:4372). Kierkegaard insists, that "in our time people have no idea at all of spiritual trial" such that anyone who would suffer from it "would also be regarded as a very extraordinary sinner" (JP 4:4023). To demonstrate that the absence of spiritual trial is an indirect proof of a lack of religiousness Kierkegaard points to the words of the preachers: "*every* man ought to relate himself to God in *all things*, ought to refer *everything* to God", where "every man" really means "John Doe", or no one, and "everything" merely means "X", or nothing. The words of the preacher are too vague and really amount to no one and nothing. "In this way, to be sure, one does not discover spiritual; and nothing more is done now — at most it is preached about" (JP 4:4372).

Yet if one were to take the words seriously and to relate oneself in one's specificity and actuality to God then the story would be quite different. Spiritual trial, as Kierkegaard here defines it, "is the divine repulsion in the *quid nimis* [anything in excess] and can never fail to appear if one is to exist religiously, consequently as an actual, definite, particular man", rather than in terms of *every man, all things,* and *everything*. Kierkegaard is explicit: spiritual trial will always appear if one exists religiously. To illustrate his point, Kierkegaard offers himself up as the example:

> I, Søren Aabye Kierkegaard, thirty-five years old, of slight build, master of arts, brother-in-law of businessman Lund, living on such and such a street — in short, this whole concretion of trivialities, that I dare relate myself to God, refer all the affairs of my life to him. No man has ever lived who has truly done this without discovering with horror the horror of spiritual trial, that he might be venturing too boldly, that the whole thing might really be lunacy (JP 4:4372).

If one dares to refer all one's concrete trivialities to God then one will encounter "the horror of spiritual trial" — a horror, even a potential madness, from which one is spared by the abstraction and generality of the preacher's words that "*every* man *always* ought to refer *all things* to God". Kierkegaard thus ventures that every individual who enters into one's hidden place, alone before God, and thinks of one's concrete particularities along with the thought of God, that one will surely encounter the infinite qualitative difference between the self and God — an abyssal difference that expresses itself in the dread of spiritual trial (JP 4:4372).

Having established the inevitability of spiritual trial in relating oneself to God, Kierkegaard proceeds to invoke and correct the esteemed opinion of Luther himself: "Luther says that as soon as Christ has come on board the storm immediately begins; this storm is spiritual trial, which Luther attributes to the devil." But for Kierkegaard, Luther's attribution of spiritual trial to the devil, like that of the old devotional writings, is "more childish than true" (JP 4:4372). Rather than situating spiritual trial between the individual and the devil, as Luther and much of the old devotional literature had done, Kierkegaard here reaffirms his earliest suspicions and makes an important innovation: he situates the tension of spiritual trial solely *between the individual and God* — as an expression of the infinite qualitative difference between the human and the divine, elicited by the existential endeavour to relate the finite to the infinite. At the intense moment of spiritual trial, the relationship between the finite and the infinite simply seems to be too much: "it is spiritual trial because it seems to the person himself as if the relationship were stretched too tightly, as if he were venturing too boldly in literally involving himself personally with God and Christ" (JP 4:4372). And yet, whereas one flees from temptation, one is to press on in spiritual trial, to become nothing before God.

However, this dialectic between temptation and spiritual trial is itself mindful of the needs of each individual. Kierkegaard also identifies a further "dialectical" element, which means that sometimes one needs diversions from spiritual trial lest one be consumed by the absolute exertion. And yet, while there are those who act from a "spiritual pride", which presumptuously "demands too much of God and of itself" and who desire to be too much (absolute) Spirit, the dialectical must again be borne in mind for there are also those who are "unwilling to be spirit", and thus will flee to the "easier expedients" since they do "not dare demand too much of God" (JP 4:4372). Those who are unwilling to be spirit or to demand much of God, Kierkegaard urges "No, do not spare yourself, just persevere." To those who wish to be too much spirit and demand too much of God, his counsel is: "Do not presume too much, or do not become a self-tormentor." In other words, while spiritual trial may increase in proportion to Spirit, each one is to remember that "you are not completely spirit" and, as such, help will not always be the help of the spirit but may be the help that comes by diversionary means (JP 4:4372).

However, Kierkegaard reminds us that this advice to seek diversionary means of relief from spiritual trial is unconventional since "Genuinely spiritual persons are so rare that they can be handled appropriately as exceptions": that is, "the sick" are encouraged to be a little easier on themselves, and on God. In general, "the rule for spiritual advisers", at least as Kierkegaard perceives them, "generally should be to advise a person not to spare himself but to endure being and becoming spirit" (JP 4:4373). In his words of counsel Kierkegaard adopts the consolatory tone of the old devotional books, though he goes beyond the "childish" identification of spiritual trial as originating from the devil. Kierkegaard also elucidates the relationship of difference between spiritual trial and temptation — a position that he again confirms in an 1849 journal entry, which suggests that temptation should be "avoided" whereas in spiritual trial one should "go straight toward it, trusting in God and Christ" (JP 4:4023).

In a further entry from this year, Kierkegaard describes what he identifies as "one of the most tormenting forms of spiritual trial": one which expresses "an anxiety about sin which avoids Christ, at least to a certain extent, and yet is related to him" (JP 4:4374). Here Kierkegaard considers one who in their anxiety about sin seeks to avoid every temptation and yet also, in an important sense, avoids

Christ as a Saviour who can conquer such thoughts. This person is ensnared in "the anxiety of spiritual trial [*Anfægtelse*]": namely, the anxious belief that it is impossible to continue to survive temptation, that it is only a matter of time before one falls into temptation, thereby succumbing to the fatalistic conviction that temptation always conquers in the end. Such a person may have *resignation* but not *faith* in the possibility "that Christ would help him conquer his temptation". This, Kierkegaard warns, "is one of the most tormenting forms of spiritual trial" (JP 4:4374).

Temptation and spiritual trial in Kierkegaard are thus both testimony to the struggle of *freedom* and *will*. They are expressions of freedom's anxiety, of the will's inevitable fall into sin, the realisation that one cannot struggle against sin alone, and, finally, that through faith Christ can help one overcome. As such, in a journal entry from the same year Kierkegaard considers spiritual trial as evidence that "a bare naked *liberum arbitrium* is a chimera" (JP 2:1260), that an unconditioned free will is a mere fantasy. The struggle is itself the evidence against it. One sees this in "spiritual trials in which a man is fighting against things beyond his control" — including forces which come from the enemy within — "fighting against them in the anxiety of death . . . until finally he gradually becomes victorious in a long, drawn-out battle" (JP 2:1260). This victory itself is not attained through the sheer exertion of self-will, but by the self-will becoming nothing before the Divine Will, through faith that Christ is the Saviour with whose help the evil can be overcome.

"The Crucifixion of One's Understanding"

In 1849 Kierkegaard returns to another important aspect of his substantial 1848 meditation on spiritual trial (JP 4:4370): the tension between *faith* and *despair*. Kierkegaard opens this journal entry by suggesting that "Humanly speaking, Job's wife was in a certain sense right" and that it is an even greater burden to endure great suffering along with "the thought that God is nevertheless love" (JP 4:4375). Such a collision is "almost enough to make a person lose his mind — and, humanly, it is far easier to despair". Following this reflection, Kierkegaard proceeds with the declaration that in "sufferings and spiritual trials [*Anfægtelser*]" the combination of "the thought of God and the thought that he nevertheless is love make the suffering far more strenuous." In such instances, according to Kierkegaard, "it is a case of faith being tested, of love being put to the test, whether one really loves God and really cannot do without him." In the face of such suffering it is justifiable, "[h]umanly speaking" (a favourite caveat of Kierkegaard's), to say that the suffering would actually be more bearable *without* the idea of God. In other words, if there were no God, or God was *not* Love, then suffering would not seem incommensurable.

Yet to know that God exists and, even more agonisingly, to know that God is supposed to be *love* yet does not rescue us serves only to intensify the suffering: a suffering also expressed "in the crucifixion of one's understanding, that in spite of all this God is love and that what happens is for one's own good". Under such suffering the collapse into despair becomes the temptation since despair alleviates the tension of suffering by agreeing that it is unbearable. Despair thus surrenders before the "strenuousness of the idea of God", which is "to have to understand that not only is the suffering to be endured but that it is a good, a gift from a God of love" (JP 4:4375).

However, it is important to remember that this is not human (mundane) suffering that Kierkegaard is referring to; rather this is *religious* suffering; or more exactly, "this is only a spiritual trial, which can be dreadful enough as long as it lasts. But blessedly to endure with God." Spiritual trial is, in contrast to human suffering, designed for the upbuilding of believers. As such, Kierkegaard discerns two "lessons" in this spiritual trial. "The first lesson is simply a matter of immediately grasping the God-idea, and then one gains alleviation." In the second lesson is found "the real spiritual trial" since here "it is as if the God-idea itself intensified one's agony." In the face of this spiritual trial "it is a matter of enduring in faith." One is to cling to God, like Jacob struggling at Peni'el — and the blessing will arise with the sun from this dark night of spiritual trial:

> If you do not let go of God, it will still end in your blessedly agreeing with God that this suffering was a benefit . . . the height of blessedness is to agree unconditionally that God is right precisely when, humanly speaking, there seems to be a case against him (JP 4:4375).

In this sense, Kierkegaard concludes, God allows believers to fall into spiritual trial in order to "jack up the price of faith infinitely high. How blessed to believe — the higher the price the more blessed it is to believe" (JP 4:4375).

This perspective on the educative, even other-worldly value of spiritual trial is also a focus for a journal entry from the same year, "concerning spiritual trial" (JP 4:4376). Kierkegaard asserts an inverse relation between "the essentially Christian" and "the universally human" whereby, for example, "Christian love from a human point of view is like cruelty (and yet again love)". Because of this inverse relation, "the horror of spiritual trial consists in this that when a person feels weak he turns around and goes back to the purely human". However, when one feels weak and turns back in the face of spiritual trial, then one returns from the essentially Christian — just as Abraham may be tempted to leave the Absolute and the paradox of faith in order to return, repentantly, to the universal and the communicable (JP 4:4376).

Spiritual trial is felt as a form of suffering, and yet it contains within itself, ineffably, the premonition of blessedness: "We have a presentiment of bliss — but for the time being it expresses itself only in the most horrible agony" (JP 4:4376). Kierkegaard's own inexpressible suffering is laid before us — though it still retains its secret interiority — in another deeply personal journal entry from this year. In speaking about the "collisions in my life", Kierkegaard refers to his "erotic collision" and his "collision with the world" (JP 6:6385). The erotic collision signifies Kierkegaard's breaking of his engagement to Regine Olsen (1822-1904) provoked by "my melancholy and repentance for my earlier life". The collision with the world refers to Kierkegaard's self-imposed "collision with the crowd", in which, Kierkegaard acknowledges, "I am the one who voluntarily exposed myself to the whole thing." Both collisions are marked by an inherent *voluntariness* — a key signifier of spiritual trial (JP 1:964), which always accompanies the existential collision. "The spiritual trial is due to the fact that I myself am the one who acts. I myself must take the decisive step; I myself must expose myself to the suffering." Alongside voluntariness, therefore, spiritual trial derives from the actuality of the one who acts, from relating all things about this single individual to God. And this in itself gives rise to a tendency to doubt the spiritual trial itself, to wonder whether it is nothing but presumption, "the spiritual trial, which always voices the thought: has not too much been ventured" (JP 6:6385). In all of Kierkegaard's collisions, erotic or worldly, there is therefore a higher collision, which raises him above the universally human. This is the collision of the God-relationship itself: in daring to relate all things in their actuality to God the thought of presumption enters and reminds him of the limit of the Absolute. As such, "in every one of my collisions there is also a collision with God [*en Collision med Gud*] or a struggle with God [*en Kamp med Gud*]" (JP 6:6385).

Again in the same year Kierkegaard makes further disclosure of the spiritual trial that besets his life, claiming that "everything is reversed, a dialectic that in every moment of spiritual trial changes into its opposite for me" (Pap. X^2 A 64). Kierkegaard describes how in his own eyes he is "more insignificant than all others, even a penitent" and for this very reason he has dared "to venture what I have ventured". And yet he remains conscious that in the eyes of others "my life expresses pride, overwhelming ambition, etc.". When spiritual trial comes to him, "it takes advantage of this, because I have no direct outwardness but continually a reversed, that is, an unalloyed, spirit-relation, which is the opposite as soon as faith is not present." Because he is a penitent, Kierkegaard confesses, he has had to learn to "cling to God on a totally different scale than other people do", meaning also that he has learned not to shy away from God, but to take unusual and courageous risks. Through this, Kierkegaard observes, "God helps me to be capable on an extraordinary scale; but it has the appearance [to the others] of pride and arrogance. What dreadful suffering, never, never, never to be understood". This dialectical reversal in Kierkegaard's life also characterises "my love relationship, which, humanly speaking, appears as cruelty". Yet it is only by living life in this manner that it has "been granted to me, to describe the truly Christian, because precisely this is Christianity" (Pap. X² A 64).

The Voluntary

In *Practice in Christianity* (1850), Anti-Climacus returns to discuss the distinctive category of Christian suffering (of which spiritual trial is a profound yet under-acknowledged form), emphasising the particular significance of *voluntariness* and *the possibility of offense* (PC, 109). Anti-Climacus thus draws an infinite difference between *losing* everything (such as, to lose or have taken away all that one owns) and *giving* everything up (as the apostles left everything to follow Christ). In contemporary Christendom these two have, Anti-Climacus argues, become conflated to such a degree that one who endures the sufferings of life's vicissitudes becomes compared with an exceptional biblical figure who voluntarily relinquished all that they possessed. As such, the contemporary pastor can be found preaching a sermon in which the recently-bereaved widower in his congregation is absurdly compared with Abraham, the one who had to endure the anxious ordeal — or what Luther calls the sublime temptation — of willingly giving up Isaac (PC, 108-109). The text proceeds with the only explicit reference to spiritual trial in *Practice in Christianity* — though it is a significant one since it not only lauds the category but it identifies its relation to *voluntariness*:

> [I]f I voluntarily give up everything, choose danger and difficulties, then it is impossible to avoid *spiritual trial* [*Anfægtelse*]. . . . But the voluntary [like *imitation*] has been completely abolished in Christendom, and in this way the possibility of offense has also been abolished, inasmuch as the voluntary is also a form of the possibility of offense (PC, 109).

Here spiritual trial is identified by Anti-Climacus as "a specifically Christian category" rather than something which, as in *The Concept of Irony*, applies to "any position in life". It is related to freedom and responsibility; and yet it has been utterly "abolished in Christendom" (PC, 109).

The question of "the voluntary" also occupies Kierkegaard in a journal entry concerning Luther's sermon on the temptation of Christ from the same year (JP 4:4950). Kierkegaard examines Luther's notion that one is not to *choose* sufferings if not directed by the Spirit to do so. Considering the difference between voluntary Christian and involuntary human suffering, Kierkegaard suggests that involuntary suffering is "factually present without my collaboration in any way", such as "being assaulted just as I am walking along the street". Voluntary suffering, however, can be seen in Luther's stepping forth and witnessing, even against the Pope. For Kierkegaard Luther's act of stepping forth actually assures the place of the voluntary, which in turn assures the place of Christianity. "When the voluntary disappears, 'spiritual trial' [*Anfægtelse*] disappears, and when spiritual trials disappear, Christianity disappears — as it has disappeared in Christendom" (JP 4:4950).

For Kierkegaard the role of the voluntary in Christianity is already assured by the kenotic freedom of Christ's suffering. "Christ's whole life is voluntary suffering, just as his coming in order to suffer is voluntary." The notion that all of Christ's suffering is essentially voluntary is borne out in Kierkegaard's treatment of the temptation of Jesus. Christ is tempted by hunger; but as divine he, unlike us, has it in his power to obtain bread to relieve his hunger. One who hungers but has not recourse to bread endures *involuntary* suffering. Christ's suffering is therefore an expression of a voluntary kenosis: he freely subjects himself to suffering that, through his divinity, he could otherwise avoid. Accordingly, "The voluntary is suffering in faith's struggle with God": that is to say that "I have it in my power to get out of it [as Christ did to an infinitely higher extreme], but there is something in me which tells me God would rather have me keep on" (JP 4:4950).

The consolation of Christ in the face of spiritual trial is revived in relation to the forgiveness of sins in 'An Upbuilding Discourse' from 20 December 1850, on 'The Woman Who Was a Sinner' (re. Luke 7:37ff; collected in *Without Authority*). She anoints the feet of Christ, she dries them with her hair, and weeps. She hears Christ say that her many sins are forgiven her because she loved much (WA, 157). And yet from her we learn that "with regard to gaining the forgiveness of sins, or *before* God, a person of capable of nothing at all" (WA, 158).

All is grace. Finally, Kierkegaard suggests, we learn from her "*that we have one comfort that she did not have*", that is "the comfort of [Christ's] death as the Atonement, the pledge that the sins are forgiven" (WA, 158). While the woman who was a sinner has consolation by hearing the words of forgiveness spoken directly to her from the mouth of Jesus, she does not yet have the "the infinite comfort" that Christ died to save her (WA, 159). As such, Kierkegaard suggests that:

> If you imagine that sometime later in spiritual trial the woman who was a sinner doubted whether her many sins also were now actually forgiven her, then she would, since she could not again hear it directly from Christ himself, find rest in hearing, as it were, Christ say: Just believe it; after all, you have heard it from my mouth. (WA, 159)

In other words, there is assurance for her in the memory of Christ speaking directly and in person to her. All she has to do is to accept it, to "Just believe it". But what of those in spiritual struggle who have not heard these words spoken directly by the person of Jesus, yet who live in the new dawn of the Atonement? For those in such doubt there is consolation in Christ's words, "I have laid down my life in order to gain for you the forgiveness of your sins; so just believe it, a stronger assurance is impossible" (WA, 159).

Having described spiritual trial in such harrowing and agonistic terms, Kierkegaard also acknowledges a particular form of spiritual trial defined not simply by the nemesis or limit of the Absolute, but by a nausea, or a "disgust for the religious" (JP 4:4377). In a further entry from 1850, Kierkegaard describes how just as a woman who has been "far too intensely preoccupied with thinking about her beloved" suddenly finds herself with a "feeling of revulsion for her beloved", so is there also a form of "religious spiritual trial, also found described by older writers, in which a disgust for the religious sets in". Such spiritual trial seems akin to the notion of *acedia* (without care) which arises in reaction to an over-occupation with one's object. The longing for the Beloved has become so intense, so ardent that unconsummated passion mutates into a moment of revulsion. Through such moments, the sufferer is simply to hold out in silent patience until bliss returns with even greater force (JP 4:4377). Patience is needed since, while Christianity is all too easily proclaimed as consolation for suffering, "there is the spiritual trial [*Anfægtelser*] that the consolation is not entirely direct, that Christianity requires suffering for the doctrine, etc. — all this is completely supressed" (JP 4:4662).

In the same year, Kierkegaard again emphasises the enduring need to cling to the thought that God is love. Trials may come from God but "The thought that God tests [*prøver*], yes, tempts [*frister*] a man ('lead us not into temptation') must not horrify us" (JP 2:1401). The test (*Prøven*) is here understood as the form of higher temptation which is *sent by God* — whereas the lower temptations derive from the flesh, the world, and the devil. The test itself can, however, engender secondary spiritual trial (*Anfægtelse*) and temptation (*Fristelse*) concerning the nature of God. In the thought that God tests (*prøver*) us, melancholy and disbelief become anxious and are tempted to imagine that God tests us in order that we should fail. The believer, by contrast, "believes that God does it *in order that* he shall meet the test [*Prøven*]". Whereas disbelief, melancholy, and anxiety fail the test because they believe that the test itself is designed for the individual to fail. Faith, by contrast, "usually conquers" because faith believes that the test is aspirational rather than condemnatory. Yet faith's belief that God desires that the believer overcomes the test "is a rigorous upbringing — this going from inborn anxiety to faith" (JP 2:1401). The tempting anxiety, which infers that God tests one in order that one should fail, "is the most terrible kind of spiritual trial [*Anfægtelse*]" marking the point prior to being "disciplined in faith". Holding fast to the thought that God is love "is the abstract form of faith, faith *in abstracto*". In holding to this thought, the bonds of anxiety are loosened and "the time will come when he will succeed in concretizing his God-relationship": that is, will come to experience "*in concreto* that God is love" (JP 2:1401).

The Restlessness of Faith

> Only one solitary man, the reformer, was disciplined in all secrecy by fear and trembling and much spiritual trial for venturing the extraordinary in God's name. Now that all want to reform . . . instead of fear and trembling and much spiritual trial, there is: hurrah, bravo, applause, balloting, bumbling, hubbub, noise — and false alarm. (JFY, 213)

Written in 1851-52, *Judge for Yourself!* was withheld from publication by Kierkegaard out of consideration to Bishop Mynster. Nonetheless the use of Luther as a mirror for contemporary Christianity is paralleled in the first part of *For Self-Examination* (1851), 'What Is Required in Order to Look at Oneself with True Blessing in the Mirror of the Word?' (re. James 1:22-27), Kierkegaard describes how Luther — "a man from God and with faith" (FSE, 16) — had articulated the message of salvation by *grace* not *works*. This message has subsequently been distorted by the "secular mentality" of contemporary Lutheranism "that no doubt wants to have the name of being a Christian but wants to become Christian as cheaply as possible" (FSE, 16). As for

Kierkegaard himself: he avers that he is *"without authority*; far be it from me to judge anyone" (FSE, 17). In light of this avowal he seeks to submit himself to judgement, that is to "test my life according to just one Lutheran qualification of faith: faith is a restless thing" (FSE, 17). In a revealing moment in his ambivalent relation to Luther, Kierkegaard imagines that Luther himself has risen from the grave and has been living for several years among contemporary Christendom. He imagines that Luther has been watching him and comes to interrogate him on whether or not he has faith. Despite Kierkegaard's assurances that he does have faith — that the restlessness (*Uro*) of faith is, after all, manifest in his various writings, Luther, rather revealingly for Kierkegaard's various spiritual trials about publication, refuses to take Kierkegaard's books as evidence of anything but a poetic aptitude for *describing* faith. What is needed to demonstrate the *restlessness of faith* is a life of genuine and authentic "witness", rather than presenting oneself as a mere "speaker" of faith, such that "faith, this restless thing, should be recognizable in his life" (FSE, 19).

Finding himself wanting by Luther, Kierkegaard turns instead to describe "the restlessness of faith" with reference to an imagined "hero of faith or witness to the truth" (FSE, 19). In this world "everyone is looking after his own business in this crisscrossing game of diversity that is actuality." And yet there is one, Kierkegaard imagines, who does things rather differently: "Meanwhile, like Luther in a cloister cell or in a remote room, there is not far away a solitary person in fear and trembling and much spiritual trial [*Anfægtelse*]" (FSE, 19). But why is this secret hero of faith hidden away in solitude? This present age has, according to Kierkegaard's probing diagnosis, invented untruth in the form of "the crowd": "that a religious reformation should come from the public is untruth". In contrast to the untruth of the crowd "there is a solitary person in spiritual trial" (FSE, 19). But such a person is a hidden exception. While Kierkegaard observes that he is recognised among his contemporaries as "one who knows the human soul (psychologist)" (FSE, 19), he admits that the phenomenology of spiritual trial, unlike that of temptation, continues to elude his observations of the present age: "I can testify I have seen people of whom I dare say they have most certainly been very exposed to temptations [*Fristelser*], but I have never seen anyone of whom I dared say: He is tried in spiritual trial [*Anfægtelse*]" (FSE, 19). And yet this absence of spiritual trial is to the impoverishment of the present age; its absence testifies to a spiritual poverty within the crowd since "one year of exposure to temptation is nothing compared with one hour in spiritual trial" (FSE, 19). Exposure to temptation can, of course, be contended with by fleeing from the temptation. Spiritual trial, by contrast, cannot be so easily escaped. On the contrary, spiritual trial cannot be evaded — it confronts, even imprisons the self:

> This is the state of that solitary person sitting there; he is sitting — or, if you wish, he is pacing, perhaps up and down the floor like a lion imprisoned in a cage; and yet what imprisons him is remarkable — he is by God or because of God imprisoned within himself (FSE, 19-20).

Whereas Johannes Climacus compares spiritual trial to a bird trapped in a cage or a fish stranded on the shore, Kierkegaard here compares the solitary person in spiritual trial to a lion pacing in captivity, in the prison of the self. Yet the solitary one is not to remain in this cloistered solitude.[1] The solitary person is to press on: "That for which he has suffered in spiritual trial must now be transposed into actuality" — a harrowing and difficult calling, which one pleads, without success, to be exempted from (FSE, 20). When the step into actuality is made terror rises up, tempting one to turn and flee:

> ... but as soon as he turns to flee he sees — he sees an even greater horror behind him, the horror of spiritual trial, and he must go forward — so he goes forward; now he is perfectly calm, because the horror of spiritual trial is a formidable disciplinarian who can give courage. — The terror rises up. Everything that closely or remotely belongs to the given actuality arms itself against this man of spiritual trial whom it nevertheless is impossible to terrify because, strangely enough, he is so afraid — of God (FSE, 20).

Even though "All attack him, hate him, curse him" (FSE, 20), the person of spiritual trial is given the courage to press on — a courage born of a holy fear: the fear of God by which the self transcends all fear of the crowd (as Jacob was delivered from fear of the other by struggling with God).

Kierkegaard opens the subsequent discourse, 'Christ Is the Way' (re. Acts 1:1-12), with a prayer that speaks to the suffering of Christ. Kierkegaard praises Christ as "you who knew your fate beforehand and yet did not draw back" even though Christ was, as Kierkegaard recurrently observes, "finally even forsaken by God" (FSE, 56). In this prayer it is possible to discern two defining characteristics of the spiritual trial of Christ: that he knew what was before him and yet

---

1 Kierkegaard has already spoken out in the beginning of this section against "the petty self-torments" and "bondage" of the monastery which turned all back into Law (FSE, 15).

did not flee (as one may flee from temptation) but pressed on (as one is to confront spiritual trial); and finally that he endured the last and most terrible spiritual trial — an ineffable anguish to which none may compare: the agony of God-forsakenness. Although his own sufferings exceed all human understanding, Christ is nonetheless the exemplar: "Christ is the way", although "this way is *narrow*" (FSE, 57). But the narrow (*trang*) way of Christ's life far exceeds the straits (*Trang*) of earthly poverty, destitution, and wretchedness. "His life from the very beginning is a story of temptation", Kierkegaard observes, but "it is not only one particular period in his life, the forty days, that is the story of temptation — no, his whole life is a story of temptation (just as it is also a story of suffering)" (FSE, 58-59).

The perennial temptation of the life of Jesus, according to Kierkegaard, derives from the fact that "he has this possibility in his power, to take his calling, his task, in vain" (FSE, 59). While in the desert Satan appears as the explicit tempter of Jesus, there are also others throughout his life "who play the role of tempter": the people around him, even the disciples. At all times, there is the temptation to become otherwise than the Messiah that God has called him to be: to become "someone important in the world, king and ruler" (FSE, 59). There exists the unrelenting temptation to transform a spiritual into a material kingdom, to triumph in the ways of the world rather than of heaven, to pursue the way of spiritlessness rather than Spirit. If "his calling, his task" represents the spiritual trial that Jesus must nonetheless fight on through, then the temptation which always accompanies it, as its shadow-side, is the seduction of the many alternative pathways — paths which lead not to the cross but to the thrones and kingdoms of this world, to "everything that a mortal heart could desire" (FSE, 59). In this sense, spiritual trial is always accompanied by temptation — the higher is always haunted by the seductions of the lower: the narrow way is always tempted by the wide and easy way. Spiritual trial and temptation can in this sense be seen as two sides of the same coin.[1]

As Christ's death approaches and the shadow of the cross draws near, the path becomes *"narrower and narrower to the end, to death"* (FSE, 61; italics original), narrowing to the point at which there is no escape from its destination — except through the temptation to forsake the path itself. Here Kierkegaard's narrative brings us, in fear and trembling, to the Garden of Gethsemane: "there he sinks down — oh, that it has happened already! He sinks down, doomed [*dødsens*]

---

1 This relationship between temptation and spiritual trial is elaborated further, with reference to Nikos Kazantzakis's depiction of the life of Jesus in *The Last Temptation*, in my 'Crucified by God: Kazantzakis and the Last *Anfechtung* of Christ'.

— indeed, was he really any more a dying man [*Døende*] on the cross than in Gethsemane!" (FSE, 63). Whereas on the cross Jesus suffered the moment of death itself, in Gethsemane he struggles with God: "If the suffering on the cross was a death agony — ah, this agony in prayer was also a mortal combat; nor was it bloodless, for his sweat fell like drops of blood to the earth" (FSE, 63). But Jesus is not broken by this struggle; he does not flee from the path, even as it narrows unto death. An angel of consolation appears to him. "Then he rises, strengthened: Your will be done, Father in heaven!" (FSE, 63).

Still there remains one final sigh. Jesus is crucified — "then just one more sigh and it is over. One more sigh, the deepest, the most terrifying: My God, my God, why have you forsaken me!" (FSE, 64). In this "humiliation" Kierkegaard discerns "the last of the suffering" (FSE, 64). There are "weak intimations" of this suffering in the Christian martyrs who follow Christ: in the "moment at the end" when "the sigh escapes, 'God has forsaken me' . . . Everything I have said was not true, was a delusion" (FSE, 64). Yet the despair of the martyr cannot compare with "the last spiritual trial" (JP 4:4699) of the God-forsaken God.[1] Here Kierkegaard refuses the consolatory reading of the crucified cry of God-forsakenness, which would redeem the words of dereliction as a triumphant invocation of the entirety of Psalm 22. Kierkegaard stares the contradiction of the crucified God in the eye. This cry of God-forsakenness issues from the mouth of one who claimed to be the Son of the Father, to be one with the Father:

> One with the Father, but if they are one, how then can the Father forsake him at any moment! And yet he says: My God, my God, why have you forsaken me! Thus it was not true that he was one with the Father. Oh, what extremity of superhuman suffering! Oh, a human heart would have burst a little sooner — only the God-man must suffer all through his final suffering. — Then he dies (FSE, 64).

Such an abyss of suffering surpasses human understanding. On the one hand, Kierkegaard infers from the cry of God-forsakenness that Jesus was not, could not be, who he said he was. On the other hand, *only* the God-man must, indeed could, endure this final superhuman suffering. Paradoxically, the cry of God-forsakenness is both a denial and an affirmation of the divinity of Christ. Here, before the God-forsaken God, the understanding is crucified.

In this same year, 1851, Kierkegaard makes several significant

---

1 Kierkegaard later reflects that in *For Self-Examination* he "too hastily" theorised that a martyr suffers something similar to Christ's voluntary cry of God-forsakenness (JP 4:4980).

journal entries on the theme of spiritual trial. One of the most agonistic references comprises a contemplation of one who believes that they are not merely abandoned by God but under the explicit wrath of God. Might such an experience of a God of wrath, Kierkegaard wonders, be as much an experience of God as the God of grace: "Does only the person who has a gracious God and Father have a God and Father? I wonder if the person who has, alas, an angry God and Father does not also have a God and Father?" (JP 2:1421). In response to this disconcerting question Kierkegaard offers words of consolation: "O, my friend, if this is your predicament, or if you have been spiritually tried [*i Anfægtelse*] in this way, continue to cling to this radical consolation; only do not let go of God, and you will find that there is help in this." Kierkegaard's counsel is, as for the devotional books, to continue to hold on to God even when God appears so dreadfully *otherwise*. One must cling to God, even when the divine assails us in the shadowy form of the stranger, in the hope that the blessing will come with the breaking of the dawn. "The one danger is to let go of God", Kierkegaard warns. The loss of God — to forsake rather than be forsaken by God — is the greatest of all dangers, more dangerous even than "if his wrath were to hang over you all your life". Such horror of spiritual trial brings the sufferer close to madness, face to face with the ostensible darkness of God. Yet such horrendous suffering is far from normative: "no doubt a man is seldom spiritually tried as hard as this" (JP 2:1421).

The Struggle of Spirit and the Temptation of Flight

Kierkegaard's recurrent contrast between temptation and spiritual trial provides the focus for an 1851 journal entry, which again invokes the words of James: "Resist the devil, and he will flee from you" (James 4:7). Kierkegaard verifies that "This, then, is the tactic. Not the reverse: Flee the devil — this can be the tactic only in relation to temptation [*Fristelse*]" (JP 4:4378). But whether or not the devil or the self is the source of temptation or spiritual trial, the response to them — fleeing temptation, confronting spiritual trial — reveals a decisive variance: "Here we see that spiritual trial lies a whole quality higher than temptation" (JP 4:4378). From this point of differentiation, Kierkegaard proceeds to reflect once more on the secondary struggles, which can emerge as a consequence of not fleeing but engaging with spiritual trial. From pressing on, "a new spiritual trial is born, because for a long time it will seem to the spiritual combatant as if he perhaps had taken on too much, as if he perhaps ought to have tried flight" (JP 4:4378). At such moments, the struggler comes to doubt their course of action in the face of spiritual trial — that is, to doubt the struggle itself. At such moments

Kierkegaard's guidance is emphatic: one must struggle on; faith must be valiant, mirroring Jacob in its refusal to relinquish its grasp. "Spiritual trial can be fought only with the rashness of faith, which charges head-on." And yet in such spiritual trial one is, Kierkegaard concedes, vulnerable to "weak moments" in which "the believer grows uneasy and fearful over this rashness of faith, as if it were a way of tempting God, which again is a spiritual trial" (JP 4:4378).

In a journal entry from the same year, Kierkegaard once more laments that the majority "live essentially without religiousness, or at most have religiousness in the same sense as they go to the theater now and then, which is nul-religiousness." For such people, "spiritual trial is completely out of the question" (JP 4:4379). There are, Kierkegaard concedes, a few who possess some degree of religiousness, "who live their daily life within religious conceptions" and for whom "God is the one they depend upon to make everything go well for them, provided they themselves are circumspect, prudent, stay out of all dangers etc.". Again, however, for such people "spiritual trial is completely out of the question." In contrast to such lives, Kierkegaard reveres "authentic Christian religiousness" — although he confesses, with a pointed indictment of his contemporaries, that "whether or not a person like this is to be found, I do not know: I have never seen one." For such a person, authentic Christian religiousness means to believe with the New Testament that one's intimacy with God will evoke suffering in the world, that witnessing to the truth carries a price of sacrifice — that "the mark or the sign of the God-relationship is the opposition of the world, persecution, suffering." For such people this opposition is evidence of "spirit, and the witness of spirit bears them up." However, such a person is not immune from the arid moments in which "they sink down from this high intensification" and begin to doubt themselves, to doubt the authenticity of their struggle. They begin to wonder whether the opposition of the world is, in truth, evidence that they are in the wrong, that venturing out in this way has been presumptuous, even arrogant, "so that they almost repent and regret as guilt what was their most honest enthusiasm" (JP 4:4379).

This doubt is, however, itself a further spiritual trial. "The natural man", according to Kierkegaard, possesses the tendency to believe that all will go well in life if one is in right relationship to God. "Spirit", in contrast to the natural man, "recognizes God's relationship in the opposition [of the world], in suffering, and has the courage and faith for an interminable polemic". To become Spirit means to endure struggle, to elicit the nemesis of the world as well as the limit of the Absolute. When one doubts the authentic God-relationship because of the spiritual trial, which is expressed through the opposition of the world, then one is actually in a further spiritual trial — a struggle in which the temptation is to repent of the God-relationship. In such a "dull and lustreless moment the spiritual man sinks down to being the natural man, and then comes spiritual trial." Such spiritual trial does not, however, befall the one who "egotistically" wants God to help him to flourish and succeed in the ways of the world. In his success, such a man "will be so bewitched that he will be blind to his true condition". Spiritual trial, by contrast, "is enough to make one lose his mind." In spiritual trial, God "lures a man out, or commands him to venture out — and then when he momentarily lets the man go, everything turns around for him" (JP 4:4379). That is to say, one is out over 70,000 fathoms, where grace neither comes too soon nor is sold too cheaply (JP 4:4380).

In a journal entry from the following year, 1852, Kierkegaard observes a similarity between spiritual trial and Greek legends in which "the divine venture" is "shaped by delaying factors or something which tempts [*frister*] one to remain behind, tempts one to sympathy" (JP 4:4381). Whereas ordinary people are commonly scared back by dangers, "the brave ones" are not frightened. To them is given spiritual trial "in the shape of sympathy" because "usually it is precisely the brave ones who are disposed to show sympathy for others." While the usual dangers do not frighten them back, sympathy is the Achilles heel of the brave ones — it tempts them to remain behind with the others who have fallen to temptation and fear. This spiritual trial must be struggled through, even though "such a thing cannot be done without making some people unhappy" (JP 4:4381).

In the same year Kierkegaard undertakes another substantial reflection on "the last spiritual trial" of God-forsakenness: "the final suffering, the most terrible of all", which is only known in its fullness by Christ and in appearance only to the most heroic of martyrs of faith, but the spectre of which seems to continually haunt Kierkegaard himself (JP 4:4699). To all their contemporaries such a person appears to be a fool as "he himself is devoid of strength and forsaken by God and must suffer this final humiliation, the last, in which God puts him to the test to see whether he will still hold fast to God." Such a test (*Prøvelse*) of *apparent* abandonment has befallen all the "magnificent" who have followed in Christ's uniquely ineffable moment of true abandonment. While only Christ has been truly God-forsaken, the sublime martyrs of faith have endured the test (*Prøvelse*) of the *appearance* of abandonment by God. Such suffering, Kierkegaard confesses, is far beyond himself: "I, who compared with the magnificent men, suffer only in a childish way". Before the final spiritual trial of God-forsakenness, Kierkegaard can only wonder in fear and trembling:

Terrible suffering! I just cannot conceive of it otherwise than that such a sufferer is with God's help still able to hold fast, that this suffering is not the truth, that this is the last spiritual trial [*Anfægtelse*], that it is just one last suffering hour to go through and then he has God again forever, eternally victorious, so that this very suffering also belongs to the consummate victory. But, nevertheless, nevertheless terrible! (JP 4:4699)

Spirit as the Death-to-Self

Kierkegaard's sense of the other-worldliness of authentic Christian religiousness — the ecstatic nature of Spirit marked by the struggle of spiritual trial — reaches an agonistic crescendo in the final years of his life. In the year before his death, the journals contain several related deliberations on spiritual trial, in which Kierkegaard speaks as both polemicist and physician of the soul. With reference to "thoughts that try the spirit [*anfægtende Tanker*]" Kierkegaard suggests the tactic of "the most absolute indifference to them [which] is itself the victory". Through indifference, or even outright anger, one subverts the devilish desire of such thoughts to make one anxious or afraid, thereby overcoming the temptation to imagine that one is guilty for spiritual trial (JP 4:4382). By anger or indifference one does not flee from these thoughts (as one does with temptation); instead one faces spiritual trial in the refusal to be made guilty by it (JP 4:4382).

However, such thoughts, which arise when a person endures "the tension of being a Christian" and "the tension of the imagination", are seemingly absent among contemporary Christians, who seem to regard the disappearance of spiritual trials "as progress, yes, progress backward". Such "progress" is likened by Kierkegaard to a physician who declares that a fever has been cured because the patient has died — "in the very same way thoughts which try the spirit have vanished, but so, of course, has Christianity" (JP 4:4382). Of course, this invites the persistent question: if spiritual trials have vanished, then to whom is Kierkegaard's counsel directed? Is this spiritual direction intended to expose a lacuna in the life of contemporary Christendom? Perhaps his counsel evokes an implicit hope that spiritual trials have not entirely vanished — after all, Kierkegaard himself confesses to them. Otherwise all consolation is merely an ironic lament over the death of Christianity.

In a related journal entry in the same year, Kierkegaard confirms his verdict that "thoughts that try the spirit are related, as mentioned before, to the imagination", adding that "pure rationalists do not know about such things" (JP 4:4383). He even insouciantly compares such thoughts with "*flatus* (wind). As such they are nothing but can certainly make one feel uncomfortable as long as they last." It is the *imagination* that makes such thoughts into more than they are. Kierkegaard warns that one is especially vulnerable to these thoughts in the moment of anxious indecision, which precedes action. It is when one's mind is not made up "that such tormenting spirits turn up, just as the morning and evening twilight is the time for ghosts." Twilight is the liminal moment of transition between light and darkness which itself wholly belong to neither. It is a moment when the imagination is tempted to run wild with possibilities.[1] In this sense, Kierkegaard identifies such tormenting spirits as "possibility, a product of possibility" (or anxiety) for which "the best remedy against them is: actuality" (JP 4:4383).

In the same year, Kierkegaard writes a substantial entry which clarifies much of his previous reflections on spiritual trial. In particular, he recapitulates his identification of the God-relationship and the individual subjectivity, which "cannot immediately and completely surrender to God", rather than the devil, as the source of spiritual trial (JP 4:4384). Spiritual trial does not only arise from the limit of the Absolute; it also arises from the limit, or nemesis of the quantum of 'self', which, refusing to be erased, resists becoming nothing before God. This emphasis upon the tension of subjectivity represents, to Kierkegaard's mind at least, a departure from the "older and better devotional literature", which speaks of "burning arrows . . . ascribed to the devil". This view "is not a truly Christian interpretation" since "such thoughts come from the individual himself, although innocently" (JP 4:4384).

In harmony with aspects of the old devotional books, however, Kierkegaard identifies a source of spiritual trial in the vestige of self-will that resists the Divine Will. Like a fire that burns the self out to Spirit, "when God loves a man and a man is loved by God, this man *qua* selfish will has to be completely demolished." Such mortification of the self-will is "what it means to die to the world, it is the most intense agony." The anguish of spiritual trial testifies to the reality of the divided will, that no matter how much one wills to become nothing, there remains an indelible trace of self-will which refuses this nothingness. Even "the religious person" who wills to die to the world "in accord with his better will" does not possess sufficient will-power to "completely get his will, his subjectivity, into the power of the better will in him". The self-will makes a desperate resistance — fighting for its life — that even if mastered for a time it remains watching "for a chance to disorganize the whole revolution that dethroned it" (JP 4:4384).

Transcendence of this nemesis of the self-will requires divine grace, since "No religious person, even the purest, has sheer, purified

---

1 "Temptation [*Fristelse*] has its power in 'the moment'" (JP 4:4745).

subjectivity or pure transparency in willing solely what God wills, so that there is no residue of his original subjectivity" (JP 4:4384). Insofar as there remains an obstinate relic of the old self (the natural person), which the new self (or the spiritual person) is unable to will into nothingness, the process of kenosis, detachment (*Abgeschiedenheit*) and releasement (*Gelassenheit*), remains incomplete. This trace is "a residue still not wholly penetrated, a remote portion of residue still uncaptured", perhaps even a hidden abyss of the self, "perhaps as yet not even really discovered in the depths of his soul." Spiritual trials signify the "reactions" of this thorn in the flesh of the old self, an inexorable shadow of self-will perhaps even confessed in Christ's prayer: "take this cup away from me, nevertheless, not my will but your will be done".

In this spiritual trial of the agonistic will there remains the temptation to despair over one's inexorable quantum of self-will. "But as the old devotional literature rightly teaches, the individual is completely innocent in this." Furthermore, the presence of such spiritual trial should not be "something to be charged against" one, but actually "prove" that one "has really become thoroughly involved and engaged". Indeed, the desire to become nothing before God will elicit spiritual trials — struggles that bring the self out of the inclosing reserve of its self-will, as through a *kenosis-in-ekstasis*, it passes into the fires of Spirit — "dying to the world, slaying his will" (JP 4:4384).

In this final year before his death, Kierkegaard returns once more to the harrowing words of "the prototype [*Forbilledet*]" Christ, "My God, my God, why have you forsaken me!" (JP 4:3903), asserting that while there is an absolute difference between the suffering of Christ and human suffering, "These words are consoling to those who imitate Christ." Every martyr, has been acquainted with "the most agonizing moment" when one is "on the verge of losing his conception of himself, as if he had been abandoned by God." But the words of Christ sanctify such suffering, even to the point of despair: "the prototype consoles by showing that this, too, belongs." Even the despair of God-forsakenness may itself form part of the "the proper emptying out of the human being standing face to face before God". As such, one should not fall into the temptation of melancholy and despair at the thought of "feeling abandoned by God, of losing the conception of oneself". Rather, "this human suffering", empties the self in order that one may receive "the conception of himself again, on the highest level" (JP 4:3903). In this sense, both God-forsakenness and the fire of Spirit aspire towards a higher mortification: the death-to-self, the becoming nothing, by which the self finds itself transfigured and resting transparently in God. It is towards this vision of Spirit as nothingness and self-becoming, as restlessness in search of rest, that the following chapter now turns.

7. The Desire of Spirit:
Restlessness and the Transparency of Rest

One says that God needs no gifts, for He is lacking naught.
Why then should it be true that He needs my pure heart?
(Angelus Silesius, 1624-77)[1]

To be *spirit* is to be *I*. God desires to have *I*'s, for God desires to be
loved [*Gud vil have »Jeger«; Gud vil være elsket*]. . . . 'Christendom'
is a society of millions — all in the third person, no *I*.
(JP 4:4350 / 1854)

To develop the Kierkegaardian vision of spiritual trial outlined so
far, this chapter moves towards a constructive theological account
of the relationship between *Spirit* and *Desire* with reference to motifs
of *restlessness* and *resting transparently in God*. According to one of
Kierkegaard's most remarkable journal entries (JP 4:4350), God's
'desire', or will, for a personal relationship of love is essential to both
the primal gift of human freedom and to the restless endeavour of
self-becoming as *Spirit*. Developing this equivalence of relational
selfhood with Spirit, I contend that while a Kierkegaardian
understanding of Spirit (*Ånd*) ostensibly evokes Hegelian structures
and the pathos of Romanticism, it ultimately invokes an explicitly
theological imagery of the *fire* of the *Holy Spirit*. In this vision, Spirit
is interpreted in personalised terms as a presence of otherness within
the individual, inspiring a burning holy desire, even a melancholy
longing, for a relationship of *kenosis-in-ekstasis* — a realisation of the
imago dei in loving union with God.

This agonistic, apophatic, and relational self-becoming is elaborated
through Kierkegaard's sense of irreducible tension, perhaps even
to the point of paradox or incommensurability, between alterity

---

1 *Angelus Silesius: The Cherubinic Wanderer* (Mahwah: Paulist Press, 1986) (Book
3, 123), 78. Angelus Silesius also discusses *Anfechtung* in his poem, 'Sie bittet
ihn um Beistand in Anfechtung', in which the poet looks to the anguished
Christ, who has borne my heavy burden, for consolation in the midst of my
suffering. He flees like a hunted dove for refuge from my enemies, hidden in
Christ. *Sämtliche poetische Werke in drei Bänden*. Band 2, Herausgegeben und
eingeleitet von Hans Ludwig Held (München: Hanser, 1952) 129-130.

and unity, abyss and ground, restlessness and rest. Becoming Spirit occurs before the ostensibly inexorable — even forbidding — infinite qualitative abyss between the human and the divine. In light of this estrangement, "Spirit is restlessness [*Ånd er Uro*]" (JP 4:4361): a desire for transfiguration in the divine image, which is articulated as both the self that struggles before God; and the self that finds its resting place grounded transparently in God ("*gjennemsigtigt grunder i Gud*"; SUD, 82). In this light, spiritual trial is understood as the agonistic realisation of Spirit within the context of spiritlessness, overcome through moments of dying to self-will in the longing to unite with the will of God. Furthermore, Christ, in overcoming all spiritual trials in his God-forsakenness, promises rest (*Hvile*) for the restless, serving through grace as the prototype for all imitation of the union of wills. The process of spiritual struggle and releasement is thereby interpreted in both negative and positive terms of *becoming nothing* and as *transfiguring* the self as *Spirit*, as an *I* which *inversely resembles* the image of God and is rendered capable by grace, *ex deo*, of loving God; as well as *ex nihilo*, from out of its own heart of subjectivity and freedom.

Spirit expresses the concession and obligation of the eternal, calling each individual from within to become a self before God (SUD, 21). However, mis-direction of the energies of Spirit can also describe the ruin of the self as well as its becoming. In this sense, the devil's despair is described as sheer Spirit (SUD, 42): a demonic internalisation of the vitality of Spirit, which desires Spirit, as life, as freedom, and as will, for itself. Such temptation struggles to take Spirit away from its longing to realise the image of God, trying in despair to forge it according to the self-will or else drown its flames in the dreaming world of spiritlessness. Either way is despair. Spiritual trial therefore expresses the latent war between Spirit and that which is not Spirit, whether manifest in the soporific nihilism of spiritlessness or the demonic defiance of self-will. It is characteristic of the emergent consciousness of Spirit that the term evades precise definition, that it is irreducible to syllogistic reasoning and can only be truly 'known' in love. Yet, Spirit is described as striving; as melancholy; as alienating; as a fire which seeks to either refine or annihilate the individual. Spirit is the synthesis of the psychical and the physical, the infinite and finite, the temporal and the eternal, freedom and necessity (CA, 43); or "the relation's relating itself to itself in the relation" (SUD, 13). Spirit is the self and the self is freedom (SUD, 13; 29)[1]; Spirit struggles

---

1 Cf. Nicolas Berdyaev, *Freedom and the Spirit*, trans. Oliver Fielding Clarke (London: Geoffrey Bles, 1935), 2: "God is spirit, and spirit is activity. Spirit is liberty. The nature of spirit is the opposite of passivity and necessity; it is for this reason that spirit cannot be a substance".

against flesh and blood, against the world, against spiritlessness (*Åndløsheden*); "spirit is to will to die, to die to the world" (JP 4:4354); "Spirit is the power a person's understanding exercises over his life" (JP 4:4340); "the more spirit the more suffering" (JP 4:4359); Spirit is dreaming — yet awakened in the anxiety of freedom (CA, 42); consciousness of Spirit is brooding in the longing and world-weariness of melancholy (E/O II, 185-186); Spirit is *I* not *we* — though it is "the divine 'We' which embraces an *I* and a third person" (JP 2:1651); Christianity is Spirit as restlessness, where Christendom is the tranquiliser, the opiate (JP 4:4361; 4362); Spirit is fire (JP 4:4355); Spirit is metamorphosis: the chrysalis that gives birth to the butterfly (JP 4:4712); God is Spirit and Spirit is the image of God (UDVS, 192); "God as 'Spirit' cannot express his love otherwise" than through suffering (JP 2:1661); "the devil is sheer spirit" and, as such, his is "the most intensive despair" (SUD, 42); "not to be conscious of oneself as spirit — is despair, which is spiritlessness" (SUD, 44).

There is evidently more in such statements than can be reduced to the logic of syllogism. In the end, Spirit, as *holy*, can only truly be spoken of indirectly. Spirit is a winged horse of infinite speed that takes us a world away in a moment. Surrender to Spirit, mount it; and Spirit will do the rest (JP 6:6832). Despite modern scepticism, such Spirit does truly exist; yet to call upon this Spirit requires "a completely different conception of God" than childish Christianity (spoiled by grace) has accustomed us to (JP 6:6832). Spirit is suffering and Spirit is also the Comforter (*parakletos*), "the dispensator of grace" (JP 2:1654). Spirit therefore crucifies understanding. It is given to each individually, praying within us bringing forth "unutterable sighs"; it is discerned within the searching of our hearts (JP 4:3915). Spirit as the Holy Spirit in each individual "unites what God has united, it links together what God has linked together — man with God and God with man . . . the image of man in God and the image of God in man". Yet Spirit as a synthesis of opposites retains difference-in-unity: "it humbles you with the representation of your unlikeness, and you sink to your knees in adoration". But though humbling Spirit also *transfigures* the divine-human relationship: "it raises you up with the hope of likeness, and you rise up humble and full of confidence" (JP 4:3915).

In other words, while Spirit is conscious of an "infinite qualitative difference" between the human and the "absolutely different", Spirit also affirms that "There is a *presence of God* in us", that "your God takes up residence within you, is within you beyond all measure, is present within you, even if you notice it first of all with his disappearance" (JP 4:3915). It is in this almost mystical sense that, as shall be explored below, spiritual trial as the struggle between Spirit and spiritlessness, affirms both union and alterity. Spirit is the synthesis of all of these, and more.

In traditional pneumatological terms, "The Spirit is the animating presence of God on earth, and in humanity, and it is the circulation of the divine life between Father and Son."[1] Expressed through Kierkegaard's personalised and existential terms, however, Spirit is also the realisation of true selfhood, in freedom and love, becoming nothing before God, through the metamorphosis of Spirit's fire, burnt out to ashes, now resting transparently grounded in God, transfigured as the image of God. Yet within this structure Kierkegaard is still, Søe claims, "able to directly accept the traditional trichotomy of the Church, according to which" humanity "consists of body, soul and spirit, a conception not primarily of gnostic origin, but mentioned already in 1. Thess. 5.23"[2] ("Now may the God of peace Himself sanctify you completely; and may your whole spirit, soul, and body be preserved blameless at the coming of our Lord Jesus Christ"). Søe concludes that "spirit signifies that by virtue of which" one "knows and evaluates" oneself and "submits to the eternal authority, or realizes that it is rebellion not to do so. Spirit has to do first and last with [one's] relationship with God".[3] This relational quality is supported by Walsh's suggestion that "For Kierkegaard, the first thing to be said about God from a Christian standpoint is that God is Spirit (cf. John 4:24), in relation to whom a human being is also defined as spirit".[4] Yet while Kierkegaard does make reparative appeal to a New Testament vision of Spirit, particularly in his critique of modern Christendom, his evocations of Spirit are not primarily intended as a recapitulation of traditional Church pneumatology. At times his reference to Spirit seems idiomatically Hegelian as well as biblical; Romantic and even mystical in meaning, nuance and expression. However, it is the role of Spirit in relation to a constructive theological anthropology rather than

---

1   Oliver Davies, *A Theology of Compassion: Metaphysics of Difference and the Renewal of Tradition* (Grand Rapids/Cambridge: William B. Eerdmans, 2001), 207.

2   N.H. Søe, 'The Human Spirit and God', Niels Thusltrup and M. Mikulvá Thulstrup (eds) *Bibliotheca Kierkegaardiana Vol. 2*, (Copenhagen: C.A. Reitzels Boghandel, 1978), 16-26, 16. On the relation between one's Spirit and the Holy Spirit, Kierkegaard affirms Hugo St. Victor's 'The Seven Gifts of the Holy Spirit', "If you pray for your spirit, you pray for Spirit (the Holy Spirit)" (JP 2:1653).

3   'The Human Spirit and God', 23.

4   Sylvia Walsh, *Kierkegaard: Thinking Christianly in an Existential Mode* (Oxford: Oxford University Press, 2009), 52.

a dogmatic or speculative pneumatology, which motivates this account of spiritual trial. Kierkegaard is not concerned with articulating the immanent Mind (*Idee*) of Spirit (*Geist*) through speculative logic or reason (*Vernunft*), but with the Spirit within and the Holy Spirit: that which is both Holy Other *and* in the depths of the human heart, speaking *de profundis* — as abyss calling unto abyss — awakening selfhood to its source in, longing for, and estrangement from the divine. Spirit in this sense is not only the "synthesis" of the physical and the psychical: it is the paradoxical (dialectical or even antinomous) synthesis — though not a Hegelian *mediation* or *sublation* — of *the human and the divine*: between which there is as yet also an infinite qualitative abyss and an interior intimacy.

Spirit and Desire: Kierkegaard and Hegel

From the requisite perspective of subjectivity, "Spirit is the self" and the self is "the relation's relating itself to itself in the relation" (SUD, 13). As is well-recognised, Anti-Climacus' idiom in this condensed passage appears self-consciously Hegelian — if also ironically or even doubly ironically so.[1] Contrasting *The Sickness Unto Death* (1849) with Hegel's *Phenomenology of Spirit* (1807) on the emergence of self-consciousness elucidates important points of elision, comparison, as

---

1   Mark C. Taylor observes that "The Hegelian language in which Kierkegaard ironically couches his description of spirit tends to obscure the unique contours of selfhood he highlights", which is intended as a contrast to Hegel's treatment. *Journeys to Selfhood: Hegel and Kierkegaard* (California: University of California Press, 1989), 169. Kierkegaard expressed his own concern over the often incongruous lyrical title of the work and its sometimes dry formulaic style (JP 5:6136), which Beabout claims "is poking fun at the abstract jargon of the Hegelians. Yet, at the very same time that he is mocking obtuse Hegelian formulas, he is using the abstract style to set forth his view of the self, a view that is crucially different from Hegel's." 'Kierkegaard on the Self and Despair: An Interpretation of the Opening Passage of *The Sickness Unto Death*', *Proceedings of the American Catholic Philosophical Association*, 62, (1988), 107. However, Jon Stewart suggests that the fact that "Hegel's philosophy was no longer in vogue in 1849 when *The Sickness Unto Death* appeared . . . would seem to undermine the point of writing a book that covertly satirizes Hegel's philosophy." *Kierkegaard's Relation to Hegel Reconsidered* (Cambridge: Cambridge University Press, 2003), 592. This may explain why, as Theunissen observes, after *Concluding Unscientific Postscript*, "[Kierkegaard's] critique of Hegel recedes dramatically. On occasion, Kierkegaard can even call Hegel a master in his journals of the late '40s." *Kierkegaard's Concept of Despair*, trans. Barbara Harshav and Helmut Illbruck (Princeton and Oxford: Princeton University Press, 2005), 153n.24.

well as difference. According to Taylor, although both Kierkegaard and Hegel view Spirit as "essentially an activity of self-relation" in which "opposites are brought together", there are "significant differences that distinguish the two interpretations of the self."[1] In seeking to overcome existential estrangement or spiritlessness both agree that the essence of Spirit is freedom, although Kierkegaard regards Hegel as only doing so in the realm of thought at the exclusion of *actuality*. Where Hegel speaks of "mediation" and "sublation" (*Aufhebung*) of opposites, Kierkegaard interprets Spirit as a restless "synthesis" of opposites,[2] while retaining an inalienable sense of the infinite qualitative difference between the human and the divine and the absolute paradox of the Incarnation, which itself reflects Spirit's structure. Kierkegaard asserts the offence, paradox, and absurdity of the Incarnation which, while calling all unto Christ (PC, 18-20), promises rest for the restless, and a setting fire to the earth (JP 4:4355). The limit that collides against understanding is the scandal of the cross, the *theologia crucis*, which opposes speculative theology.

---

1   *Journeys to Selfhood*, 144. As Walsh explains: "Kierkegaard was introduced to the Hegelian concept of spirit in Martensen's lectures on speculative dogmatics. . . . Like Hegel, he made the New Testament identification of God as spirit central to his theology, but while he affirms the doctrine of the Trinity, it is not an organising principle of his theology as in Hegel and Martensen's, nor it is understood as a process of actualisation of the one universal spirit through a historical objectification and mediation of itself in and through nature and culture. Rather, for Kierkegaard, the individual God-relationship is the lens through which the Trinity is encountered and known in human existence." *Kierkegaard: Thinking Christianly in an Existential Mode*, 53.

2   According to Hegelian monism, difference, opposition, is finally illusion. Kierkegaard thus rejects Hegel's mediation of contraries in deference to a view in which "otherness and difference are abiding features of experience which finally can be overcome, if at all, only eschatologically." Taylor, *Journeys to Selfhood*, 166. Despite being often read as proposing a triad of thesis — antithesis — synthesis, Hegel actually avoids referring to Spirit as "synthesis", since "the very expression *synthesis* easily recalls an *external* unity and mere combination of entities which are *in and for themselves separate*." (Hegel, *Science of Logic*. trans. A.V. Miller (New York: Humanities Press, 1969), 589. Kierkegaard, as Taylor describes, "seeks to abolish mediation and reinstate synthesis" understood as "the conjunction of two mutually exclusive opposites effected by a "positive third."'" *Journeys to Selfhood*, 171. For Kierkegaard, Hegel's dialectic ultimately violates the infinite qualitative difference, "and ends in the pantheistic dispersion of the divine and dissipation of the human" (171). The human Spirit, as the paradox of the incarnation, "is a freely sustained coincidence of opposites. Freedom, be it human or divine, synthesizes antitheses" (172). In this respect, spiritual trial reflects the struggle between opposites.

Spiritual trial, therefore, is not only elicited by the dark cloud of unknowing that veils the unknowable Godhead. Nor does it only arise between the wrath of the Father and the sinner, to be mediated by Christ. Spiritual trial, as offence and a cruciform boundary with which faith struggles, also arises between the individual and Christ himself. As such, there may be spiritual trial before the agony of Christ, in the face of the ineffable image of the crucified and God-forsaken God. There may be spiritual trial before the infinite abyss between one's suffering and the unfathomable *passio Christi*. Before the Incarnation, the understanding collides with the absolutely different (PF, 46); yet even when "the unknown" reveals itself in the Incarnation, the individual is halted by the paradox, by the absurd, and also by the revelation of sin, the revelation of oneself as the cause of absolute difference (PF, 47). In all these spiritual trials, the understanding is crucified such that, as Bonhoeffer, writes, "there are only two ways possible of encountering Jesus: man must die or he must put Jesus to death".[1]

For Kierkegaard, spiritual trial arises not only in relation to the Father and the Son but also between the individual and Spirit, between the lower self-will and the higher spiritual will, between the spirit and the flesh, and between Spirit and the spiritlessness it seeks to transubstantiate into itself. In this respect, Kierkegaard's notion of Spirit expresses both the interiority and alterity inherent to the *agonia* of spiritual trial. Kierkegaard's vision of Spirit as the relationship between self and God retains an inexorable sense of God as Wholly Other, which does not fully succumb to sublimation — though the relationship between self and God is transfigured through Spirit's realisation of the self as the image of God. Hegel, by contrast, defines God as Spirit as differentiating himself from himself through a movement of love, becoming an object to himself and yet becoming absolutely self-identical in this very differentiation in and through world-history. Whereas Spirit within Hegel's cosmogony "overcomes alienation by reconciling, without dissolving, the opposites between which spiritlessness is torn",[2] for Kierkegaard the individual human self, becoming transfigured as Spirit, is a process of synthesising opposites that is continually confronted and disturbed by spiritual trials, which are themselves essential expressions of the restlessness and absolute difference between the human and the divine, as well the finite and the infinite, the temporal and the eternal etc. Spiritlessness does not merely express absence or estrangement but also total war and enmity against Spirit, even if only implicitly or unconsciously.

---

1 Dietrich Bonhoeffer, *Christology* (London: Collins, 1978), 35.
2 Taylor, *Journeys to Selfhood*, 154.

It is the paradox of the God-Man, which "discloses the passionate coincidence of opposites which must be repeatedly constituted in the life of the self. Spiritual sojourners remain distended between the conflicting extremes they struggle to join."[1] According to Taylor, such "spiritual tensions" (we might add *spiritual trials*) culminate in the "passion . . . created by the conjunction of opposites" that cannot be grasped by the understanding, which, I suggest, afflicts the understanding in spiritual trial. Ultimately, therefore, "The passion of the individual's crisis of decision reflects the passion of the God-Man's crucifixion"[2] — a passion which is elaborated by Kierkegaard and his sources in terms of spiritual trial's struggles with doubt, will, and the resolve of faith. In this sense, "The tension generated by the recurrent crisis of decision is the cross upon which authentic spirit hangs",[3] a perennial struggle that can be understood in terms of the endurance of spiritual trials.

Furthermore, Hegel's progressive view of Spirit as also social selfhood, the "I that is we and we that is I"[4] manifest in the shared "ethical life" (*Sittlichkeit*), is rejected by Kierkegaard on the painfully degenerative evidence of the bourgeois spiritlessness of Christendom. Although the "The Holy Spirit is the divine 'We' which embraces an *I* and a third person (an objective world, a realm of existence)" (JP 2:1651), the social or ecclesial congregation is a concession to our individual inability to endure becoming purely Spirit (JP 4:4341). In its ideal form, to become Spirit is to become an individual (JP 2:2074) in the irreducible secret solitude of interiority, a self alone before God — meaning that the shadow-side, or the "negative" and melancholy definition of Spirit is thus "not to be like the others"; "Of all anguish, the greatest is this — to have the task of being spirit and then to have to live among men" (JP 4:4325).

Yet in terms of coming to self-consciousness, both Hegel and Kierkegaard relate Spirit with *desire* — though where Hegel focuses on inter-personal desire Kierkegaard's sense of this, I suggest, pertains more explicitly to the desire between God and the soul expressed in devotional theology. In chapter four of the *Phenomenology of Spirit*, Hegel claims that "self-consciousness is desire itself [*Begierde überhaupt*]" and that the desire of "self-consciousness attains its satisfaction only in another self-consciousness." The desire of self-consciousness is not only challenged by the mimetic desire of another

---

1   *Ibid.* 142.
2   *Ibid.* 178.
3   *Ibid.* 179.
4   G.W.F. Hegel, *Phenomenology of Spirit*, trans. A.V. Miller (Oxford: Oxford University Press, 1977), § 177.

who desires the same objects, it is refused by the subjectivity of the other — as expressed in the Master-Slave relation: a life and death struggle of desire for being-in-and-for-itself which gives birth to the estrangement of "the version of Christianity" Hegel names as The Unhappy Consciousness.[1] *Unity-with-itself* thus becomes the "elusive desideratum", which is attained "not in a 'Beyond' but in all of reality as itself rational, by ultimately, as Reason".[2] Yet while Hegel articulates the problem of estrangement and desire in inter-personal terms, Kierkegaard envisions self-alienation as overcome, yet not yet full reconciled, in relationship with an irreducibly Holy Other. For Kierkegaard Spirit as desire is not merely desire for self-unity but *desire for God as Other*: Spirit's desire aspires beyond a striving for the self, beyond the inter-personal, inter-subjective, or the social. It is an ecstatic desire for a Wholly Other God, which responds to, and is given possibility by, God's desire for the self to realise its own freedom and subjectivity in loving God. In striving for its Wholly Other, the self discovers that there is only one who truly possesses self-consciousness in-and-for-itself: that is the unknowable God (CD, 43).

In terms of both the Master-Slave paradigm and the anxiety of spiritual trial, however, it might be claimed that the human self is effectively subjected to the point of negation by this Wholly Other Subjectivity such that it can only become object for an unknowable Absolute Self. It is captured in the infinite qualitative abyss which forbids its appropriation of God as object of desire and condemns it to being an inescapably guilty object of the divine subject's gaze of disgust. The self is negated by God; or else, in recognition of its humility (as but dust and ashes) it negates itself before God in devotional acts of self-mortification: the dying-to-self by which it avoids the struggle to the death, the theophany of the One whose Face means Death.

Yet while the self-God relationship may be experienced in such harrowing terms — as expressed in the excesses of *Anfechtung* or in

---

1 See Robert B. Pippin, *Hegel on Self-Consciousness: Desire and Death in Hegel's Phenomenology of Spirit* (Princeton, N.J.: Princeton University Press, 2011), 98. For Hegel, the problem is that "I seem rather just to be subject to the imperatives or demands of life for my species. *Rather than being the subject of my desires, I am subject to my desires*" (32). Life, as the aperture between present and future, is what "is meant by calling consciousness *desire* as lack or gap" (35). In terms of this space of self-alienation, Hegel "describes human existence itself as a 'wound' ('*Wunde*'), but one which, he says, has been self-inflicted and which (one infers, which *therefore*) can be healed, even 'without scars' ('*ohne Narben*')" (52-53).

2 Pippin, *Hegel on Self-Consciousness*, 97.

the divine gaze which elicits the deicidal resentment of Nietzsche's Ugliest Man — this *appearance* is itself to be struggled against by clinging, *adhaesio dei*, to the Love of God. This struggle of love is itself the way through the fires of spiritual trial to the realisation of the restless self as Spirit, resting transparently in God. This relationship is not motivated by the inclosing desire of self-will, or even the desire for self-identity as negotiated in-and-through-an-other. Rather, becoming Spirit before and in God is a relationship of love, which proceeds *ex deo* as a divine love which incorporates, while also exceeding and negating, the language of *apage* and *eros*, *passio* and *com-passio*. Its essence can, once again, be glimpsed in the affirmation that "To be *spirit* is to be *I*. God desires to have *I*'s, for God desires to be loved" (JP 4:4350). Becoming Spirit is a *kenosis-in-ekstasis*, which itself springs forth from a kenotic love in which divine omnipotence, withdraws in order to create the possibility for an *other* self to become itself in freedom. God hopes, or desires, that this self will enter into a free relationship of love with its hidden origin; but the self is also free to internalise desire for itself and its own inevitably tragic self-will, to transfer its kenotic and ecstatic desire for a Holy Other to its own self, or even to the external objects in which it invests its self.

For both Hegel and Kierkegaard, therefore, the origin, becoming, and recognition of selfhood seems to originate in a form of desire. Yet in Hegel, as Kojève and Taylor both observe, there appears to be no deduction of or justification for the origin of desire itself: it is simply necessary to motivate the self's (Spirit's) coming to self-consciousness.[1] Yet does this not, as Neuhouser explains, raise a problem concerning the origin of desire, which threatens to undermine the very consistency of Hegel's "claim to be doing a rigorous and presuppositionless phenomenology"? After all, 'recognition' appears to derive from a prior desire, the origins of which "is itself no less mysterious". Therefore, "How is it that the capacity for desire is suddenly attributed to a self-consciousness which at its inception was nothing more than the certainty that it 'was'?"[2]

What then is the origin and justification of desire? Does it arise from a prior unknowable dialectic? Is this desire, as in some of the mystical thinking (e.g. Eckhart and Boehme), which inspires Hegel's speculative philosophy, God's desire for Godself? Yet if all desire

---

1 Alexandre Kojève, *Introduction to the Reading of Hegel*, trans. James H. Nichols, Jr, ed. Allan Bloom (New York: Basic Books, 1969), 3. Charles Taylor, *Hegel* (Cambridge: Cambridge University Press, 1975), 150.

2 Frederick Neuhouser, 'Deducing Desire and Recognition in the Phenomenology of Spirit', *Journal of the History of Philosophy*, 24 (2), April 1986, 243-262, 243.

begins in God's desire what then is the origin of God's desire for Godself? Does God naturally desire Godself as the only object worthy of such a subject's desire? In order to conceptualise this insatiable and excessive desire, must one postulate *alterity* within God — as Lover, Beloved, and Love itself? Is desire then simply a necessary given, the Absolute's *causa sui* — the Prime Mover moved only by itself? If such a vision of immanent Trinitarian Narcissism is valid, then what of the relationship between Creator and Creation? Is there an infinite qualitative difference between Creator and an *ex nihilo* Creation? Is *Creation* then God's (Wholly) *other* in relation to which God desires to behold Godself as if in a mirror?

Such speculations, as Kierkegaard wisely cautions, tempt us far away from the existential task of realising Spirit in the personalised God-relationship and, consequently, from spiritual trial itself. Desire, as such, should be interpreted from the perspective of subjectivity rather than *sub species aeternitatis*. For Kierkegaard, the desire that motivates the self in despair is a desire to will or not to will to be oneself (desire here understood as the conscious or unconscious prior motivation of *will*; desire which, as yet unconscious of itself being, is experienced in nascent form as *restlessness*). The desire that motivates the self in despair, willing to be or not to be itself, is, as Boehme recognises, the desire for the self-will, the internalisation of the vitality of Spirit in inclosing reserve, which is tragically the enslavement of the freedom of Spirit to the *demonic will* or to *spiritlessness*. The desire that motivates authentic selfhood before God as *Spirit*, however, is the desire *for God*: a desire which, as I will suggest with reference to mystical theology, is a desire that originates freely from God and a desire whose melancholy and restlessness expresses its estrangement from its source and its destiny.

Such longing proceeds from God, *ex deo*, in terms of a God who is the hidden spring of Love (WL, 9-10) and who first loves us: a God who desires us to become *Is*, Spirit as the selfhood and subjectivity to freely love God (the *Desideratum*) in a relationship of alterity *ex nihilo*. As created via divine kenosis *ex nihilo*, the self is gifted the freedom and subjectivity to become or refuse itself, to love God from the source of love which proceeds *ex deo*; but which in the gift of selfhood as personalised Spirit, forms its own heart from which it loves God as a self. God does not simply love Godself through myself as Spirit, as if the human self becomes the annihilated mediator of divine self-love. Alterity and consequently the freedom and inviolability of the self is assured by the infinite qualitative difference between the human and the divine.

Because of this paradox and impasse, the relationship of love realised through freedom requires struggle and spiritual trial: it requires not only the desire of God but also the free desire of the self — even a self which wills the death of its self-will in the Divine Will. Insofar as Spirit persists in tension with its conscious and it unconscious shadow-aspects (respectively, *the demonic* and *spiritlessness*), which each resist Spirit's synthesis, Spirit will elicit spiritual trial. There is no easy synthesis, no simple reconciliation, mediation or sublation of opposites. In the spiritual trial which arises in the endeavour to relate oneself to God, Spirit is awakened as restlessness striving for its place of rest. Here, I suggest, Kierkegaard's treatment of Spirit unveils significant affinities with treatments of love in mystical theology.

Spirit and Desire: Mystical Theology

As broached in chapter one, perhaps the most canonical expression of spiritual desire and inquietude is found in the opening of Augustine's *Confessions*, 1.1, "because you have made us for yourself [or towards yourself — *ad te; ad imaginum* — towards God's image] our heart is restless [*inquietum*] until it finds rest [*requiescat*] in thee". Augustine's anxiety is such that, resonant with the dialectic of spiritual as I have elsewhere suggested, he can only express his desire in the plea: "Hide not Thy face from me. Even if I die, let me see Thy face lest I die" (*Confessions* 1.5). The *tremendum et fascinans* of Augustine's religious melancholy is epitomised here: the absence of the face of the Beloved means an arid living death; the desired theophany of the face seems to promise annihilation.[1] In Augustine's model, as George Pattison explains, "the religious life is figured as something like a passionate love-affair between the soul and God" in which the *telos* is a fusion of the soul with "the ultimate object of its most powerful longings." External to this, "the soul, like any romantic lover, feels that it has no existence worth talking of. Whatever else the world may offer is just illusion, surface, deception."[2] In this dialectic the erotic and disillusioned elements of Spirit's melancholy can be glimpsed through its lack of fulfilment in the world of spiritlessness. Spirit's desire is a search for Truth, and not simply for ecstatic rapture, such that for Augustine "both the Socratic *eros* and the reasons of the heart are equally prominent: the

1 See further my *Kierkegaard and the Self Before God*, 65-67.
2 George Pattison, 'Desire, Decreation and Unknowing in the God-Relationship: Mystical Theology and its Transformation in Kierkegaard, Simone Weil and Dostoevsky', Arne Grøn, Iben Damgaard, and Søren Overgaard (eds), *Subjectivity and Transcendence* (Tübingen: Mohr Siebeck, 2007), 193-211, 193.

God-relationship is characterized both in terms of ardent, heartfelt longing and as a quest for wisdom or knowledge."[1] And yet, as Pattison rightly articulates, the quest for knowledge of God is frustrated by the Wholly Otherness of desire's intended 'object', or other. To see the Holy Other God is death; yet the unconsummated desire to behold God is a living death of melancholy longing and restless despair.[2]

This ambivalence is elaborated further in the treatment of love and desire in apophatic theology. In this respect, Pattison attends to *The Cloud of Unknowing*'s distinction between a God who is unknowable to the intellect yet knowable to love. Yet this love of God does not originate *ex nihilo* from the will of "a ready-made pre-existent self". Rather it emerges as "a response to a movement or prompting of grace" such that the subjectivity it constitutes "is not only for-another but from-another. One does not so much intend the love of God as allow the intention of loving God to become the defining formative drive of the (non)subject."[3] In terms of the desire of Spirit, love, which forms the (non-)self becoming nothing yet transfigured as Spirit, could be understood as the personalisation of the love of God, which proceeds from God. What Boehme discerns as the inner spark, which desires divine grace in the midst of spiritual trial, is the Holy Spirit, which is "the divine desire itself",[4] sanctifying the heart through its presence within each individual.[5]

This erotic sense of Spirit's desire might suggest that the kenotic selflessness of 'Christian' love as *Agape* is not so decisively contrasted

---

1   Pattison, 'Desire, Decreation and Unknowing in the God-Relationship', 194.

2   See further my 'To Die and Yet Not Die: Kierkegaard's Theophany of Death'.

3   Pattison, 'Desire, Decreation and Unknowing in the God-Relationship', 198.

4   *The Way to Christ*, 263. Cf. Eckhart: with reference to Romans 5:5, "God's love is shed abroad in our hearts", Eckhart equates God's gift of God's love with the gift of the Holy Spirit such that when one loves with a divine one loves with the love with which God loves Godself. Sermon 27, *Werke I*, 310; *Meister Eckhart: Werke I, II*; Bibliothek des Mittelalters, vol. 20, 21; ed. & trans. Nicholas Largier (Frankfurt am Main: Deutsche Klassiker Verlag, 1993).

5   Pattison discerns a comparable move in Kierkegaard's and Simone Weil's conceptions of what might be called apophatic desiring non-selfhood. "It is the desiring itself that is to be desired: to know one's need of God is a person's highest perfection, to will the Good: it is intention not 'state' that matters" (202). With reference to *The Cloud*, Kierkegaard, and Weil, Pattison concludes that "God is the wholly other and the wholly immanent and neither of these, since these, after all, are descriptions fetched from the world of knowledge and concepts. Our consciousness, in the encounter with God (which, of course, is not an 'encounter'), is both our consciousness of the selves we actually are in the lives we live, and yet the utter decreation of self-consciousness" (207).

with so-called 'pagan' conceptions of *Eros*. The realisation of Spirit through the movement between spiritual trial and releasement, *Anfechtung* and *Gelassenheit*, might be understood as a *kenosis-in-ekstasis*: a self-sacrificial love that is drawn out in desire to be with the Other. After all, even in its egocentricity, *Eros*, in its physical and spiritual expressions, is understood Platonically as desire under divine guidance.[1] Furthermore, Kierkegaard himself does not use *Kjærlighed* and *Elskov* as formal technical differentiation throughout his authorship: he employs both terms with reference to both erotic *and* Christian neighbour love — from which Furtak infers that "Kierkegaard uses the different words for love in order to distinguish various aspects or manifestations of love, not to demarcate absolutely dissimilar categories which can only be locked in violent conflict".[2] In this sense, I suggest that *Eros* does not exclusively belong to temptation (*Fristelse*) and *agape* to spiritual trial (*Anfægtelse*). On the contrary, the entreaty to press on through the struggle of spiritual trial is itself envigorated by the higher desire and restlessness of Spirit. Nonetheless, such desire is itself dialectical insofar as one can desire to be too much Spirit as well as be unwilling to become Spirit (JP 4:4372).

As Jack Mulder, Jr also submits: "the whole dialectical movement toward eternal happiness is itself a movement of love for God in Kierkegaard", and as such "the love for God in Kierkegaard is, in the deepest sense, a kind of eros."[3] Here Mulder acknowledges Daphne Hampson's prior observations that Kierkegaard's view of love of God occupies a fertile space between traditionally distinctive Lutheran and Catholic views. Comparing Kierkegaard's *Works of Love* with Anders Nygren's *Agape and Eros* (1930/1936), Hampson elucidates an important difference between the two, in many ways, similar texts. Whereas Hampson regards Nygren as understanding the human as "a mere 'channel' between God and neighbour" through whom divine love flows, she astutely points to

---

1   Rick Antony Furtak, 'Symposium: Kierkegaard and Platonic Eros', in Jon Stewart & Katalin Nun (eds), *Kierkegaard and the Greek World: Tome I: Socrates and Plato* (Aldershot: Ashgate, 2010), 105-114, 106.

2   Furtak, 'Symposium', 112. Furtak acknowledge that though there may be important differences between preferential and selfless love, "it would be a mistake to speak as if there were an absolute ontological difference between the love that Kierkegaard discusses in his religious writings and the love that is the topic of Plato's erotic dialogues, as if human beings were subject to a fundamentally Manichean duality of motives, one good and the other evil" (113).

3   Jack Mulder Jr, *Kierkegaard and the Catholic Tradition: Conflict and Dialogue* (Indianapolis: Indiana University Press, 2010), 94-95.

Kierkegaard's notion that the human person must "form a 'heart' (a core we may say) out of which he [sic] loves"[1]. In this sense, Hampson concludes that "although he is apparently speaking of *agape*, sometimes the way in which Kierkegaard expresses love of God would seem to approximate more closely to a higher *eros*".[2] Indeed, Kierkegaard's works repeatedly invoke the allegory of lover and beloved when speaking of the relationship between the self and God (e.g. PF, 29-30). Through the gift of love, the Lover gives the beloved the capacity to reciprocally consider God (the Lover) as the heart's Beloved. As such, Kierkegaard also retains a profoundly Lutheran sense of humanity's incapacity for following a 'natural' love for God — while also suggesting that love's *works* can become transformative with reference to becoming transfigured as Spirit. All love begins in God's love — a love that descends but which, nonetheless, does not simply pass through the heart: it transforms the heart, forming the heart itself, out of which one is enabled to love, to become Spirit, even an *I*, not merely to play passive, even entirely negated, host to Spirit. Kierkegaard therefore writes of the eternal gaining control over, almost possessing, the person; while also establishing itself eternally within, forming a heart which is irreducibly one's own (WL, 12-13).

Yet desire or need, while a human being's highest perfection (EUD, 300ff), in and of itself is not sufficient for this transfiguration of the will. While the nature of desire may be shaped in accordance with its source and object,[3] the mere presence of desire is not sufficient to logically prove the existence of the source or object of desire itself.[4] Insofar as it endures in the apparent absence of that which evokes it or that which it aspires towards, desire is apophatic — "*desire* for something unknown".[5] Though desire may be

---

1 *Christian Contradictions*, 260.

2 *Christian Contradictions*, 260. See also Hampson, *Kierkegaard: Exposition and Critique*, 254.

3 See further Brian Harding, 'Dialectics of Desire and the Psychopathology of Alterity: From Levinas to Kierkegaard via Lacan', *The Heythrop Journal*, XLVIII (2007), 406-422.

4 See further Gary J. Deverell, 'The Desire of God', *The Heythrop Journal*, XLVIII (2007), 343-370. "While human desire is not enough to guarantee God's arrival, desire perseveres on the basis of a mysterious sense of call or promise which, while experienced and apprehended within the self, nevertheless appears to emanate or broadcast as from another place" (343).

5 Bruce Milem, 'Four Theories of Negative Theology', *The Heythrop Journal*, XLVIII (2007), 187-204, 187. Adriaan T. Peperzak also suggests that God's transcendence to human desire afflicts as "the highest or deepest form of suffering and utter disappointment. What apophatic theology does in

heralded as the presence of the Spirit as Love, restlessness itself also suggests that rest is elusive. Furthermore, as Kierkegaard cautions, no one in this world is able to fully realise becoming *wholly Spirit*. The denial, suppression, deferral, or un-consummation of Spirit's restless longing grieves the Spirit, inducing melancholy — "the hysteria of the spirit" (E/O II, 188) — perhaps even causing it to fall into despair. The call of the eternal induces restlessness, which oppresses the nascent 'self' (in which Spirit is dreaming; CA, 42). The eternal is a fire, the fire of Spirit (eternity's obligation to become a self), which burns but cannot consume the self (SUD, 20-21). This is its sickness unto death: its inability to die, its inability to either fully realise or annihilate Spirit. And yet, despite the consolations offered to the soul in spiritual trial by Boehme and Kierkegaard, the notion that desire is itself a trace, or even proof, of a divine presence-in-absence is not immune from doubt.[1] That is to say that this consolation itself may be vulnerable to spiritual trial, which in turn can bring Spirit to grief.[2]

> For self-scrutiny [*Selvbetragtning*] breeds unrest [*Uro*] and unrest breeds spiritual trial [*Anfægtelse*] and spiritual trial breeds despondency [*Mismod*] and despondency halts the growth and grieves [*bedrøver*] the Holy Spirit. (JP 4:3915)

---

words, affectivity experiences as an overwhelming emptiness, night, and desert". 'Affective Theology, Theological Affectivity', ed. Jeffrey Bloechl, *Religious Experience and the End of Metaphysics* (Bloomington: Indiana University Press, 2003), 94-105, 101.

1   In a similar sense, Millem questions Peperzak by contending that: "The mere existence of a desire for God would not by itself shed any light on the question of God's existence, and it would certainly be possible to desire God even if God does not exist, in or outside the world. In this sense, one could understand negative theology as the expression of a desire for God yet remain agnostic or even doubtful that God exists." Millem, 'Four Theories of Negative Theology', 194.

2   Kierkegaard writes that "being loved of God is suffering . . . the closer to God the more suffering, yet with the consolation [*Trøst*] of eternity and with the Spirit's testimony that God is love, this is what it is to dare to love God" (JP 2:1433). As Walsh explains, God as Spirit and as infinitely qualitatively different may appear as otherwise than love. Yet "Kierkegaard admits that one must be very spiritually advanced in order to be able to understand suffering in this way. In fact, this apparent cruelty of God constitutes another form of spiritual trial (*Anfægtelse*) for the Christian striver. . . . This is the *ultimate inversion* concerning suffering that Christians are required to make." Sylvia Walsh, *Living Christianly: Kierkegaard's Dialectic of Christian Existence* (Pennsylvania: Pennsylvania State University Press, 2005), 148.

Spirit and the *Imago Dei*

Echoing this dialectic between presence and absence, I suggest that in Kierkegaard Spirit is not understood in terms of desire consummated in a state of divine union in which difference vanishes, but as desire for a self-God relationship in which profound alterity is honoured — even though such alterity may be expressed through the fires of spiritual trial, which attest to the ultimately eschatological nature of becoming Spirit. Spirit transfigures the self with reference to the image of God and re-inscribes the self's relation to 'the world' and to 'the other', expressed through *works* of *love* by which one *inversely reflects* the *invisible divine image*. This notion of Spirit as the invisible image of God can be elaborated with reference to the final of Kierkegaard's eighteen upbuilding discourses, 'One Who Prays Aright Struggles in Prayer and is Victorious — in that God is Victorious' (1844) and the 1847 discourse 'On the Occasion of a Confession', 'Purity of Heart Is To Will One Thing'. Through the "transfiguration" of prayer the self is reconciled to the paradox of alterity and intimacy, struggle and rest, which determines the relationship between Spirit and spiritual trial. In the loving struggle of prayer, the restless self before God seeks to rest transparently in God. God and humanity are separated by an infinite qualitative difference since "God is solely spirit", whereas the human being as Spirit is an anxious synthesis of restless opposites. And yet it can also be said that "the God to whom [one] prays is human" insofar as God is "moved by the struggler's cry". In the transfiguration of prayer, it appears that the chasmic abyss of human-divine alterity dissolves, insofar as the one who prays is *illuminated* by God to the extent that they come to "resemble" God (EUD, 399).[1]

In imagery evocative of Eckhart,[2] Kierkegaard elaborates this resemblance by appealing to the way in which the image of Heaven sinks deeply into the still depths of the ocean — no longer a raging

---

1   This section is expounded further in my 'The Abyss of the Heart: Transfiguration and the *Imago Dei*', Králik *et al* (eds), *Acta Kierkegaardiana VI: Kierkegaard and Human Nature* (Toronto and Šal'a: Kierkegaard Circle, 2013), 88-104.

2   "I take a bowl of water and place a mirror in it and set it under the disc of the sun. Then the sun sends forth its light-rays both from the disc and from the sun's depths, and yet suffers no diminution. The reflection of the mirror in the sun is a sun, and yet it is what it is. So it is with God. God in the soul with His nature, with His being and with His Godhead, and yet He is not the soul. The reflection of the soul in God is God, and yet she is what she is." Eckhart, Sermon Fifty-Six, *The Complete Mystical Works*, 293.

abyss of offense and despair; but resting and receptive, a deep, silent nothing. The ocean embraces heaven's image, allowing the glittering sun to permeate it; then from its deepest nothingness, it reflects heaven back to itself. In the resting moment of *transfiguration*, the one who struggles thus comes to *resemble* God. As such, prayer is "a life and death struggle" (EUD, 401) consonant with spiritual trial and the alterity of Spirit. Yet prayer is also the resting ground for a moment of ineffable intimacy between the soul and God: a moment when "explanation" (*Forklaring*) gives way to "transfiguration" (*Forklarelse*) and the image of God comes to rest within the abyss (*Afgrund*) of the restless heart.

As developed in 'Purity of Heart Is To Will One Thing', Kierkegaard's notion of becoming "nothing" (UDVS, 193) in inverse resemblance is a development of the Scriptural dictum that "*God created the human being in his image*" (UDVS, 192). The lily of the field, for example, is more resplendent than even Solomon in his glory; but it does not resemble God. It bears a mark, which in turn bears witness to its creator; but it does not bear the creator's *resemblance* — thus confirming an infinite qualitative difference between the created and a creator whose trace the lily nonetheless bears. Yet while for the human being there also exists an infinite qualitative difference between creature and creator, there is also a relationship of resemblance whereby the creature is also in the image of the creator. Again with recourse to the imagery of "the mirror of the ocean", Kierkegaard elaborates this image of God in the human being further, describing how it is different from a visual image: it is an *invisible image*. "When a person sees his image in the mirror of the ocean," Kierkegaard observes, "he sees his own image, but the ocean is not his image, and when he departs the image disappears. The ocean is not the image and cannot keep the image" (UDVS, 192).[1] Here is image as *reflection*: the image is only visually but not substantially present on the surface of the water. It exists contingently: the resemblance is ephemeral and superficial insofar as it only exists for the moment at which the gaze itself is present to perceive it on the water's surface. The visible form, therefore, is essentially powerless to "reproduce itself in another in such a way that the other keeps the image when the form departs" (UDVS, 192). When the face is turned away from the water, the image vanishes. The image has never penetrated the hidden depths of the ocean. The image, it might be said, has not entered into a state of union.

The reflection of the *image of God*, however, differs from the visible

1 Eckhart again compares the soul to a mirror which holds the image as long as the object stands before it. If the mirror were to be shattered, the image would vanish since it is not *in* the mirror. Sermon 9, *Werke* I, 113.

form of the human face. "God is spirit, is invisible," Kierkegaard continues, "and the image of invisibility, of course, is in turn invisibility. Thus the invisible Creator reproduces himself in the invisibility, which is the qualification of spirit, and the image of God is explicitly the invisible glory" (UDVS, 192). As such, no one can visibly resemble the invisible God. Yet since the image of the unknowable God is *Spirit*, "To be spirit . . . is the human being's invisible glory" (UDVS, 193). While the visual face is *reflected* superficially and transiently on the surface of the water, the image of God saturates the still resting depths of the ocean, uniting with and infusing it with its invisible glory, transfiguring it as Spirit, by which it *resembles* the divine, by which the ocean invisibly reflects the sky above it.

The infinite qualitative difference is, as Anti-Climacus reveals, ultimately grasped through the *mysterium* of *forgiveness* rather than in the abyss of *sin* (SUD, 122). And yet, this is a wholly *other* forgiveness, which the soul is nonetheless called to reflect in its interaction with the other. In such works of love, the soul reflects (rather than channels) the image of God, just as the ocean reflects the image of the heavens (WL, 380). In this, one resembles God, not directly or visibly, but *inversely* and *invisibly*, by *worship*, by the regeneration and blossoming of Spirit in the heart made manifest in works of love toward 'the other' who, through Spirit, now becomes 'the neighbour'. In this Kierkegaard's vision of the image of God seeks to resist what he suspects as the more ecstatic or unitive flight from actuality of mystical theology by re-inscribing the self in the world. While the horizon of *Gelassenheit* may provide glimpses of an eschatological state, which is, as Boehme envisions, a restoration of a prelapsarian relationship, the endurance of spiritual trials serves as a reminder that we are not wholly Spirit, that we are not God. After all, God desires *Is* because God desires to be loved in and through the divinely relinquished gift of freedom. And the self is freedom; and Spirit is the self (SUD, 13; 29).

The Difference Burns

As has been observed, Tauler refers to *Anfechtung* as an agonistic reminder that the self is ultimately not God;[1] and the *Theologia Deutsch* speaks of the suffering in the process of union of all that is contrary to the divine.[2] In this sense, spiritual trial is the essential expression of absolute difference within the God-relationship (CUP, 461). Yet in union with God, in resting transparently in God, or in becoming Spirit, does difference vanish? In one of his most striking

---

1 *The Sermons and Conferences*, 573.
2 *The Theologia Germanica*, 89-90.

sermons, Eckhart illustrates how it is the *difference* that *burns*, the
burning negation or distinction; that which the hot coal in my hand
contains, which my hand is *not*. It is not self-will that burns in hell,
it is negation (*niht*). If I were of one nature with fire then all the fire
in the world poured upon me could not burn me. This difference,
this *not*, between God and those who stand before God "torments the
souls in hell more than self-will or any fire".[1] As Williams clarifies,
insofar as I am not you and you are not me, it is the "*not* that upholds
our very distinction. It is the *not* which distinguishes one thing from
another thing. For without this negation, neither of us would be
distinct. Were the hand and the coal 'one' in God, then they would
be the same in that neither would have what the other has *not*. But in
themselves, what one is, the other necessarily is *not*".[2] In other words,
difference burns; or the difference is burning. If we were one then
there would be no otherness, no boundary or limit between us to
experience as burning.

This notion of difference dissolved in union derives from
Eckhart's understanding of creation *ex nihilo* in terms of in terms
of *exitus-reditus*, the nothingness of the human being who returns
to God, the source of its being. As made in the image of God, the
uncreated ground of the soul (*Grund der Seele*) (re-)unites with
the divine at the level of *intellect*.[3] While Kierkegaard is sceptical
about the speculative excesses of the thinking that derives from
such notions, he is, moreover, concerned that at the existential
level of actuality God's omnipotence is manifest precisely in
creating a being *ex nihilo* who is then encouraged to become a
fragile *something* "independent of that omnipotence", a subjectivity
before God (JP 2:1251; CD, 133). In freely becoming a self before

1   Sermon 13(b), *The Complete Mystical Works*, 109.

2   Duane Williams, 'Meister Eckhart and the Varieties of Nothing', *Medieval
     Mystical Theology*, 20 (2011), 85-98, 87. Williams traces this understanding
     of negation to Plato's *Sophist* where negation is understood as a relatively
     differentiated *other* rather than absolute 'nothing' or 'nonbeing' (87-88).
     God, for Eckhart, is One and thus the negation of negation, or otherness,
     since nothing is outside of God — though this negation is itself negated
     in God (90-93). Through this negation of a negation of a negation, it can
     be said that God is beyond being but not non-existent, as such: "Although
     God is 'nothing', which is to say, 'no-thing', God nevertheless *is* — as
     Nothing. Eckhart is not simply saying that 'God is not', he is saying that
     'God is *not*, any-thing'. And although God is not any-thing, for Eckhart,
     God nevertheless is as *isness* itself" (94).

3   The ground of the soul as intellect, however, "does not belong to the soul's
     created nature *ad imagem*". Bernard McGinn, *The Harvest of Mysticism in
     Medieval Germany* (New York: Herder & Herder, 2005), 150.

God, however, the self must *become nothing*, in terms of a kenosis of the self-will, which evidently reflects mystical theology;[1] yet at the same moment as it rests transparently in God, its expression of the image of God is an *inverse resemblance* in which the personal alterity of self as Spirit is also affirmed. As such, one does not "merge in God through a pantheistic fading away or in the divine ocean through the blotting out of all individual characteristics, but in an intensified consciousness . . . the union with God still takes place in the personality clarified through the whole process" of sin and grace, difference and unity (JP 4:3887).

Yet through this process of clarification or transparency of selfhood, *difference* — or that which opposes God in terms of the struggle between self-will and the Divine Will — also undergoes reconciliation. "Spirit is fire. . . . As gold is purified in fire, in the same way the Christian is purified" (JP 4:4355) in the purity of heart which is to will one thing.[2] Yet in the fire of Spirit, Kierkegaard also warns that "not all are burned out to spirit, a few are burned out to ashes — that is, they do not become spirit in the fire" (JP 4:4355). Entering into the fire of spiritual trial, the desire to become Spirit should remain mindful of the limits of difference, the restlessness of the synthesis of opposites, and the ultimately eschatological nature of its consummation. No one is purely Spirit and none can sustain an absolute relation to the Absolute. "Alas, but we all carry the Spirit in fragile vessels" (JP 4:3915).

For Kierkegaard, as for Eckhart and Boehme, creation is restless in its desire to rest in the Creator.[3] Yet Kierkegaard's vision of Spirit as the self resting transparently in God is more fraught by the spiritual trials of the infinite qualitative difference than the more serene Eckhartian vision of union and *Gelassenheit*. "Wherever the eternal is, there is rest; but there is unrest where the eternal is not present" (UDVS, 258). Awakening to the call of the eternal is manifest in the restlessness of Spirit, the *restlessness* of the self before God

---

1 See further Christopher B. Barnett's illuminating essay 'The Mystical Influence on Kierkegaard's Theological Anthropology', *Acta Kierkegaardiana Volume 6: Kierkegaard and Human Nature*, 105-122.

2 According to one master, Eckhart suggests that as the image of God the soul can be called spirit, relating to God as spirit to spirit. Furthermore, "the soul is called a fire because with her desire she keeps pace with God like the fire in the heavens, for the soul can never rest except in God." Sermon Seventy-Five, *The Complete Mystical Works*, 381.

3 Eckhart suggests that the desire of the Creator in creating, and the natural desire of all creatures, and of the soul is *rest*. To the same extent that the soul rests in God, so does God rest in the soul, whether resting only in part or resting completely. Sermon 60; *Werke* I.

that desires the rest of being transfigured, through purity of heart and simplicity of will, in the image of God. The metamorphosis of becoming Spirit is undergone in the crucible of spiritlessness. Resting, or being grounded transparently in God (*gjennemsigtigt grunder i Gud*; SUD, 82), struggles with the restlessness, or abyss (*Afgrund*) of the infinite qualitative difference between the self and God. This struggle is a struggle of *faith* rather than a union of *intellect*, since "Faith expressly signifies the deep, strong, blessed restlessness that drives the believer so that he cannot settle down at rest in this world" (UDVS, 218).

Spirit, therefore, might be envisioned as a stranger awakened within, leading us back to the divine origin — the echo of God's image, the quantum of divinity within us, longing restlessly to rest in its source. Repressed, supressed, stifled, denied, unconscious, grieved. Fallen but not beyond redemption. Fallen yet rendered pure in heart and will. The *passio* of Spirit's *eros* is the spiritual trial of desire before the Holy Other it desires yet cannot possess, even in union. In life's journey across the infinite qualitative abyss, rest for the restless Spirit, in all its spiritual trials, is ultimately found in the call of Christ to 'come unto me' given to those "whose residence has been assigned among the grave": that is, to the one who is "not buried, yet dead . . . belonging neither to life nor to death . . . you, too, come here, here is rest [*her er Hvile*], and here is life!" (PC, 18).

In spiritual trial, love passes through the fire of the infinite qualitative difference. Love struggles with the darkness of God in which the desire of Spirit is as if tempted to despair of the impossibility of the love of God. Here the possibility of consolation is offered in the thought that the love for God is the presence of God, the Spirit of God within which proceeds secretly from God. Through love's struggle with the dark night of God, the soul in spiritual trial "has been so shaken that he became spirit by understanding that", despite the appearance of impossibility and despair, "God *is* that all things are possible" (SUD, 173-174). Appositely, Kierkegaard's final words on the love of God are also his final, and perhaps most difficult, written words. Even greater than the praise of angels to God's ears is the praise of a human being who "when God seemingly changes into sheer cruelty" in suffering's dark night "nevertheless continues to believe that God is love, that God does it out of love." The secret of such faith is that a person, *qua* Spirit, loves God even when God appears as *otherwise* than a God of love. "Such a human being becomes an angel" (JP 6:6969).

8. The Temptation of Spiritual Trial

> ... that God could create human beings free over against himself
> is the cross which philosophy could not bear but upon which it
> has remained hanging. (JP 2:1237)

Given a more nuanced idiomatic understanding, the term *the temptation of spiritual trial* seems problematic. In light of Kierkegaard's innovative differentiation between *lower* temptation (*Fristelse*) and *higher* spiritual trial (*Anfægtesle*), the *temptation* of *spiritual trial* might even appear paradoxical. And yet insofar as Luther employs the German *Anfechtung* as a form of the Latin *tentatio* it could be said that spiritual trial emerges under the rubric of temptation. However, the subsequent development of higher and more spiritual forms of temptations, trials, and tribulations — those of the flesh, the world, the devil, and the self; even those of the absolute difference, or the divine itself — demands a more rarefied appreciation of the distinctiveness of spiritual trial. Yet, even as spiritual trial occupies the transfiguring heights of Spirit, struggling with God, *temptation* always lingers in its shadow.

To summarise what has been explored in this work, a Kierkegaardian theology of spiritual trial could be characterised by the following key features. Firstly, the silence, ineffability and secrecy of spiritual trial. Spiritual trial is hardly spoken about; yet, while this silence should be broached by a theology of consolation, its discrete individual content remains an inexorable secret between self and God. While the idiom and tension of spiritual trial can be applied to any position in life, its distinctively theological sense is oriented in relation to the self's encounter with the absolute difference and the struggle between Spirit, spiritlessness, and the demonic. Spiritual trial (*Anfægtelse*) is differentiated from temptation (*Fristelse*) insofar as it is 'higher' and subsists within 'the religious'; whereas temptation is an enticement by what is 'lower' and belongs in 'the ethical'. Yet in an even higher and more ineffable form than spiritual trial there lies the category of the ordeal (*Prøvelse*) — analogous to Luther's idea of the sublime *tentatio* and reserved only for such figures as Abraham and Job.

Spiritual trial is both the "essential expression" and the *nemesis* of the God-relationship, the Absolute limit of the Absolute, which rises up against the individual's attempt to relate to the Absolute. Its sources are ultimately traceable to the anxiety of the infinite qualitative abyss, to the awakening of freedom and the tension of becoming Spirit, and even to the excesses of the human imagination (*Phantasie*), rather than the temptations of the devil. Yet one is to press on rather than flee from spiritual trial — even when it confronts one with the appearance of God as wrath, as "otherwise" than changeless love. At such moments, one is to struggle against the *appearance* of wrath, examining the possibility of its psychogenic origins and clinging to the love of God. The love of God is itself to be understood as the presence of God as Spirit, as the love which issues forth as grace from its secret divine spring. In awakening oneself to Spirit and love, spiritual trial can therefore be understood as intended for one's upbuilding. As such, no one is tried or tempted beyond what is endurable. In light of this consolation, one is to look to the *passio Christi* in which Christ *voluntarily* undertakes and overcomes all temptation and spiritual trial. In voluntary *imitatio Christi* and with the consolation of the Holy Spirit as Comforter, the struggler is maintained even in the appearance of God-forsakenness — "the last spiritual trial", which Christ assumes and in assuming ultimately spares all from.

Passing through fire, the process of spiritual trial is the reconciliation of the burning of difference, of alienation and estrangement between the self and God, between the self-will and its authentic self-becoming as Spirit. Through spiritual trial, one struggles with God against oneself, against 'the world', 'the flesh', and 'the devil' within me, so that becoming nothing before God, the restless self might be transfigured as Spirit, coming to rest grounded transparently in God and reflecting in inverse resemblance the image of God. Yet as this transfiguration passes through the fire of Spirit it encounters a fire that threatens to burn to ashes those who desire to be too much Spirit, those who attach themselves to stringently to the idea of an absolute relation to the Absolute. The recurrence of spiritual trials, in this respect, reminds us that while the *via mystica* may flow from *Anfechtung* to *Gelassenheit*, in actuality one must remain mindful that one is, after all, a human being in whom Spirit is personalised as self in a restless synthesis of the physical and the psychical, the finite and the infinite, the temporal and the eternal. Though restless and passionate, we are only fragile beings.

It is in this sense, among others, that one might speak of the *temptation of spiritual trial*: that is, the *temptation* to desire an absolute relation to the Absolute, to deny life in its embodiment and actuality, to flee from the world, whether in self-apotheosis, in despair, or in the *mortido* of self-annihilation in the divine abyss.[1] Spiritual trial tempers such desire by reminding us of the infinite qualitative difference, by reminding us of the anxiety of freedom and the desire of God that each individual should become a *fragile something* rather than an obliterated nothing before God, even in union with God. As this concluding chapter will explore further, spiritual trial is at once a subjecting creature feeling — the consciousness of oneself as but dust and ashes — and also the making of subjectivity as reaching, desiring, beyond its limits and in relation to the Holy Other, through a *kenosis-in-ekstasis*.[2]

Educing the role of the desire, the previous chapter has sought to render more explicit the implicit role of spiritual *eros* in spiritual trial, expressed in terms of the restlessness of Spirit. As *kenosis-in-ekstasis*, becoming Spirit signifies a process of emptying the self from its lower self-will in order to draw the self out from its inclosing reserve and into relation with the other. This inducement of the desire of Spirit is not a temptation in the sense of a lower seduction, which is in continuity with one's lower self — a fall into oneself and the despairing desire of the self-will. Rather, the 'temptation' of Spirit is something that draws one out of oneself, as an *ekstasis* through which the self-will becomes nothing. In seeking *ecstasy*, lower temptation draws the self out of itself in desire for fulfilment, or even obliteration of the self in an object in which it invests or even seeks to lose its self-identity (in this temptation can express both forms of despair-to-will and not-to-will to be oneself). Spiritual trial, by contrast, as an awakening of Spirit within spiritlessness (the despair not to will to be oneself which is the hidden root of all despair) seeks union with an Other who transfigures the self in becoming itself through a union of love, lover, and beloved.

---

1 Gregor describes how "In its most intense forms, temptation appears with an urgency that fills the horizon. In the moments of its ascendance, it occludes everything else, clouding my perception, refusing to let me see beyond the possibility it discloses. At its highest pitch, temptation is given as though it were the only thing of significance." 'Kierkegaard and the Phenomenology of Temptation', 136-137. I suggest that a similar domination of one's horizon can be encountered in the desire to relate absolutely to the Absolute, to become wholly Spirit.

2 In reference to Vladimir Lossky on Negative Theology and *Personal Being*, Williams described *ekstasis* and *kenosis* as "self-transcending and self-forgetting, the overcoming of the boundaries of mutual exclusion that define individuals over against each other". Rowan Williams, 'Eastern Orthodox Theology', ed. David Ford, *The Modern Theologians* (Oxford: Blackwell, 2005), 572-588, 579.

In temptation, as Gregor describes, "an enticing project, a possible course of action, is given, and at the same time I am aware of an obligation to resist its solicitations."[1] A similar dialectic is, I suggest, discernible within spiritual trial: a possibility is given which in some sense, if only *sub specie aeternitatis* or through the gaze of Spirit, is desirable as the *desideratum* of Spirit's longing. In spiritual trial, Spirit is restlessness in search of its place of rest — in God. At the same time, the self is conscious of a *resistance* in relation to the Absolute. Resistance may be encountered form the *Eros* of the demonic self-will or even the *Thanatos* of spiritlessness. The resistance is also the limit, which is understood as both of the self and of the Absolute itself — as, analogously, the anxiety of dizziness resides both in the abyss and in the eye that gazes within it (CA, 61). In the throes of spiritual trial, the self is intended to struggle on, resisting the temptations of resistance to the Absolute — while also temperately mindful of the relativity of one's relation to the Absolute. God is given at the same time as the absolute alterity of God — the infinite qualitative abyss — enforces itself upon the individual. It does so by evoking fear (CUP, 459), perhaps even a fear of the good or the holy concerning which even the demons know and tremble.

Kierkegaard describes how temptation occurs in continuity with the self; while spiritual trial asserts discontinuity with the self, as it arises from the alterity of the Absolute.[2] Yet it might be said that while the continuity of temptation is in accordance with the desires of the lower self, the ethical self, the higher spiritual self as Spirit desires is in continuity with spiritual trial and in discontinuity with temptation. It is *Spiritlessness* in its tranquilisation of the self, and *the demonic* in its wilful self-enslavement, which are in discontinuity with the primal God-given *I* as freedom, transfigured as the image of God.

Both temptation and spiritual trial, therefore, may be understood in terms of "being drawn", whether drawn down into the abyss of anxiety or drawn out of oneself before God. In this sense, *Practice in Christianity* refers to John 12:32, "And I, when I am lifted up from the earth, will draw all to myself" (PC, 158, 159).[3] A vital difference between the seduction of temptation and the drawing of all unto Christ is that temptation deceptively (*bedragende*) draws (*drage*) one downward, whereas Christ draws unto himself in an "intersubjective . . . relation between selves" such that "The self is constituted in and through being drawn (PC, 159)."[4] In this drawing

---

1 Gregor, 'Kierkegaard and the Phenomenology of Temptation', 128.
2 Gregor, 'The Phenomenology of Temptation', 130 and 132.
3 See also Gregor, 'The Phenomenology of Temptation', 134.
4 Gregor, 'The Phenomenology of Temptation', 134-135.

of self unto self, Christ offers rest for the restless Spirit. And yet, as spiritual trial knows well, the cross, as *mysterium crucis*, while drawing all unto Christ, also establishes a halt, a limit, a paradox and an offence. Beneath the shadow of the cross, the self may also be struck down by the anguished conscience, even a fear of the good or the Holy, which is also a consciousness, even a fear of itself as evil, as unholy. Before such a forbidding limit of the abyss of sin, the self might again be drawn down into temptation, the temptation to despair over the forgiveness of sins.[1]

If a strict Kierkegaardian distinction between temptation (*Fristelse*) and spiritual trial (*Anfægtelse*) is pressed to the point of dichotomy then it would be misleading, if not contradictory, to speak of a temptation of spiritual trial. However, in qualifying Kierkegaard's claim, I would elicit the observation that temptation and spiritual trial are often, if not always, dialectically related: that where one is in spiritual trial one is always tempted to flee from struggle, to flee from God and to turn back to the lower things (whether in self-will or spiritlessness). At the same moment when one is in temptation, therefore, spiritual trial itself may also be latently present: that is, when one is tempted by the lower things one can always turn away and face that which is higher. When temptation becomes conscious of itself as such, is this consciousness not itself constituted by the awareness of something 'higher', of a limit or boundary? In this sense, temptation in Eden is attended by the horizon of spiritual trial, even if it is only construed as the word of prohibition that the serpent manipulates — as the devil often attempts to entwine himself within the word of God in order to bring one into spiritual trial, as Luther warns. That God is encountered as spiritual trial in the fall into temptation is exemplified for Luther in the fear of God, which induces Adam and Eve to hide from the divine presence. In Boehme's terms, in temptation they have fallen from that state of *Gelassenheit* with God into one of *Anfechtung* before the Face of God whom none may see and live.

The dialectic of temptation and spiritual trial can also be discerned in the Pauline dialectic of the Spirit and the flesh. The temptation is a temptation to fall away from what is higher and, as such, Spirit is already presupposed, even if only as a presence-in-absence. Without the horizon of Spirit there is no temptation, there is only the wanton

---

1 Gregor notes that both the highest and the lower engage the imagination "in order to draw to itself" or "to 'draw downward' to itself" (137). In spiritual trial, however, the imagination can be awakened to the point of tempting the individual to despair of the fear of God: anxiety about the good and fantastic delusions of God-forsakenness.

gratification of a lustful and selfish nature. Similarly, without the existence of God there is no despair in willing or not willing to be a self, since all willing/non-willing is relative to strictly human accounts of 'bad faith' or the 'death of the self'.[1] Within a theological horizon, however, temptation proposes both a pessimistic view of sinful human desire and also a positive sense of the *Eros*, which remind us of our true nature as Spirit. This also points towards the second sense in which spiritual trial can be spoken of as a form of temptation: specifically as a 'temptation' of Spirit. Spiritual trial arises with the arousal of the consciousness of the desire of Spirit (the lusts of the Spirit lusting against the lusts of the flesh). In this sense, spiritual trial can be spoken of as a 'temptation' of Spirit, an excitation of desire *for*, which initially derives *from* that which is the highest. Yet at the same time it is conscious of a limit, of a gravity that draws the self back to its lower desires and grieves the Spirit. In this dialectical relationship, spiritual trial is also not fully what it is without the shadow of temptation. As such, in the temptation of Jesus by the devil, spiritual trial is implicit as a call to proceed along the higher path, the presence of the Spirit, which temptation seeks to entice Jesus away from, even tempting the Spirit within him. Reciprocally, in the spiritual trial of Gethsemane, temptation is present as the possibility of fleeing from death. Spiritual trial therefore evokes temptation, as its shadow-side. And temptation exists under the abyssal firmament of spiritual trial. This seemingly relentless dialectic or struggle between the two is the anxiety of freedom, without which neither is possible. For some, though perhaps not for many, the enduring dialectical struggle between spiritual trial and temptation captures the human condition as an eternal struggle between the Spirit and the flesh. Even graceful moments of detachment (*Abgeschiedenheit*) and releasement (*Gelassenheit*), of resting transparently in union with God, are unsustainable before the fall back into the struggle of actuality.

The dialectic can be illustrated further in relation to the spiritual trial of God-forsakenness. Here the temptation is to despair of the love of God (*tentatio desperationis*). From this temptation one must flee, fleeing the wrath of God by clinging to the God of grace, overcoming God and oneself through God, as Jacob struggles to hold on for a blessing from one who appears as his enemy. In this spiritual trial, one struggles with God against God, against the temptation to despair of the darkness of God. As such, as I shall return to below, there is an *agonistic apophaticism* to spiritual trial. Insofar as it invites the self to struggle with its own wrathful God-images, perhaps even

---

1 Podmore, *Kierkegaard and the Self Before God*, 23.

revealing such wrath as a projection of the self's own fear of God and despair of itself, spiritual trial deconstructs the idols of 'God', even of the 'Wholly Other'. Through the struggle of spiritual trial, the self comes to realise that God is not ultimately known as the Wholly Other of irredeemable estrangement but as the *Holy Other* of union-in-alterity.

After Kierkegaard: The Spiritual Trial of Theology

Despite this belated contemporary attempt to (re-)construct a Kierkegaardian theology of spiritual trial, it should be noted that while Kierkegaard's emphases upon freedom, subjectivity, anxiety, and despair have been preserved and reinterpreted within the existentialist traditions of the twentieth century; his more devotional attempt to rehabilitate the pathos of *spiritual trial* from the arcane pages of old devotional books appears, for the most part, to have fallen on stony ground. In a sense, therefore, his impassioned and solitary plea for a revival of the idiom of spiritual trial within the spiritless milieu of modern Christendom has been a lamentable failure. It was left to the proverbial Luther Renaissance of the early twentieth century (represented, among others, by such scholars as Karl Holl and Albrecht Ritschl in Germany; Gustav Aulén, Gustav Wingren and Anders Nygren in Sweden, and Regin Prenter in Denmark) to reinvigorate key themes within Lutheran theology. However, insofar as Kierkegaard provides a re-energised vision of Luther in a context where Luther was rarely studied in depth, his role in rehabilitating the existential pathos of Luther's thought perhaps remains undervalued.[1] By the time that German and Scandinavian Luther research had been mediated to English-language audiences in Rupp's *The Righteousness of God*, *Anfechtung* had seemingly acquired characteristic resonances with prevailing existentialist philosophies, such that Rupp himself suggests that "We might call it [*Anfechtung*] an existential word since it concerns man as he grapples with himself and the universe". Yet at the same moment Rupp also warns that "we must not be misled into supposing that this is mere subjectivism" insofar as *Anfechtung* is oriented around bringing the individual to an awareness of one's irreducible existence *coram Deo* and the need for divine grace which this awakens.[2]

Following the preceding contemporary renaissance of Luther

---

1 See Hinkson, 'Will the *Real* Martin Luther Please Stand Up!', 75.

2 Rupp, *The Righteousness of God*, 106. See further my *Kierkegaard and the Self Before God*, 123-126.

studies, Paul Tillich's 1945 essay on 'The Transmoral Conscience' described Luther's *Anfechtungen* as "tempting attacks", which express "the state of absolute despair" of "the bad conscience".[1] In 1950's 'The Recovery of the Prophetic Tradition', Tillich states more explicitly that Luther "anticipates all modern Existentialism, including Pascal and Kierkegaard" in his descriptions of *Anfechtung*, "meaning daemonic attacks in which every meaning was lost."[2] Furthermore, in a sermon on Psalm 139 ('Whither shall I flee from thy presence?', 139:7), 'The Escape From God,' Tillich reads Lutheran *Anfechtung* in relation to Nietzschean *ressentiment*, claiming that the "Presence of God created the same feeling in Luther as it did Nietzsche"[3] — namely the desire to escape, whether through self-mortification or deicide, both of which, for Kierkegaard, signify manifestations of despair's unwillingness to be revealed to itself.

Bonhoeffer recapitulates much of Luther's theology of *tentatio* in *Versuchung*, which despite its title, also refers to "the highest spiritual trial of Christ" as *"die höchste Anfechtung Christi"*.[4] The account of temptation that Bonhoeffer elaborates mirrors his assertion in *Creation and Fall* that "In the destroyed world between God's curse

---

1 Originally published in *Crozer Quarterly*, XXII (4), 1945, this essay subsequently reappeared in 1948 in James Luther Adams' collected translation of several of Tillich's essays, *The Protestant Era* (Chicago, Illinois: The University of Chicago Press, 1948; 2nd impression 1951), 145-146.

2 'The Recovery of the Prophetic Tradition', *Theological Writings Volume 6*, ed. Gert Hummel (Berlin; New York: De Gruyter; Berlin: Evangelisches Verlagswerk, 1992), 340. See also Tillich, *The Religious Situation* (New York: Holt, 1932) (originally published in Germany in 1925 as *Die religiose Lage der Gegenwart*) and *The Interpretation of History* (New York: Charles Scribner's Sons, 1936). For a perceptive account of temptation in Tillich, in relation to Kierkegaard and Augustinian tradition (though without mention of *Anfechtung*), see Peter Slater, 'Tillich on the Fall and the Temptation of Goodness', *The Journal of Religion*, 65 (2), April, 1985, 196-207. Whereas Karl Barth develops a form of the Lutheran view that *Anfechtung* is "dialectically aligned with the saving action that is concealed under what appears to be its opposite", Tillich "mediates it with an experience of existential threat and loss of meaning that no longer needs to be articulated theistically", thereby detaching *Anfechtung* from the dialectic of sin and forgiveness and articulating its overcoming in terms of a more humanistic "courage to be". Hans-Martin Barth, 'Temptation', 336. Tillich also proposes a view of *Gelassenheit* "as the sympathetic coming together of man's will/being and God's Will/being thereby overcoming the tensions extant within the opposition of autonomy *vs.* heteronomy." Steven T. Katz, 'Mysticism and Ethics in Western Mystical Traditions', *Religious Studies*, 28, 407-423, 415n30.

3 Tillich, 'The Escape From God', *The Shaking of the Foundations*, 44.

4 Bonhoeffer, *Versuchung* (Munich: Chr. Kaiser Verlag, 1954), 60.

and promise man is tempted. . . . Man does not adhere to God in peace but in enmity and conflict".[1] However, as a struggle with God in the wound of the infinite qualitative abyss, temptation is not to be misconstrued as the testing of one's strength. On the contrary, "it is of the very essence of temptation in the Bible that all my strength — to my horror, and without my being able to do anything about it — is turned against me".[2] In view of such horror, one is to humbly echo Christ's prayer, "Lead us not into temptation" (Matthew 6:13), since temptation is not the proving of oneself in *ascesis*, but the assault in which one is "abandoned by all his powers — indeed, attacked by them — abandoned by all men, abandoned by God himself."[3] Faced with such desolation one is "not to yield in stoic resignation to temptation, but to flee from that dark bond, in which God lets the devil do his will, and call to the open divine freedom in which God tramples the devil under foot."[4]

Whereas it may appear that Bonhoeffer is contradicting Kierkegaard's exhortation to press on in spiritual trial, his notion of fleeing temptation attests to the dialectic of temptation and spiritual trial, insofar as one flees the temptation of despair by fleeing "to the Crucified".[5] By cleaving to God, the one "tempted in Adam" is now "tempted in Christ", such that "the Christ in us is tempted — in which case Satan is bound to fall."[6] Though the one tempted *in Adam*, who flees into one's own inner resources rather than to God, is destined to fall, Bonhoeffer, perhaps echoing Kierkegaard's concept of anxiety, asserts that the one who is tempted is as yet innocent in temptation: "Indeed the tempter is only to be found where there is innocence; for where there is guilt, he has already gained power."[7] In this sense,

---

1 Dietrich Bonhoeffer, 'Creation and Fall', *Creation and Fall/Temptation: Two Biblical Studies* (New York: Simon & Schuster, 1997), 94; *Schöpfung und Fall* (Munich: Chr. Kaiser Verlag, 1937).

2 Bonhoeffer,'Temptation', *Creation and Fall/Temptation*, 112.

3 *Ibid.* 112.

4 *Ibid.* 114.

5 *Ibid.* 133.

6 *Ibid.* 115.

7 *Ibid.* 116. Bonhoeffer also maintains that "God himself tempts no one [James1:31]. The source of temptation lies in my own self" (126). Gregor also observes that "In terms reminiscent of Kierkegaard, Bonhoeffer describes temptation as the 'sudden.'" 'The Phenomenology of Temptation', 136. On the relation between Bonhoeffer and Kierkegaard see further Matthew D. Kirkpatrick, *Attacks on Christendom in a World Come of Age: Kierkegaard, Bonhoeffer, and the Question of 'Religionless Christianity'* (Eugene: Pickwick Publications, 2011); Christiane Tietz, 'Dietrich Bonhoeffer: Standing "in the Tradition of Paul, Luther, Kierkegaard, in the Tradition of Genuine Christian

Jesus can be tempted yet remain in innocence. Temptation, however, still suffers, even in its innocence. As such, "the Spirit leads Jesus into the wilderness, into solitude, into abandonment." It is as if Spirit leads Jesus into the desert of spiritlessness. Just as "temptation must find Jesus weak, lonely, and hungry", so "God leaves man alone in temptation". In this way, as Luther and Kierkegaard recognise, "So Abraham had to be quite alone on the mountain in Moriah. Yes, God himself abandons man in the face of temptation."[1]

Bonhoeffer classifies Jesus's prototypical three temptations by the devil as "the temptation of the flesh [*die fleischliche Versuchung*]", higher "spiritual temptation [*die hohe geistliche Versuchung*]" and the "complete temptation [*die vollkommene Versuchung*]", which is the temptation to deny God and submit to Satan, a complete temptation of spirit and flesh, "the temptation to sin against the Holy Ghost" (cf. SUD, 125).[2] In all his temptations, Christ "is left with nothing but the saving, supporting, enduring Word of God, which holds him firmly and which fights and conquers for him." The Word also struggles for him when "The night of the last words of Jesus — 'My God, my God, why has thou forsaken me' — has fallen", following "the hour of this temptation as the last fleshly-spiritual, complete temptation of the Saviour."[3] Bonhoeffer identifies *death* as "the last temptation", in which he also echoes Luther's and Kierkegaard's affirmation of God-forsakenness as the last spiritual trial overcome in the God-forsakenness of Christ. While it is in death that one "loses everything, where hell reveals its terror", Christ's cry assures that "even here life has broken in upon the believer."[4] Through Christ's endurance and conquering of the wrath of God, one "finds behind the God of wrath who tempts him the God of grace who tempts no one."[5] In relation to the three temptations of Jesus in the wilderness, Bonhoeffer also refers to "the last temptation" as a full unconcealed demonopathy of Satan, which tempts one to deny God and worship him, offering worldly happiness and power. Foreshadowing the cry of God-forsakenness,

---

Thinking"', ed. Jon Stewart, *Kierkegaard's Influence on Theology: Tome I German Protestant Theology* (Aldershot: Ashgate, 2012), 43-64; and Geoffrey Kelly, 'Kierkegaard as 'Antidote' and as Impact Upon Dietrich Bonhoeffer's Concept of Christian Discipleship', *Bonhoeffer's Intellectual Formation: Theology and Philosophy in his Thought* (Tübingen: Mohr Siebeck, 2008), 145-166 (which also considers Kierkegaard's critique of Lutheranism). However, none of these works contain explicit treatments of temptation or spiritual trial.

1   Bonhoeffer, *Creation and Fall/Temptation*, 118.
2   *Ibid.* 118-121.
3   *Ibid.* 121.
4   *Ibid.* 129.
5   *Ibid.* 129.

this unveiling of the satanic presence tempts one to despair of divine absence and also to forsake God, to sin against the Holy Spirit. Once again in harmony with both Luther and Kierkegaard, Bonhoeffer qualifies this harrowing vision with the consolation that "Just as temptations of the spirit are not experienced by all Christians, since they would go beyond their powers, so this last temptation certainly comes only to a very few men."[1]

Following quotations from Luther's lectures on Genesis, Bonhoeffer proceeds to outline seven thoughts, in which Luther's words again resonate, for consoling those in such temptation. Firstly, one should remember that it is the devil who is manipulating God's Word. Secondly, that one should only discuss one's sins with Jesus and not with the devil. Thirdly, that one should remind the devil that Jesus called sinners and not the righteous. Fourthly, that in this temptation our sin is punished by God's wrath. Fifthly, one should thank God for the judgement that expresses divine love. Sixthly, that one should recognise that the devil places one into "the highest temptation of Christ [die höchste Anfechtung Christi] on the cross, as he cried: 'My God, my God, why hast thou forsaken me.' But where God's wrath broke out, there was reconciliation. Where I, smitten by God's wrath, lose everything, there I hear the words: 'My grace is sufficient for thee; for my power is made perfect in weakness' (II Cor. 12.9)." Finally, Bonhoeffer affirms Luther's consolation that "in gratitude for temptation overcome I know, at the same time, that no temptation is more terrible than to be without temptation."[2]

---

1   "He who has experienced this temptation [to sin against the Holy Spirit] and has conquered, has indeed won the victory over all temptations." *Ibid.* 142. Ultimately, "All temptation is temptation of Jesus Christ and all victory is victory of Jesus Christ" (143).

2   *Ibid.* 141-142. Luther: "*Keine Anfechtung haben ist die schwerste Anfechtung*" (WA 3, 420); "*Nulla tentatio — omnis tentatio*" (LW 44, 47). Bonhoeffer also refers to this in 'Psychologie', *Dietrich Bonhoeffer Werke, Volume 12, Berlin: 1932-1933*, Carsten Nicolaisen and Ernst-Albert Scharffenorth (eds) (Gütersloh: Chr. Kaiser/Gütersloher Verlagshaus, 1997), 181; and in his 1936 lecture on pastoral counselling, *Dietrich Bonhoeffer Werke, Volume 14, Illegale Theologenausbildung: Finkenwalde 1925-1937*, Otto Dudzus and Jürgen Henkys, with Sabine Bobert-Stützel, Dirk Schulz, and Ilse Tödt (eds) (Gütersloh: Chr. Kaiser/Gütersloher Verlagshaus, 1996), 584. See further Wolf Krötke, 'Dietrich Bonhoeffer and Martin Luther', ed. Peter Frick, *Bonhoeffer's Intellectual Formation: Theology and Philosophy in his Thought* (Tübingen: Mohr Siebeck, 2008), 53-82, 80n206. Krötke laments the observation that "Bonhoeffer scholarship hardly recognizes that Bonhoeffer's emphasis on his certitude in prison belongs to the context of his perception of Luther's existential temptations." 'Dietrich Bonhoeffer and Martin Luther', 81; on temptation see 79-82. Krötke also notes that "Bonhoeffer unfortunately deleted Luther's word *tentatio facit*

While Kierkegaard had lamented the silence surrounding spiritual trial as well as affirming the irreducible singularity, even incommunicable secrecy of spiritual trial for the solitary individual before God, for a swathe of theologians and philosophers, including Tillich, Bultmann, Barth, Jaspers, Jüngel, and Thielicke, the existential rhetoric of *Anfechtung* also resonated with the *Angst* of a civilisation in crisis, a European conscience wrestling with its scruples in the shadow of world war.[1] Before the Second World War, *Anfechtung* was invoked in The Barmen Declaration of 1934 to describe the Church's time of common need and crisis.[2] The post-war situation in Germany has been poignantly captured in Helmut Thielicke's 1951 theological study of nihilism.[3] Deriving from crowded lectures delivered to the disillusioned youth of war-

---

    theologum (temptation makes the theologian) [though for Luther this is part of a tripartite pedagogy: *oratio, meditatio, tentatio faciunt Theologum*] from the manuscript [of *Versuchung*] — most likely because the topic for the biblical interpretation was that of 'temptation'" rather than *tentatio* as *Anfechtung*. 'Dietrich Bonhoeffer and Martin Luther', 80n202. *Versuchung* conforms to the German of the Lutheran Bible (lead us not into temptation), and Bonhoeffer does replace Jesus' reference to his own *Anfechtung* from Luther's Bible in Luke 22:28 with *Versuchung*. However, he does invoke Anfechtung in this work as well as elsewhere. Furthermore, his treatment of *Versuchung* borrows heavily from Luther's wider treatments of *tentatio* and *Anfechtung*.

1 See further L. Pinomaa, *Der existentialle Charakter der Theologie Luthers*; and Randall Stephens, 'An Examination of Luther's Theology According to an Existentialist Interpretation', *Quodlibet Journal*, 2 (2), Spring 2000. For *Anfechtung* in Barth see, for example, Karl Barth, *Die christliche Gemeinde in der Anfechtung* (Basel: Gaiser & Haldimann, 1942). On Barth and Bultmann see further Klaus Bockmühl, *Atheismus in der Christenheit, Anfechtung und Überwindung. 1. Teil, Die Unwirklichkeit Gottes in Theologie und Kirche* (Wuppertal: Aussaat, 1969). Jüngel also invokes Luther's dictum: "Theology must not only call the trials of faith by name, but also think them through with such thoroughness that theology as a whole becomes a theology of testing: *tentatio facit theologum*." Eberhard Jüngel, *Theological Essays II*, ed. and trans. John Webster (Edinburgh: T & T Clark, 1995), 18-19. See also Eberhard Jüngel, *Anfechtung und Gewissheit des Glaubens oder die der Kirche wieder zu ihrer Sache komm. Zwei Vorträge* (Munich: Kaiser, 1976). *Anfechtung* was also a critical feature of the theology of Barth and Bultmann's teacher Wilhelm Herrman, who describes it as the experience of guilt and despair before the good, which precedes the way to religion. Wilhelm Herrmann, *The Communion of the Christian with God*, trans. J.S. Stanyon (London: Williams & Norgate, 1906), 100.

2 See Michael Weinrich, 'God's Free Grace and the Freedom of the Church: Theological Aspects of the Barmen Declaration', *International Journal of Systematic Theology*, 12 (4), October 2010, 404-419, 409.

3 *Der Nihilismus*, translated into English ten years later with the bold title *Nihilism: Its Origins and Nature — with a Christian Answer*.

ravaged Germany at the University of Tübingen in 1945, Thielicke's book sought to penetrate the gloom and despair of a generation who had come face to face with the abyss of nothingness:

> Before us sat a generation of youth which had been shrewdly and cruelly misled by the holders of power. And now they faced a world of rubble and ruins; not only their homes, but also their idealism, their faith, their concepts of value were shattered. But the vacuum in their hearts cried out to be filled. At the same time these young people were profoundly skeptical. Whatever we professors said they turned it about in their minds ten times before they would accept it: these burnt children dreaded the fire, because it might contain the coals of fresh seductions.[1]

Thielicke's conclusion to the book, 'Where Do We Go From Here?', invokes the notion of *Anfechtung* in a distinctly existentialist and Heidegerrian context of fallenness and confrontation with 'Nothingness' (*Nichts*):

> In theological terms, this means that he must face absolute temptation (*Anfechtung*). The sustaining environment in which he has parasitically rooted himself and on which he lives illegitimately must be knocked from under him. He must face doubt and the calling in question of all the forces that sustain him, in order to see whether he is still a 'self' apart from these things or whether he completely disappears within his sham self.[2]

This "confrontation with Nothingness . . . expresses itself in anxiety, in *horror vacui*, a dreadful feeling of being adrift, exposed, and helplessly abandoned."[3] In this final sense resides Thielicke's conclusion that Nothingness cannot be overcome by the defiance or detachment of atheistic existentialism; but by a faith which "is either struggle or it is nothing",[4] and which draws the individual into a confrontation with "the abyss of Nothingness":

> He who wants to die 'in order' to become has not really died at all. In such cases theology speaks of temptation (*Anfechtung*).

---

1 Thielicke, 'Preface to the American Edition', *Nihilism: Its Origins and Nature — with a Christian Answer*, trans. John W. Doberstein. (New York: Harper & Brothers, 1961), 11. See also Thielicke's *Theologie Der Anfechtung* (Tübingen, 1949) and *Between God and Satan* (Grand Rapids, 1958).

2 Thielicke, *Nihilism*, 168.

3 *Ibid.* 169.

4 *Ibid.* 177.

Not until a man is in the fiery furnace of utter bewilderment and despair does he see what is really genuine. This is what Luther meant when he said that *'tentatio facit theologum'* (temptation makes the theologian).[1]

Anfechtung is re-affirmed as the theological motto for the modern individual's struggle of faith in the face of despair, doubt, and the abyss of Nothingness. Echoing Kierkegaard, Thielicke regards the authentic engagement with despair as a salve against the opiate of a perfunctory modern religiousness that numbs itself against the arrows of doubt and therefore also the full force of "the miracle of grace"[2] — which is not reducible to a dialectical *via negativa* of dying-in-order-to-become.

Thielicke's sense of existential post-war doubt and anxiety is confirmed by the psychiatrist and philosopher Karl Jaspers (1883-1969). The theme of *Anfechtung*, moderately translated into English by E.B. Ashton as "doubt" and "self-doubt", emerges at the conclusion to Jasper's 1962 exploration of philosophical faith, *Der philosophische Glaube angesichts der Offenbarung*.[3] Here Jaspers emphatically asserts that, "The experience of self-doubt [*Anfechtung*] is unknown only to the thoughtless 'enlighteners' and positivists, to those who live in the obtuse self-certainty of conventions, whether ecclesiastic or non-

---

1 *Ibid.* 178. Like Bonhoeffer, Thielicke appears to oppose the view of *Anfechtung* as a dialectical dying-in-order-to-become. Treating *Anfechtung* as a necessary dialectical *via negativa* renders it in almost ascetical terms that threaten to mitigate the actuality of despair and the radical nature of grace in rescuing one from the utter abyss of *Anfechtung*.

2 *Ibid.*

3 Jaspers, *Der philosophische Glaube angesichts der Offenbarung* (München: R. Piper and Co., 1962), translated by E.B. Ashton as *Philosophical Faith and Revelation* (New York: Harper & Row, 1967). Jaspers' concluding section on *Anfechtung* is preceded by a section dealing with 'The Situation After Kierkegaard' (*Kierkegaards Kampf* in the original). However, this section outlines and evaluates Kierkegaard's critique of the fraudulence of Christendom and makes no mention of spiritual trial. Although an interpreter and admirer of Kierkegaard, Jaspers here states that, "I myself have tried hypothetically to understand Christianity along Kierkegaard's lines, but I cannot help finding this concept of the faith unbelievable — or something, at least, of which there is not a rudiment in my own experience of belief. . . . I repeat: a Christian faith that uses Kierkegaard's theological construct to comprehend itself as incomprehensible, as necessarily absurd — thus justifying itself, so to speak, in a modern world — would be as apt to mean the end of this Christianity and this church as would Kierkegaard's exposure of ecclesiasticism." *Philosophical Faith and Revelation*, 349-50.

ecclesiastic."[1] Such struggles with *Anfechtung* afflict "the believer in revelation"; but equally, Jaspers maintains, "the philosophical believer [*Der philosophisch Glaubende*]". As such, "The conquest of their doubts [*Anfechtungen*] is what makes both sides recognize each other's faith, if they are honest."[2] Here *Anfechtung* provides an opportunity for recognition and dialogue between the believer in revelation and the philosophical believer: the authentic conquest of *Anfechtung*, Jaspers proposes, may furnish us with the possibility for mutual communication and recognition in the modern struggle with faith, revelation, and reason, and a meeting point between philosophy and theology.[3] This meeting point, or clearing (*Lichtung*), might be explored further with reference to one of the most decisive interlocutors for these twentieth-century exponents of *Anfechtung*, Martin Heidegger (1889-1976).

Heidegger: *Destruktion* and *Tentatio*

The theological concerns of Bultmann, Tillich, Thielicke, and Jaspers were each indebted to the *Existenz* philosophy of Heidegger, as well as to Kierkegaard's thought. In turn Heidegger's own debt to Kierkegaardian themes is well recognised; but, unlike *Angst*, Kierkegaard's notion of *spiritual trial* is not explicit in Heidegger's writings. However, this does not preclude the possibility that Heidegger was familiar with "proto-phenomenological descriptions of *Anfechtung*"[4] via his earlier studies of Luther. In this vein, Crowe has made a compelling argument for Luther's influence suggesting that:

---

1 Jaspers, *Philosophical Faith and Revelation*, 361.

2 *Ibid.* 362.

3 Through this consideration of *Anfechtung* as the recognition of (self-) doubt, "Jaspers believed that the gulf between philosophical and religious faith could be overcome by *Anfechtung* combined with a critical rationality capable of recognizing the 'limits' of reason in order to, as in Kant, 'make room for faith.'" Alan M. Olson, 'Faith and Reason: Isaac and Ishmael Revisited', *Existenz: An International Journal in Philosophy, Religion, Politics, and the Arts*, 1 (1-2), Fall 2006.

4 Brian Gregor, *A Philosophical Anthropology of the Cross: The Cruciform Self* (Bloomington: Indiana University Press), 170. For an illuminating contrast of theological and philosophical doubt, see Gregor's juxtaposing of Luther's *Anfechtung* with Descartes' attempt to escape radical doubt through the light of reason. While both speak in relation to a God who has seemingly withdrawn from the sense, Descartes' *credo/cogito, ergo sum* offers little consolation to the soul falling into doubt and despair in *Anfechtung* (170-172).

Heidegger saw his own work as bringing to completion the dismantling of the metaphysical tradition that began with Luther [particularly Luther's attack on medieval Aristotelian philosophy and scholasticism]. . . . Luther's emphasis on the concrete experience of Christian life under the cross, afflicted by *Anfechtung*, and his critique of the pride (*superbia*) of metaphysical speculation, exerted a powerful influence over Heidegger's new hermeneutics.[1]

As discussed in chapter three, *Anfechtung* operates as a central element of Luther's theology, humbling the theologian *coram Deo* and averting the temptations of speculative theology. *Anfechtung*, even as a devilish form of pedagogy, therefore signified the destruction (*Destructio*) of one's own attempts at natural knowledge of God by confrontation with the alien work of God (*opus alienum*). Luther's investment of the whole being in the struggle for salvation, Crowe argues, was particularly influential for Heidegger's own search for an authentic philosophical form of thinking.[2] Furthermore, as a vital element of *Destructio* — "Luther's name for God's dismantling of the idols of human egotism . . . concretely experienced in spiritual trial, in the pangs of conscience, and, ultimately, in total despair"[3] — *Anfechtung* can be seen to nurture Heidegger's own Germanised version of "*Destruktion*". However, as Crowe also submits, while "Heidegger shared, for the most part, Luther's pessimistic assessment of the human condition . . . unlike Luther, he was aware of what to him was an authentic mode of living", which is not radically dependent upon a personal relationship with divine grace. "Accordingly, he

---

1 *Heidegger's Religious Origins* (Bloomington and Indianapolis: Indiana University Press, 2006), 45.

2 "The experiences of awe before the power of God, and heart-wrenching *Anfechtung* . . . no doubt had a strong influence on Heidegger's well-known discussions of *Bekümmerung* [worry, concern] and *Angst*." *Heidegger's Religious Origins*, 57. However, McGrath also observes that "Heidegger's implicit assent to the Lutheran concept of God-forsakenness is philosophically problematic. To be God-forsaken is not to be ignorant of God [Godlessness]; it is to be abandoned by God, to have a history of dealing with God that has resulted in a decisive rupture and distance. But if this is a theological position, as Luther would be the first to argue, it can be justified only theologically." Sean J. McGrath, 'The Facticity of Being God-forsaken: The Young Heidegger and Luther's Theology of the Cross', *American Catholic Philosophical Quarterly*, 79 (2), 2005, 273-290, 273. See further McGrath, *The Early Heidegger and Medieval Philosophy: Phenomenology for the God-forsaken* (Washington: The Catholic University of America Press, 2006).

3 Crowe, *Heidegger's Religious Origins*, 66.

began to conceive of philosophy not merely as a handmaiden to the sciences (positivism), or as a construction of *a priori* values (neo-Kantianism), or even as the proclamation of ideology (philosophy of life), but as a comrade in the struggle against inauthenticity. Learning from Luther, Heidegger called this philosophy *'Destruktion.'*[1] Yet in dissolving the centre-piece of the human being *coram Deo*, Heidegger develops elements of *Anfechtung* in orientations which deviate decisively from the theological stances of both Luther and Kierkegaard.

However, while Heidegger evidently re-inscribes such terminology within his own distinctive philosophy, there may also be discernible traces of Luther and Kierkegaard in Heidegger's discussion of Augustine and temptation (*tentatio*).[2] As explored previously, the confession of sin and the possibility of temptation is already rendered enigmatic by the ineffability and impossibility of a complete self-consciousness of sin. In a similar sense, Heidegger reflects upon Augustine's avowed difficulty in confessing an unknowable self. "Yet there is something in the human being which is unknown even to the spirit of man . . . I do not know which temptations I can resist and which I cannot. *quibus tentaionibus resistere valeam, quibusve non valeam'* [*Confessions*, X, 5, 7]."[3] In reference to Augustine's observation, "For life is really nothing but a constant temptation. *'Numquid non tentatio est vita humana super terram sine ullo interstitio'*",[4] Heidegger elaborates a nuanced Augustinian phenomenology of temptation. The First Form of *tentatio* is "*concupiscentia carnis* [desire of the flesh]", spoken of in relation to three phenomena: "(1) *concupiscentia carnis* [desire of the flesh], (2) *concupiscentia oculorum* [desire of the eyes], (3) *ambition saeculi* [secular ambition]."[5] Under *Voluptas* (Pleasure), Heidegger considers "*Illecebra odurum* [The allurement of smell]"; "*Voluptas aurium* [The pleasure of the ear]"; "*Voluptas oculorum* [The pleasure of the eye]"; and "*Operatores et sectatores pulchritudinum exteriorum* [The artists and followers of external beauty]".[6] The Second Form of *tentatio* is listed as "*concupiscentia oculorum* [the desire of the eye]",

---

1 *Ibid.*
2 Heidegger, *The Phenomenology of Religious Life*, trans. Matthias Fritsch and Jennifer Anna Gosetti-Ferencei (Bloomington and Indianapolis: Indiana University Press, 2010); Martin Heidegger, *Phänomenologie des religiösen Lebens* (Frankfurt am Main: Vittorio Klostermann, 1995). See further McGrath, *The Early Heidegger and Medieval Philosophy*, 197-203.
3 Heidegger, *The Phenomenology of Religious Life*, 130.
4 *Ibid.* 152.
5 *Ibid.* 155-156.
6 *Ibid.* 158-165.

which encompasses "*Alia forma tentaionis: concupiscentia oculorum, curiositas supervacanea cognoscendi* [A different form of temptation: 'the desire of the eye,' 'the superfluous curiosity of knowing']."[1] The Third Form of *tentatio* is found in "*ambitio saeculi* [secular ambition]", which can be expressed in (169) "*Timeri velle* [wishing to be feared] and *amari velle* [wishing to be loved]" by one's others.[2] Ensuing from this is the temptation of "*Amor laudis* [love of praise]": "Finding joy in being praised as such is a taking-oneself-to-be-important, and in the context of *tentatio*, it is a falling, since the human being, according to its significance, is a 'nothingness' before God."[3]

As Heidegger recognises through Augustine, temptation discloses hidden aspects of the self to oneself and to others. It elicits the unknown and the unconfessed enigma of the self into an anxious clearing. "*In tentatione apparet, quails sit homo* [In temptation appears what kind of human being one is]" — "*Nescit se homo, nisi in tentatione discat se* [You do not know a human being unless you have gotten to know him in temptation; *Sermones* II 3, 3]."[4] In temptation, one faces the question 'What am I?' and 'What do I love?', which as suspended between fall and redemption "forms the possibility of losing and of winning myself."[5] In further notes and sketches for Heidegger's 1920-21 lecture course on the phenomenology of religious life, *tentatio* is referred to as "an existential sense of enactment, a How of experiencing. . . . Not such that it is present self-sufficiently, significantly, not in absorption, but that a 'possibility' is experienced, that *significance* refers, in terms of content, toward something else, cf. 'conflict.'"[6] In terms which are more of less lifted from *The Concept of Anxiety*, "Guilt" is described as "a more concrete conception, which becomes more and more possible in the relation of possibility to freedom" (cf. CA, 109). Furthermore, "whosoever becomes guilty also becomes guilty of that which occasioned the guilt. For guilt never has an external occasion, and whoever yields to temptation is himself guilty of the temptation" (cf. CA, 109).[7]

A debt to Kierkegaard appears even more evident in Heidegger's notes on "The Counter-Expected? (*Wider-wärtige*), the Temptation [*Versuchung*], the Appeal (*Anfechtung* [perhaps a more legalistic modern translation than intended by Heidegger])". In terms that

---

1 *Ibid.* 165.
2 *Ibid.* 169-171.
3 *Ibid.* 173, 175.
4 *Ibid.* 181.
5 *Ibid.* 184.
6 'Appendix I: Notes and Sketches for the Lecture Course', *Ibid.* 186.
7 *Ibid.* 192.

echo Kierkegaard's characteristic differentiation, Heidegger sketches, "The temptation [*Versuchung*] (ethical): the 'lowly' one lures, and seeks to pull down what is 'higher.'" In contrast to which he poses, "The Appeal [*Anfechtung*] (religious): What is higher (jealously, as it were) limits the individual away from itself, increases with religiosity. The absolute's own resistance."[1] Supplementary notes from the philosopher Oskar Becker, while of limited verifiability, suggest the possibility of further veiled references to Kierkegaard and to Luther. Becker notes two different meanings of *tentatio*: namely, "*tentatio deceptionis* [temptation of deception]: with the tendency to bring-to-a-fall", and "*tentatio probationis* [temptation of probation]: with the t[endency] to test. In the first sense only the devil (*diabolus*) tempts, in the second, God tempts too."[2] He furthermore adds that "the real *tentatio*" is "the *tentatio tribulationis*, so that the human being becomes a question to himself [Augustine]" in the context of which *Anfechtung* is also invoked.[3]

Though Heidegger bears the trace of Lutheran and Kierkegaardian reflections on spiritual trial and temptation, these do not serve as decisive hermeneutical keys to this thinking.[4] While Heidegger's concern with *Destruktion* is most prevalent in his work during the 1920s, there is, for instance, no clear mention in 1927's *Being and Time* of *Anfechtung* or even of the sense of Affliction (*Bekümmerung*),[5] which, though important in his study of Christian mysticism, becomes replaced with *Angst*.[6] Echoes and traces of Luther's and Kierkegaard's ideas are certainly discernible in Heidegger's thinking, but the former's irreducible concern with the soul seeking to work out its salvation with fear and trembling *coram Deo* has dissipated.

---

1 *Ibid.* 202.

2 Appendix II: Supplement from the Notes of Oskar Becker', *Ibid.* 206.

3 *Ibid.* 206. Becker's notes later add, "What kind of *delectatio* [delight] is dominant will become decisive for one's comportment in the appeal [*Anfechtung*] and in coping with it" (207).

4 On the presence of Luther and Kierkegaard in Heidegger's phenomenology of religious life see further Matheson Russell, 'Phenomenology and Theology: Situating Heidegger's Philosophy of Religion', *Sophia* 50 (2011), 641-655. Russell, however, makes no reference to *Anfechtung*.

5 Alfred Denker, *Historical Dictionary of Heidegger's Philosophy* (Lanham, Maryland, and London: The Scarecrow Press, 2000), 43. Denker's dictionary also contains no entry on temptation (*Versuchung* or *Anfechtung*).

6 Heidegger, *Being and Time*, trans. John Macquarrie and Edward Robinson (New York & Evanston: Harper & Row, 1962). Heidegger does state that "Being-in-the-world is in itself *tempting* [*versucherisch*]" (221), but his subsequent discussion of "falling" and "throwness" (222-224) take him far from Lutheran theology.

Yet even insofar as this orientation of the individual in relation to the Absolute *qua* Spirit is absent, there may be elements of Heidegger's thinking which re-connect with and even rehabilitate the old devotional way of spiritual trial and might contribute, even by way of *opposita juxta se posita magis illucesunt* [the opposites appear more clearly by juxtaposition] (SUD, 122), to a contemporary account of theology as spiritual struggle.

The Struggle of *Aletheia* and the Releasement of *Gelassenheit*

In temptation, the latent enigma of the self is disclosed, though not necessarily in ways that the self can integrate. Only through encountering temptation have hidden desires and weaknesses become manifest and only now do they threaten to disrupt the self's mastery of itself. In spiritual trial, moreover, the self is confronted with itself, with the revelation of the consciousness of sin, and also, in the darkest moments, with its vision of the wrath of God. At the same time, however, the struggle of spiritual trial is the awakening of Spirit, the revealing of the self to itself, which draws the self out of the inclosing reserve of the demonic and the dreaming of spiritlessness. Aspects of this sense of unveiling can, I suggest, also be recognised in Heidegger's notion of truth as *aletheia*, or unconcealment. *Aletheia*, like the theology of *Anfechtung* and *Destructio*, is not primarily concerned with the assertion of certitude over doubt and propositional correctness. *Aletheia* "must be gained by struggle. Unconcealment is wrested from concealment, in a conflict with it."[1] *Struggle* is an integral facet of the process of bringing to light (*lichtung*) that which has been concealed, hidden, veiled, masked — the struggle of *aletheia*, which strives to bring truth into the light of being and disclosure (*Erschlossenheit*), and out of the darkness of ignorance and forgetfulness.

This process has been pertinently illustrated by Haim Gordon and Rivca Gordon with reference to the struggle to recognise the epoch-shaking discoveries of Copernicus.[2] The publication of Nicolaus Copernicus' *De Revolutionibus Orbium Celestium Libri IV* in 1543 presented astronomical findings which *demonstrated* the scientific truth of heliocentric cosmology. However, the struggle to *realise* this truth as *aletheia* took more than half a century of debate between scientists, theologians, and philosophers concerning

1 Heidegger, *Parmenides*, trans. Andre Schuwer and Richard Rojcewicz (Bloomington: Indiana University Press, 1992), 17.

2 Haim Gordon and Rivca Gordon, *Heidegger on Truth and Myth: A Rejection of Postmodernism* (New York: Peter Lang, 2007), 11-13.

the place of the earth — and therefore of humanity itself, of each individual self — in the wider cosmos. "As a result of that struggle, an important cosmological truth was wrested from concealment."[1] The *fact* of the earth's orbit of the sun already lay in concealment, and while Copernicus' scientific observations sought to demonstrate this truth, it was actually the wider struggle to *recognise* and *realise* the unconcealment of the truth of the Copernican Revolution, which expressed the true struggle of *aletheia*. For Heidegger truth comes from concealment into unconcealment in the light that our way of being in the world opens up: "within the open space, the newly unconcealed truth about the Being of certain beings is illuminated, and illuminates additional truths."[2] Copernicus opened the first two aspects of Heidegger's "fourfold openness": namely the openness "(1) of the thing, (2) of the region between the thing and man"; and yet it took further decades of struggle to open the further aspects of "(3) of man himself with regard to the thing, and (4) of man to fellow man."[3]

Theologically, the truth of heliocentrism presents potential for illustrating an understanding of both temptation and spiritual trial. By threatening to unsettle humanity from its cosmic centre, the Copernican Revolution suggests a limit and a trial to current understanding. It is, for some, an *offence*. But *as offence* it must be *struggled with* — neither blithely accepted nor repressed, but struggled with and thereby existentially integrated into theological reflection, even though it may suggest unsettling ideas and even doubts about God, creation, and our own identity. The same might be said of the revelation of the consciousness of sin — a revelation of oneself, which can never become an object of the self's knowing, though it may overwhelm it in the fantasy of despair. The *temptation*, therefore, is to remain in concealment, to enter into a forgetfulness of oneself and of difficult truths. The temptation is to remain inclosed in dreaming, or to attempt to actively forget by holding to the old truths, even by distraction, by intoxicating ourselves with other things which take our minds away from difficult truths. Or else the temptation is to despair. The spiritual trial, however, is felt in the nemesis of difficult truths, the limit to understanding, which also urges us to struggle beyond ourselves, beyond interiorised self-knowing and beyond despair — through a *kenosis-in-ekstasis* in which false beliefs are released and

---

1 *Ibid.* 11.

2 *Ibid.* 12

3 *Ibid.* 12. On this fourfold openness see further Heidegger, *Basic Questions of Philosophy: Selected 'Problems' of 'Logic'*, trans. Richard Rojcewicz and Andre Schuwer (Bloomington: Indiana University Press, 1994), 18-19.

emptied out in order to relate beyond our self-inclosed horizons to the truth as other. *Aletheia* for theology is therefore attended by the struggle between such temptation and spiritual trial to bring all into the unconcealed openness of the human being in relation to God. As *kenosis-in-ekstasis*, Spirit is truth.

In this sense, the struggle of *aletheia* and of spiritual trial is also a letting-go or a letting-be. The truth of Spirit is not the dominance of subject over object fought for in the Master-Slave struggle for recognition. *Aletheia* as Spirit cannot be reduced to an object for the self. Even in the revelation of the consciousness of sin, the self is not given as object for itself, since, as Luther warns, the self would be unable to integrate the full disclosure of its sinfulness. Likewise, in spiritual trial the self is confronted with the impossibility of grasping God as object. It is confronted by the limit of the absolutely different — even with the apophatic realisation that its own sense of wrath of God does not, in truth, equate to a theophany of God-in-Godself. Ultimately the struggle of spiritual trial (*Anfechtung*) brings the self to the moment of letting-go or letting-be (*Gelassenheit — lassen*, to let).

Again, dialogue with Heidegger's thinking may help to enlighten how this might be understood theologically, even if ultimately by way of contrast. In his 1955 'Discourse on Thinking', Heidegger invokes the old word *Gelassenheit* as "releasement towards things [*die Gelassenheit zu den Dingen*] and openness to the mystery", illustrative of a difference between a more masterful or active "calculative thinking [*das rechnende Denken*]" and a more passive "meditative thinking [*das besinnliche Denken*]", which should express both a "yes" and a "no", in this case towards technology. Heidegger also appeals to *Gelassenheit* as indicative of a "non-willing [*Nicht-Wollen*]" form of thinking in *Conversation on a Country Path about Thinking* (written between 1944 and 1945, first published in 1959).[1] Desiring non-willing, or the willing renunciation of willing, is the way towards a releasement of the desire to master, control, or dominate objects in voluntaristic or scientific knowing, which manifests a secret will-to-power — even, theologically speaking, a speculative will-to-power over the idea of *God*. In light of Luther's *Destructio, Gelassenheit* encounters truth as *aletheia* rather than through the metaphysical lens of onto-theological thinking or speculative philosophy.[2]

---

1 These works were published together in *Discourse on Thinking*, trans. John M. Anderson and E. Hans Freund (New York: Harper and Row, 1966), see 54-55, 58-60.

2 However, while Heidegger refers *Gelassenheit* explicitly to Eckhart, he is not concerned with the devotional goal of *Gelassenheit* as divine union. Despite his studies of mysticism, it remains imperative and cautionary to observe

While Heidegger invokes both Eckhart and Angelus Silesius, it is the to the poetry of that latter which Jacques Derrida principally refers in his treatment of *Gelassenheit* as a "serene indifference" to all that can be said of God, since *tout autre est tout autre* (every other is wholly other). As Caputo notes, Derrida suggests that in speaking of *Gelassenheit*, "why not speak of love, so that saying *tout autre est tout autre* would be a way of loving and letting others be, the 'hospitality' of a 'passage to the other'? After all, Meister Eckhart said that in its highest reaches *Gelassenheit* is love, that love is 'without why' and love is 'letting the other be.'"[1] In this sense, *Gelassenheit* is an expression, perhaps contra

---

"how much this religious mysticism [Meister Eckhart in particular] differs from Heidegger's own path, how much Heidegger is not a mystic." John Caputo, *The Mystical Element in Heidegger's Thought* (New York: Fordham University Press, 1986), xxi. On the relationship between *angst* and *Gelassenheit* in Eckhartian speculative mystical thought and its return "in secularized or postsecualrized form in contemporary Heideggerian philosophy" see Luca D'Isanto, 'Kenosis of the Subject and the Advent of Being in Mystic Experience', *Qui Parle, Special Issue: Thinking Alterity, Reprise,* 17 (1), Fall/ Winter 2008, 147-173, 147. See also Sonya Sikka, 'Call and Conscience in Tauler and Heidegger', *The Heythrop Journal,* XXXIII (1992), 371-398 (Sikka also engages with Kierkegaard's critique of mysticism). Clifton-Soderstrom has lucidly outlined how "Heidegger's phenomenology of humility changed from an Eckhartian conception of detachment culminating in the *unio mystica* to a Lutheran conception of humiliation and Anfechtung", such that "Heidegger's break from a mystical phenomenology of humility parallels Luther's own break from that tradition, and anticipates contemporary developments in the continental philosophy of religion." Karl Clifton-Soderstrom, 'The Phenomenology of Religious Humility in Heidegger's reading of Luther', *Continental Philosophy Review,* 42 (2009), 171–200, 171.

1   John D. Caputo, *The Prayers and Tears of Jacques Derrida* (Bloomington: Indiana University Press, 1997), 49 (see also 60, 226, 248). However, Marko Zlomislić contends that "Caputo folds Derrida onto Heidegger. The problem however is that Derrida's ethics of dissemination is not Heidegger's ethics of *Gelassenheit*. *Gelassenheit* requires letting individuals be whereas dissemination requires letting person become." (Marko Zlomislić, *Jacques Derrida's Aporetic Ethics*, Plymouth: Lexington books, 2007, 267). In reference to Derrida's essay, *Sauf le nom/On the Name*, Steven Shakespeare elucidates how, "The name of God effaces itself, opens itself to being substituted. The process by which it dies is the process by which it lives on. The dereliction of God is also what releases a kind of bliss: not an escape into eternal beatification, but a return to the play of the world and the innocence of becoming." *Derrida and Theology* (Edinburgh: T & T Clarke, 2011), 115. See also Jacques Derrida, 'Post-Scriptum: Aporias, Ways and Voices', Harold Coward and Toby Foshay (eds), *Derrida and Negative Theology* (Albany, NY: State University of New York Press, 1992), 283-324. Derrida notes that "Silesius writes in the tradition of the *Gelassenheit* that goes from Eckhart, at least, to Heidegger. It is necessary to leave all, to leave

speculative or onto-theology of letting God be God.[1] However, as Derrida himself acknowledges, *difference* and deconstruction do not lay claim to the hyperessentiality (*superessentialité*) he discerns as underwriting even the most apophatic of negative theology.[2]

Theologically speaking, therefore, can one truly have *Gelassenheit* without *Anfechtung*; or *apophasis* without *agonia*? Alongside letting the other be, spiritual trial also witnesses to the Other who does not simply let me be: that is, to the Absolutely Different who, in the fear and trembling of alterity, appears in the night to struggle with the self, though ultimately out of a hidden love, the light of which is breaking out of the darkness. In this sense, one might also acknowledge the apophatic unthinkableness of God, which, for Marion, effaces "the idolatrous quotation marks" around 'God' with the G⊗d who "crosses out our thought because he saturates it; better, he enters into our thought only in obliging it to criticize itself."[3] In crossing out our thinking in this way, might Marion's apophatic theology, as a *theologia crucis* in which *hyperousious* is interpreted not as "above" or "beyond" being but "otherwise than being" , open the way to spiritual trials in which God may appear as "otherwise"? Luther, however, might resist any elision with literality insofar as the *experience* of spiritual trial is struggled with by clinging in the face of dreadful alterity — which is itself a form of presence, even as presence-in-absence or *absconditus* — to the God of Love. In other words, a theology of spiritual trial struggles with *apophasis* as desolation, grasping on to the consolation of the *deus revelatus*. Yet in its confrontation with the abyssal difference of the Absolute, the theology of spiritual trial is humbled before the unknowableness of the *deus nudus*. Its agonistic apophaticism resides in the concomitant sense of creature-feeling (*Kreaturgefühl*) — the consciousness of

---

every 'something' through love of God, and no doubt to leave God himself, to abandon him, that is, at once to leave him and (but) let him (be beyond being-something)" (316-317). In the secret abandonment (*Die geheimste Gelassenheit*) Silesius's poetry speaks of "the abandonment *to* this *Gelassenheit* does not preclude pleasure or enjoyment [it is not *apatheia*]; on the contrary, it gives rise to them. It opens the play *of* God (of God and with God, of God with self and with creation); it opens to the enjoyment of God" (317).

1   On *Gelassenheit* in Heidegger, Derrida, and Eckhart see further Ian Almond, 'Doing Violence upon God: Nonviolent Alterities and Their Medieval Precedents', *The Harvard Theological Review*, 92 (3), July 1999, 325-347.

2   See further the brilliant essay by Mary-Jane Rubenstein, 'Unknow Thyself: Apophaticism, Deconstruction, and Theology After Ontotheology', *Modern Theology*, 19 (3), July 2003, 387-417.

3   Jean-Luc Marion, *God Without Being: Hors Texte*, trans. Thomas H. Carlson (Chicago and London: The University of Chicago Press, 1991), 46.

oneself as but dust and ashes — before God. In this, spiritual trial represents the *destructio* of the self as well as the self's idols of God. Yet it also points to the transfiguration of the dis-integrated self as Spirit, as reflecting the image of God through becoming nothing.

Kenosis: Subjectivity and Subjection

The theology of spiritual trial is therefore confronted with the *kenosis-in-ekstatsis* of the self-will, beyond which it cannot think in onto-theological terms of the hidden kenosis of the Godhead. But this is not to say that the inexorable subjectivity of spiritual trial's struggle with God is reducible to subjectivism. On the contrary, spiritual trial assumes the transcendent divinity beyond the infinite qualitative abyss at that same time that it struggles with the causes of absolute difference revealed within the self (PF, 47). As struggle with the limit of the Absolute, spiritual trial is only made possible by the kenosis of the Absolute, which gives itself, as given in the form of the stranger who wrestles with Jacob. Without this kenosis, difference is utterly indifferent; or else the Absolute annihilates and overwhelms all that is not the Absolute. Furthermore, through the struggle of spiritual trial, the self, becoming Spirit, comes to realise the secret presence of God as love. Yet the love of God is also expressed in the divine withdrawal that gifts the freedom and possibility of becoming a fragile something, an *I* capable of loving, or even hating, God in return. Becoming Spirit through spiritual trial, however, does entail becoming nothing: that is, the kenosis of the self-will, of spiritless and the demonic. The kenosis of spiritual trial is not only the releasement (*Gelassenheit*) of wilful forms of knowing. It also attests to the subjection of the self-will.

In this respect, does spiritual trial, as the forming of the self as Spirit, represent a notion of subjectivity formed through subjection? As Judith Butler writes, with reference to Michel Foucault's *Discipline and Punish: The Birth of the Prison*, "Subjection is, literally, the making of a subject, the principle of regulation according to which a subject is formulated or produced." In other words, subjection manifests a power that "not only unilaterally *acts on* a given individual as a form of domination, but also *activates* or forms the subject." Subjectivity wrought in subjection therefore represents a path between domination and production of selfhood, designating "a certain kind of restriction *in* production, a restriction without which the production of the subject cannot take place, a restriction through which that production takes place."[1]

---

1   Judith Butler, '3: Subjection, Resistance, Resignification: Between Freud and Foucault', *The Psychic Life of Power: Theories in Subjection* (Stanford: Stanford University Press, 1997), 83.

Autonomy develops in response to subjection by and dependence upon a heteronomous power — a power which restricts the autonomy of the imprisoned subject while also restricting its own ability to dominate. Might such a dialectic be resonant with Kierkegaard's vision of a God who restricts divine omnipotence enough to allow the relative freedom for the emergence of a *fragile something*, while at the same time subjecting that subjectivity with the spiritual trial of the nemesis of the Absolute Difference? After all, while Foucault is concerned with the *subjectivation*, which occurs through the body of the prisoner, Johannes Climacus suggests that even "the prisoner in the narrowest prison cell [is] not as captive as the person who is captive in his conception of God, because, just as God is, the captivating conception is everywhere present and at every moment" (CUP, 484). In other words, as Luther discovers in the *Anfechtung* of being guilty before a God, from whom one flees but cannot escape, does spiritual trial seek the breaking and making of subjectivity through subjection to the self-limiting power of the Wholly Other?

This may be so, I suggest, if one conceives of the God-relationship as ultimately one of a Master-Slave struggle in which true subjectivity is only attained through dominance of objects. However, spiritual trial is ultimately concerned with transfiguring this relationship such that the vision of a life-and-death struggle between a sinful object who trembles before the wrath of an Absolute Subject is itself struggled against in the name of God as Love. As such, Kierkegaard subtly nuances Johannes Climacus description when he states that the one in spiritual trial "is by God or because of God imprisoned within himself" (FSE, 19-20). In other words, whereas Climacus speaks of being captive in the absolute *conception* of God — and not necessarily God-in-Godself or even the *deus revelatus* — Kierkegaard transposes the prison of the Absolute to the interiority of the self. Yet these are mutually compatible insofar as the potentially dysmorphic conception of God as a subjecting Wholly Other is formed in part by the psychogenic elements of subjectivity, which spiritual trial urges one to struggle against. In this sense, like Luther, one is to struggle against one's vision of the absolute wrath of God by cleaving, like Jacob, to the God of love — struggling *against* God *with* God, thereby also struggling against the self-will, which secretly wills to have God against itself (CD, 67). Through spiritual trial, therefore, one struggles, or is struggled free of the prison of the self's inclosing reserve (*Indesluttethed*) which, within the horizon of its hidden despair, cannot conceive of God as anything other than the Wholly Other.

Yet, insofar as the self-will must become nothing, is a theology of spiritual trial, in its longing for the reprieve of *Gelassenheit*, vulnerable to the critique that an emphasis upon kenosis valorises weakness and thereby proliferates the injustice that flourishes in its space? While spiritual trial might suggest an implicit form of subjectivation, it also affirms the desolation of the will. In this sense, Kierkegaard suggests "The stronger the natural will, the deeper the break can be and the better the Christian": a form of subjectivation he expresses via "the new obedience" whereby "A Christian is a man of will who no longer wills his own will but with the passion of his crushed will — radically changed — wills another's will" (JP 6:6966). What is inescapable in this is that it is the "man of will" whose will is crushed such through the passion of which he is able to will the will of the other.[1] Such a position seems exposed to Daphne Hampson's critique that, while men have been able to cultivate a will that is then mortified in relation to God, women have themselves been denied a robust sense of self through their calling (by men) to cultivate virtues of *selflessness*: self-sacrifice, humility, self-denial, self-emptying (*kenosis*). Kenosis thereby becomes disempowering for women insofar as it contains no "grammar" for resistance: "Moreover, if the doctrine of self-sacrifice and the paradigm of powerlessness are held up as exemplary before those who are struggling to change their lot, it may serve to undercut them. For resistance to injustice then comes to look un-Christ-like."[2] Kenosis thus legitimises and participates in the subjugation of female autonomy by valorising obedience and submission to the heteronomous will of God. It is regarded as a self-emptying which is tantamount to a breaking of the self — a self that in the first place it has been the privilege of men to nurture and mortify but has generally been denied to women. The masculine paradigm of subjectivity through subjection thus becomes subjugation, which denies female subjectivity from ever arising. The path from *Anfechtung* to *Gelassenheit*, which Christ symbolises in his prayer, "nevertheless, not my will but your will be done", thereby becomes the heroic paradigm of male spiritual struggle; while women seemingly lack the will with which to struggle, such that the 'virtue' of women's kenosis is represented by the *Gelassenheit* of the Mother Mary, which makes the kenotic incarnation possible: according to your will (Luke 1:38).[3]

---

1 See further Sylvia Walsh, 'On "Feminine" and "Masculine" Forms of Despair,' ed. Robert Perkins, *International Kierkegaard Commentary: The Sickness Unto Death* (Macon: Mercer University Press, 1987), 121-134.

2 Daphne Hampson, 'On Power and Gender,' *Modern Theology*, 4 (3), July 1988, 239.

3 See further Rose Ellen Dunn, 'Let It Be: Finding Grace With God Through the *Gelassenheit* of the Annunciation', in Chris Boesel and Catherine Keller (eds), *Apophatic Bodies: Negative Theology, Incarnation, and Relationality* (New

In response to Hampson's powerful critique, however, Sarah Coakley suggests that kenosis should be interpreted in terms of *subversion* rather than subjugation, contending that the kenosis of Christ actually subverts the classic paradigms of power, powerlessness, and empowerment within which she suggests Hampson's position remains entrenched.[1] Christ's kenosis thereby transfigures vulnerability as a "special sort of human strength" that transcends and even empties patriarchal power.[2] As such, kenosis aspires beyond the temptations of power that afflict those who are disempowered victims of power. The victims desire the same power that oppresses and disempowers them; whereas kenosis, like spiritual trial, seeks different expressions of overcoming, even to the point of conquering God through ostensible weakness.

Where victims remain caught in the dialectic of a mimetic desire for the very power that disempowers them, it might be said that the 'lower' is tempting. The spiritual trial therefore becomes a 'higher' struggle, which transcends the paradigm of oppression, subjection, and mimesis. In this view of kenosis as the free choice to refuse certain forms of power, Coakley identifies a form of resistance in kenosis: specifically the resistance to the expressions of power that patriarchy enforces. Through this reading, Jesus' resistance of the temptation of the devil for worldly power could be interpreted as a form of kenosis: a refusal of the demonic self-will-to-power, which also contains an implicit spiritual trial, a higher struggle with God, a struggle of love against the forces of hatred, aggression, and fear.[3] It

---

York: Fordham University Press, 2010), 329-348. See Mary Daly's objection that in Mary's submission to the annunciation, "Like all rape victims in the male myth she submits joyously to this unspeakable degradation." *Pure Lust* (Boston: Beacon, 1984), 74. When Luther praises the Cannanite woman as one who overcame God, he valorises her active stance towards God but is only apparently able to acknowledge it by bestowing a *male* term of honour: a knight of faith (LW 6, 139-141).

1   Sarah Coakley, 'Kenosis and Subversion: On the Repression of 'Vulnerability' in Christian Feminist Writing', ed. Daphne Hampson, *Swallowing a Fishbone?: Feminist Theologians Debate Christianity* (London: SPCK, 1996), 82-111.
2   Coakley, 'Kenosis and Subversion', 101.
3   Carolyn A. Chau also suggests this kenotic implication of Jesus' resistance of temptation. '"What Could Possibly be Given?", 'Towards an Exploration of Kenosis as Forgiveness — Continuing the Conversation Between Coakley, Hampson, and Papanikolaou', *Modern Theology*, 28 (1), January 2012, 1-24, at 21n41. This excellent article provides an extensive framework for this discussion of kenosis. Chau develops a profound view of forgiveness as kenosis, which requires an element of *ascesis*: forgiveness as the self-emptying of fear or wrath (12-19).

is ultimately in contemplative prayer that Coakley discerns the self's "transformation and expansion into God",[1] which also "undermines all previous certainties and dogmatisms".[2] In contemplative prayer Coakley affirms the potential for a freely willed self-effacement before a loving divine presence, which does not seek the obliteration of the self.

The relationship of a theology of spiritual trial to these issues is, however, far from resolved. Critiques of self-mortification continue to provide vital admonition against any normative theology that presents spiritual trial as a necessary and prescriptive dialectical *via* to 'true' spirituality or interiority. The temptation of a theology of spiritual trial is to fetishize spiritual trial itself, to valorise suffering to the extent that it becomes a normative signifier of the most authentic and intensified God-relationship. Such a temptation is the temptation to desire to be too much Spirit. Yet at the same moment, I suggest that theology must remain attentive to the loneliness of Kierkegaard's plea to break the silence of spiritual trial. The self-God-relationship is evidently not universally recognised in such solitary and agonistic terms. Perhaps there are those who find the presence of God on more intimate grounds, even those for whom some form of *Gelassenheit* is closer at hand. Yet this too should not become normative, lest theology forgets the 'sick souls' who otherwise, as Kierkegaard did within the old devotional books, will be left to find one another across the centuries of silence. In this respect, without enforcing it within the hearts of every individual, a theology of spiritual trial might at least hold open the hermeneutic question of the darkness of God.

Conclusion: Resting in the Heart of Struggle
Towards a Theology of Spiritual Trial

By holding this question in openness, I suggest that a theology of spiritual trial might also resist the temptation to resolve all desolation into consolation. It is tempting to sublimate spiritual trial (*Anfechtung*) through releasement (*Gelassenheit*), but, even in *imitatio Christi* of "nevertheless, not my will but your will be done", the *nevertheless* passes over a vast abyss between self-will and Divine Will. As Hugh Pyper provocatively and profoundly suggests, this single word "nevertheless" might be read as a cypher for the whole Bible itself.[3] While *Gelassenheit* might shine forth as

---

1 Coakley, 'Kenosis and Subversion', 108.
2 Coakley, 'Kenosis and Subversion', 148.
3 Hugh S. Pyper, *The Joy of Kierkegaard: Essays on Kierkegaard as a Biblical*

the blessed horizon for souls in spiritual trial, there are undoubtedly many (perhaps Luther and Kierkegaard included) for whom it may be only glimpsed in rare moments of transfiguration. Many strugglers tarry in the paradoxical liminality of the "nevertheless". Full consummation of *Gelassenheit*, or of transfiguration of the self as Spirit, resting transparently grounded in God and reflecting the image of God in inverse resemblance, may remain an eschatological vanishing point for those who, for now, struggle to hold on to God in the darkness of night.

Spirit is restless in its struggle to synthesise unity and alterity, the infinite qualitative difference and the intimacy of God. Spirit holds these together in a temporal relationship marked by moments of struggle and release. This movement between struggle and release is suggestive of the prayer of Spirit in the face of spiritual trial — reflecting Coakley's ultimate appeal to contemplative prayer and the invocation of prayer as a loving struggle with God in the introduction of this work. While Bonhoeffer, Jüngel, and Thielicke all make the Lutheran invocation of *tentatio facit theologum* (temptation makes the theologian), it is significant that this dictum is adapted from Luther's tripartite formation *oratio, meditatio, tentatio faciunt Theologum* — prayer, study, and temptation make the theologian. Temptation, in other words is inseparable from reflection and prayer in the formation of a theologian and in Luther's account disrupts and displaces speculative theology (*contemplatio/theoria*). The way of prayer from spiritual trial to releasement has been acknowledged with reference to Christ's prayer at Gethsemane. Here, like Jacob he is met with an angel in the night. Yet an allegory for prayer is also discernible in Jesus' cry of God-forsakenness, an invocation of Psalm 22 in the face of the last spiritual trial. Here it seems that God is absent, there is desolation without consolation. As proposed in the introduction, his cry can itself be read as a voice of protest amidst the darkness and silence of God.[1] As such, it struggles with God, even after Gethsemane's *Gelassenheit* of the will in the face of spiritual trial. This cry therefore suggests that prayer might be an enduring dialogue between moments of struggle and release.

Returning to the original imagery of Jacob's *agonia* at Peni'el as an allegory for prayer in the face of spiritual trial, one might discern a Jacob who struggles with God, against God and the self. In his refusal to let go of his stranger assailant, Jacob might express a state

---

Reader (Sheffield/Oakville: Equinox, 2011).
1 See also 'My God, My God, Why Have You Forsaken Me? Between Consolation & Desolation'.

of detachment (*Abgeschiedenheit*) from all other things. But in refusing to let go, in *desiring* to know the name of his combatant, might he also express an attachment to the 'God' whom he can hold in his grasp. As night is vanishing into dawn, the stranger asks him to let go. Receiving his blessing, Jacob finally must let go, entering state of releasement (*Gelassenheit*) in which, in Kierkegaard's terms, he does not receive *explanation* (the name of the stranger) but rather *transfiguration* (the gift of a new name and new relation to God). His transfiguration is confirmed in the struggle and releasement through which he has beheld the Face of God and lived. He has struggled on beyond the limits and nemesis of spiritual trial Not only that, he is blessed.[1]

Yet, insofar as the stranger vanishes with the dawn, perhaps no blessing is sufficient consolation for the absence of God. God has seemingly become tangibly present in the flesh and blood struggle at Peni'el. The Wholly Other renounces absolute otherness in order to engage with humanity, and by doing so gives of itself. In this sense, the night at Peni'el symbolises the dark night of spiritual trial in which all idols of self-image and God-image are brought to nothing as the self struggles with God in the most visceral and intimate encounter. And yet the kenosis of the divine presence is itself withdrawn. Prayer must also endure in the silence of absence as well as the struggle of presence. Yet as it sinks into silence, the restlessness of prayer might still discover the rest of *Gelassenheit*. Here in the silence of struggle's absence, the presence of the love for God affirms the presence of the love of God as Spirit. As Kierkegaard's 1841 student sermon expresses, at its deepest level of silence and unknowing, prayer becomes the blessed prayer of the Spirit itself, praying within the individual in the secret and hidden interior life "alone with your God". In Spirit, prayer enters into the middle voice of *Gelassenheit*, between the activity and passivity of will.[2] "It is not our life, it is the Spirit's life in us, it is a divine growth . . . your God takes up residence within you, is within you beyond all measure, is present within you, even if you notice it first of all with his disappearance" (JP 4:3915).

---

1 In terms resonant with spiritual trial, Delwin Brown comments: "Jacob confronts a divine limitation that cannot be escaped. But Jacob can respond. Not only can he resist facile subjugation, but he can even place his own demands on the angel-he demands a blessing. What Jacob gains in the struggle is not without its price; the myth says Jacob is injured in the struggle." Delwin Brown, 'Struggle Till Daybreak: On the Nature of Authority in Theology', *The Journal of Religion*, 65 (1), January 1985, 15-32, 28.

2 See further David Lewin, 'The Middle Voice in Eckhart and Modern Continental Philosophy', *Medieval Mystical Theology*, 20 (2011), 28-46.

We return, therefore to the vision of Spirit as the presence of divine love, personalised through the becoming of selfhood in relation to God, transfigured as the image of God. Kenosis, once more, is neither merely passive self-surrender nor active self-mortification of will, but an entering into a process greater than oneself. Kenosis is an act of self-giving towards otherness: a *kenosis-in-ekstasis* which is motivated by a desire for the other.[1] By transcending limitation kenosis is an agonistic self-overcoming which aspires beyond rather than merely negating the self. It also, in Kierkegaardian vision, discovers itself in relation to an Other who heals the possibility of becoming oneself, *a single individual*, not merely the broken and abased remnant ashes of a 'self' which has been burnt up and absorbed within the fire of God, but a self transfigured as Spirit, as an *I* capable of loving God from the divinely-given (kenotic) freedom of its own heart of love.

A theology of spiritual trial might, under these conditions, approach something akin to Abraham Joshua Heschel's notion of a Depth Theology, operating at the ineffable level within the heart, in numinous moments of the Spirit, which cannot be articulated but which constructive theology attempts to sustain and uphold in their absence. In his account of this Depth Theology, Heschel "finds both the Kotzker [the legendary Hasidic Rebbe Menachem Mendel Morgensztern of Kotz (1787–1859)] and Kierkegaard to be partners".[2] Yet Heschel discerns a decisive difference between these two figures, which, I suggest, is vital to a theology of spiritual trial.

Reflecting on the Kotzker's withdrawal into solitude for the final twenty years of his life, Heschel suggests that the great Rebbe was shifting the battlefront from a struggle with men to a struggle with God. Drawing upon Abraham's 'dust and ashes' intercession for the people of Sodom and Gomorrah (Genesis 18:22-32), Heschel contends that the individual should *not* always become *as nothing*

---

1 In this sense Papanikolaous contends that "*Kenosis* is not primarily self-sacrifice but a state of being that liberates *eros*, the desire to be in relation with the other. It is a precondition for relations of love and freedom, the only context in which the self is truly given." Aristotle Papanikolaou, 'Person, Kenosis and Abuse: Hans Urs von Balthasar and Feminist Theologies in Conversation', *Modern Theology*, 19/1 (January, 2003), 41–65, at 59.

2 Jack Mulder Jr, 'Abraham Joshua Heschel: Heschel's Use of Kierkegaard as a Cohort in Depth Theology', ed. Jon Stewart, *Kierkegaard Research: Sources, Reception and Resources: Kierkegaard's Influence on Theology Tome III: Catholic and Jewish Theology* (Aldershot: Ashgate, 2012), 155-170, at 159. Mulder Jr concludes that Heschel's "appreciation for 'depth theology' allowed him to appreciate a thinker as committed to Christianity (Kierkegaard) as Heschel was to Judaism" (168).

before God, but that there are moments when one must stand up and say *no* to God in the face of suffering.[1] As Jack Mulder Jr elucidates, "Kierkegaard would need to correct the impression from Heschel that submitting to God, becoming nothing in the deepest sense, is inconsistent with pleading and struggling with God in the temporal sense."[2] While Kierkegaard may be taken as an advocate of silent self-abnegation, of *becoming nothing* before God in the face of suffering, he also lauds Abraham's agonistic stance before God in Genesis 18 (EUD, 66-67; FT, 22). Furthermore, I suggest that Kierkegaard can be read as exploring a view of silence before God, which is itself a form of struggling with God.[3] In other words, in the affirmation of the *I* as Spirit, even as a *fragile something* that relates in freedom before God, a Kierkegaardian theology spiritual trial need not flee from the possibility of protest — as sanctified in the cry of God-forsakenness — by becoming nothing in an abyss of *Gelassenheit*. The endurance of spiritual trials suggests that we are perhaps still within the night, struggling with the infinite qualitative difference, even through moments of transfiguration. As the theology of spiritual trial affirms, one is not lost to silent resignation in the face of the darkness of God, but one is inspired, by the secret divine presence of love itself, to struggle with God against the God who appears as "otherwise".

Yet in the end, perhaps all we can truly say of the possibility of a theology of spiritual trial is to echo the words of Kierkegaard's young man, A, concerning Hegel's writings on the problem of the Unhappy Consciousness: "happy is the one who has nothing more to do with the subject than to write a paragraph about it; even happier the one who can write the next" (E/O I, 222). Such a one seems to know too little about the subject if they are able to write systematically about it. Ultimately a theology of spiritual trial can only be written in the realisation that it is itself always being written by the spiritual trial of theology.

---

1   Heschel, *A Passion for Truth* (New York: Farrar, Straus and Giroux, 1973), 269-271.
2   Mulder Jr, 'Abraham Joshua Heschel', 167.
3   I develop this further in my 'The Sacrifice of Silence'.

Bibliography

See also *Abbreviations* for main works by Kierkegaard and Luther.

Almond, Ian, 'Doing Violence upon God: Nonviolent Alterities and Their Medieval Precedents', *The Harvard Theological Review*, 92 (3), July 1999, 325-347.

Andic, Martin, 'The Secret of Sufferings', Robert Perkins (ed.), *International Kierkegaard Commentary: Upbuilding Discourses in Various Spirits [IKC: UDVS]*, (Macon, G.A.: Mercer University Press, 2005) 199-228.

Angelus Silesius, *Angelus Silesius: The Cherubinic Wanderer*, trans. Maria Shrady (Mahwah: Paulist Press, 1986).

——, *Sämtliche poetische Werke in drei Bänden*, Band 2, Herausgegeben und eingeleitet von Hans Ludwig Held (München: Hanser, 1952).

Appel, Helmut, *Anfechtung und Trost im Spätmittelalter und dei Luther* (Leipzig: M. Heinsius Nachfolger, 1938).

Arbaugh, G.E., 'The Devil', *Bibliotheca Kierkegaardiana Vol. 5: Theological Concepts in Kierkegaard*, ed. Niels Thusltrup and Marie Mikulová Thulstrup (Copenhagen: C.A. Reitzels Boghandel, 1980).

Arndt, Johann, *True Christianity*, trans. Peter Erb (New York/Ramsey/ Toronto: Paulist Press, 1979).

——, *True Christianity*, trans. A.W. Boehm, [1712]; new American ed. / revised, corrected, and furnished with additional matter from the original German, together with a general introduction by Charles F. Schaeffer (Philadelphia, P.A.: General Council Publication House, 1917).

——, *Weiland Generalsuperintendenten des Fürstenthums Lüneburg, Vier Bücher vom Wahren Christenthum nebst dessen Paradiesgärtlein* (Berlin: Trowitzsch und Sohn, 1831).

Arunguren, José Luis L., 'Sobre el talante religioso de Miguel de Unamuno', *Arbor*, XI, 1948, 485-503.

Auster, Paul, 'Book of the Dead: an Interview with Edmond Jabés', ed. Eric Gould, *The Sin of the Book: Edmond Jabés* (Lincoln N.E. and London: University of Nebraska Press, 1985).

Bachmann, C. Charles, 'Luther as Pastoral Counselor', *Pastoral Psychology*, 3 (1952) 35-42.

Bainton, Roland, *Here I Stand: A Life of Martin Luther* (Peabody: Hendrickson, 1977).

——, 'Luther's Struggle For Faith', *Church History*, 17 (1948).

Baker, Armand F., 'The God of Unamuno', *Hispania*, 74 (4), December 1991, 824-833.

Barnett, Christopher A., 'Gerhard Tersteegen: Reception of a Man of "Noble Piety and Simple Wisdom"', ed. Jon Stewart, *Kierkegaard Research: Source, Reception and Resources Volume 5, Kierkegaard and the Renaissance and Modern Traditions: Tome II: Theology* (Aldershot: Ashgate, 2009), 245-257.

——, *Kierkegaard, Pietism and Holiness* (Farnham: Ashgate, 2011).

——, 'The Mystical Influence on Kierkegaard's Theological Anthropology', Králik *et al* (eds), *Acta Kierkegaardiana VI: Kierkegaard and Human Nature* (Toronto and Šaľa: Kierkegaard Circle, 2013), 105-122.

Barrett, Lee C., 'Jacob Böhme: The Ambiguous Legacy of Speculative Passion', ed. Jon Stewart, *Kierkegaard Research: Source, Reception and Resources Volume 5, Kierkegaard and the Renaissance and Modern Traditions: Tome II: Theology* (Aldershot: Ashgate, 2009), 43-61.

——, 'The Joy of the Cross: Kierkegaard's Appropriation of Lutheran Christology in "The Gospel of Suffering"', ed. Robert Perkins, *IKC: UDVS* (Macon, G.A.: Mercer University Press, 2005), 257-285.

Barth, Hans-Martin, 'Temptation', ed. Erwin Fahlbusch, *The Encyclopedia of Christianity: Si-Z. Volume 5* (Grand Rapids: Wm Eerdmans, 2008), 335-336.

Barth, Karl, *Die christliche Gemeinde in der Anfechtung* (Basel: Gaiser & Haldimann, 1942).

Barthes, Roland, 'La Lutte avec l'ange: analyse textuelle de Genese 32.23-33', *Analyse structural et exegise biblique* (Neuchitel: Delachaux et Niestle Editeurs, 1971), 27-39.

——, 'Wrestling with the Angel: Textual Analysis of Genesis 32:32-32', ed. Graham Ward, *The Postmodern God: A Theological Reader*, ed. Graham Ward (Oxford: Blackwell, 1997), 84-95.

Bayer, Oswald, 'Hermeneutical Theology', *Scottish Journal of Theology*, 56 (2), May 2003, 131-147.

——, *Theology the Lutheran Way*, ed. and trans. Jeffrey G. Silcock and Mark C. Mattes (Grand Rapids: William B. Eerdmans, 2007).

Ballan, Joseph, 'Johann Arndt: The Pietist Impulse in Kierkegaard and Seventeenth-Century Lutheran Devotional Literature', ed. Jon Stewart, *Kierkegaard and the Renaissance and Modern Traditions*, 21-30.

Beabout, Gregory R., 'Kierkegaard on the Self and Despair: An Interpretation of the Opening Passage of *The Sickness Unto Death*', *Proceedings of the American Catholic Philosophical Association*, 62 (1988).

Begalke, M. Vernon, 'Luther's *Anfechtungen*: An Important Clue to His Pastoral Theology', *Consensus*, 8 (July 1982), 3-17.

Beintker, Horst, *Die Überwindung der Anfechtung bei Luther: Eine Studie zu seiner Theologie nach den Operationes In Psalmos 1519-21* (Berlin: Evangelische Verlagsanstalt, 1954).

Berdyaev, N.A., *Freedom and the Spirit*, trans. Oliver Fielding Clarke (London: Geoffrey Bles, 1935).

——, 'Iz Etiudov O Ya. Beme. Etiud I. Uchenie Ob Ungrund'e I Svobode', *Journal Put'*, 20, February 1930, 47-79.

Blanchot, Maurice, *L'Entretien infini* (Paris: Gallimard, 1969).

Blank, Sheldon H., 'Men against God: The Promethean Element in Biblical Prayer', *Journal of Biblical Literature*, 72 (1), March, 1953, 1-13.

Blumenthal, David, 'Despair and Hope in Post-*Shoah* Jewish Life', *Bridges: An Interdisciplinary Journal of Theology, Philosophy, History, and Science*, 6 (3/4), Fall/Winter 1999, 1-18.

——, *Facing the Abusing God: A Theology of Protest* (Louisville, K.Y.: Westminster/John Knox, 1994).

Bockmühl, Klaus, *Atheismus in der Christenheit, Anfechtung und Überwindung. 1. Teil, Die Unwirklichkeit Gottes in Theologie und Kirche* (Wuppertal: Aussaat, 1969).

Jacob Boehme, *The Way to Christ*, trans. Peter Erb (New York/Ramsey/ Toronto: Paulist Press, 1978).

Bonhoeffer, Dietrich, *Act and Being*, trans. Bernard Noble (London: Collins, 1962).

——, *Christology* (London: Collins, 1978).

——, *Creation and Fall/Temptation: Two Biblical Studies* (New York: Simon & Schuster, 1997).

——, *Dietrich Bonhoeffer Works in English, Volume 9, The Young Bonhoeffer: 1918-1927*, Paul Matheny, Clifford J. Green, and Marshall Johnson (eds), trans. Mary Nebelsick and Douglas W. Scott (Minneapolis, M.N.: Fortress Press, 2001).

——, *Dietrich Bonhoeffer Werke, Volume 14, Illegale Theologenausbildung: Finkenwalde 1925-1937*, Otto Dudzus and Jürgen Henkys, with Sabine Bobert-Stützel, Dirk Schulz, and Ilse Tödt (eds) (Gütersloh: Chr. Kaiser / Gütersloher Verlagshaus, 1996).

——, 'Psychologie', *Dietrich Bonhoeffer Werke, Volume 12, Berlin: 1932-1933*, Carsten Nicolaisen and Ernst-Albert Scharffenorth (eds) (Gütersloh: Chr. Kaiser / Gütersloher Verlagshaus, 1997).

——, *Schöpfung und Fall* (Munich: Chr. Kaiser Verlag, 1937).

——, *Versuchung* (Munich: Chr. Kaiser Verlag, 1954).

Bornkamm, Heinrich, *Luther und Böhme* (Bonn: Marcus und Weber, 1925).

——, 'Renaissancemystik, Luther und Böhme', *Jahrbuch der Luther-Gesellschaft*, 9 (1927), 156-197.

Boulton, Matthew, 'Forsaking God: a Theological Argument for Christian Lamentation', *Scottish Journal of Theology*, 55 (1), 2002, 58-78.

Brown, Delwin, 'Struggle Till Daybreak: On the Nature of Authority in Theology', *The Journal of Religion*, 65 (1), January 1985, 15-32.

Bühler, P.T., *Die Anfechtung bei Martin Luther* (Zürich: Zwingli Verlag, 1944).

Bukdahl, Jørgen, *Søren Kierkegaard and the Common Man*, ed. and trans. Bruce H. Kirmmse (Grand Rapids/Cambridge: Williams B. Eerdmans, 2001).

Bulgakov, Sergii, *Sergii Bulgakov: Towards a Russian Political Theology*, ed. Rowan Williams (Edinburgh: T & T Clark, 1999).

——, *Unfading Light: Contemplations and Speculations*, trans. Thomas Allan Smith (Grand Rapids: Wm. B. Eerdmans, 2012).

Burton, Robert, *The Anatomy of Melancholy* (New York: The New York Review of Books, 2001).

Butler, Judith, *The Psychic Life of Power: Theories in Subjection* (Stanford, C.A.: Stanford University Press, 1997).

Caputo, John D., *The Mystical Element in Heidegger's Thought* (New York: Fordham University Press, 1986).

——, *The Prayers and Tears of Jacques Derrida: Religion Without Religion* (Bloomington, I.N.: Indiana University Press, 1997).

Capps, Donald, *Men, Religion, and Melancholia* (New Haven, C.T.: Yale University Press, 1997).

de Chardin, Teilhard, *Hymn of the Universe* (London: William Collins & Co., 1970).

Chau, Carolyn A., '"What Could Possibly be Given?", Towards an Exploration of Kenosis as Forgiveness — Continuing the Conversation Between Coakley, Hampson, and Papanikolaou', *Modern Theology*, 28 (1), January 2012, 1-24.

Clair, André, 'La Catégorie Kierkegaardienne de Tribulation: Discriminer Entre L'Éthique et le Religieux-Chrétien', *Revue des Sciences Philosophiques et Théologiques*, 5 (81), October 1997.

Clément, Olivier, *The Roots of Christian Mysticism* (London: New City, 1997).

Clifton-Soderstrom, Karl, 'The Phenomenology of Religious Humility in Heidegger's reading of Luther', *Continental Philosophy Review*, 42 (2009), 171-200.

Coakley, Sarah, 'Kenosis and Subversion: On the Repression of 'Vulnerability' in Christian Feminist Writing', ed. Daphne Hampson, *Swallowing a Fishbone?: Feminist Theologians Debate Christianity* (London: SPCK, 1996), 82-111.

Cobb, Kelton, 'Theology and Culture', *The Blackwell Guide to Theology and Popular Culture* (Oxford: Blackwell, 2005).

Cohen, Arthur A., *The Tremendum: A Theological Interpretation of the Holocaust* (New York: Crossroad, 1981).

Cole, Jr, Allan Hugh, 'A Spirit in Need of Rest: Luther's Melancholia, Obsessive-Compulsive Disorder, and Religiosity', *Pastoral Psychology*, 48 (3), 2000, 169-190.

Connors-Nelson, Catherine, 'Touched by the God of Grace: The *Anfechtung* of Luther and the Dark Night of John of the Cross', *Studies in Spirituality*, 9 (1999), 109-139.

Cook, Christopher, *The Philokalia and The Inner Life: On Passions and Prayer* (Cambridge: James Clarke & Co., 2011).

Crowe, Benjamin D., *Heidegger's Religious Origins: Destruction and Authenticity* (Bloomington and Indianapolis, I.N.: Indiana University Press, 2006).

Culpepper, R. Alan, *Eternity as a Sunrise: the Life of Hugo H. Culpepper* (Macon, G.A.: Mercer University Press, 2002)

Cunningham, Valentine, 'It is no Sin to Limp', *Journal of Literature and Theology*, 6 (4), December 1992, 303-309.

Dąbrowski, Kazimierz, *Positive Disintegration* (Boston: Little Brown, 1964).

Daly, Mary, *Beyond God the Father* (Boston: Beacon, 1985).

——, *Pure Lust* (Boston: Beacon, 1984).

Dargan, Geoffrey, 'Trial, Test, Tribulation', Steven Emmanuel, William McDonald and Jon Stewart (eds), *Kierkegaard Research: Sources, Reception and Resources: Volume 15: Kierkegaard's Concepts: Tome VI* (Aldershot: Ashgate, forthcoming).

Davies, Oliver, *A Theology of Compassion: Metaphysics of Difference and the Renewal of Tradition* (Grand Rapids/Cambridge: William B. Eerdmans, 2001).

Denker, Alfred, *Historical Dictionary of Heidegger's Philosophy* (Lanham, M.D., and London: The Scarecrow Press, 2000).

Derrida, Jacques, 'Post-Scriptum: Aporias, Ways and Voices', Harold Coward and Toby Foshay (eds), *Derrida and Negative Theology* (Albany, N.Y.: State University of New York Press, 1992), 283-324.

Deutsches Wörterbuch von Jacob und Wilhelm Grimm (16 Bde. in 32 Teilbänden. Leipzig 1854-1961. Quellenverzeichnis Leipzig 1971).

Deverell, Gary J., 'The Desire of God', *The Heythrop Journal*, XLVIII (2007), 343-370.

Dunn, Rose Ellen, 'Let It Be: Finding Grace With God Through the *Gelassenheit* of the Annunciation', in Chris Boesel and Catherine Keller (eds), *Apophatic Bodies: Negative Theology, Incarnation, and Relationality* (New York: Fordham University Press, 2010), 329-348.

Meister Eckhart, *The Complete Mystical Works of Meister Eckhart*, trans. Maurice O'C Walshe (New York: Crossroad, 2009).

——, *Meister Eckhart: Werke I, II*; Bibliothek des Mittelalters, vol. 20, 21; ed. and trans. Nicholas Largier (Frankfurt am Main: Deutsche Klassiker Verlag, 1993).

Erikson, Erik, *Young Man Luther: A Study in Psychoanalysis and History* (New York: W.W. Norton & Company Inc., 1962).

Evans, Jan E., 'Miguel de Unamuno: Kierkegaard's Spanish "Brother"', ed. Jon Stewart, *Kierkegaard Research: Sources, Reception and Resources: Volume 9: Kierkegaard and Existentialism* (Aldershot: Ashgate, 2011), 375-392.

——, *Unamuno and Kierkegaard: Paths to Selfhood in Fiction* (Lanham, M.D.: Lexicon Books, 2005).

Fabiny, Tibor, 'The "Strange Acts of God:" The Hermeneutics of Concealment and Revelation in Luther and Shakespeare', *Dialog: A Journal of Theology*, 45 (1), Spring 2006, 44-54.

Ferreira, M. Jamie, *Love's Grateful Striving: A Commentary on Kierkegaard's Works of Love* (Oxford: Oxford University Press, 2001).

Florin, Frits, 'Was Kierkegaard Inspired by Medieval Mysticism? Meister Eckhart's *Abgeschiedenheit* and Kierkegaard's *Udsondring'*, Dario González *et al* (eds), *Kierkegaardiana 22* (Copenhagen: C.A. Reitzels Forlag, 2002).

Francis, Pamela J., 'Reading Kazantzakis through Gregory of Nyssa: Some Common Anthropological Themes', Darren J.N. Middleton (ed.), *Scandalizing Jesus: Kazantzakis's The Last Temptation of Christ Fifty Years On*, (New York/London: Continuum, 2005).

Freud, Sigmund, 'Civilization and its Discontents' (1930 [1929])', The Pelican Freud Library, Volume 12: *Civilization, Society and Religion: Group Psychology, Civilization and its Discontents and Other Works*, trans. James Strachey, ed. Albert Dickson (Harmondsworth: Penguin Books, 1985).

Furtak, Rick Antony, 'Symposium: Kierkegaard and Platonic Eros', in Jon Stewart & Katalin Nun (eds), *Kierkegaard and the Greek World: Tome I: Socrates and Plato* (Aldershot: Ashgate, 2010), 105-114.

Garrett, Catherine, 'Making Sense of Healing: Meaning and Spirituality in Stories of Chronic Illness', Peter L. Twohig and Vera Kalitzkus (eds), *Making Sense of Health, Illness and Disease* (Amsterdam/New York: Rodopi, 2004), 105-124.

Gerhardt, Ferdinand August, *Untersuchung über das Wesen des mystischen Grunderlebnisses. Ein Beitrag zur Mystik Meister Eckharts, Luthers und Böhmes* (Greifswald: Doctoral Thesis, 1923).

Gill, Jerry H., 'Kazantzakis and Kierkegaard: Some Comparisons and Contrasts', Darren J. Middleton and Peter Bien (eds), *God's Struggler: Religion in the Writings of Nikos Kazantzakis* (Macon, G.A.: Mercer University Press, 1996).

Gordon, Haim, and Rivca Gordon, *Heidegger on Truth and Myth: A Rejection of Postmodernism* (New York: Peter Lang, 2007), 11-13.

von Görres, Joseph, *Die christliche Mystik* (Regensburg and Landshut, 1836-42).

Gottschall, Dagmar, 'Eckhart's German Works', ed. Jeremiah H. Hackett, *A Companion to Meister Eckhart*, (Leiden: Brill, 2013), 137-184.

Gowland, Angus, 'The Problem of Early Modern Melancholy', *Past & Present*, 191 (May 2006), 77-120.

Gregor, Brian, 'Kierkegaard and the Phenomenology of Temptation', ed. Jeffrey Hanson, *Kierkegaard as Phenomenologist: An Experiment* (Evanston, I.L.: Northwestern University Press, 2010), 128-148.

——, *A Philosophical Anthropology of the Cross: The Cruciform Self* (Bloomington, I.N.: Indiana University Press).

Grislis, Egil, 'The Experience of the *Anfechtungen* and the Formulation of Pure Doctrine in Martin Luther's Commentary on Genesis,' *Consensus*, 8 (April 1982).

——, 'Luther's Understanding of the Wrath of God', *The Journal of Religion*, 41 (4), October 1961, 277-292.

Gritsch, Eric W., *Martin — God's Court Jester: Luther in Retrospect* (Ramsey, N.J: Sigler Press, 1991).

Haar, Michel, 'Nietzsche and the Metamorphosis of the Divine', ed. Philip Blond, *Post-Secular Philosophy* (London and New York: Routledge, 1998).

Haggemark, Steven A., *Luther and Boehme: Investigations of a Unified Metaphysic for Lutheran Theological Discourse* (Luther Northwestern Theological Seminary: ThD Dissertation, 1992).

Hamilton, Victor P., *The Book of Genesis: Chapters 18-50* (Grand Rapids: William B. Eerdmands Publishing Company, 1995).

Hampson, Daphne, *Christian Contradictions: The Structures of Lutheran and Catholic Thought* (Cambridge: Cambridge University Press, 2001).

——, *Kierkegaard: Exposition and Critique* (Oxford: Oxford University Press, 2013).

——, 'On Power and Gender,' *Modern Theology*, 4 (3), July 1988.

Harding, Brian, 'Dialectics of Desire and the Psychopathology of Alterity: From Levinas to Kierkegaard via Lacan', *The Heythrop Journal*, XLVIII (2007), 406-422.

Heidegger, Martin, *Basic Questions of Philosophy: Selected 'Problems' of 'Logic'*, trans. Richard Rojcewicz and Andre Schuwer (Bloomington, I.N.: Indiana University Press, 1994).

——, *Being and Time*, trans. John Macquarrie and Edward Robinson (New York and Evanston, I.L.: Harper & Row, 1962).

——, *Discourse on Thinking*, trans. John M. Anderson and E. Hans Freund (New York: Harper and Row, 1966).

——, *Parmenides*, trans. Andre Schuwer and Richard Rojcewicz (Bloomington, I.N.: Indiana University Press, 1992).

——, *Phänomenologie des religiösen Lebens* (Frankfurt am Main: Vittorio Klostermann, 1995).

——, *The Phenomenology of Religious Life*, trans. Matthias Fritsch and Jennifer Anna Gosetti-Ferencei (Bloomington and Indianapolis, I.N.: Indiana University Press, 2010).

Hein, Steven A., 'Tentatio', *Lutheran Theological Review*, X (1997-98) 38-39.

Hegel, G.W.F., *Phenomenology of Spirit*, trans. A.V. Miller (Oxford: Oxford University Press, 1977).

——, *Science of Logic*, trans. A.V. Miller (New York: Humanities Press, 1969).

Herbstrith, Waltraud, *Therese von Lisieux: Anfechtung un Solidarität* (Frankfurt: Verlag Gerhard Kaffke, 1974).

Herrmann, Wilhelm, *The Communion of the Christian with God*, trans. J.S. Stanyon (London: Williams & Norgate, 1906).

Heschel, Abraham Joshua, *A Passion for Truth* (New York: Farrar, Straus and Giroux, 1973).

Hinkson, Craig, Hinkson, 'Luther and Kierkegaard: Theologians of the Cross', *International Journal of Systematic Theology*, 3 (1), March 2001, 27-45.

——, 'Will the *Real* Martin Luther Please Stand Up! Kierkegaard's View of Luther versus the Evolving Perceptions of the Tradition', ed. Robert L. Perkins, *International Kierkegaard Commentary, Volume 21: For Self-Examination and Judge for Yourself!* (Macon, G.A.: Mercer University Press, 2002), 41-76.

Hong, Edna, *The Gayety of Grace* (Northfield, MN: Postscript, Inc., 2008).

Hyde, J. Keith, *Concepts of Power in Kierkegaard and Nietzsche* (Farnham: Ashgate, 2010).

Hyppolite, Jean, *Studies on Marx and Hegel*, ed. and trans. John O'Neill (New York, Evanston, I.L., San Francisco, London: Harper and Row, 1973).

D'Isanto, Luca, 'Kenosis of the Subject and the Advent of Being in Mystic Experience', *Qui Parle, Special Issue: Thinking Alterity, Reprise*, 17 (1), Fall/ Winter 2008, 147-173.

Ivarsson, Henrik, 'The Principles of Pastoral Care According to Luther', *Pastoral Psychology*, 13 (1), 1962, 19-25.

James, William, *The Varieties of Religious Experience* (London and New York: Routledge, 2008).

Jaspers, Karl, *Der philosophische Glaube angesichts der Offenbarung* (München: R. Piper and Co., 1962).

——, *Philosophical Faith and Revelation*, trans. E.B. Ashton (New York: Harper & Row, 1967).

Ji, Won Yong, 'The significance of *Tentatio* in Luther's Spirituality', *Concordia Journal*, 15 (April 1989), 181-188.

Johnson, Roger A. (ed.), *Psychohistory and Religion: The Case of Young Man Luther* (Philadelphia, P.A.: Fortress Press, 1977).

De Jonge, Michael P., *Bonhoeffer's Theological Formation: Berlin, Barth, and Protestant Theology* (Oxford: Oxford University Press, 2012).

Juan de los Angeles, *The Loving Struggle Between God and the Soul*, trans. Eladia Gómez-Posthill (London: The Saint Austin Press, 2001).

Jüngel, Eberhard, *Anfechtung und Gewissheit des Glaubens oder die der Kirche wieder zu ihrer Sache komm. Zwei Vorträge* (Munich: Kaiser, 1976).

——, *Theological Essays II*, ed. and trans. John Webster (Edinburgh: T & T Clark, 1995).

Kadai, Heino O., 'Luther's Theology of the Cross', *Concordia Theological Quarterly*, 63 (3), July 1999, 169-204.

Kangas, David and Curtis L. Thompson, *Between Hegel and Kierkegaard: Hans L. Martensen's Philosophy of Religion* (New York: Oxford University Press, 1997).

Kangas, David, *Kierkegaard's Instant: On Beginnings* (Bloomington & Indianapolis, I.N.: Indiana University Press, 2007).

——, 'The Very Opposite of Beginning with Nothing: Guilt-Consciousness in Kierkegaard's "The Gospel of Sufferings" IV', *IKC: UDVS* (Macon, G.A.: Mercer University Press, 2005), 187-314.

Katz, Steven T., Shlomo Biderman, and Gershon Greenberg (eds), *Wrestling with God: Jewish Theological Responses During and After the Holocaust*, (Oxford: Oxford University Press, 2007).

Katz, Steven T. 'Mysticism and Ethics in Western Mystical Traditions', *Religious Studies*, 28, 407-423.

Kazantzakis, Nikos, *The Last Temptation*, trans. Peter Bien (London: Faber and Faber, 1975).

——, *Report to Greco*, trans. Peter Bien (New York: Simon and Schuster, 1965).

——, *The Saviors of God: Spiritual Exercises*, trans. Kimon Friar (New York: Simon & Schuster, Inc., 1960).

Keeley, Louise Carroll, 'Spiritual Trial in the Thought of Kierkegaard', ed. Robert Perkins, *International Kierkegaard Commentary: Concluding Unscientific Postscript* (Macon, G.A.: Mercer University Press, 1997).

Kelly, Geoffrey, 'Kierkegaard as 'Antidote' and as Impact Upon Dietrich Bonhoeffer's Concept of Christian Discipleship', *Bonhoeffer's Intellectual Formation: Theology and Philosophy in his Thought* (Tübingen: Mohr Siebeck, 2008), 145-166.

Kierkegaard, Søren, *Le Concept De L'Angoisse*, trans. P. Petit (Paris, Gallimard, 1935).

——, *El Concepto de la Angustia* (Madrid: Ediciones Guadarrama, 1965).

——, *The Diary of Søren Kierkegaard*, ed. Peter P. Rhode and trans. Gerda M. Anderson (New York: Philosophical Library, 1960).

——, *The Journals of Søren Kierkegaard: A Selection*, ed. and trans. Alexander Dru (London, New York, Toronto: Oxford University Press, 1951).

——, *Kierkegaard's Journals and Notebooks: Volume 1 Journals AA-DD*, Bruce H. Kirmmse general editor (Princeton, N.J. and Oxford: Princeton University Press, 2007).

——, *Kierkegaard's Journals and Notebooks: Volume 1 Journals EE-KK*, Bruce H. Kirmmse general editor (Princeton, N.J. and Oxford: Princeton University Press, 2008).

——, *Post-scriptum aux miettes philosophiques*, trans. P. Petit (Paris, Gallimard, 1949 and 1989).

——, *Søren Kierkegaard Papers and Journals: A Selection*, ed. and trans. Alastair Hannay (London: Penguin Books, 1996).

——, *Søren Kierkegaard: The Last Years, Journals 1853-1855*, ed. and trans. Ronald Gregor Smith (London: Collins, 1965).

——, *Søren Kierkegaards Skrifter 17 Journalerne AA. BB. CC. DD* [SKS], eds Niels Jørgen Cappelørn *et al* (København: Fonden for Søren Kierkegaard Forskningscenteret, 2000).

Kirkconnell, W. Glenn, *Kierkegaard on Ethics and Religion: From Either/Or to Philosophical Fragments* (London: Continuum, 2008).

Kirkpatrick, Matthew D., *Attacks on Christendom in a World Come of Age: Kierkegaard, Bonhoeffer, and the Question of 'Religionless Christianity'* (Eugene, O.R.: Pickwick Publications, 2011).

Kitcher, Philip, *Living With Darwin: Evolution, Design, and the Future of Faith* (Oxford: Oxford University Press, 2007).

Kleinig, John W., '*Oratio, Meditatio, Tentatio*: What Makes A Theologian?', *Concordia Theological Quarterly*, 66 (3), July 2002.

Kojève, Alexandre, *Introduction to the Reading of Hegel*, trans. James H. Nichols, Jr, ed. Allan Bloom (New York: Basic Books, 1969).

Kristeva, Julia, *Black Sun: Depression and Melancholia*, trans. Leon S. Roudiez (New York: Columbia University Press, 1989).

Krötke, Wolf, 'Dietrich Bonhoeffer and Martin Luther', ed. Peter Frick, *Bonhoeffer's Intellectual Formation: Theology and Philosophy in his Thought* (Tübingen: Mohr Siebeck, 2008), 53-82.

Law, David, *Kierkegaard as Negative Theologian* (Oxford: Clarendon Press, 1993).

——, 'Kierkegaard's Anti-Mysticism', *Scottish Journal of Religious Studies*, 14 (1993), 102-111.

——, *Kierkegaard's Kenotic Christology* (Oxford: Oxford University Press, 2013).

——, 'Wrongness, Guilt, and Innocent Suffering in Kierkegaard's *Either/Or*, Part Two*, and *Upbuilding Discourses in Various Spirits*', *IKC: UDVS* (Macon, G.A.: Mercer University Press, 2005), 315-348.

Levinas, Emmanuel, 'Existence and Ethics' in *Kierkegaard: A Critical Reader*, ed. J. Reé and J. Chamberlain (Oxford: Basil Blackwell, 1998).

Lewin, David, 'The Middle Voice in Eckhart and Modern Continental Philosophy', *Medieval Mystical Theology*, 20 (2011), 28-46.

Lindberg, Carter, 'Introduction', *The Pietist Theologians* (Oxford: Blackwell, 2005).

López Cuétara, José Miguel, 'El misticismo alemán en la obra de Fr. Juan de los Ángeles', *Verdad y vida*, 64 (247), 2006, 577-612.

Luther, Martin, *The Table Talk of Martin Luther*, ed. and trans. William Hazlitt (London: H.G. Bohn, 1857).

McCarthy, Vincent A., *The Phenomenology of Moods in Kierkegaard* (The Hague and Boston: Martinus Nijhoff, 1978).

McGinn, Bernard, *The Harvest of Mysticism in Medieval Germany* (New York: Herder & Herder, 2005).

——, '*Vere tu es Deus absconditus*: The Hidden God in Luther and Some Mystics', Oliver Davies and Denys Turner (eds), *Silence and the Word: Negative Theology and Incarnation* (Cambridge: Cambridge University Press, 2004).

McGrath, Alister, *Luther's Theology of the Cross* (Oxford/New York: Basil Blackwell, 1985).

McGrath, Sean J., *The Early Heidegger and Medieval Philosophy: Phenomenology for the God-forsaken* (Washington, D.C.: The Catholic University of America Press, 2006).

——, 'The Facticity of Being God-forsaken: The Young Heidegger and Luther's Theology of the Cross', *American Catholic Philosophical Quarterly*, 79 (2), 2005, 273-290.

McLaughlin, R. Emmett, 'Truth, Tradition, and History: The Historiography of High/Late Medieval and Early Modern Penance', ed. Abigail Firey, *A New History of Penance* (Leiden: Brill, 2008), 19-71.

McNeill, John T., 'The Cure of Souls in Lutheranism', *Pastoral Psychology*, 2 (5), 1951, 11-19.

Mahn, Jason, *Fortunate Fallibility: Kierkegaard and the Power of Sin* (Oxford: Oxford University Press, 2011).

Malysz, Piotr J., 'Luther and Dionysius: Beyond Mere Negations', *Modern Theology*, 24 (4), October 2008, 679-692.

Marion, Jean-Luc, *God Without Being: Hors Texte*, trans. Thomas H. Carlson (Chicago and London: The University of Chicago Press, 1991).

Marius, Richard, *Martin Luther: The Christian Between God and Death* (Cambridge, M.A.: The Belknap Press of Harvard University Press, 1999).

Marks, Herbert, 'Biblical Naming and Poetic Etymology', *Journal of Biblical Literature*, 114 (1), Spring 1995, 21-42.

Martensen, Hans, *Jacob Boehme: His Life and Teaching or A Study in Theosophy*, trans. T. Rhys Evans (London: Hodder and Stoughton, 1885).

——, *Meister Eckhart: A Contribution to the Elucidation of Mysticism in the Middle Ages (Mester Eckart: Et Bidrag til at oplyse Middelaldrens Mystik* (Copenhagen: C.A. Reizel, 1840).

Martin, H.V., *The Wings of Faith: A Consideration of the Nature and Meaning of Christian Faith in the Light of the Work of Søren Kierkegaard* (London: The Lutterworth Press, 1950).

Matheson, Peter, 'Angels, Depression, and "The Stone": A Late Medieval Prayer Book', *Journal of Theological Studies*, 48 (2), October 1997, 517-530.

Mikulová Thulstrup, Marie, *Kierkegaard og Pietismen* (Copenhagen: Munksgaard, 1967).

——, 'Kierkegaard's Encounter with Mysticism through Speculative Idealism', *Liber Academiæ Kierkegaardiensis Tomus V 1983*, ed. Niels Thulstrup (København: C.A. Reitzels Forlag, 1984), 31-91.

——, 'The Role of Asceticism', ed. Marie Mikulová Thulstrup, *Bibliotheca Kierkegaardiana: Vol. 2: The Sources and Depths of Faith in Kierkegaard*, (Copenhagen: C.A. Reitzels Boghandel, 1978), 154-55.

——, 'Studies of Pietists, Mystics, and Church Fathers', ed. Marie Mikulová Thulstrup, *Bibliotheca Kierkegaardiana: Vol. 1: Kierkegaard's View of Christianity*, (Copenhagen: C.A. Reitzels Boghandel, 1978).

——, 'Suffering', *Bibliotheca Kierkegaardiana Vol. 7: Kierkegaard and Human Values*, ed. Niels Thusltrup and M. Mikulvá Thulstrup (Copenhagen: C.A. Reitzels Boghandel, 1980).

Milem, Bruce, 'Four Theories of Negative Theology', *The Heythrop Journal*, XLVIII (2007), 187-204.

Miller, Arlene A., 'The Theologies of Luther and Boehme in the Light of their Genesis Commentaries', *Harvard Theological Review*, 63 (1970), 261-303.

Mulder, Jr., Jack, 'Abraham Joshua Heschel: Heschel's Use of Kierkegaard as a Cohort in Depth Theology', ed. Jon Stewart, *Kierkegaard Research: Sources, Reception and Resources: Kierkegaard's Influence on Theology Tome III: Catholic and Jewish Theology* (Aldershot: Ashgate, 2012), 155-170.

——, 'Bernard of Clairvaux: Kierkegaard's Reception of the Last of the Fathers', ed. Jon Stewart, *Kierkegaard Research: Sources, Reception and Resources Volume 4: Kierkegaard and the Patristic and Medieval Traditions* (Aldershot: Ashgate, 2008), 23-45.

——, *Kierkegaard and the Catholic Tradition: Conflict and Dialogue* (Indianapolis, I.N.: Indiana University Press, 2010).

Nelson, Christopher, A.P., 'Kierkegaard, mysticism, and jest: The story of little Ludvig', *Continental Philosophy Review*, 39 (4), 2006, 435-464.

Neuhouser, Frederick, 'Deducing Desire and Recognition in the Phenomenology of Spirit', *Journal of the History of Philosophy*, 24 (2), April 1986, 243-262.

Nietzsche, Friedrich, *The Portable Nietzsche*, ed. and trans. Walter Kaufmann (London: Penguin, 1982).

——, *Twilight of the Idols*, trans. R.J. Hollingdale (London: Penguin Books, 1990).

Ngien, Dennis, 'The Art of Dying: In Luther's Sermon on Preparing to Die', *The Heythrop Journal*, XLIX (2008), 1-19.

Nugent, Donald Christopher, 'Mystical and Evangelical Theology in Martin Luther and St John of the Cross', *Journal of Ecumenical Studies*, 28 (Fall, 1991), 555-565.

Oberman, Heiko A., *Luther: Man Between God and the Devil*, trans. Eileen Walliser-Schwarzbart (New York: Doubleday, 1992).

Olson, Alan M., 'Faith and Reason: Isaac and Ishmael Revisited', *Existenz: An International Journal in Philosophy, Religion, Politics, and the Arts*, 1 (1-2), Fall 2006.

O'Regan, Cyril, *Gnostic Apocalypse: Jacob's Boehme's Haunted Narrative* (Albany, N.Y.: State University of New York Press, 2002).

Orlov, Andrei A., 'The Face as the Heavenly Counterpart of the Visionary in the Slavonic *Ladder of Jacob*', Craig A. Evans (ed.), *Of Scribes and Sages: Early Jewish Interpretation and Transmission of Scripture: Volume 2: Later Versions and Traditions* (London: T & T Clark, 2004), 59-76.

Otto, Rudolf, *Das Heilige: Über das Irrationale in der Idee des Göttlichen und sein Verhältnis zum Rationalen* (München: Verlag C.H. Beck, 2004).

——, *The Idea of the Holy: An Inquiry into the non-rational factor in the idea of the divine and its relation to the rational*, trans. John H. Harvey (London: Oxford University Press, 1950).

Ozment, Steve E., 'An Aid to Luther's Marginal Comments on Johannes Tauler's Sermons', *The Harvard Theological Review*, 63 (2), April 1970, 305-311.

Pannenberg, Wolfhart, 'Der Einfluß der Anfechtungserfahrung uaf den Prädestinationsbegriff Luthers', *Kerygma und Dogma*, 3, (1954) 109-39.

Papanikolaou, Aristotle, 'Person, Kenosis and Abuse: Hans Urs von Balthasar and Feminist Theologies in Conversation', *Modern Theology*, 19 (1), January, 2003, 41-65.

Pattison, George, 'Desire, Decreation and Unknowing in the God-Relationship: Mystical Theology and its Transformation in Kierkegaard, Simone Weil and Dostoevsky', Arne Grøn, Iben Damgaard, and Søren Overgaard (eds), *Subjectivity and Transcendence* (Tübingen: Mohr Siebeck, 2007), 193-211.

——, *Kierkegaard: The Aesthetic and the Religious* (London: SCM Press, 1999).

——, *Kierkegaard's Upbuilding Discourses: Philosophy, Theology, Literature* (London/New York: Routledge, 2002).

Pederson, Ann M., 'Saviors of God: Soteriological Motifs in the Theologies of Kazantzakis and Luther', Darren J. Middleton and Peter Bien (eds), *God's Struggler: Religion in the Writings of Nikos Kazantzakis* (Macon, G.A.: Mercer University Press, 1996).

Peperzak, Adriaan T., 'Affective Theology, Theological Affectivity', ed. Jeffrey Bloechl, *Religious Experience and the End of Metaphysics* (Bloomington, I.N.: Indiana University Press, 2003), 94-105.

Pfeiffer, Andrew, 'The Place of *Tentatio* in the Formation of Church Servants', *Lutheran Theological Journal*, 30 (1996), 111-119.

Philo, *De mutatione nominum*, (Les Œuvres de Philon d'Alexandrie 18) (Paris: Cerf, 1964).

Pinomaa, L., *Der existentialle Charakter der Theologie Luthers* (Helsinki: Akateeminen Kirjakauppa, 1940).

Pippin, Robert B., *Hegel on Self-Consciousness: Desire and Death in Hegel's Phenomenology of Spirit* (Princeton, N.J.: Princeton University Press, 2011).

Podmore, Simon D., 'The Abyss of the Heart: Transfiguration and the *Imago Dei*', Králik *et al* (eds), *Acta Kierkegaardiana VI: Kierkegaard and Human Nature* (Toronto and Šal'a: Kierkegaard Circle, 2013), 88-104.

——, 'Crucified by God: Kazantzakis and The Last *Anfechtung* of Christ', *Literature and Theology*, 22 (4), December 2008, 419-435.

——, 'The Dark Night of Suffering & the Darkness of God: God-forsakenness or Forsaking God in "The Gospel of Sufferings"', ed. Robert Perkins, *International Kierkegaard Commentary: Upbuilding Discourses in Various Spirits* (Macon, G.A.: Mercer University Press, 2005), 229-256.

——, *Kierkegaard and the Self Before God: Anatomy of the Abyss* (Bloomington, I.N.: Indiana University Press, 2011).

——, 'Lazarus and the Sickness Unto Death: An Allegory of Despair', *Religion and the Arts*, 15 (2011), 486-519.

——, 'The Lightning and the Earthquake: Kierkegaard on the *Anfechtung* of Luther', *The Heythrop Journal*, XLVII (2006), 562-578.

——, 'My God, My God, Why Have You Forsaken Me? Between Consolation & Desolation', ed. Christopher C.H. Cook, *Spirituality, Theology & Mental Health: Multidisciplinary Perspectives* (London: SCM Press, 2013), 193-210.

——, '*Mysterium Horrendum*: Mystical Theology and the Negative Numinous', Louise Nelstrop and Simon D. Podmore (eds), *Exploring Lost Dimensions in Christian Mysticism: Opening to the Mystical* (Aldershot: Ashgate, 2013).

——, 'Mysticism's Secret: A Silent Prayer of Unknowing', ed. Hartmut von Sass, *Stille Tropen: Zur Rhetorik und Grammatik des Schweigens* (München: Karl Alber, 2013), 218-239.

——, 'The Sacrifice of Silence: *Fear and Trembling* and the Secret of Faith', *International Journal of Systematic Theology*, 14 (1), January 2012, 70-90.

——, 'Struggling with God: Kierkegaard/Proudhon', Roman Králik, *et al* (eds) *Acta Kierkegaardiana. Vol. II: Kierkegaard and Great Philosophers*, (Mexico City and Barcelona: Sociedad Iberoamericana de Estudios Kierkegaardianos, University of Barcelona, Kierkegaard Society in Slovakia, 2007), 90-103.

——, 'To Die and Yet Not Die: Kierkegaard's Theophany of Death', Patrick Stokes and Adam J. Buben (eds), *Kierkegaard and Death* (Bloomington, I.N.: Indiana University Press, 2011), 44-64.

Pyper, Hugh S., *The Joy of Kierkegaard: Essays on Kierkegaard as a Biblical Reader* (Sheffield/Oakville: Equinox, 2011).

Rasmussen, Joel D.S., 'Thomas à Kempis: *Devotio Moderna* and Kierkegaard's Critique of "Bourgeois-Philistinism"', ed. Jon Stewart, *Kierkegaard Research: Sources, Reception and Resources Volume 4: Kierkegaard and the Patristic and Medieval Traditions* (Aldershot: Ashgate, 2008), 289-298.

Ross, Allen P., 'Jacob at the Jabbok, Israel at Peniel', *Bibliotheca Sacra*, 137 (1980), 338-354.

Rubenstein, Mary-Jane, 'Unknow Thyself: Apophaticism, Deconstruction, and Theology After Ontotheology', *Modern Theology*, 19 (3), July 2003, 387-417.

Rubenstein, Richard, *After Auschwitz: History, Theology, and Contemporary Judaism* (Baltimore, M.D. and London: The Johns Hopkins University Press, 1996).

Rupp, Gordon, *The Righteousness of God: Luther Studies* (London: Hodder and Stoughton, 1953).

Russell, Matheson, 'Phenomenology and Theology: Situating Heidegger's Philosophy of Religion', *Sophia*, 50 (2011), 641-655.

Šadja, Peter, 'Abraham a Sancta Clara: An Aphoristic Encyclopedia of Christian Wisdom', ed. Jon Stewart, *Kierkegaard Research: Source, Reception and Resources Volume 5: Kierkegaard and the Renaissance and Modern Traditions: Tome II: Theology* (Aldershot: Ashgate, 2009), 1-20.

——, 'Does Hegelian Philosophy of Religion Distort Christian Dogmatics and Ethics? (The Debate on Speculative Mysticism)', *Acta Kierkegaardiana Volume 4: Kierkegaard and the Nineteenth-Century Religious Crisis in Europe*, Roman Králik *et al* (eds) (Toronto and Šaľa: Kierkegaard Circle, 2008), 64-83.

——, 'François de Salignac de La Moth-Fénelon: Clearing the Way for *The Sickness Unto Death*', ed. Jon Stewart, *Kierkegaard Research: Source, Reception and Resources Volume 5: Kierkegaard and the Renaissance and Modern Traditions: Tome II: Theology* (Aldershot: Ashgate, 2009), 129-147.

——, 'Lucovicus Blosius: A Frightful Satire on Christendom', ed. Jon Stewart, *Kierkegaard Research: Source, Reception and Resources Volume 5: Kierkegaard and the Renaissance and Modern Traditions: Tome II: Theology* (Aldershot: Ashgate, 2009), 30-41.

——, 'Meister Eckhart: The Patriarch of German Speculation who was a *Lebemeister*: Meister Eckhart's Silent Way into Kierkegaard's Corpus', ed. Jon Stewart, *Kierkegaard Research: Sources, Reception and Resources Volume 4: Kierkegaard and the Patristic and Medieval Traditions* (Aldershot: Ashgate, 2008), 237-253.

——, 'On Some Aspects of Kierkegaard's Reading of Abraham a Sancta Clara', *Acta Kierkegaardiana Volume II: Kierkegaard and Great Philosopher*, ed. Roman Králik *et al* (Toronto and Šal'a: Kierkegaard Circle, 2007), 80-89.

——, 'Tauler: A Teacher in Spiritual Dietethics: Kierkegaard's Reception of Johannes Tauler', ed. Jon Stewart, *Kierkegaard Research: Sources, Reception and Resources Volume 4: Kierkegaard and the Patristic and Medieval Traditions* (Aldershot: Ashgate, 2008), 276-77.

——, '"The wise men went the other way": Kierkegaard's Dialogue with Fénelon and Tersteegen in the Summer of 1849', *Acta Kierkegaardiana III: Kierkegaard and Christianity*, Roman Králik *et al* (eds) (Toronto and Šal'a: Kierkegaard Circle, 2008), 89-105.

Scaer, David P., 'The Concept of *Anfechtung* in Luther's Thought', *Concordia Theological Quarterly*, 47 (1), January 1983, 15-30.

Schweid, Eliezer, *Wrestling Until Day-Break: Searching for Meaning in the Thinking on the Holocaust* (Lanham, New York and London: University Press of America, 1994).

Schweizer, Bernard, *Misotheism: The Untold Story of Hating God* (Oxford: Oxford University Press, 2011).

Schulz, Heiko,'Das entfallene Herz. Zur Dialektik der Anfechtung bei Søren Kierkegaard', *Anfechtung nd Reflexion, vol. II: studien zur philosophie und theologie sören kierkegaards* (Berlin/Boston: Walter de Gruyter 2013).

Screech, M.A., *Montaigne and Melancholy: The Wisdom of the Essays* (London: Gerald Duckworth and Co. Ltd., 1983).

Scupoli, Lorenzo, *The Spiritual Combat* (London: Longmans, Green and Co., 1910).

Shakespeare, Steven, *Derrida and Theology* (Edinburgh: T & T Clarke, 2011).

Sibelman, Simon P., 'The Dialogue of Peniel: Elie Wiesel's Les Portes de la forêt and Genesis 32:23-33', *The French Review*, 61 (5), April, 1988, 747-757.

Sikka, Sonya, 'Call and Conscience in Tauler and Heidegger', *The Heythrop Journal*, XXXIII (1992), 371-398.

Slater, Peter, 'Tillich on the Fall and the Temptation of Goodness', *The Journal of Religion*, 65 (2), April, 1985, 196-207.

Soderquist, K. Brian, *The Isolated Self: Truth and Untruth in Søren Kierkegaard's On the Concept of Irony* (Copenhagen: C.A. Reitzel, 2007).

Søe, N.H., 'The Human Spirit and God', Niels Thusltrup and M. Mikulvá Thulstrup (eds) *Bibliotheca Kierkegaardiana Vol. 2*, (Copenhagen: C.A. Reitzels Boghandel, 1978).

Spitz, Lewis W., 'Headwaters of the Reformation: Studia Humanitatis, Luther Senior et Initia Reformationis', ed. Heiko Oberman, *Luther and the Dawn of the Modern Era* (Leiden: Brill, 1974), 103-104.

——, 'Psychohistory and History: The Case of *Young Man Luther*', Roger A. Johnson, *Psychohistory and Religion: The Case of Young Man Luther* (Philadelphia, P.A.: Fortress Press, 1977), 70-77.

Stan, Leo, 'Chrysostom: Between the Hermitage and the City', ed. Jon Stewart, *Kierkegaard Research: Sources, Reception and Resources Volume 4: Kierkegaard and the Patristic and Medieval Traditions*, (Aldershot: Ashgate, 2008), 46-65.

Stephens, Randall, 'An Examination of Luther's Theology According to an Existentialist Interpretation', *Quodlibet Journal*, 2 (2), Spring 2000.

Steinmetz, David C., 'Ecstasy in Staupitz and the Young Luther', *The Sixteenth Century Journal*, 11 (1), Spring, 1980, 23-38.

Stewart, Jon, *Kierkegaard's Relation to Hegel Reconsidered* (Cambridge: Cambridge University Press, 2003).

Tauler, Johannes, *The Sermons and Conferences of John Tauler*, trans. Walter Elliott (Washington, D.C.: Apostolic Mission House, 1910).

Taylor, Charles, *Hegel* (Cambridge: Cambridge University Press, 1975).

Taylor, Mark C., *Journeys to Selfhood: Hegel and Kierkegaard* (California: University of California Press, 1989).

The Theologia Germanica of Martin Luther, trans. Bengt Hoffman (New York/ Ramsey/Toronto: Paulist Press, 1980).

Theologia Deutsch, herausgegeben von Herm. Mandel (Leipzig: A. Deichert, 1908).

Theunissen, Michael, *Kierkegaard's Concept of Despair*, trans. Barbara Harshav and Helmut Illbruck (Princeton N.J. and Oxford: Princeton University Press, 2005).

Thielicke, Helmut, *Between God and Satan* (Grand Rapids, 1958).

——, *Nihilism: Its Origins and Nature — with a Christian Answer*, trans. John W. Doberstein (New York: Harper & Brothers, 1961).

——, *Theologie Der Anfechtung* (Tübingen, 1949).

Thulstrup, Niels, 'Trial, Test, Tribulation, Temptation', ed. Marie Mikulová Thulstrup, *Bibliotheca Kierkegaardiana: Some of Kierkegaard's Main Categories* (Copenhagen: C.A. Reitzels Forlag, 1988), 116-117.

Tietz, Christiane, 'Dietrich Bonhoeffer: Standing "in the Tradition of Paul, Luther, Kierkegaard, in the Tradition of Genuine Christian Thinking"', ed. Jon Stewart, *Kierkegaard's Influence on Theology: Tome I German Protestant Theology* (Aldershot: Ashgate, 2012), 43-64.

Tillich, Paul, *The Protestant Era* (Chicago, Illinois: The University of Chicago Press, 1948; 2nd impression 1951).

——, 'The Recovery of the Prophetic Tradition', *Theological Writings Volume 6*, ed. Gert Hummel (Berlin; New York: De Gruyter; Berlin: Evangelisches Verlagswerk, 1992).

——, *The Religious Situation* (New York: Holt, 1932).

——, *The Shaking of the Foundations* (New York: Charles Scribner's Sons, 1952).

Turchin, Sean, 'Temptation', Steven Emmanuel, William McDonald and Jon Stewart (eds), *Kierkegaard Research: Sources, Reception and Resources: Volume 15: Kierkegaard's Concepts: Tome VI* (Aldershot: Ashgate, forthcoming).

Unamuno, Miguel de, *The Agony of Christianity and Essays on Faith*, trans. Anthony Kerrigan (London: Routledge & Kegan Paul, 1974).

——, *Tragic Sense of Life*, trans. J.E. Crawford Flitch (New York: Dover Publications, 1954).

Vallée, Gérard, 'Luther on Monastic Theology: Notes on *Anfechtung* and *Compunctio*,' *Archiv für Reformationsgeschichte*, 75 (1984), 290-296.

Walsh, Sylvia, *Kierkegaard: Thinking Christianly in an Existential Mode* (Oxford: Oxford University Press, 2009).

——, *Living Christianly: Kierkegaard's Dialectic of Christian Existence* (Pennsylvania: Pennsylvania State University Press, 2005).

——, 'Moral Character and Temptation', Paul Moser and Michael McFall (eds), *The Wisdom of the Christian Faith* (Cambridge: Cambridge University Press, 2012).

——, 'On "Feminine" and "Masculine" Forms of Despair,' ed. Robert Perkins, *International Kierkegaard Commentary: The Sickness Unto Death* (Macon, G.A.: Mercer University Press, 1987), 121-134.

Watkin, Julia, *Historical Dictionary of Kierkegaard's Philosophy* (Lanham, M.D., and London: The Scarecrow Press, 2001).

Weeks, Andrew, *Boehme: An Intellectual Biography of the Seventeenth-century Philosopher and Mystic* (Albany, N.Y.: SUNY, 1991).

Weil, Simone, *Gravity and Grace*, trans. Emma Crawford (London: Routledge, 2002).

Weinrich, Michael, 'God's Free Grace and the Freedom of the Church: Theological Aspects of the Barmen Declaration', *International Journal of Systematic Theology*, 12 (4), October 2010, 404-419.

——, *Waiting for God*, trans. Emma Crawfurd (London: Harper Perennial, 2009).

Widenman, Robert, 'Kierkegaard's Terminology — and English', ed. Niels Thulstrup, *Kierkegaardiana VII* (København: Munksgaard, 1968).

Wiesel, Elie, 'Art and Culture after the Holocaust', ed. Eva Fleischner, *Auschwitz: Beginning of a New Era? Reflections on the Holocaust* (New York: KTAV Publishing House, 1977).

Williams, Duane, 'Meister Eckhart and the Varieties of Nothing', *Medieval Mystical Theology*, 20 (2011), 85-98.

Williams, Rowan, 'Eastern Orthodox Theology', ed. David Ford, *The Modern Theologians* (Oxford: Blackwell, 2005), 572-588.

Van Winden, J.C.M., 'Quotations from Philo in Clement of Alexandria's "Protrepticus"', *Vigiliae Christianae*, 32 (3), September, 1978, 208-213.

Wolfson, Elliot, *Through a Speculum That Shines* (Princeton, N.J.: Princeton University Press, 1997).

Yoon-Jun Kim, David and Joel D.S. Rasmussen, 'Martin Luther: Reform, Secularization and the Question of His "True Successor"', ed. Jon Stewart, *Kierkegaard Research: Source, Reception and Resources Volume 5: Kierkegaard and the Renaissance and Modern Traditions: Tome II: Theology* (Aldershot: Ashgate, 2009), 173-217.

Yoreh, Tzemah, 'Jacob's Struggle', *Zeitschrift für die Alttestamentliche Wissenschaft*, 117. Bd., S., 95-97.

Žižek, Slavoj, *The Parallax View* (Cambridge, M.A. & London: MIT Press, 2006).

Zlomislić, Marko, *Jacques Derrida's Aporetic Ethics* (Plymouth: Lexington books, 2007).

Index

guilt, 112, 113n1, 125, 144, 172, 184, 188, 210, 212, 223, 245, 248n1, 254, 262; and innocence, 50, 97, 164, 184, 213-214, 245-246

Hamann, Johann Georg, 38, 100
Hampson, Daphne, 20n1, 21n3, 34n2, 159n1, 228-229, 263-264
Hannay, Alastair, 68
Hegel, G.W.F., 21, 77, 219-226; Hegelianism, 20-21, 51, 87, 141-142, 159-160, 215, 218-219
Heidegger, Martin, 251-260
Herrman, Wilhelm, 248n1
Heschel, Abraham Joshua, 268-269
Hinkson, Craig, 108n2, 119n1, 243n1
Holocaust (also Shoah), 27n1, 40-42
Holy, the (also the Holy One), 19, 65, 66, 174, 195
Hong, Howard and Edna, 65-66, 68-69; Edna, 66
hope, 43, 101, 114, 116, 121, 123, 132-134, 166, 168, 188-189, 190, 209, 217
Hyde, Keith J., 26

imagination, 34, 65, 114-115, 140, 146, 148-153, 184, 190-191, 204, 212-213, 238, 241n1; fantasy (also the fantastic), 106n1, 150-153, 184, 198
impossibility, 43n2, 51, 69, 119, 149, 165-166, 183, 198, 201-203, 236; and divine possibility, 165-166, 183
inclosing reserve (also Indesluttethed), (see also despair) 50, 138, 146, 174, 191, 193, 214, 225, 239, 256, 258, 262
infinite and finite, 41, 79, 178, 181, 191, 195-196, 216, 221, 238
infinite qualitative difference (also absolute difference), 20, 36, 64n2, 65, 78, 79-80, 87, 171, 182, 193-196, 214, 217-218, 220-221, 225, 231-239, 261-262, 266, 269
irony, 157, 164
Isaac, 13n2, 48, 119-120, 158-159, 161, 165

Jabés, Edmond, 41
Jacob (also Yisra'el), 13-18, 26, 31, 37n4, 38n4, 40, 42, 44, 47, 48n2, 55n2, 119-123, 130, 151-152, 169, 206, 210, 242, 261, 262, 266-267
James, William, 102-103, 109
Jaspers, Karl, 250-251
Jihad, 46n1
Job, 55, 116-118, 121, 134, 163-166, 168, 184, 198, 237
John of the Cross, 45, 51n1, 81
Juan de los Angeles, Fray, 44
Jüngel, Eberhard, 248

Kabbalah, 77n3, 139
Kangas, David, 51n1, 88, 137-138
Kant, Immanuel, 251n3
Kazantzakis, Nikos, 27-29, 37
Keeley, Louise Carroll, 130n2, 137n1
Kenosis, 29, 51, 86, 88n1, 101, 188, 190, 202, 214, 225, 235, 261-265, 267-268; in-ekstasis, 144, 193, 214, 215, 224, 228, 239, 257-258, 268
Kierkegaard, Søren: authorship, 170, 175, 182, 228; and father, 72, 74
Kirkconnell, Glenn, 159n2, 164n1
Kirmmse, Bruce, 70n2
Kojève, Alexandre, 224
Kristeva, Julia, 18, 112n5
Krötke, Wolf, 247n2

Law, David R., 51n1, 81n2
Lazarus, 124
Levinas, Emmanuel, 21n2
Lewin, David, 267n2
Logos, 15
Lowrie, Walter, 60
Luther, Martin, 15-16, 24-25, 28, 29-30, 36n5, 38n6, 42-43, 45n1, 46, 48n2, 52, 54-56, 60-63, 66-67, 78n3, 86, 90, 96-99, 100-126, 127-133, 139-143, 149, 152-153, 158-159, 166, 183, 196, 201-202, 204-205, 237, 241, 243-248, 250, 251-255, 258-260, 262, 266
Lutheran, 16, 34, 50, 54, 78-79, 104n1, 108n2, 111n1, 129, 138n5, 139-141, 143, 204-205, 229, 244

93, 101, 107n2, 117-118, 122, 127,
131-132, 144-148, 152, 167, 175,
188, 191, 193, 206-208, 214, 217-
218, 231-233, 245, 263, 265, 266-268
Proudhon, Pierre-Joseph (*see also*
antitheism), 26
Pseudo-Dionysus, 87
Pyper, Hugh, 265

Rasmussen, Joel, 84n2; and David
Yoon-Jun Kim, 104n1, 107-108
reason, 32, 68-69, 92, 146, 155, 170,
216, 219, 223, 226, 251
releasement (*also Gelassenheit*) 16, 18,
46, 80, 86, 88n2, 89, 98, 102n4, 125-
126, 127, 139, 140n1, 141-148, 152,
164, 169, 193, 214, 216, 228, 233,
235, 238, 241, 242, 244n2, 256-269
religious, the, 34, 49, 53, 57, 70, 83,
159-160, 174, 175-178, 181, 185,
203, 237
repentance, 102, 143-146, 159-161,
167, 172-173, 192, 200
repetition, 165-166
resignation, 18, 31, 126n1, 134, 146,
160, 164, 188-190, 198, 245, 269
Resurrection, 115, 123-125
revelation, 15, 24, 33, 78, 82, 99, 115,
141n2, 171, 221, 251, 256-258
Rivero, Demetrio G., 63
Rubenstein, Richard, 41-42
Rupp, Gordon, 43n1, 60, 110, 243

sacrifice, 18, 28, 48, 72, 119, 122, 158,
161-163, 210, 263, 268n1
Šadja, Peter, 75-77, 84-86, 89-90
Scaer, David P., 100n2
Schelling, F.W.J., 77, 137-138
Schweizer, Bernard, 26n4, 27n1
Scupoli, Lorenzo, 31-34
secret (*also* secrecy), 20, 23, 29, 33,
43, 47-51, 66, 70, 98, 133-135, 154,
157-158, 162-167, 179-181, 183,
204-205, 220, 236-238, 248, 261-
262, 267-269
self, the (*also* selfhood, personhood;
see also Spirit): abasement (*also*
abnegation; becoming nothing;

negation), 23, 35, 88n2, 148, 180,
192, 193, 198, 213-216, 218, 227,
238, 261, 269; apotheosis, 26,
29-30, 25, 72, 78, 92, 239; before
God, 23, 48, 193, 216, 223, 231,
235-236, 240; death to, 22-23, 55,
90, 98, 103, 117, 130, 148, 212-214;
divine gift of, 215; knowledge
of (*also* failure/impossibility of
knowing), 32, 100, 117, 170; self-
consciousness, 222-224, 227n5,
253; transparency, 19, 23-24, 47,
87, 193, 214-218, 224, 231, 233-
236, 238, 242, 266; will, 23, 31,
35, 142, 144-148, 153, 160n1, 167,
175, 188, 191, 213-214, 216, 221,
224-226, 234-235, 238-241, 261-
265
Shakespeare, Steven, 259n1
Shakespeare, William, 102n2, 113n1
silence, 16n1, 39-44, 47-54, 98, 134,
147, 154, 159, 162-165, 179, 190,
194, 203, 232, 266-267
sin (*also* consciousness of sin; sin
of despair), 26, 30, 35-36, 39, 61,
69, 85-86, 93, 97-99, 109, 114-122,
125-126, 129, 138, 145-151, 159-
160, 171-174, 185-188, 191-192,
197-198, 221, 223, 133, 241, 247,
253, 256-258; as revelation, 115,
221, 256-258, (*see also* revelation);
unforgivable sin, sin against the
Holy Spirit. *See* forgiveness
single individual, the, 48, 53, 159-
162, 166, 190, 200, 268
Smith, Ronald Gregor, 64, 68
soul (*also* psychical), 16n1, 22, 25,
31-34, 37, 43n1, 44, 46, 71, 76n5,
78-82, 85-86, 88n2, 89-99, 102-103,
105-106, 109n5, 111-117, 125, 131-
153, 156-157, 166-169, 173, 186,
189-190, 205, 214, 216, 218, 219,
226, 231-236, 238
Soul-care, 85, 154
Spirit (*see also* self), 19-21, 23-24, 27-
30, 34-39, 43-45, 47, 49, 52, 55n1,
57, 63-67, 71-72, 80, 87, 91-95,
98, 103n1, 114, 130-133, 138, 140,